Pastor Gary Landers
Val Caron, ON
897-6200

4 95

Introduction
to
Christian Theology

by
H. Orton Wiley, S.T.D.
and
Paul T. Culbertson, Ph.D.

BEACON HILL PRESS OF KANSAS CITY
Kansas City, Missouri

DEDICATION

To all those entering upon a preparation for the Christian ministry or missionary service, and to Christian laymen who desire to heed the admonition of St. Peter: "Sanctify the Lord God in your hearts; and be ready always to give an answer to every man that asketh you a reason of the hope that is in you," this volume is affectionately dedicated.

First Printing, 1946

Printed in United States of America

PREFACE
TO
INTRODUCTION TO CHRISTIAN THEOLOGY

The material in this volume is drawn primarily from *Christian Theology* by H. Orton Wiley, and is adapted and arranged by Paul T. Culbertson. The essential purpose of the authors is to provide a text for introductory courses in Theology, and to present Christian doctrine in a brief, yet substantial form for the general use of the laity of the Church. It is hoped, therefore, that the volume will be useful not only for those who are looking forward to a further study of Theology, but for students in missionary training schools, and all those Christians who desire a preparation which will enable them to give a ready and adequate answer for the hope that is within them.

The material has been carefully organized into seven units, each consisting of three to five chapters. Each unit is preceded by a preview, and by an outline which is carefully followed in the text of the unit. Any topic can easily be found by a quick reference to the general table of contents and the appropriate unit outline.

The doctrinal emphasis of this volume is Arminian and Wesleyan. Our aim has been to present Christian doctrine positively and fairly, with adequate evidence in the form of quotations from the Holy Scriptures. A devotional tone and a practical emphasis has been continually sought.

For those who may desire a more definitive treatment of any of the various themes considered herein, an annotated bibliography of selected titles will be found at the close of Unit VII.

H. ORTON WILEY
PAUL T. CULBERTSON

CONTENTS

INTRODUCTION

The subject and object of theology is God. The scope of theology includes not only God, but creation, man, the fall, redemption, final destiny, with many other important implications.

One's concept of God and one's attitude toward Him are the determining factors in building both life and character. Thus, it is obvious that the study of theology is both a supreme privilege and inescapable duty. In this study lies hope of finding a right understanding of God. The right attitude toward God may be found in an open mind, a seeking heart, and an obedient will. The privilege and the duty to study theology applies both to the ministry and to the laity.

This Introduction to Theology by Dr. H. Orton Wiley will fill a distinct need in the literature of the church. All young ministers and many older ones who have not had the opportunity to study theology under competent teachers in recognized theological institutions will find this volume of untold value. The subjects are clearly outlined; the language is simple and understandable. It is adapted especially for young ministers in the first year of the Course of Study. This treatise on theology in its simplicity and yet thoroughness is especially adapted to the needs of laymen. A strenuous effort should be made to influence every Christian layman to purchase, to read, and to study this Introduction to Theology. Is it not just as important for laymen to be sound in doctrine as for ministers?

Dr. Wiley is eminently qualified in every way to give to the church and to the Christian world the sort of study in theology urgently needed at this particular time. First, he is a man of unimpeachable character and of rich Christian experience, having spent many years in the laboratory of scholastic training. His scholarship entitles him, together with his sound theology, to the complete confidence of the reader. It is a great consolation for one to take food, either physical or mental, knowing such food contains no trace of poison.

It is my sincere wish that this volume will find its way into the hands of all ministers, especially the younger group and those who have not had opportunity to spend years in the classroom for exhaustive study. May God grant that it may fall into the hands of every Christian layman, that each one may have a better understanding of God and of His work, that all may be sound in doctrine, rich in Christian experience, and useful in service.

Roy T. Williams

UNIT I

INTRODUCTION

Preview

Foundations are important! We all know that there is a logical relationship between the kind of foundation we prepare and the type of superstructure we hope to build. Just a clearing of the ground's surface is sufficient in order to stretch a tent, but we need to strike bedrock in order to erect a skyscraper. As the skyline of a city goes up, its foundations must necessarily go down. Foundations *are important*.

What is so obviously true in the physical realm is no less valid in the area of thought and belief. Therefore, in this introductory unit our purpose is to describe the firm foundation upon which the structure of Christian doctrine securely rests. To do so we begin with a survey of the nature and scope of Christian Theology. We find it to be a systematic study of the great *realities* of the Christian faith.

In Chapter II we reach the heart of our introduction in the discovery that the basic foundation of Christian truth is found in the personal and written Word of God. We then focus our attention more precisely upon the exact nature of this special revelation of God in and through the Word. In particular, we study the inspiration of the Scriptures, and examine the development and integrity of the canon of the Old and New Testaments.

A careful and diligent study of this unit will pay rich dividends as we begin and continue the erection of our temple of Christian truth. Look well to your foundations!

UNIT I

INTRODUCTION

Chapter I. *Nature and Scope of the Subject*

I. THE NATURE OF CHRISTIAN THEOLOGY

  A. Reasons for Studying Christian Doctrine.

  B. Terminology.

  C. Definitions of Theology.

  D. Nature and Scope of Theology.

  E. Christian Theology a Study of Reality.

  F. Systems of Theology.

  G. Qualifications for the Study of Theology.

II. THE RELATIONS AND DIVISIONS OF THEOLOGY

  A. The Relations of Theology.

    1. Relation to Religion.

    2. Relation to Revelation.

    3. Relation to the Church.

  B. The Divisions of Theology.

    1. Natural Theology.

    2. Exegetical Theology.

    3. Historical Theology.

    4. Systematic Theology.

    5. Practical Theology.

Chapter II. *Sources and Methods of Theology*

I. THE SCIENCE OF THEOLOGY

  A. The Scientific Nature of Theology.

  B. Methods of Organization and Presentation.

II. THE PRIMARY SOURCE OF CHRISTIAN THEOLOGY

  A. The Bible as the Primary Source.

  B. Contrast of Protestant and Catholic Views of the Bible.

Introduction to
Christian Theology

CHAPTER I

NATURE AND SCOPE OF THE SUBJECT

"The study of Christian theology is not only instructive, but elevating and delightful. No subject in all the range of human thought is to be compared with it. As a science, it rises above all other sciences, and is, when properly understood, the basis of all science. . . . . In studying theology we are brought into companionship with the purest and best minds of all ages. We enter into companionship, and, if we will, into fellowship with Jesus Christ. . . . . What study can be more delightful and of deeper interest than that of Christian Theology? Especially since we find in it what we cannot find elsewhere, and realize that it meets a want in the soul which human reason and philosophy never have satisfied, and never can."—BISHOP JONATHAN WEAVER.

I. THE NATURE OF CHRISTIAN THEOLOGY

A. *Reasons for Studying Christian Doctrine.*

In recent years there has been a tendency in liberal religious circles to discredit the importance of doctrinal study. Frequently an impression has been given that sincerity of attitude was more important than the content of belief. While no one would discount the necessity of sincerity, no right-thinking person believes that sincerity can or should be substituted for a knowledge of the truth. To believe a falsehood, however sincerely, is disastrous, and the greater the degree of sincerity the more dire are likely to be the consequences. It is only a knowledge of the truth that makes men either free or safe. And if this be true, as it is, in the physical and material realms of life, how much more important it is in the realm of spiritual values with their eternal consequences.

An anonymous writer has well expressed the intimate relation between belief, activity, character, and destiny in the following lines:

> "Sow a thought, reap an act;
> Sow an act, reap a habit;
> Sow a habit, reap a character;
> Sow a character, reap a destiny."

Exactly so! Ideas are motor. They eventuate in acts. Acts, repeated, become habits out of which character evolves. Thus does Holy Writ affirm that out of the heart are the issues of life, and "as a man thinketh in his heart, so is he." There is a chain of unbroken continuity between what one believes in the here and now, and the kind of person he will be and the place of his abode in the hereafter. It is clear, therefore, that belief is vital in determining personal activity, moral character, and eternal destiny!

A man's belief is also directly related to his influence on others. For this reason St. Paul admonished Timothy in a familiar passage, *Study to shew thyself approved unto God, a workman that needeth not to be ashamed, rightly dividing the word of truth* (II Timothy 2:15). Paul further advised him to *Meditate upon these things; give thyself wholly to them; that thy profiting may appear to all. Take heed unto thyself, and unto the doctrine; continue in them: for in doing this thou shalt both save thyself, and them that hear thee* (I Timothy 4:15-16). And this obligation is binding upon the laity as well as the ministry. Every Christian is admonished to *be ready always to give an answer* ("apology") *to every man that asketh you a reason of the hope that is in you with meekness and fear* (I Peter 3:15).

The study of Christian doctrine is therefore an obligation binding upon every Christian. It is not something divorced from life. It is not a place for carelessness, indifference, idle speculation, or quibbling over nonessentials. Personal salvation, sound character, and holy influence are dependent on the acquisition of correct tenets of faith. Every individual is responsible within the limits of his capacity and opportunity to discover and accept Christian doctrine.

However, the study of Christian theology is not simply an obligation. It is also a source of inspiration and delight. No subject in all the range of human thought is to be compared with it. In studying the great truths of the Bible, one enters into companionship with some of the purest and best minds of the ages—St. Paul,

St. Augustine, Thomas Aquinas, John Calvin, John Wesley—to mention only a few. Best of all, as Bishop Weaver declared, we "enter into companionship, and, if we will, into fellowship with Jesus Christ!" What study, then, could be of greater delight or of more profound interest than that of Christian theology?

B. *Terminology.*

In order to achieve a greater degree of exactness, every science develops its own distinctive vocabulary. Theology, the "Queen of the Sciences," is no exception. At the very outset a few key terms should be clearly defined. We therefore turn at once to examine the meaning of certain of these basic words and concepts.

Christian doctrine is most commonly presented under the broader title of Christian theology, or the more technical term, Christian dogmatics. As here used, it is an analytical study of the great body of truth which furnishes the material of theology and is commonly known as the Christian faith. A distinction is sometimes made between doctrine and dogma—the former term applying to the systematized teaching of the Scriptures on any theological subject, the latter to the form which the doctrine has assumed in consequence of its development. Thus, for example, the Scriptures set forth certain facts concerning water baptism, but through the centuries dogmas have developed with reference to mode, acceptable candidacy, exact significance of the rite, and so on. It is the dogmas which have given rise to Dogmatic Theology, and mark many differences in the various branches of the church.

The term *theology* is derived from two Greek words— *theos* (θεός), God, and *logos* (λόγος), a discourse, and originally signified a discourse about God. The ancient Greeks used the word in its literal sense, and hence applied the term *theologoi* or theologians, to those who wrote the history of the gods and their exploits. Pherecydes is supposed to have been the first so denominated, and his work was entitled *Theologia* or Theology. Aristotle applied the term theology to his highest or first philosophy. In this sense also, Homer, Hesiod, and Orpheus, "Who with poetic inspiration sang of the gods and divine things," were known as *theologoi* or theologians. In its most general sense, therefore, the term theology may be applied to scientific investigations of real or supposed sacred persons, things, or relations. However crude the content of these treatises may be, usage allows it to be called theology if the subject matter is concerned with that which is regarded as sacred. The term is therefore elastic and somewhat vague, and must be rendered more definite and specific by the use of such qualifying terms as Christian theology or Ethnic (non-Christian) theology.

C. *Definitions of Theology.*

One of the simplest definitions of theology is that which is implied in the foregoing paragraph, namely, "Christian theology is the systematic presentation of the doctrines of the Christian faith." Dr. Samuel Wakefield, who edited Watson's *Institutes* and added some valuable material of his own, defines theology as "That science which treats of the existence, the character, and the attributes of God; His laws and government; the doctrines which we are to believe, the moral change we must experience, and the duties we are required to perform." Dr. Charles Hodge gives the following definition: "Theology is the exhibition of the facts of Scripture in their proper order and relation with the principles or general truths involved in the facts themselves, and which pervade and harmonize the whole." Perhaps no definition, however, exceeds in adequacy or comprehensiveness, that of William Burton Pope, the eminent Methodist theologian, who defines theology as "The science of God and divine things, based upon the revelation made to mankind in Jesus Christ, and variously systematized within the Christian Church."

D. *Nature and Scope of Theology.*

Christian theology comprehends in its scope a wide range of investigation, with particular emphasis upon certain well-defined fields of thought. If the above definitions be carefully analyzed, they will be seen to include the following subjects: (1) God—the subject, source, and end of all theology; (2) Religion—as furnishing the basic consciousness of the supernatural, without which man would have no capacity to receive the revelations of divine truth; (3) Revelation—as the primary source of the facts out of which systematic theology is constructed; (4) Jesus Christ—the personal and eternal Word, in whom all truth finds its center and circumference; and (5) the Church—in which the truth has been systematized and developed under the supervision and control of the Holy Spirit.

E. *Christian Theology a Study of Reality.*

We cannot overemphasize the fact that Christian theology is an exposition of the *facts* and *realities* of a divine revelation. Just as the natural scientist concerns himself with the objective reality or external facts which underlie nature, so the Christian theologian is interested in the great objective realities of the kingdom of God. When and if theology cuts loose from this basis it becomes a mere system of philosophy, ethics, or psychology. The Bible does not speculate or argue—it reveals and announces divine truth with assurance and certitude.

Dr. Henry B. Smith has given an excellent statement of the reality which forms the foundation of Christian theology. He writes, "If the expression be duly guarded, it is useful to say that there is a Christian realism which is absolutely fundamental in Christian theology. That is, there is a grand series of facts, constituting the very life of the Christian system, which have an objective reality and validity, and without which the whole of Christian theology is, in principle, no better than a mere philosophical system.

"An immense practical power is given to the Christian revelation by its resting in such quietness and strength on those central, integral facts, the grandest in the annals of the race—that God has established in this world a real kingdom, centering in the person and work of our gracious Lord, who for us became incarnate and suffered and died; and that He sent forth His Spirit to renew, teach, and sanctify His chosen ones; and that this kingdom is to go on doing its mighty work until all the elect of the Lord are gathered in; and that all that it gives to man here only foreshadows that full measure of blessedness and glory which is to be the consummation of the same kingdom in the unnumbered ages of eternity. Men say that the volume of divine revelation is a 'popular book.' But it is a real book—a book of divine realities, and it makes men feel and know their power" (SMITH, *Introduction to Christian Theology,* pages 5-7). It is with these glorious *realities* that Christian theology is concerned.

F. *Systems of Theology.*

Despite the objective reality which furnishes the ground of Christian theology various systems have been developed by individuals and groups within the Christian Church. These theological systems, being the creations of human minds, differ as regards certain fundamental positions and in a multitude of details. This is not unexpected when we consider the many-sidedness of Bible truth, the finiteness of human understanding, the inadequacy of human language in expressing spiritual realities, the incompleteness of our knowledge of the Scriptures, and the fact that sin has darkened man's understanding. While we recognize that human systems of Christian theology differ at many points, it should be remembered that the points of essential agreement are of equal or greater significance. For example, within the theological systems of Protestantism there is general agreement as to the fundamental importance of such facts as the existence of God, the holy Trinity, the deity of the Lord Jesus Christ, the necessity of redemption from sin through the atonement of our Lord, and so on. Often the differences are simply or primarily matters of emphasis which, for understanding, demand clear analysis, careful study, and considered judgment on the part of the student. This brings us to a consideration of the intellectual and other requisites necessary for the most fruitful study of theology.

G. *Qualifications for the Study of Theology.*

In his *Introduction to Christian Theology* (pages 25-33), Dr. Henry B. Smith has given an excellent statement of "the spirit that should animate a true student of theology." First among such necessary qualifications is the requisite that the student should be spiritually minded. This does not mean a mere abstract knowledge *about* spiritual things, nor a general sentiment of good will, but a spiritual mindedness which is in its inmost nature an expression of the reality of God's kingdom as centering in the person and work of Jesus Christ. It is a spiritual mindedness which results from vital, personal contact with Deity.

Second among the characteristics which should be possessed by the sincere student of theology is a spirit of reverential humility. "Such humility," says Smith, "is not to be confounded with abasement before dogmatism; that is the mark, not of a humble, but of a cowering spirit. It is, however, the opposite of self-sufficiency— He cannot be a true divine who is not awe-struck and reverential, a humble learner, before the mysteries of the Incarnation and of the Atonement, who does not feel and know that in these grand facts there is that which calls upon him to put off his shoes from off his feet; who has not the conviction that here is holy ground."

The third characteristic of the theological inquirer should be an honest love of the truth for its own sake. "As with virtue, so with truth; both are good in and of themselves, and are to be loved and pursued for their own sake. Many men love truth for the sake of their party; some for the sake of their church; the plurality of mankind, perhaps, from personal interests; others because they cannot or will not unlearn what they have learned; but the preacher should love and preach the truth, because it is the truth."

A fourth qualification which the student of theology should possess is a trustful spirit; that is, a belief that, under the illumination of God's Spirit, the truth which

is the substance of theology may be found. "And as the
illumination of that Spirit is promised and vouchsafed
to all who commit themselves to His guidance, they may
confidently expect that they shall come to know, if they
be faithful, whatever is needful to be known in order
that they may do their Master's work here on earth."

The theological student should also have a profes-
sional zeal for his work. This is particularly true of those
who are called to the Christian ministry. Such a student should "feel and live, day by day, and week by
week, as if theology was his proper and beloved work,
giving to it his best time and his most earnest powers,
and his patient labor."

To the foregoing list of requisites, so well set forth
by Dr. Smith the following may be added. *First,* an adequate knowledge of the Bible, the Word of God. "Exegesis precedes theology, and the work of systematic
theology should be preceded by work in biblical theology, or the systematic study of the doctrinal contents
of the Bible" (CLARKE, *Outlines of Christian Theology,*
pages 5-6). There is no substitute for a personal, adequate knowledge of what the Bible itself teaches regarding doctrine. In order to ascertain the meaning of the
Scriptures, a knowledge of the original languages, especially Greek, is valuable. *Second,* a broad understanding of other fields of knowledge is helpful in studying
Christian theology. This is particularly true as regards
those areas of knowledge such as philosophy, history,
religion, and psychology which are more intimately related to the study of theology. *Third,* those mental characteristics which are summed up in the concept, "a
disciplined mind," are of inestimable value to the student of theology. Regarding such a mind, Dr. A. H.
Strong, eminent Baptist theologian, says, "Only such a
mind can patiently collect the facts, hold in its grasp
many facts at once, educe by continuous reflection their
connecting principles, suspend final judgment until its
conclusions are verified by Scripture and experience"
(STRONG, *Systematic Theology,* I, p. 38). Such a mind is
marked by the courage and will to cast aside prejudices

when their true nature becomes evident. It *proves all things and holds fast to that which is good;* and grasps intuitional truths as well as those which are acquired merely by logic and reason. It is a mind which is not wholly dominated by rational process, but one which possesses spiritual insight as well as mental understanding.

II. THE RELATIONS AND DIVISIONS OF THEOLOGY

A. *The Relations of Theology.*

Aside from the divine source of theology, there are three outstanding relations which it sustains—to religion, to revelation, and to the Church. By a relation we mean a particularly close or intimate interconnection, and mutual dependence.

1. *Relation to Religion.* Theology is closely linked to religion in that the latter furnishes the basic consciousness in man without which human nature would not be able to receive the revelation of God. It is the awareness that he is made for higher things, and that he has kinship with the unseen Power upon which he feels himself dependent. Added to this is man's sense of need which expresses itself in the consciousness of sin and a desire for communion with a higher spiritual power. It is the task of theology to gather up and systematize these human needs and desires.

Religion is both an individual and a social phenomenon. Those who have been brought into communion with God feel the necessity of imparting this spiritual knowledge to others, and hence there arise various religious societies. These in turn crystallize into fixed institutions, designed to hand down to posterity the religious insights of the past. God, who is subject, source, and objective of Christian theology, is also central in this personal and collective phenomenon—religion. Theology and religion are, therefore, related "as effects in different spheres of the same cause."

2. *Relation to Revelation.* Theology also depends upon a higher type of experience—the Word incarnate in Jesus Christ—and known as the Christian Revela-

tion. Christian faith is, therefore, not merely subjective and self-created. It has its source and validity in an objective, written revelation—the Word of God. The same Holy Spirit who communicates the inner or subjective knowledge of God in religious experience, has also brought about an external record of it. This makes possible the extension of religious truth to others than those who at first received it. Both the internal revelation and its external interpretation furnish the objective facts necessary as the material of a true science.

3. *Relation to the Church.* It is to the Church that God has committed the Scriptures, and these have become its rule of faith and practice. As the earlier oracle had its ark, so the Christian Church has become the receptacle of the latter oracle—the faith which was *once delivered unto the saints* (Jude 4). With the coming of the incarnate Christ, and the gift of the Holy Spirit on the day of Pentecost, the foundations of the Church were laid. With the enlargement of its mission, it was necessary also that its oracles be increased, and hence we by divine inspiration have the New Testament. Becoming the repository of a new dispensational truth, the Church was and is under obligation, both as a teacher and defender of the faith, to create a theology by means of which it could systematically present its truth in doctrinal form.

B. *Principal Divisions of Theology.*

To facilitate understanding, scholars have organized and systematized the materials of theology in various ways. We mention only a few of the principal terms used in designating the several branches of this "science of God and divine things."

1. *Natural Theology.* This branch of theology treats of the being, attributes, and will of God as revealed in the various phenomena of nature: *The heavens declare the glory of God: and the firmament sheweth his handywork.* In the great book of nature we find evidence concerning the existence of God, His power, and His purposes. In the material universe and in the constitution

of man, God is dimly, though unmistakably revealed. It is the province of natural theology to gather up and systematize this evidence.

2. *Exegetical Theology.* This is a careful, analytic study of the Scriptures classified according to doctrines. It comprehends a wide range of investigations, including the age, origin, content, and character of the sacred writings; the integrity of the original text; the authenticity of the several books; and, the principles of biblical interpretation, exposition, and application.

3. *Historical Theology.* This branch of theology deals with the historical development of doctrine. It consists of two main divisions: a study of the progressive development of the doctrines of the Bible, and a survey of the historical development of doctrine in the Church since apostolic times. Tribute is laid upon secular, biblical and ecclesiastical history for the contribution they can make to an understanding of doctrinal growth.

4. *Systematic Theology.* The materials furnished by natural, exegetical, and historical theology are here arranged in logical and methodical form in order to facilitate understanding and promote practical application. Through systematic arrangement and presentation the vital connection and symmetry of the whole of Christian truth can be perceived and appreciated. One is thus enabled to see theology steadily and to see it as a whole. Systematic theology is commonly subdivided into such categories as ethics, dogmatics, and polemics.

5. *Practical Theology.* This division of theology has to do with the practical application of the fruits of theological inquiry, particularly as they relate to the work of the Christian ministry. Included in this study are such topics as homiletics, which treats of the composition and delivery of sermons; catechetics, which deals with the instruction of the young in preparation for church membership; and liturgics, a study of the forms of worship and devotion.

CHAPTER II

SOURCES AND METHODS OF THEOLOGY

"As the facts of nature are all related and determined by physical laws, so the facts of the Bible are all related and determined by the nature of God and His creatures. As He wills that man should study His works and discover their wonderful organic relation and harmonious combination, so it is His will that we should study His Word and learn that like the stars, its truths are not isolated points, but systems, cycles, and epicycles in unending harmony and grandeur."—DR. CHARLES HODGE.

I. THE SCIENCE OF THEOLOGY

A. *The Scientific Nature of Theology.*

It is common usage among theologians to speak of their study as a science. In the representative definitions of theology given in Chapter I this tendency is evident. Pope speaks of theology as "the science of God and divine things." Hodge points out the importance of order, systematic presentation, and the development of general truths and principles.

There are some who are unwilling to admit that theology is a true science, comparable to physics or biology, history or psychology. It is contended that theology draws its facts from Revelation or personal experience, and that these facts are not comparable to those which come out of the laboratory, from the case study, or which result from the introspective report of a subject concerning his mental states.

The question as to whether or not theology is a science is not of sufficient importance to warrant extended discussion, but a few observations may be of value in making more evident the exact nature of theology. There is considerable difference of opinion as to whether such subjects as history, which bases its conclusions on testimony and evidence; and psychology, which deals to a considerable extent with human consciousness have yet attained the status of true sciences. In the two respects mentioned theology is similar to both history and psychology.

24

Science is characterized by two principal features: its method and its spirit. The method of science involves a systematic inquiry into truth and an orderly presentation of the discovered facts, revealing causal relationships and general truths or laws. The spirit or attitude of science is that of open-minded, unprejudiced inquiry into all relevant facts, both objective and subjective. Karl Pearson has significantly observed that this scientific attitude, rather than the exact nature or source of the facts, constitutes the common element in all sciences.

As in the case of history and psychology, theology is a science to the degree that it partakes of the spirit and method of science. To the degree that its facts are systematized, revealing relationships and laws, and to the degree that its spirit is that of open, unbiased search after truth—to that extent theology is a science. The science of theology seeks to discover through all legitimate means, both objective and subjective, the whole truth and nothing but the truth.

If it be objected that faith is not a part of science, one needs only to recall that the physical sciences themselves rest on a foundation of faith: faith in an orderly universe; faith in the testimony of the senses; faith in our own existence.

It may even be contended that all science ends in theology, which thus becomes the "Queen of the Sciences." This conclusion is derived from the fact that theology is primarily concerned with a study of God— the ultimate source of all truth and reality. Thus all sciences in their search after truth find their ultimate in God, and in His personal relationship to the universe.

B. *Methods of Organization and Presentation.*

There are numerous valid arguments for the systematic arrangement of the truths of the Bible. As Dr. Hodge has stated, "Such, evidently, is the will of God. He does not teach men astronomy or chemistry, but He gives them the facts out of which these sciences are constructed. Neither does He teach us systematic theology, but He gives us in the Bible the truths which, properly understood and arranged, constitute the science of theology." Through such organization rich and beautiful harmonies among Christian doctrines become clear. Truths become pregnant with meaning as their interrelationships are delineated. Such an orderly and coherent presentation of doctrine not only appeals to the very constitution of man's mind, but enables an individual to effectively teach others. Thus strong and useful Christian character results when the great tenets of the Christian faith are carefully organized, systematically presented, and firmly grasped.

With such valid reason for the systematization of Bible doctrine, it is not surprising that numerous plans have been utilized in organizing Christian theology. In the early history of the Church the trinitarian method of organization was prominent. Doctrines were set forth as they were related to the Father, Son and Holy Spirit. A later development was the federal method in which the idea of two covenants, that of works and that of grace, constituted the central factor in organization. A Christocentric method in which Christ and His redemption form the central core of thought has been widely used. Perhaps the most commonly utilized method, however, is the synthetic type of organization. As described by Hagenbach, this method "starts from the highest principle, God, and proceeds to man, Christ, redemption, and finally to the end of all things." The basic principle of organization is its logical order of cause and effect. This method has been used effectively by such notable theologians as Strong, Pope, Miley, Ralston, and others. Despite its frequent use, it has not lost its freshness and attractiveness. The present study utilizes a modification of this method of organization.

II. The Primary Source of Christian Theology

A. *The Bible as the Primary Source of Christian Theology.*

Christian theology as the science of the one true and perfect religion is based upon the documentary records of God's revelation of Himself in Jesus Christ. Thus the Bible is the divine rule of faith and practice, and the only authoritative and primary source of Christian theology. The Holy Scriptures constitute the quarry out of which are mined the glorious truths utilized in constructing the edifice of Christian doctrine. This view of the Bible as fundamental and central in Christian theology is one of the basic elements and points of emphasis in Protestantism.

However, in a deeper sense, Jesus Christ, our ever-living Lord, is Himself the fullest revelation of God. He is the Word of God—the outlived and outspoken thought of the Eternal. Thus, while we honor the Scriptures in giving them a central place as our primary source in theology, we are not unmindful that the letter killeth but the spirit maketh alive. Christ, the Living Word, must ever be held in proper relation to the Holy Bible, the written Word. If the latter would be vital and dynamic, we must through the Holy Spirit, be ever attuned to that Living One whose matchless words, incomparable deeds, and vicarious death constitute the great theme of that Book of books.

B. *Contrast Between Protestant and Catholic Views of the Bible.*

In contrast to the Protestant view of the Scriptures, just stated, is that of the Roman Catholic Church. The latter is unwilling to concede to the Bible an exclusive and central position as the ultimate standard of faith and practice. Roman Catholics hold that only the Vulgate or Latin version of the Scriptures, including most of the Apocryphal books, is authoritative. In addition, tradition—and practice handed down in the church from generation to generation—is also accepted as authoritative. In fact, in increasing degree the authority of the church itself as expressed in formal papal pronouncements has become the supreme criterion in interpreting both Scriptures and tradition. Thus the church has been placed in an abnormal relation to Jesus Christ, and the decrees of the church have superseded the direct revelation of God in the Holy Scriptures. To such views Protestants cannot and will not give assent.

III. SECONDARY SOURCES OF CHRISTIAN THEOLOGY

A. *Nature as a Source of Theology.*

Numerous passages in the Holy Scriptures teach that nature reveals somewhat of God and divine things. The words of the psalmist are very familiar, *The heavens declare the glory of God; and the firmament sheweth his handywork. Day unto day uttereth speech, and night unto night sheweth knowledge. There is no speech nor language where their voice is not heard. Their line is gone out through all the earth, and their words to the end of the world* (Psalms 19: 1-4). Nature thus speaks with a universal language of the power and glory of God.

From various statements of the Apostle Paul we gather that nature reveals God sufficiently to lead men to seek after Him and worship Him (Acts 14: 15-17; 17: 22-34). However, that revelation is vague and imperfect. Revealing something of the power and resources of God, nature is silent concerning His moral attributes, and has no word of assurance concerning the gracious means provided for the salvation of man. Nature, therefore, as a source of Christian theology is subsidiary, secondary, and incidental.

B. *Experience as a Source of Theology.*

In the study of Christian Theology one must ever keep in mind the basic fact that true Christian experience involves a vital, intimate, *personal* relationship between God and man. It is more than an intellectual apprehension or acceptance of truth. In its ultimate nature truth is personal, and our Lord himself declared, *I am the truth.* To know Him is not merely to adhere to a creed but to receive Him wholeheartedly and to love Him devotedly. To those who thus receive Him, He gives the glorious right and gracious ability to become the sons of God. This filial relationship between Jesus Christ and man has its root in likeness of character. It is a relationship which is begotten and nourished by the Holy Spirit. This spiritual knowledge, based on personal, vital contact with God through the Spirit, constitutes a rudimentary but true subsidiary source of theology.

Spiritual contacts, right ethical and spiritual relationships, and personal obedience to the divine will thus lead to a true knowledge of God. This knowledge may not be elaborate, but it is characterized by certainty and assurance. Even the unlearned, the "whosoever" may possess it if they will: *If any man willeth to do his will, he shall know of the teaching, whether it is of God, or whether I speak from myself* (John 7:17, R.V.). And from this knowledge, assured to the obedient by the Master, valid conceptions of God may be intellectually constructed and systematic knowledge developed.

C. *Creeds as Sources of Theology.*

A creed is a confession of faith, a group of doctrines set forth for acceptance, or articles of belief. Creeds may be individual or collective, written or unwritten, valid or invalid. The great generally accepted credal statements of the Church grew up from within. They epitomize the collective experience of the Church, tested by many believers over long periods of time, and formulated into clear and concise statements. They represent the outgrowth of the religious experience of the Church which owes its life to Jesus Christ through the Spirit. As such they may be accepted as subsidiary sources of theology. They remain valid only so long as they represent true convictions based on Christian experience. When persons or groups drift away from a vital relationship with Jesus Christ, creeds tend to become increasingly elaborate, formal, and less valid as sources of Christian theology. It is to be remembered that all credal statements, among Protestants at least, are not set forth as substitutes for the Scripture itself. They are supposedly or actually grounded in the Holy Scriptures. Thus they are derived or secondary rather than primary sources.

The three great Ecumenical Creeds of the early undivided Christian Church are of particular value in revealing the substance of belief in that day. These three credal statements are the Apostles' Creed, the Nicene Creed, and the Athanasian Creed.

1. *The Apostles' Creed.* This familiar creed was not written by the apostles, but is so named because it represents a summary of their teaching. It is usually dated early in the second century A.D., and was then in substantially the same form as it is now. This creed may well be hidden in the hearts and minds of all believers and should be often upon their lips. The creed is as follows:

> I believe in God the Father Almighty, Maker of heaven and earth;
>
> And in Jesus Christ, His only Son our Lord; who was conceived by the Holy Ghost, born of the Virgin Mary; suffered under Pontius Pilate; was crucified, dead, and buried; He descended into hell; the third day He rose again from the dead; He ascended into heaven, and sitteth on the right hand of God the Father Almighty; from thence He shall come to judge the quick and the dead.
>
> I believe in the Holy Ghost; the Holy Catholic Church; the communion of saints; the forgiveness of sins; the resurrection of the body; and the life everlasting. Amen.

2. *The Nicene Creed.* This creed was formulated and adopted at the First Ecumenical Council, held in Nicaea in Bithynia during the summer of A.D. 325. The council was called by the Emperor Constantine who was not yet a baptized Christian. A large number of bishops attended—318 being the traditional but somewhat questionable number. They represented a great and glorious company of Christian fathers, and many showed evidence of having suffered for the faith. Eusebius, the father of Church history, was present and graphically describes this heroic group. They met for serious business. The Arian heresy was greatly distracting the Church and threatening much that many held dearer than life. Arius had sought to find a place for Christ above that of creation and yet outside the Godhead. The effect of his teaching was to make both Christ and the Holy Spirit created beings. This teaching aimed a mortal blow at the devotional consciousness of the followers of Christ. If Christ were not God, then to worship Him was idolatry. If He were neither God nor man, He could not be mediator, and thus Arianism destroyed the ground of redemption in Christ.

Led by the great Athanasius, who fought a life-long battle against this heresy, the formulators of the Nicene Creed erected a barrier against this insidious tide of evil. The text of the creed was subsequently changed somewhat, and it is quoted below in the modified form.

I believe in one God, the Father almighty, Maker of heaven and earth, and of all things visible and invisible.

And in one Lord Jesus Christ, the only begotten Son of God; begotten of His Father before all worlds, God of God, Light of light, Very God of very God, begotten, not made; being of one substance with the Father; by whom all things were made; who for us men and for our salvation came down from heaven, and was incarnate by the Holy Ghost of the Virgin Mary, and was made man; and was crucified also for us under Pontius Pilate; He suffered and was buried; and the third day He arose again according to the Scriptures; and ascended into heaven; and sitteth on the right hand of the Father; and He shall come again, with glory, to judge both the quick and the dead: whose kingdom shall have no end.

And I believe in the Holy Ghost, the Lord and Giver of Life, who proceedeth from the Father and the Son; who with the Father and Son together is worshiped and glorified; who spake by the prophets; and I believe in one Catholic and Apostolic Church; I acknowledge one baptism for the remission of sins; and I look for the resurrection of the dead; and the life of the world to come. Amen.

3. *The Athanasian Creed.* This creed is of a later and uncertain date, possibly as late as the seventh century A.D. It was never officially adopted by a general council but has been widely accepted as a valid source of Christian belief. In its teaching concerning the Trinity and the incarnation it is more detailed than the creeds cited above. It is too long for common use in worship, and too detailed and abstruse in some of its distinctions for wide appreciation or for full understanding.

IV. HISTORICAL DEVELOPMENT OF CHRISTIAN THEOLOGY

A. *The Earlier Period.*

The history of theology in the Church is a very extensive subject of which only a bare outline can be given here. During the first seven centuries of the Christian Era the Church fathers wrought out through patient endurance and often at the price of martyrdom the materials of Christian theology. They had to contend with paganism without and repeated heresies within the Church. They were frequently men of great talent and deep devotion. Theology was a sacred business of heart and life to these defenders of the faith. This early period was notable in that all but one of the seven Ecumenical

Councils were called to consider matters of doctrine. Among the most important writers of the period are Origen, whose *First Principles* is the first formal attempt at systematic theology; Augustine, whose influence is still very strong in theological thought; and John of Damascus, whose *Summary of the Orthodox Faith* is by many considered the first work worthy to be known as systematic theology. John of Damascus is the great theologian of the Greek Catholic Church. Theophanes states that he was called Chrysorrhoas, Stream of Gold—literally pouring forth gold—"because of that grace of spirit which shines like gold both in his doctrine and in his life."

B. *The Medieval Period.*

This era covers about seven centuries, from the death of John of Damascus to the beginning of the Reformation early in the sixteenth century. This was pre-eminently a period during which the doctors or schoolmen were actively engaged in developing well-ordered systems of theological thought. This scholastic era reached its climax in the thirteenth century when the theology of the period was co-ordinated and systematized by means of a new principle derived from Aristotelian philosophy. Among the great names associated with this phase of development we mention Anselm, Abelard, Peter Lombard, and Thomas Aquinas. Peter Lombard's *Four Books of Sentences* included arrangement of excerpts from the writings of Augustine and other Church Fathers in systematic order. It was used as a textbook in theology for more than five hundred years. The *Summa Theologica* of Thomas Aquinas represented the climax of theological work in the Scholastic Period. This work is still standard in the Roman Catholic Church. It is said that Thomas Aquinas thought of ten thousand objections to his own ideas and answered them all—at least to his own satisfaction. His achievement in philosophy, theology, and exegesis was monumental, and yet he died before the age of fifty.

C. *The Reformation Period.*

This was a period of controversies and credal formulations marking the transition from the medieval to the modern world. Separation of the Church into two main divisions, Roman Catholicism and Protestantism, gave rise to two radically different types of theology. While there are certain elements in common, there are also marked differences at almost every essential point in theology. Protestantism accepted certain early credal statements such as that of Nicaea, and most of the Augustinian doctrines of sin and grace. It rejected the absolute authority of ecclesiastical tradition and the findings of the Church councils. It maintained the supreme authority of the Scriptures in faith and morals, and the doctrine of justification by faith alone.

Theology of the Reformation Period, as regards Protestant thought, falls into two broad divisions—the Lutheran and the Reformed. The former may be characterized as more deeply sacramentarian, while the latter is more intellectual and doctrinal. One of the most significant Lutheran theologians of this period was Luther's friend, Melanchthon. His *Loci Communes* was published first in 1521, and ran through eighty editions during the lifetime of its author. However, the epochal work of this period was undoubtedly John Calvin's *Institutes of the Christian Religion*. This monumental study appeared first in 1536, and consisted of four books and one hundred and four chapters. The arrangement is essentially trinitarian, and the central idea is the sovereignty of God. Few, if any, books in the history of Christian thought have been more influential than Calvin's *Institutes*.

D. *The Confessional Period.*

This period in theological development spans the seventeenth and eighteenth centuries (A.D. 1600-1800). During these years the doctrinal statement of the larger communions were worked out in systematic form and were given to the Church as varying types of Christian dogmatics. Theologians of the period were sometimes called Protestant Scholastics, for they often tended to follow the same or similar principles of systematization as were used by the schoolmen of the Medieval Period.

It should not be assumed that theologies of varying types were original with the doctors of the Confessional Period. In fact, different types of theology are observable in the work of the New Testament writers themselves. For example, there is Peter with his practical emphasis; Paul, the logician and systematizer; and John, the seer who announces dogmatically what he had seen by intuition. Subsequent developments in Christian thought reveal many interesting variations in emphasis and content, only a few of which can be mentioned here.

Theology in the Greek Catholic Church was marked by its philosophical and speculative tendency. In contrast to Roman Catholic thought, it rejected the doctrine of the papacy, modified the seven sacraments, denied the immaculate conception of the Virgin Mary, circulated the Bible in the vernacular, and asserted its own supremacy.

The features which differentiate Roman Catholicism and Protestantism are marked and numerous. The Roman Catholic Church is sacramentarian, teaching that the Church is the one divinely appointed instrument through which spiritual blessings are communicated by means of the sacraments. The Protestant Church is evangelical, holding that God saves men directly by entering into personal and spiritual relations with them. Protestantism maintains that the true Church is composed of all those who are redeemed through Christ, and derives its authority from the living spiritual relation existing between the constituent members and the divine Head of the Church, Jesus Christ. Roman Catholic theology practically identifies the Church with its visible organization which derives its authority, not from any personal relation between Christ and any of its members, but from the original commission given by Christ to His disciples. From these divergent views as to the nature of the Church, the following differences in Catholic and Protestant theology obtain: (1) Protestantism maintains the universality of the priesthood of believers, in contrast to the special order of priesthood as asserted by Roman Catholicism. (2) Protestantism insists that grace is communicated through the truth received in faith as over against that which vests it solely in the sacraments. (3) Protestantism exalts the preaching of the Word above the sacramental ministry of the altar. (4) Protestantism declares that grace is received directly from Christ through the Spirit, and that this gives membership in the Church as Christ's spiritual body. On the other hand, Roman Catholics insist that a spiritual relationship with Christ must be established through the church.

It should be noted also that the Confessional Period was marked by the development of divergent lines of thought among various groups of Protestants. These differences were evident in the formulation of Lutheran, Reformed, Arminian, and lesser types of dogmatic systems. Space does not permit a consideration of these divergent views at this point. In our subsequent study we shall give particular attention to Arminianism, contrasting and comparing it with other types of Protestant thought. (See also *Annotated Bibliography* after Chapter XXII.)

E. *The Modern Period.*

In this survey only brief mention can be made of the very extensive developments in theological thought since 1800. Theologians of this era, especially the nineteenth century, may be roughly classified into schools of thought as follows: (1) The School of Schleiermacher which emphasized the Christian faith as having its seat in the consciousness of man. Religion was conceived as a "feeling of dependence," and Christ and His redemption were made the center of the theological system. (2) The Rationalistic School in which theology was extensively influenced by certain modern German philosophers. (3) The Mediating School which included a group of outstanding theologians who sought to maintain evangelical principles and yet combine them with the best thought of modern times. (4) The Ritschlian School which insisted strongly upon the recognition of the historical Christ, and the acceptance of the Scriptures as the record of revelation.

American theologians—Arminian, Reformed, and Lutheran—have been influenced by and are dependent upon European thought. Theologians of the Reformed Church in the United States are commonly classified into the Old School, which adheres rather closely to the views of Calvin and Augustine as regards human depravity and grace; and the New School, which has modified many of the original tenets of Calvinism in the direction of Arminianism. Jonathan Edwards was the first notable exponent of the latter school.

The writings of John Wesley constitute the foundational elements in the doctrinal standards of Methodism. The saintly John Fletcher, though an Anglican, was in some respects an apologist of Methodism. This "Arminian of Arminians" wrote convincingly and definitively in his *Checks to Antinomianism*, which is still the best treatise on the subject. Richard Watson's *Theological Institutes* (1823) was the first complete system of doctrine formulated by a Methodist. William Burton Pope in his *Compendium of Christian Theology* is the first British writer to compare favorably with Watson. Among other notable works which represent the Arminian type of theology we mention the following: Raymond's *Systematic Theology*, Ralston's *Elements of Divinity*, Sheldon's *System of Christian Doctrine*, Sumner's *Systematic Theology*, and Miley's *Systematic Theology*.

For a brief list of standard works in theology, with concise explanatory comments on each, the reader is referred to the *Annotated Bibliography* which follows Chapter XXII.

CHAPTER III

THE CHRISTIAN REVELATION

"The Bible contains the mind of God, the state of man, the way of
salvation, the doom of sinners, the happiness of believers. Its doctrines
are holy, its precepts are binding, its decisions are immutable. Read it
to believe, believe it to be safe, practice it to be holy. It contains light
to direct you, food to support you, and comfort to cheer you. It is the
traveler's guide, the pilgrim's staff, the pilot's compass, the soldier's sword,
and the Christian's charter. Here paradise is restored, heaven opened
and the gates of hell disclosed. Christ is its grand subject, our good its
design, and the glory of God its end. It should fill the memory, rule the
heart, and guide the feet. Read it slowly, daily, prayerfully. It is a mine
of wealth, a paradise of glory, and a river of pleasure. It is given you in
life, will be opened at the judgment, and will be remembered forever.
It involves the highest responsibility, will reward the greatest labor, and
condemn all who trifle with its contents."—WHITEHEAD.

Christian theology is based upon the revelation of
God in Christ, the record of which in its preliminary and
perfect stages is given in the Old and New Testaments.
In the following discussion of the Scriptures as the Rule
of Faith, our subject is divided into four principal topics:
I. The Nature of General Revelation; II. The Nature of
Special Revelation; III. The Inspiration of the Scriptures;
and, IV. The Canon of Holy Scripture. The first three of
these will be considered in this chapter and the fourth in
Chapter IV.

I. THE NATURE OF GENERAL REVELATION

A. *Definitions of General Revelation.*

It is customary to divide the subject of revelation
into two major categories: General Revelation and Special Revelation — sometimes designated Natural and
Supernatural, or External and Internal. By General
Revelation we mean the disclosure of Himself which
God makes to all men in nature, in the constitution of
the mind, and in the progress of human history.

B. *Revelation Through Nature.*

Nature is filled with the divine Spirit and reveals
God as the atmosphere is filled with sunlight and reveals

the sun. But the language of nature falls upon darkened intellects and dulled sensibilities and must be read in the dim light of a vitiated spiritual nature. When, however, the individual is spiritually renewed through faith in Christ, the revelation of God in nature becomes clearer, fuller, and replete with meaning and blessing.

Our perception of God in nature is also dulled by our very familiarity with its wonders. Some have thought that if God would only reveal Himself repeatedly in miraculous occurrences then surely belief in Him would be universal. But, as Dr. Samuel Harris pointed out, repetition of the miraculous would, through repeated acquaintance with it, soon lead many to discount or deny it as miraculous or as a revelation of God. Thus to adequately appreciate and realize the revelation of God in nature, one needs first to know Him in vital Christian experience. Perception — "seeing" — whether physical or spiritual, is essentially a subjective or inner experience, and man's outlook is always conditioned by his insights.

C. Revelation in the Nature and Constitution of Man.

Man knows himself to be a spiritual, personal being, and in the unity of this personality he finds three major aspects: intellect, feeling, and will. Man knows himself also to have a conscience from which arises a sense of duty to an Overmaster or Lord. Conscience is the self apprehending God and distinguishing itself from God, even as consciousness is the self distinguishing itself from the natural environment. Carlyle defined conscience as "that Somewhat or Someone within us which pronounces as to the rightness or wrongness of the choice of motives."

Here is the voice of the Eternal speaking in the inmost recesses of man's soul. It is not of our earth-born nature. In its essence it is timeless and eternal and personal—"a vital concrete personal Presence." Thus as consciousness is that quality of the self which knows itself in relation to external things, and cannot exist apart from its object in the temporal order; so also conscience cannot exist without a Personal Object in the timeless and eternal order.

God also becomes known through man's powers of reasoning and intuition. He is known directly and immediately in consciousness, and indirectly through the evidences of God which man perceives in the universe. Man thus becomes aware of God as the evidence of His existence flashes upon him from a multitude of sources. Man is at once a creature of nature and a personal being transcending nature. He is therefore aware that he is a spiritual being made for communion with the Supernatural. By means of these spiritual capacities which distinguish him from all other organic beings in God's created universe, man has contact with his spiritual or supernatural environment. Dulled though these spiritual sensibilities may be because of the effects of sin, he nevertheless has certain perceptions concerning the spiritual order.

D. *The Revelation of God in History.*

The progress of human history reveals the purposes of God in a higher manner than is possible in the constitution of a single individual. The Christian philosophy of history has as its basic proposition the fact that God's plans and purposes will ultimately be achieved in the affairs of men and nations. This does not mean that the volitional activity of men in determining historical development is questioned. But, in addition to the human element, there is the Directing Presence and Authoritative Will behind the human scene. History is viewed as a pyramid with the apex representing the coming of Jesus Christ, God manifest in the flesh. In the light of His coming previous centuries take on added meaning. In the light of His mission and the ultimate triumph of His Church, succeeding centuries gather added significance. By His presence the course of history continues to develop in spite of the darkness and antagonism of sin until that glorious day when all things are gathered together in one, both in heaven and in earth, even in Him (Eph. 1: 10).

II. The Nature of Special Revelation

A. *Definition of Special Revelation.*

By special revelation we refer to the redemptive purpose of God manifested in Christ Jesus, as over against the more general revelation of His power and Godhead in the created universe, the constitution of man, and human history. Through special revelation man may come to know God, not as a mere force or law, but as a Supreme Personality who created man specifically for communion with Himself. Since man was thus created for personal fellowship, it is reasonable to suppose that God would make disclosures of Himself to human personality. The fact that sin entered the world subsequent to man's creation, destroying the intimate personal relationship between God and man, suggests that if that communion was ever to be restored, God's attitude toward sin must be understood and His redemptive purpose and plan made known. Thus a special revelation of God and His will was made imperative. In it we find the unfolding of the eternal counsel of God as it concerns the redemption of man through Christ.

Three preliminary observations may well be made in this introduction to special revelation. *First,* the redemptive purpose of God is revealed in Christ. He is the sum of all revelation, *the brightness of his glory, and the express image of his person, and upholding all things by the word of his power, when he had by himself purged our sins, sat down on the right hand of the Majesty on high* (Heb. 1:3). In Christ, all the prophets with all their lamps; all the priests with all their altars and sacrifices; and all the kings with their thrones and scepters are lost in Him who is our Prophet, Priest, and King.

Second, the Scriptures contain and are the Word of God. Not merely Christ's words or His acts, but He himself was the revelation of God as manifested in His words and acts. His testimony is the spirit of prophecy— the last word of objective revelation. It is because this testimony is perfected in the Scriptures that they become the Word of God objectified. Here we find the final

testimony of Jesus Christ with reference to sinful men
and the means whereby they may be redeemed.

Third, the revelation of God given to man in the Holy
Scriptures is addressed primarily to the principle of faith
in man, and only secondarily does it present its credentials to his reason.

B. *The Christian Book.*

In any discussion of the Christian revelation the
first major subject must of necessity be the Christian
Book since here alone are to be found its documentary
records. Our first inquiry in this connection deals with
the nature and function of the Scriptures as the Oracles
of God. The Bible occupies an intermediate position between the partial revelation of God in nature and the
perfect revelation of God in Christ—the Personal Word.
If we place at the very center of Revelation the idea of
the Eternal Word and draw about it a series of concentric
circles, the first and nearest would represent the Word
incarnate, or the revelation of God in Christ, the Personal Word. The second circle farther removed would
represent the Bible as the Written Word. It is in this
sense that the Bible is at once the Word of God and the
record of that Word. It bears the same relation to the
Living and Personal Word that our spoken and recorded
words bear to our own persons. The third and outer
circle would represent the revelation of God in nature
and the created universe. In order, therefore, to correctly understand the Bible as the written Word, we
must estimate it in its relation to nature on the one hand
and the Personal Word on the other.

The revelation of God in the Holy Scriptures is not
meant to supersede His revelation in nature, but to add
to it. From observation of the natural realm, the mind
is able to grasp spiritual conceptions. Jesus spoke of
the lilies of the field and taught a lesson in the providential care of the Father. He mentioned the vine and the
branches and called attention to our dependence on Himself for our spiritual sustenance. The earth and the
Bible are God's two texts, each having its place, time,

and function in progressive revelation. Nature reveals something of God and divine things, the Bible supplements that revelation. The first tells us somewhat of His eternal power and Godhead, the other of His mercy and love. Without the Bible, the universe would be a riddle; without Nature, the Bible would be meaningless.

As already noted, the Bible must ever be held in proper relation to the Personal Word lest men substitute the written Word for Christ, the Living Word. When that is done men become bound by legal rather than by spiritual bonds. Religious knowledge becomes formal rather than spiritual. Christ tends to become a mere historical figure, not a living Reality. More attention is given to creeds than to Christ. Christian experience is likely to become a mere intellectual assent to a creed than a vital personal contact with Deity. The Bible thus divorced from the mystical connection with the Personal Word becomes in a sense a usurper, a pretender to the throne.

In the nineteenth century a movement, popularly known as "destructive criticism," endeavored to enthrone Reason, sever the Bible from its Living Source, and debase it to the position of a mere book among books. In protest against this a group arose to the defense of the full inspiration of the Bible, as well as its genuineness, authenticity, and authority. The tendency of these defenders of the faith was to resort to a legalistic defense, depending upon logic, reason, and debate. Spiritual men and women—those filled with the Holy Spirit— are not unduly concerned with criticism of the Bible. They do not rest merely in the letter which must be defended by argument. The more excellent basis of their faith is in their risen Lord, the glorified Christ. They know the Bible is true, not primarily through the efforts of the apologists, but because they are acquainted with the Author. The Spirit which inspired the Word dwells within them and witnesses to its truth.

C. *The Christian Faith.*

By the Christian faith we mean the acceptance by man of the revelation of God given by Christ and recorded in the Holy Scriptures. It is the revealed truth incorporated in personal life, and made vital and dynamic by being thus embodied in human personality.

The body of Christian truth is addressed primarily to faith. The faculty of believing is the highest exercise of man as a personal being, and calls into action the full range of his powers: intelligence, affections, and will. The revelation of God to man is personal, and is to the whole of man's personality. If the feelings be overemphasized in our knowledge of God, we have mysticism. If the understanding be overemphasized, the result is rationalism.

Mysticism leads to the error of claiming for itself an inspiration equal to the utterances of Holy Writ, and rationalism falls short of a true knowledge of God. To those who by faith receive the truth, revelation becomes an organic whole. To them it is both objectively and subjectively the Christian faith—objectively as a body of revealed truth, subjectively as having become their own in faith and assurance. It is more than a philosophy of life or a rich tradition. It is the richer inheritance of the Holy Spirit, who has quickened their belief into assurance of personal knowledge and experience.

While the Christian faith is addressed primarily to the principle of believing in man, it also appeals to reason as subordinate to that faith. The experiential aspect of the knowledge of God is to be checked at all times by the body of Christian truth as given in the Bible, and by the voice of reason, humbled and purified by the indwelling Spirit. Faith honors reason when thus restored to soundness, and gives it perfect authority in that field over which reason should preside. The Scriptures of revelation and the voice of sound reason blend into one perfect and harmonious whole.

D. *The Credentials of Revelation.*

We now consider the Christian revelation as presenting its evidences to reason. The believer is exhorted to be ready and prepared to give a reason or apology for the hope that is within him (I Peter 3: 15). He must not overlook the value of the credentials of revelation as a means of bringing the unbeliever to listen to the voice of revelation. Of course, these external evidences apart from the internal demonstration of truth by the Holy Spirit cannot have the same strength as the combined credential, and therefore too much cannot be expected of this form of evidence.

It is to be remembered that the Christian revelation evidences its value in that it appeals directly to a preparation in the human spirit. Augustine expressed a universal truth when he said, "Thou hast created us for Thyself, and our hearts are restless till they rest in Thee." Throughout the whole of Scripture the voice of the Creator speaks directly to the inner needs of His creatures. There is no possible question growing out of created human nature to which response is not given by the Creator. Not only so, but Christianity comes as the culmination and final answer to the earlier and less complete revelations of God. It is the explanation of all the preparatory disclosures and the consummation of them all. In the words of Dr. Pope, "It is the last of many words, and leaves nothing to be desired in the present estate of mankind."

1. *The Evidence of Miracles.* An intervention of divine Power in the established course of nature beyond man's understanding is regarded as a miracle; while the same divine intervention in the realm of knowledge is termed prophecy. Miracles do not represent a violation of natural law nor a suspension of it. God is a free Personal Being and is not bound by natural forces of His own creation. God may introduce a sufficient cause for any effect that He chooses to produce without destroying the integrity of the natural order.

A number of scriptural terms are used to describe miracles. One of these words is *powers.* This signifies the agency by which miracles are produced—the power of God. A second term denotes *wonders,* and emphasizes the effect produced on the spectators. A third term is that of *signs.* This stresses the significance of miracles as seals by which God placed the stamp of approval upon the persons by whom the miracles were wrought. These three terms *wonders, signs,* and *powers* occur three times in connection with one another. Thus in the healing of the paralytic (Mark 2: 1-12), it was a *wonder* for "they were all amazed"; it was a *power,* for at Christ's word the man took up his bed and went out before them all; and it was a *sign* for it was a token that One greater than man was among them. A fourth term, signifying *works,* occurs only in the Gospel of John (John 10: 38, 15: 24). Taken in connection with the deity of Christ, the term suggests that what men regarded as wonders, requiring the exercise of mighty power, were in the estimation of the Lord himself simply works, and required no more exertion at His hand than that which was common or ordinary with Him as divine.

The chief value of miracles as evidences lies in the fact that they constitute an authentication of the messengers of God to their contemporaries. This fact was expressed by Nicodemus in words addressed to Christ, *Rabbi, we know that thou art a teacher come from God; for no man can do these miracles that thou doest, except God be with him* (John 3: 2).

The miracles recorded in the Scriptures meet all tests or criteria of genuineness, and are thus important as credentials of revelation. They are always faithful to the character of God, revealing either His power, wisdom, mercy, or justice. They are worthy of God. They are guaranteed as historical facts by many infallible proofs. This is especially true of the resurrection of Christ, the central miracle of the Bible. This was believed by a large number of mentally sound and conscientious persons, many of whom sealed their faith with their blood.

2. *Prophecy as a Credential of Revelation.* Unlike miracles, prophecy is *cumulative* in its evidential value, each fulfilled prediction becoming the basis for further prediction. It is a credential of the highest order. Prophecy is a declaration, a description, a representation, or a prediction of that which is beyond the power of human

wisdom to discover. It is a miracle in the field of knowledge. As prediction it is the divine impartation of future
knowledge. Prophecy in this sense of foreannouncement
was intended to be a permanent credential in the Church.
Thus Jesus Christ declared, *And now I have told you
before it come to pass, that when it is come to pass ye
might believe* (John 14:29).

Prophecy follows certain well defined principles. Dr.
Pope, in his discussion of the subject, calls attention to
four laws of prophetic prediction. (1) Christ is its Supreme Subject. It is to Him that all the prophets gave
witness. (2) The law of progression, according to which
each age is under the sway of some governing prophecy,
the accomplishment of which introduces a new order of
prophetic expectation. (3) The law of reserve, by which
God has so ordered that in every prediction and every
cycle of predictions, sufficient is given to encourage hope
and anticipation, and enough concealed to shut up the
prediction to faith. (4) Prophecy has been constituted
a sign to each succeeding generation. The books of the
prophets furnish an inexhaustible fund of information
and instruction apart from the predictive elements, and
this makes it clear that prophecy was intended to be an
abiding credential throughout the whole course of time.

3. *The Unique Personality of Christ.* The supreme
credential of Christianity is Christ. He is the Great Fulfillment of all prophecy. To Him is given all power in
heaven and in earth (Matt. 28:18). In His sacred presence the sphere of miracles is immediately enlarged. His
advent was a miracle, and His words and works, His
life, death, resurrection and ascension were but a continuation of one great miracle.

Prophecy also takes on a new aspect when considered
in direct relation to the unique personality of Christ. No
earthly biography was ever preceded by such a preface
as that furnished our Lord in the Messianic prophecy.
For a thousand years, a picture was gradually unfolded
of One who should be Son of man and Son of God; and
who should within His unique personality manifest the

full range of divine and human attributes in glorious harmony.

The wealth of Christ's person, however, transcends even the most glowing predictions of prophecy. That God should Himself create a living creature in His own image, a reflection of Himself, is glorious; but that God himself in the Person of His Son should appear in the flesh, and take upon Him the likeness of man transcends in glory all other manifestations, human or divine. When we consider that the incarnation was in itself redemptive as representing a new order of creation; and that it was provisional in its relation to the crucifixion, resurrection, and ascension; and, further, that to this glorious Being was given the power of so transforming a sinful creature as to bring him into possession of the divine holiness, and so exalt a debased and groveling worm of the dust that he shall sit with Him on the throne of His majesty; then this is not only indescribable but inconceivable! Yet here the glory of God and the glory of man are conjoined. In Him we not only find our calling's glorious hope, but in Him likewise we are made the praise of His glory.

4. *The Witness of the Holy Spirit.* The last evidence of revelation is found in the presence of the Holy Spirit in the Church, and His witness to sonship in the hearts of individuals. The Holy Spirit was not given to supersede Christ, but to enlarge and make more effective the work begun in the incarnation (John 16: 7, 14; 15: 26). The early Church clearly recognized the importance of the witness of the Holy Spirit. Thus Peter, speaking to the council declared, *We are his witnesses of these things, and so also is the Holy Ghost, whom God hath given to them that obey him* (Acts 2: 32, 33; 5: 32). The Apostle Paul builds a strong argument upon the witness of the Holy Spirit, maintaining that the presence of unbelief regarding the Christian revelation is due directly to the rejection of the Spirit (I Cor. 12: 3). The Author of the Epistle to the Hebrews gives expression to the thought that the Holy Ghost attests the truth of the atoning and intercessory work of Jesus Christ (Heb. 10: 12-15).

We are therefore urged and warned to take heed lest we refuse the One who now speaks from heaven (Heb. 12: 25, 26).

III. The Inspiration of the Scriptures

Christian theology as the science of Christianity is based upon the documentary records of God's revelation of Himself in Christ Jesus. The Holy Scriptures, containing these records, constitute the primary and true source. It is necessary and proper, therefore, that our inquiry be directed toward the nature and authority of the Bible. That authority lies in the fact that the Scriptures constitute an inspired revelation of God to man.

A. *Definitions of Inspiration.*

In general, inspiration signifies the operation of the Holy Spirit upon the writers of the books of the Bible in such a manner that their productions became the expression of God's will. The term "inspiration" is derived from a Greek word which signifies literally "the breathing of God" or "the breathing into." As Dr. Hannah states, it is "That extraordinary agency of the Holy Spirit upon the mind in consequence of which the person who partakes of it is enabled to embrace and communicate the truth of God without error, infirmity, or defeat." This applies to the subjects of communication whether they consist of that which was immediately revealed to the writers or that with which they were previously acquainted. Dr. Strong shifts the emphasis of inspiration from a mode of divine agency to the body of truth which is a product of this agency; and further, he holds that inspiration applies only to the whole body of Scripture when taken together, each part being viewed in connection with what precedes or follows. His definition is as follows: "Inspiration is that influence of the Spirit of God upon the minds of the Scripture writers which made their writings the record of a progressive divine revelation, sufficient when taken together and interpreted by the same Spirit who inspired them to lead every honest inquirer to Christ and salvation." While the views of the Church concerning theories of inspiration have varied widely, there is no subject upon which there has been closer agreement than the fact of inspiration. To summarize: inspiration is the actuating energy of the Holy Spirit by which men chosen of God have officially proclaimed His will as revealed to us in the sacred Scriptures.

B. *Inspiration and Revelation.*

By *revelation* we understand a direct communication from God to man of such knowledge as is beyond the power of his reason to attain, or for whatever cause was not known to the person who received it. By *inspiration* we mean the actuating energy of the Holy Spirit by which holy men were qualified to receive religious truth and to communicate it to others without error. Revelation made the writers wiser; inspiration enabled them to communicate the revelation without mistake. The disclosure of the mind of God is Revelation when viewed from the standpoint of the truth unveiled; it is inspiration when viewed in relation to the method of its impartation and transmission.

C. *The Possibility and Necessity of Inspiration.*

Undoubtedly the Creator of men may act upon the minds of His creatures, and this action may be extended to any degree necessary in order to attain the fulfillment of His purposes. If men can communicate their thoughts by means of language and make themselves understood by others, most certainly the Author of our being can reveal Himself to men if He chooses to do so. Our inability to explain this extraordinary action of God on the human mind is no valid objection to the doctrine of inspiration. It is unreasonable to suppose that God, the "Father of spirits" does not have it in His power to communicate truth to the minds of men, or to instruct them in those things which concern their eternal well-being.

The necessity of inspiration grows out of the nature of the subjects which the Scriptures unfold. There are truths, such as the facts concerning creation and Antediluvian times, which could not otherwise be known except by special inspiration. Granting the possibility that written accounts and oral tradition had been handed down from former times, even then inspiration was necessary in order that a true and inerrant account be given. Again, the authoritative language of the Scriptures argues the necessity of inspiration. The writers of the books of the Bible do not present to us their own thoughts, but they preface their remarks with such statements as *Thus saith the Lord,* or *The word of the Lord came.* It is said that these and synonymous statements occur 3,808 times in the Old Testament alone. It follows, then, that either the sacred writers spoke as they were moved by the Holy Spirit, or they must be acknowledged as impostors—a conclusion invalidated by the quality and enduring character of their works and other evidences. Our conclusion is that the Scriptures were given by plenary inspiration to the degree that they became the infallible Word of God, the authoritative Rule of Faith and Practice in the Church.

D. *Theories of Inspiration.*

Various theories have been advanced in an attempt to harmonize and explain the relation of the divine and human elements in the inspiration of the Scriptures. Christianity, however, is based upon the fact of inspiration and is not dependent upon any particular theory as to the origin of the Sacred Writings. The theories of inspiration may be conveniently classified as follows: (1) the Mechanical or Dictation Theory, which emphasizes the supranaturalistic element; (2) the Intuition and Illumination Theories, which stress the human element: and (3) the Dynamical or Mediating Theory.

1. *The Mechanical or Dictation Theory.* This theory emphasizes the supranaturalistic element to such a degree that the personality of the writer is set aside, and he becomes under the direction of the Holy Spirit a mere amanuensis or penman. As one writer states this extreme view, "They neither spoke nor wrote any word of their own, but uttered syllable by syllable as the Spirit put it into their mouths." Holders of this theory admittedly have difficulty in accounting for the peculiari-

ties of individual expression which is so evident in the
books of the Bible. In addition, this theory is weak in
that it denies the inspiration of persons and holds only to
the inspiration of the writings; whereas, the Scriptures
plainly teach that *holy* MEN *of God spake as they were
moved by the Holy Ghost* (II Peter 1: 21). Also, this
mechanical theory does not agree with all of the facts. It
is evident from the Scriptures themselves that the writers
were aroused to action in different ways—though by the
inspiration of one Spirit. Some disclosures of truth were
made in audible words (Num. 7: 89; Acts 9: 5). But the
writers in a number of instances refer to sources, or they
used their own knowledge of history, or recorded their
own experiences. Such is clearly the case in Luke's
Gospel and in the Acts of the Apostles. Finally, mechanical inspiration is out of harmony with the known manner in which God works in the human soul. The higher
and more exalted the divine communications, the greater
the illumination of the human soul and the more fully
does man come into possession of his own natural and
spiritual faculties.

2. *The Intuition and Illumination Theories.* According to the intuition theory, inspiration is only the natural
insight of men lifted to a higher plane of development.
It is rationalistic in the extreme, and virtually denies the
supernatural element in the Scriptures. The Bible is debased to the plane of literary works created by mere
human genius. The great weakness of this theory is
that man's insight into truth is rendered ineffective and
perverted by a darkened intellect and wrong affections
(I Cor. 2: 14).

The illumination theory differs from the preceding
in that it holds to an elevation of the religious perceptions instead of the natural faculties. It has been likened
to the spiritual illumination which every believer receives from the Holy Spirit in Christian experience. The
inspiration of the writers of sacred Scripture, according
to this theory, differed only in degree, not in kind, from
that which belongs to all believers. While illumination
through intensification of experience may prepare the

mind for the reception and appreciation of the truth already revealed in the Scriptures, it is not in itself a communication of that truth.

3. *The Dynamical or Mediating Theory.* This is a mediating theory that explains and preserves the proper harmony between both the divine and human factors in the inspiration of the Bible. It maintains that the sacred writers were given extraordinary aid without any interference with their personal characteristics or activities. God spoke through human agencies, but these were not reduced to mere passive instruments or robots. In opposition to the intuition theory, the dynamical theory maintains that there is a true supernatural element in inspiration. In harmony with the illumination theory, it maintains that there was a special spiritual preparation of heart and mind for the reception of the message, but, in addition, insists that there must be a divine communication of truth. Against the dynamical theory little objection can be urged.

E. *Scriptural Proofs of Divine Inspiration.*

The Scriptures claim to be divinely inspired. Our consideration of this testimony of the Bible will be summarized under the following topics: (1) the Witness of the Old Testament; (2) the Declarations of our Lord; and, (3) the Testimony of the Apostles.

1. *The Witness of the Old Testament.* Communications of divine truth were given at various times and in divers manners to the writers of the Old Testament. The special privilege of creating the first body of literature known as Sacred Scripture was given to Moses, of whom it was recorded *that there arose not a prophet since in Israel like unto Moses, whom the Lord knew face to face* (Deut. 34:10). His messages were given by divine authority, and no phrase is of more frequent recurrence than the words *The Lord spake unto Moses.*

David, the poet-king of Israel, laid claim to divine inspiration in the declaration: *The Spirit of the Lord spoke by me, and his word was in my tongue* (II Sam. 23:2). The later prophets delivered their messages not only in the name of the Lord, but as messages immediately inspired by the Spirit. Thus Isaiah, Jeremiah, Ezekiel, and a number of minor prophets clearly and repeatedly declared that the words they spoke were inspired by the Spirit of God.

2. *The Declarations of our Lord.* Jesus Christ declared the Old Testament to be of divine authority, and His testimony must be the final word as to the nature and results of inspiration. He regarded the Old Testament as a completed canon, and expressly declared that the least ordinance or commandment must have its perfect fulfillment. Jesus quoted from four of the five books of Moses, from the Psalms, Isaiah, Zechariah, and Malachi. He recognized the threefold division of the Scriptures which was common among the Jews—the Law, the Prophets, and the Psalms (Luke 24: 44, 45). He declared that these testified of Himself. He expressly stated that the Old Testament was the Word of God (Matt. 15: 3, 6), and declared that the Scriptures, the Word of God, cannot be broken (John 10: 35). He recognized the whole content of Scripture in its unity, and declared significantly that it referred to His own Person and work (Luke 24: 27). This is testimony of unquestioned validity, for it comes from One of supreme authority: *For he whom God hath sent speaketh the words of God: for God giveth not the Spirit by measure unto him* (John 3: 34).

3. *The Testimony of the Apostles.* Repeatedly the apostles gave testimony concerning the inspiration of the Scriptures. St. Paul often quotes from the Old Testament in his writings, and declares in II Timothy 3: 16, 17, that *All scripture is given by inspiration of God and is profitable for doctrine, for reproof, for correction, for instruction in righteousness: that the man of God may be perfect, throughly furnished unto all good works.* In the gathering of apostles and disciples immediately before Pentecost, Peter declared, *Men and brethren, this scripture must needs have been fulfilled, which the Holy Ghost by the mouth of David spake before concerning Judas, which was guide to them that took Jesus* (Acts 1: 16). The nature of the Epistle to the Hebrews is such

that the whole composition depends upon the Old Testament as Holy Scripture. This it regards as the oracles of God, spoken by the Holy Spirit and preserved to the Christian Church in a book quoted as authoritative and infallible.

The apostles were also united in their belief that their own messages were from the Lord Jesus Christ and by His Holy Spirit. Everywhere the fact of inspiration is implied by themselves and is understood to be such by those who received them. Revelation made by the Old Testament prophets and those made by New Testament apostles are placed side by side as being of equal authority (II Peter 3:2). The writings of St. Paul are classed with the *other scriptures* by the Apostle Peter (II Peter 3:16). St. Paul himself ascribed his revelations to Christ, but his inspiration to the Holy Spirit (Compare Gal. 1:16; Eph. 3:3; I Cor. 2:12, 13). St. John speaks of *an unction from the Holy One* (I John 2:20), and declares that he was *in the Spirit* (Rev. 1:10) when revelations were given. Comparing this with Revelation 22:6 it is clear that John used this expression in the sense that it was used in the Old Testament by those who spoke by inspiration. We conclude this brief summary of evidence concerning the inspiration of the New Testament with the words of the Apostle Paul: *Now we have received, not the spirit of the world, but the spirit which is of God; that we might know the things that are freely given to us of God. Which things also we speak, not in the words which man's wisdom teacheth, but which the Holy Ghost teacheth; comparing spiritual things with spiritual* (I Cor. 2:12, 13).

E. *Holy Men and a Holy Bible.*

As the subject of the inspiration of the Scriptures is concluded, a number of observations should be made. *First,* the Holy Spirit, proceeding from the Father and the Son, is the sole basis of communication between God and man. The Holy Spirit is alone the Author of inspiration. We conclude, therefore, "that while the Scripture is God-inspired, only the Spirit is the inspiring God." *Second,* the Bible clearly has in it a human element. Not only did the Holy Spirit speak through David, but David also spoke. *Holy men,* we are told, *spake as they were moved by the Holy Ghost.* An even better rendering is: *Holy men spake from God, being moved by the Holy Ghost.* Just as the Personal Word of God was both human and divine, so also the written Word of God must be viewed. The Bible possesses as a result of the combination of the human and divine elements both divine authority and human appeal. The holy, inspired men who wrote the Bible had both character and preparation. They were holy in heart and life for only such could have grasped spiritual truth under divine inspiration. They were men possessed of the full range of their powers, but these faculties were prepared by the immediate influence of the inspiring Spirit in order that they might bring into being the Sacred Scriptures. Lastly, the utterances of these holy men through whom God spoke constitute a body of divine truth, the Holy Scriptures. As such we regard the Bible as given to us by plenary inspiration. By this we mean that the whole and every part is divinely inspired. It is therefore the final and authoritative Rule of Faith in the Church.

CHAPTER IV

THE CANON OF HOLY SCRIPTURE

"When the selection and collection of sacred books was made, first of the Old Testament and then of the New, it was not done by direct commandment or authority from God, nor was it done by any formal agreement of men or by churchly decree. The Church gathered into sacred wholes the writings that it held sacred separately; and it held them sacred partly because of their contents, and partly because it believed them to have been written by men especially honored and inspired. The process was gradual, because genuine and natural. It is sometimes imagined that councils fixed the canon; but in fact councils scarcely did more than recognize and ratify the judgment of the common Christian body. The canon was the outcome of the religious life that sprang from the divine revelation: that is to say, revelation first produced its own divine life in men, and then through that life produced, collected, and organized its records and other literary memorials. The judgment by which the canon was formed was the religious judgment of the believing people."—WILLIAM NEWTON CLARKE.

In Chapter III we examined the subject of revelation as the divine unveiling of the truth, and as the Christian faith received by man. Also we described the divine-human manner in which that revelation was committed to writing through the inspiration of the Spirit. In the present chapter we complete our study of revelation by considering in greater detail the specific character of the Bible as containing the divinely authorized documents of the Christian faith. This leads us to a study of the Canon of the Holy Scripture.

By the canonicity of a book is meant its right to a place in the collection of Christian sacred writings. The word "canon" means literally a straight rod or measuring reed. Some scholars believe that the word was originally used to designate a catalogue or list of things that belonged to the Church.

It was applied particularly to the publicly approved list of books that might be read in the Church for edification and instruction. In this sense it is thought to discriminate between the *canonical* books which might be read authoritatively, and the *apocryphal* books which might be read for instruction but not as a standard or rule of faith. At any rate, the word "canon" came to be commonly used in a twofold sense—as a test or standard of measurement, and as applied to that which is measured. The canonical books are therefore those that have been measured up to the standard tests. The word has been used in this twofold sense since the fourth century A.D. Subsequently in our discussion we shall note some of the tests or standards by which the canonicity of a book was determined. Limitations of space necessarily require that our survey of this important theme be rather sketchy. Those interested in a more definitive study of the Canon are referred to the appropriate citations in the *Annotated Bibliography* listed after Chapter XXII.

I. The Old Testament Canon

A. *Divisions of the Old Testament.*

The Old Testament Scriptures are arranged in three great divisions: the Law, the Prophets, and the Writings or the "Psalms." The first division included the Pentateuch, that is, the five books of Moses. The second was divided into the Former or Earlier Prophets which included the historical books of Joshua, Judges, Samuel, and Kings; and the Latter Prophets: Isaiah, Jeremiah, Ezekiel, and the Twelve (Minor Prophets). The third division included Psalms, Proverbs, Job, Daniel, Ezra, Nehemiah, the Chronicles, Songs of Solomon, Ruth, Lamentations, Ecclesiastes, and Esther. Since the Psalms formed the first book in this third group, the Scriptures are sometimes referred to as the Law, the Prophets, and the Psalms (Matt. 11:13; Luke 16:16).

B. *Development of the Old Testament Canon.*

The beginnings of the canon of the Old Testament are shrouded in mystery. We are told that before his death Moses wrote a book of the law which he commanded the Levites to put in the side of the ark, *that it may be there for a witness against thee* (Deut. 31:26). In this book of the law, it was enjoined upon every future king that *it shall be, when he sitteth upon the throne of his kingdom, that he shall write him a copy of this law in a book out of that which is before the priests the*

Levites: and it shall be with him, and he shall read there-in all the days of his life (Deut. 17:18, 19). Later we are informed that Joshua made a covenant with the people and wrote these words in the book of the law of God (Joshua 24:26). Subsequently, the Prophet Samuel wrote *in a book and laid it up before the Lord* (I Sam. 10:25). Under the reforms of Jehoshaphat the people were taught out of the book of the law (II Chron. 17:9).

A landmark in the formation of the Old Testament canon occurred in 621 B.C. It was then that Hilkiah the high priest discovered the book of the law in the temple. This happened during the earlier part of the reign of Josiah (II Kings 22:8, 10). After the book had been read before the king, he called a great gathering composed of the elders, priests, prophets, and all the people of Judah and Jerusalem. The account informs us that the king *read in their ears all the words of the book of the covenant which was found in the house of the Lord .... to perform the words of this covenant that were written in this book. And all the people stood to the covenant* (II Kings 23:1-3). This incident is rightly considered an epochal event in the history of the canon. Here in a solemn religious act, king and people accept the book read before them as expressing the divine will and as binding upon themselves.

In the fifth century B.C. two significant events in the development of the Old Testament canon took place. The first was the occasion in the time of Ezra and Nehemiah when the Law of Moses was read before the people and a covenant was made which was sealed by the princes, Levites, and priests (Neh. 9:38; 10:1ff). During the same century the Samaritan Pentateuch was created. This was composed of the five books of Moses. These the Samaritans had eagerly adopted in order to substantiate their claim of being descended from ancient Israel. It appears from these two developments that the Law, the first division of the Hebrew Scriptures, was accepted as canonical by 440 B.C.

The second division of the Old Testament canon, commonly known as the "Prophets," was also gradual in its development. It is probable that the canon of this division was well on its way toward being closed in the century that marked the close of the canon of the Law. Possibly this explains why the books of Ezra and Nehemiah are not contained in the "Prophets." According to the best available evidence, the canon of this second division of the Old Testament was closed by at least 200 B.C.

The third division, the Writings or Psalms, contains writings of a diverse character. The first reference we have to these "other writings" as a group occurs about 130 B.C. The best available evidence indicates that this third division of the Old Testament canon was closed about 100 B.C.

C. *Witnesses to the Canon of the Old Testament.*

Jewish authorities recognized the present canon of the Old Testament as being in existence at the time of Christ. Josephus, the great Hebrew historian, makes the following statement concerning the Hebrew Scriptures: "We have only twenty-two books which are to be trusted as having divine authority, of which five are the books of Moses. From his death to the reign of Artaxerxes, king of Persia, the prophets, who were the successors of Moses, have written thirteen books. The remaining four contain hymns to God, and documents of life for human edification." Our English Bible contains thirty-nine books, considering the minor prophets as twelve books instead of one, and making certain other divisions not found in the Hebrew Bible. The action taken by the Council of Jamnia, A.D. 90, may well be regarded as the final stage in fixing the Jewish canon. This action approved all of the books in the English Old Testament and no others.

The highest witness to the canon of the Old Testament as divinely inspired is found in the fact that it was ratified by our Lord and His apostles. The importance of this supreme testimony can hardly be overemphasized in establishing the Old Testament as the infallible Oracles of God. It is this fact which seals the Jewish canon as Christian Scripture. Of this evidence Dr. Pope writes that their divine origin is guaranteed to the Church by the fact "That the Saviour has given His authenticating testimony to the whole body of them in their integrity. That sanction, first, makes the Old Testament the revelation of Christ. As it testified of Him, so He testifies of it. He took it into His hands and blessed it, and hallowed it forever as His own. As revelation is Christ, and Christ is the subject of the Old Testament, the Old Testament is of necessity the revelation of God. Knowing better than any human critic can know all its internal obscurities, He sealed it nevertheless for the reverence of His people. The canon of the ancient oracles, precisely as we hold them now, no more, no less, He sanctified and gave to the Church as the early preparatory records of His own gospel and kingdom. That sanction, secondly, assures us that the New Testament is His own authoritative completion of the Scriptures of revelation" (POPE, *Compend Chr. Th.*, pp. 39, 40).

II. THE NEW TESTAMENT CANON

A. *Early History of the New Testament Canon.*

The formation of the New Testament canon was a gradual process extending over a considerable period of time—the first four centuries of the Christian Era. Doubt concerning any of the books had vanished by A.D. 400. In II Peter 3:16, we find evidence of an early collection of Pauline Epistles in which St. Peter admits that there "are some things hard to be understood." St. Paul requests in Col. 4:16 that *when this epistle is read among you, cause that it be read also in the church of the Laodiceans; and that ye likewise read the epistle from Laodicea.* There is some evidence that the Epistles to the Ephesians and to the Romans were both originally in the nature of circular letters. It will be readily understood how the early churches would preserve the epistles directed to them, and how they would cherish circular letters which came to rest in their collections. Thus unconsciously began the growth of the New Testament.

B. *Early Canons and Catalogues.*

The earliest mention of a definite canon for the New Testament is in A.D. 140. However, the Muratorian Canon (A.D. 200) is far more significant. This contained a list of books regarded as authoritative in Rome. In it are found all the books of our present New Testament except Hebrews, St. James, and John's Third Epistle. The Second Epistle of Peter is regarded as doubtful. It is probable that by this time the concept of the New Testament as the scriptural companion of the Old Testament was being recognized.

During the third and fourth centuries several church fathers drew up lists of the books of the New Testament. These vary somewhat, though some of them, such as the catalogues of Athanasius, Ruffinus, and Augustine contain the full list of the New Testament books as now acknowledged. The list of Eusebius (A.D. 315) is of particular interest because he mentions all the books accepted by his contemporaries, which he divided into two groups: the acknowledged, and the disputed books. In addition, he adds a third class of spurious or rejected books. In the list of fully accepted books he includes the four Gospels, the Acts, the Epistles of St. Paul, I Peter, and I John, and with some hesitation he mentions the Apocalypse. In the disputed class he includes James, Jude, II and III John, II Peter, and again mentions the Apocalypse. Hebrews is probably included among the Pauline Epistles, although he admits the authorship of it is disputed in the Roman Church. It should be emphasized that these are merely disputed, not rejected books. Judgment was suspended either because authorship was uncertain, or because some had been written to the Church at large and had not been under the protection of any single church. Others were addressed to individual persons and were thus not readily accepted. The rejected group included the Acts of Paul, Hermas, the Apocalypse of Peter, the Epistle of Barnabas, and the "Teaching of the Apostles." These spurious books were not placed in this category because they were necessarily untruthful, but only as not having sufficient warrant for

canonicity. It is clear that the Apocalypse had not yet
been classified.

C. *Conciliar Action.*

The Synod of Carthage (A.D. 397 or 419) was the
first Church council to formally ratify the canon as it
now stands. The action of this and subsequent confirmatory councils *did not authorize* the present canon of
Scripture. They only confirmed what had already been
accepted by general usage. "So we may sum up the history of the Canon as the gradual work of the collective
consciousness of the Church, guided by the Holy Spirit.
It was a task of not only collecting but sifting and re-
jecting. . . . . It was a work in which all members of the
body played their part. The devotional taste of the multitude was guided and corrected by the learning and
spiritual enlightenment of its leaders. Their decisions
approved themselves to the mind and conscience of the
whole Church" (BICKNELL, *The Thirty-nine Articles,*
p. 182).

D. *The Apocrypha.*

As we have noted, the Jewish canon of the Old
Testament was completed about 100 B.C. However,
edifying books continued to be written, which were
widely used and quoted, but they were not regarded as
on the same plane with the canonical Scriptures. This
was true only in Palestine. The Hellenistic Jews, particularly those of Alexandria, took an entirely different
attitude. Not only did they adopt a different arrangement of the canonical books but included for the most
part those books now regarded as apocryphal.

As the early Christian Church extended its borders
beyond Palestine, it was confronted with a greater and
lesser canon. The great body of the Church followed
and used the Greek Bible and the Alexandrian canon.
But Jerome and other learned men who understood the
Hebrew language recognized that there was a narrower
and truer canon. This fact Jerome accepted and defended. He was opposed by Augustine, through whose
influence the apocryphal books were declared to be

canonical Scripture by Church councils late in the fourth century.

The word "Apocrypha" as applied by Jerome to these books, and as commonly understood now, means simply noncanonical. Protestantism rejected the Apocrypha and accepted the Jewish rather than the Alexandrian canon, the Jewish Scriptures rather than the Septuagint. What is commonly called the New Testament Apocrypha is a collection of spurious writings which were never published in connection with the canonical Scriptures. There is no evidence that can be claimed for them as inspired writings.

III. The Canon as a Rule of Faith

A. *The Rule of Faith.*

The canonical books of the Old and New Testaments, exclusive of the apocryphal books, constitute the Rule of Faith in its application to the Christian Church. The statement of the *Manual* (Article IV) in this regard is as follows: "We believe in the plenary inspiration of the Holy Scriptures, by which we understand the sixty-six books of the Old and New Testament, given by divine inspiration, inerrantly revealing the will of God concerning us in all things necessary to our salvation; so that whatever is not contained therein is not to be enjoined as an article of faith."

The New Testament represents the consummation or completion of Scripture, filling out or completing the revelation made through the Old Testament. This brings us to the interesting and important problem of the relation between the Old and New Testaments.

B. *The Relation of the Old Testament to the New Testament.*

One of the first problems to arise in the early Church was that of its relation to the Jewish law. The Jewish Christians were reluctant to give up any part of their regulations, and the Gentiles were loath to receive them. The problem became acute when St. Paul declared that it was not necessary for the Gentiles to become Jews before they could become Christians.

Paul's Epistle to the Galatians is his declaration of independence as it concerns Judaism in itself. So serious became the controversy that a council of elders was called in Jerusalem (A.D. 51). The Pharisees demanded that the Gentiles be circumcised and that they keep the law of Moses. Peter, Paul, and Barnabas recited their experiences. They told of the miracles and wonders which God had wrought among the Gentiles. Then James, the presiding officer of the council, rendered the final verdict in these words: *Wherefore my sentence is, that we trouble not them, which from among the Gentiles are turned to God; but that we write unto them, that they abstain from pollutions of idols, and from fornication, and from things strangled, and from blood* (Acts 15: 19, 21). This was a victory for the liberal party, but the problem has been persistent in every succeeding age of the Church.

At the opening of the Reformation Period the issue became particularly serious again. It took the form of a minifying of the Old Testament on the one hand, and an attempt to enforce the minute ceremonial regulations on the other. The present Article VII of the Anglican Confession represents not only the conclusions of English Protestantism on this subject, but is in accord with all Protestantism. The solution took the form of three declarations. *First*, the Old Testament was not to be considered contrary to the New Testament, but to be regarded as an earlier and preparatory stage for Christianity. The Old Testament progressively unfolds God's will. Men and their actions at each stage are to be judged in accordance with the accepted standards of their times and in harmony with the amount of divine light accorded them. *Second*, God's promises to the Jews carried with them not only promises of material blessing but of spiritual light and salvation. They are therefore to be regarded as revelations on various levels and in varying degrees of the one Messianic hope which found its perfect fulfillment in Christ (Cf. Heb. 1: 1). *Third*, the relation of the Church to the Jewish law was solved by making a distinction between the civil and ceremonial law on the one hand and the moral law on the other. This is admittedly a radical distinction, for to the Jew every part of the law was equally sacred. Nor could it have been made unless our Lord himself had first abrogated that part of it which belonged solely to the earlier or Jewish economy. Thus, that which was in Judaism as a necessary accompaniment, and essential to its earlier expression, is to be superseded by other and more spiritual forms of expression—though through all there abides the truth eternal. Christ's superiority to the law and His purposes concerning it are repeatedly expressed in word and deed (Cf. Matt. 5: 38, 39, 43, 44; Mark 2: 28). To the testimony of Christ may be added that of the Council of Jerusalem which claimed specific direction of the Holy Ghost, and Paul's Epistles to the Galatians and Romans. All bear witness to the fact that the ritual and ceremonial law was abolished by One who had the authority to do so.

The relation of the Christian Church to the Jewish law may be summed up as follows: The civil portions of the law belonged to Israel as a nation. These civil restrictions could not possibly be binding upon the Church. This new and spiritual Israel demanded new and universal laws, for in Christ *There is neither Jew nor Greek, neither is there bond nor free, there is neither male nor female; for ye are all one in Christ Jesus* (Gal. 3: 28). This new law must be applicable to all nations, all peoples, all degrees of civilization and culture, and without distinction as to sex. It can be nothing less than the law of faith (Rom. 3: 21-28).

Likewise, also, the ceremonial rites attained their purposes in the proper instruction of those who observed them. They pointed forward to Christ as their perfect fulfillment (Gal. 4: 3-5; Gal. 3: 24, 25). As respects the moral law, Christ did not abolish it, but declared His intention to deepen and vitalize it. The moral law is God's will for all men, and it is not necessarily entangled with the accidents of religious ceremonies or civil obligations. Not only so, but the Christian is inspired by the new law of love as an inner impulsive power, and therefore exceeds a forced obedience to an outwardly imposed law.

C. *Evidences of the Rule of Faith.*

We can make only brief mention of the evidences which are urged in favor of the Scriptures as the authoritative rule of faith and practice in the Church. These evidences belong to the extensive field of study known as Apologetics. This field is peculiarly difficult, and its adequate consideration demands the attention of not only mature and well-prepared students, but those who have access to the literature of modern research.

The development of modern historical research and the recent discoveries in philology and archaeology have in each instance served to strengthen and confirm the faith of the Church in the authenticity of the sacred Scriptures. But in addition to this evidence, the Christian also possesses the *testimonium Spiritus Sancti*, the witness of the Holy Spirit. The Spirit dwelling within the hearts of true believers through the atoning work of Jesus Christ is found to be the same Spirit who breathes in the pages of the Holy Scriptures. Hence, the strongest evidence for the authority of the Scriptures is to be found in the fact that the Spirit of inspiration to whom we are indebted for the authorship of the Bible is Himself the divine Witness of its genuineness and authenticity.

1. *Genuineness and Authenticity of the Old Testament.* A book is genuine when it is the production of the author whose name it bears. The term genuineness has reference solely to authorship. It is frequently confused with *authenticity* which refers not to the authorship but to the truth of a book's contents. In this sense a book may be genuine without being authentic, or authentic without being genuine. In practice, however, the words are used with varying shades of meaning, and it is usually difficult to sharply distinguish between the two in any discussion of Christian evidences. If a book is not written by the author that it acknowledges, then not only is the question of genuineness involved but that of its authen-

ticity as well. For this reason it is common practice to treat both subjects under one head, as we do here.

In substantiation of the claims of the Old Testament to genuineness and authenticity, we may mention: (1) The wealth of evidence from ancient secular historians concerning the antiquity of the Old Testament, and the fact that Moses was the founder and leader of the Jewish state. (2) The Septuagint translation of the Old Testament, which was made from the Hebrew into Greek for the use of the Alexandrian Jews about 287 B.C., is positive proof that the Pentateuch existed at that time, and strong evidence that it also existed in the days of Ezra, for the circumstances of the Jews in captivity were such as to preclude its authorship between these two dates. (3) The Samaritan Pentateuch, one of the two extant copies of the law of Moses, clearly indicates that the latter existed before the Jewish kingdom was divided. The foregoing, and other lines of evidence, leaves no good ground for denying the Mosaic authorship of the Pentateuch. (4) Archaeological discoveries are constantly increasing the wealth of evidence which confirms the genuineness and authenticity of the Old Testament.

The *Code of Hammurabi,* dating from 2250 B.C., represents conditions in Egypt precisely as they are related in Genesis and Exodus. Until recent times critics have discredited the biblical statements concerning the ancient and powerful people known as Hittites, but the discoveries of archaeology have confirmed the biblical accounts and added another proof to the authenticity of the Scriptures. So the testimony of the spade continues to confirm the validity of the Old Testament.

2. *Genuineness and Authenticity of the New Testament.* Among the various lines of evidence which serve to confirm the authenticity of the New Testament, we mention the following: (1) The numerous quotations from the New Testament which are found in the writings of the Church fathers. Some of these citations date back to the first century A.D. (2) The testimony of opponents of Christianity during the days of the early

Church, all of whom bear witness to the existence of the New Testament in their day. (3) The early catalogues of the books of the New Testament. (4) The Roman historians Suetonius and Tacitus, who mention Christ as the Founder of Christianity. (5) The style of the books in each case is suited to the age and circumstances of the reputed writer, and the characteristic differences are evidence that the work was not that of one person but of many. (6) The character of the writers is evidence in favor of the authenticity of their writings. They were holy, trustworthy men. Their writing has a forwardness, artlessness, and frankness that testifies of its truthful character. (7) The writers refer to incidents, persons, and places which can readily be confirmed by history and geography, and which an impostor would overlook or conceal. It has been said that in the New Testament we have stronger evidence for the genuineness and authenticity of the books which compose it than is afforded by books of any other class, sacred or profane.

3. *The Integrity of the Scriptures.* Have the sacred books, even though divinely inspired, been transmitted to us in an uncorrupted manner? By the integrity of the Scriptures we mean that they have been kept intact and free from essential error, so that we may be assured of the truth originally given by the inspired authors. Here we can present only a brief summary of the available evidence. (1) There is no evidence that the Scriptures have been corrupted. No proof has yet been furnished of essential alterations, and the burden of proof is upon the objectors. (2) The Jews had strong motives for preserving the Old Testament. Not only did they have high veneration for their sacred books, but these books contained the articles of their religious faith and the laws of their land. (3) The multiplication of copies, their wide distribution, and the public reading in the synagogues every Sabbath day tended to prevent alteration and to preserve their purity. So jealous were the Jews of their scriptures that a law was enacted making the slightest alteration an inexpiable sin. (4) The exceeding care of the Jewish copyists reduced to a minimum errors in

transcribing. Enoch Pond discussing this writes, "The Jewish copyists were at some periods, excessively, I had almost said superstitiously, exact. . . . . They ascertained the middle letter of the Pentateuch, the middle clause and letter of each book, and how many times each letter of the alphabet occurs in all the Hebrew Scriptures. Thus Aleph, they tell us, occurs 42,377 times; Beth, 32,218 times. I mention these facts to show the excessive care and particularity of these ancient copyists, and how unlikely it is that any considerable change could occur under their hands." (5) In the case of the New Testament there is the agreement of the ancient manuscripts. Dr. Kennicott, who examined six hundred and fifteen manuscripts, declared that he had "found many variations, and some grammatical errors; but not one of which affected, in the smallest degree, any article of faith and practice." (6) The numerous quotations from the New Testament found in the writings of the early Church fathers not only prove the authenticity of the Scriptures but the integrity of the text as well. (7) The various commentaries and helps have served to preserve the original text. For the Old Testament there are the Targums, the Talmud, and the Septuagint. For the New Testament there are the various translations, such as the Syriac version (A.D. 150), the old Latin Version (A.D. 160), the Vulgate translated by Jerome (latter part of the fourth century), the Coptic, Ethiopic, and Gothic versions of the fourth century, and the Armenian translation of the fifth century. Dr. Philip Schaff says that "in the absence of the autographs, we must depend on copies or secondary sources. But these are fortunately far more numerous and trustworthy for the Greek New Testament than for any ancient classic." It is clear, therefore, that evidence concerning the integrity of the Scriptures is sufficiently ample and adequate to convince any sincere inquirer.

UNIT II

THE DOCTRINE OF GOD

Preview

With the foundation of Christian Theology laid in the eternal Word of God, our task is now to begin the erection of our temple of Christian truth. The doctrine of God may well be called the cornerstone of this edifice, for on it so much depends. This is reflected in the very meaning of the word theology—"a study of God."

Not only is the doctrine of God of fundamental importance, but it is also singularly difficult. God is infinite. We are finite. Only the Infinite can fully comprehend the Infinite. The finite human mind can never adequately conceive of the infinite God. Yet, God has chosen to reveal Himself; and, while our grasp of this revelation is imperfect because of our limitations, we may have a true and satisfying revelation of Him. When we add to our finite limitations the inadequacy of language in expressing our most precious experiences of God, our difficulties increase all the more.

In our treatment of this doctrine we first consider the various lines of evidence concerning the existence of the Divine Being. The Scriptures are then examined to learn of His glorious nature. We turn next to an analysis of His attributes, considering them under the threefold division: absolute, relative, and moral. Lastly, we give attention to the doctrine of the Holy Trinity, emphasizing the deity of our Lord Jesus Christ, and the personality and deity of the blessed Holy Spirit.

In studying this unit, let us not forget that *the fear of the Lord is the beginning of wisdom.* God is not One who is to be known primarily through the mind, but One who is to be worshiped and loved. Moral likeness alone leads to the true knowledge of the Eternal One. None but the pure in heart see God.

UNIT II

THE DOCTRINE OF GOD

Chapter V. *The Existence and Nature of God*

I. THE EXISTENCE OF GOD

    A. The Idea of God Intuitive.
    B. The Testimony of the Scriptures.
    C. The Confirmatory Arguments.
        1. The Cosmological Argument.
        2. The Teleological Argument.
        3. The Ontological Argument.
        4. The Moral Argument.
        5. The Historical Argument.
        6. The Religious Argument.

II. THE NATURE OF GOD

    A. Definitions of God.
    B. The Names of God.
    C. The Christian Conception of God.
        1. God is Spirit.
        2. God as a Spirit is Life.
        3. God as a Spirit is Light.
        4. God as a Spirit is Love.

Chapter VI. *The Attributes of God*

I. CLASSIFICATION OF DIVINE ATTRIBUTES

    A. Divine Attributes, Perfections, and Predicates.
    B. Errors to be Avoided in Considering the Divine Attributes.
    C. Classification of the Attributes of God.

II. THE ABSOLUTE ATTRIBUTES OF GOD

    A. Spirituality as an Attribute of God.
    B. Infinity as an Attribute of God.
    C. Eternity as an Attribute of God.
    D. Immensity as an Attribute of God.

IV. ANTITRINITARIAN THEORIES
   A. Sabellianism.
   B. Arianism.
V. THE EVANGELICAL DOCTRINE OF THE TRINITY
   A. The Unity of Substance or Essence.
   B. The Trinity of Persons.
   C. Conclusions Regarding Evangelical Doctrine of the Trinity.

CHAPTER V

THE EXISTENCE AND NATURE OF GOD

"Upon the conception that is entertained of God will depend the nature and quality of religion in any soul or race, and in accordance with the view that is held of God, His nature, His character, and His relation to other beings, the spirit and the substance of theology will be determined. It may almost be said that when one has stated his conception of God he has written his theology. A system of theology is weak unless it is grounded in a clear and satisfying conception of God, and a vital change in the thought of a man or an age concerning Him is sure to be attended by a sweeping change throughout the field of theology. Here, therefore, we need all the qualifications for the discovery of truth. Humility, devoutness, and diligence must be our constant companions." —DR. WILLIAM NEWTON CLARKE.

Student of theology: "Bishop, about what should a young minister preach?"

Bishop Stubbs: "Young man, preach about God, and preach about twenty minutes."

Man needs only to look about him at the wonderful order and harmony in the universe, the magnificence of the heavens, the beauty of the earth, and all the charming variety of plants and animals in order to come to the conclusion that these things could not have come into being of themselves. The universe must have had a Creator. This was the conclusion of the Psalmist when he said, *The heavens declare the glory of God, and the firmament sheweth his handywork* (Psalms 19:1). All nations have believed that which the psalmist declared, even from the remotest ages of antiquity. Nor has this idea ever been lost; but in every age, belief in God has been the foundation upon which every religion, whether natural or revealed, has rested. From the ancient Athenians to the Incas of Peru, altars have been raised and homage paid to the "One who animates the Universe: unknown, unseen, shapeless, formless—the Cause of Causes."

Two questions immediately arise: How may we account for this universal belief in a supernatural Being? and, What may be known of this One? Reduced to a theological statement we have before us two funda-

75

mental theological considerations: (1) The Existence of God; and (2) The Nature and Attributes of God. The first is a fundamental concept and therefore a determinative factor in theological thought; while the second gives color to the whole system of religious thought and life.

I. THE EXISTENCE OF GOD

God alone can reveal Himself to man. This He has done in a primary revelation found in the works of nature and the constitution of man; and a secondary or higher revelation of Himself through the Spirit to the consciousness of man. The first finds its culmination in the Word made flesh; while the second has its source in the glorified Christ through the Holy Spirit.

A. *The Idea of God Intuitive.*

How may we account for the universal belief in the existence of God? There can be but one satisfactory answer: the knowledge of God is intuitive. This is what Dr. Miley calls "the faculty of immediate insight into truth." It is God's primary revelation—a supreme truth wrought into the very constitution of human nature by its Creator. It is a first truth which precedes and influences all observation and reasoning. When we speak of the idea of God as intuitive, we do not mean that it is a concept written upon the soul prior to consciousness, an actual knowledge with which the soul finds itself in possession at birth, or an idea imprinted upon the mind in such a manner that it necessarily develops apart from observation and reasoning. We do mean that human nature is such that it necessarily develops the idea of God through revelation, in much the same manner that the mind develops a knowledge of the external world through the data of the senses. There are three important factors united in this knowledge of God, namely, intuitive reason, or the power of immediate insight, which endows men with a capacity for the knowledge of God; revelation, or the presentation of the truth to intuitive reason as a *light which lighteth every man coming into the world;* and, as a consequence of the union of the two previous factors, the universal and necessary idea of God.

B. *The Testimony of the Scriptures.*

It is a fact of great significance that the written revelation opens with the words, *In the beginning God.* His existence is assumed without any attempt at proof. In addition, the Scriptures assert that there is in man's nature a consciousness of the Supreme Being, and consequently makes an appeal to the *law written in their hearts.* Holy Writ declares that it is in God that *we live, and move, and have our being,* and that *we are also his offspring* (Acts 17: 27-28). We must therefore boldly declare on the authority of the Scriptures that *The invisible things of him from the creation of the world are clearly seen, being understood by the things that are made, even his eternal power and Godhead.* Not only so, but this primary intuitive revelation is of such clearness and strength, that the apostle declares that men are without excuse (Rom. 1: 20). The only atheism recognized by the Scriptures is a practical atheism which grows out of a stubborn will or a reprobate mind. It is the fool who has said in his heart, *There is no God,* that is, "There is no God for me" (cf. Rom. 1: 28; Psalms 14: 1; Eph. 2: 12).

C. *The Confirmatory Arguments.*

While intuitive truths are self-evident, and are usually regarded as above logical proof, there are some truths which are intuitional in a portion of their content, and are yet acquired in either an experiential or a logical manner. Such is the truth of the existence of God. This fact is intuitive as an immediate datum of the moral and religious consciousness, and yet it is also a truth to be demonstrated by reason. The philosophical proofs of God's existence do not properly belong to the sphere of Christian dogmatics. However, they ought not to be entirely neglected in Christian theology for at least three reasons: *first,* because the statement that God's existence does not need to be demonstrated is sometimes misapplied in a way to promote unbelief and skepticism;

second, because these proofs when taken together furnish a scientific defense for faith in God, sufficient to brand unbelief as folly and sin; and, *third,* because these philosophical proofs illustrate the paths over which the mind travels in the confirmation of its belief in the existence of God.

The Confirmatory Arguments are generally arranged under two different heads, namely, those drawn from the contemplation of the world, and those drawn from the contemplation of man. Under the first division are classified the Cosmological, the Teleological, and the Historical Arguments; under the second, the Ontological, Moral, and Religious Arguments. Those are sometimes reduced by including the Historical and Religious Arguments in the other four.

1. *The Cosmological Argument.* This is an argument from change or effect to the cause of that change or effect. It may be stated logically as follows: (1) Every event or change must have a sufficient and pre-existing cause; (2) the universe consists of a system of changes; (3) therefore, there must be a self-existent and necessary Being as the cause of these events and changes. This argument is set forth in the Scriptures in such instances as *Every house is builded by some man; but he that built all things is God* (Heb. 3:4). *And, thou, Lord, in the beginning hast laid the foundation of the earth; and the heavens are the works of thine hands* (Heb. 1:10). *Before the mountains were brought forth, or ever thou hadst formed the earth and the world, even from everlasting to everlasting thou art God* (Psalms 90:2).

The elemental nature of the mind is such that it must believe in adequate causes. Even an intelligent child has been known to trace these back to a first cause and then ask "Who made God?" This reasoning in the child becomes a confirmed habit of mind in the man who knows that he must assume a First Cause, itself uncaused, or else assume a beginning of things without a cause.

Let us take the negative argument and assume that the Creator does not exist. Then the world must be self-explained. But to whatever simple form of existence we conceive that the whole might be traced back, it is inconceivable that it should be traced back to nothing at all. Some philosophers have sought to explain the world by matter or force. Now it seems clear that there could be no motion without matter, and matter must, therefore, be the more original. But, if it be assumed that matter is eternal, how shall we account for mind, which is greatly superior and which itself has the power of inducing motion? In this instance we should have an effect greater than the cause. But all matter is mutable, subject to change, and hence in the very nature of things cannot be eternal. If not eternal, it cannot be a First Cause. God only is unchangeable and eternal, and therefore He is the only First Cause of all that is.

Nor can the theory of evolution explain the origin of the world, for evolution, like motion or force, must itself be explained. That the world is thought to move to a higher level by slow processes and over a vast stretch of time is no explanation. Again, as we know motion, it tends to grow less and less, that is, it goes from the higher to the lower; while evolution on the contrary is supposed to move from the lower to the higher. This, too, must be explained. In fact, this demands even more explanation than that of simple motion. Therefore, the theory of evolution which was once thought to dispense with God in reality demands God all the more, for it involves Him not only at the beginning of the creation process but as constantly working through that process, and adequate at every stage. Then no matter what assumptions have been made by the evolutionists, they cannot establish as a fact the proposition that the universe was evolved from nothing. The Scriptures tell us that it was spoken into existence, and without the Word of God there *was not anything made that was made* (John 1: 3).

2. *The Teleological Argument.* This argument is commonly known as the Design Argument. It is one of the oldest and simplest of all the proofs, and never fails to commend itself to the popular mind. This argument is essentially, that there are adaptations of means to ends

in the universe, and that these show purpose or design, and hence a designing or intelligent mind. The earliest expression of purpose in the world is found in Genesis, where it is said that the stars are for light, and that fruit is for food. It is stated more directly in Psalms 94: 9-10. *He that planteth the ear, shall he not hear? he that formed the eye, shall he not see? he that chastiseth the heathen, shall not he correct? he that teacheth man knowledge, shall not he know?* "This I consider to be a legitimate inductive inference," says J. S. Mill. "Sight, being a fact, not precedent but subsequent to the putting together of the organic structure of the eye, can only be connected with the production of that structure in the character of a final, not an efficient cause. That is, it is not sight itself, but an antecedent idea of it, that must be the efficient cause. But this at once marks the origin as proceeding from an intelligent Will." There are many marks of an intelligent purpose in nature. These adaptations in the universe extend from the orbits of the suns to the adjustment of an insect's eye. To deny that these are the results of an intelligent Designer is to suppose that all these things are due to a blind and uncaused law. To disbelieve in God, then, is to reduce the whole world to chaos. We may say, therefore, that while the cosmological argument gives us an idea of God as power, the teleological argument conducts us a step farther and gives us the idea of God as a Person, with freedom, intelligence, and purpose.

3. *The Ontological Argument.* The term "ontological" is derived from two Greek words that mean "the science of existence." It is an attempt to establish the fact of "real existence, or existence in its absolute reality, as distinguished from phenomena, or things as they appear to us." The germs of the Ontogolical Argument appear in Plato and Aristotle, and in Augustine and Athanasius, but the argument itself belongs properly to more recent times. Anselm (A.D. 1033-1109) was the first to state it in syllogistic form as follows: "All men have the idea of God, and this idea of God is the idea of an absolutely perfect being, one whom we cannot imagine to

have a superior. The idea of such a being necessarily implies existence, otherwise we might imagine a greater being." Dr. Banks gives a more simple statement of this argument as follows: "We have ideas of infinite goodness, truth, and holiness. Are these merely ideas? Or, is there a Being to whom they belong? If they are mere ideas, how can we account for their existence? Thus there is some measure of truth in Anselm's position, that the very idea of an absolutely perfect Being involves His existence; at least to this extent; that the existence of the idea is best explained on the supposition that it arises from the fact. Otherwise, the noblest ideas known to man are the veriest illusions" (BANKS, *Manual of Christian Doctrine*, pp. 44-45). This argument conducts us one step farther in our confirmatory knowledge of the existence of God, and to the idea of personal Being it adds the incommunicable perfections of Deity.

4. *The Moral Argument.* This argument is based upon the revelation of God as right, and is but another application of the causal principle here applied to the moral instead of the natural realm. The argument is frequently stated in two forms. *First*, there is a conscience in man which marks the distinction between right and wrong, and which gives him a sense of responsibility and accountability. The fact of the existence of a conscience, which means "to know with" another, is evidence that there is a supreme Law-giver and Judge to whom man is accountable. There is no escape from the conclusion that the human mind is always conscious of a Being higher than its highest possible thought. So far from being the creation of human thought, it discovers it to be above anything it can conceive. Man therefore has a sense of duty, a responsibility to an overmaster or Lord, and this in itself would be unexplainable without the existence of a personal God. The *second* form of the argument rests upon the fact that in this world virtue is often unrewarded and vice unpunished. This requires another world in which the necessary adjustments can be made. Man's consciousness cannot be explained without recognizing this supreme moral law, and argues

a righteous Governor and Judge. Thus our own moral nature compels us to believe in a personal God.

5. *The Historical Argument.* The Historical Argument is closely related to the Teleological Argument on the one hand, and to the Moral Argument on the other. It holds that there are evidences of design in the moral as well as in the natural course of history, and that this argues the existence of a moral Governor of the world. The idea of a divine government in history was first recognized by Christianity, and is elaborated at length by the Apostle Paul in the Acts and in the Epistles.

6. *The Religious Argument.* The argument from religion is but a specialized form of the Moral Argument, and derives its proofs from the personal religious experiences of Christians. In some respects it can be more easily applied than the other arguments, for to one who has experienced the grace of God in Christ, there can be no stronger argument. The witness of the Spirit must ever be considered the highest form of testimony. However, for this very reason, this proof finds its full force only in those who have tasted the good Word of God.

Closely allied to the Religious Argument is that which is sometimes advanced from direct reference to the Scriptures. Thus Bishop Weaver draws from the Scriptures the following proofs: (1) the exact fulfillment of prophecy, for none but an infinite mind can foretell future events which are dependent upon human choices; (2) the performance of miracles, which can be explained only on the basis of the power and volition of Deity; (3) the unity of the Scriptures, which can be understood only on the theory of one divine Author who inspired the forty or more different persons, who, over a period of some sixteen hundred years, wrote the Holy Bible; (4) the remarkable preservation of the Scriptures, which evidences a wise and gracious divine Providence; and (5) the complete adaptation of the Scriptures to the needs of mankind, which is standing proof that the Author must have been the supreme Mind, the eternal Father.

In concluding this survey of the evidences concerning the existence of God, it is well to emphasize again that the burden of Holy Writ and Christian theology is not to answer by reason or argument the question: is there a God? On the contrary, the question that is central in the Scriptures, which is primary in the teaching of the prophets, the apostles, and Jesus Christ himself is, "Which God will you choose?" Elijah on Mount Carmel cried out, *How long halt ye between two opinions? if the Lord be God, follow him: but if Baal, then follow him.* The Master solemnly affirmed, *Ye cannot serve God and mammon.* Thus the alternative of supreme importance for each person is not a choice of God or no God, but whether or not he will declare as did Joshua, *As for me and my house, we will serve the Lord* (Josh. 25:15).

II. THE NATURE OF GOD

It has sometimes been declared that it is not the existence of God that is in dispute, but His nature; it is not whether God is, but what He is. Since the mind can define only by limiting the object of its thought, it is evident that the finite human mind can never adequately conceive of the infinite God, and in this sense cannot properly define the nature of His Being. Only the Infinite can comprehend the Infinite. This the New Testament explicitly states when it speaks of God as *dwelling in the light that no man can approach unto; whom no man hath seen or can see* (I Tim. 6:16). God, therefore, can be known only through His own revelation of Himself; and while these manifestations are imperfect because of our human limitations, yet insofar as they are comprehended by us, they must be regarded as affording a true knowledge of God.

A. *Definitions of God.*

With the limitations above mentioned, we call attention to some of the more important creedal statements as furnishing the most widely accepted definitions of God. Our own statement is as follows: "We believe in one eternally existent, infinite God, Sovereign of the universe. That He only is God, creative and administrative, holy in nature, attributes and purpose. That He, as God, is Triune in essential being, revealed as Father, Son, and Holy Spirit" (*Manual*, p. 25, Art. I). The *Thirty-nine Articles* of the Church of England give us the following definition: "There is but one living and true God, everlasting, without body, parts, or passions; of infinite power, wisdom, and goodness; the Maker and Preserver of all things both visible and invisible. And in the unity of this Godhead there be three Persons, of one substance, power, and eternity; the Father, the Son, and the Holy Ghost" (Article I). The *Twenty-five Articles of Methodism* are the same as those of the Church of England with the exception that the word "be" is changed to "are," and the word "passions" omitted. The *Westminster Catechism* defines God as "A Spirit, infinite, eternal, and unchangeable in His being, power, holiness, justice, goodness, and truth." All of these definitions are but various summaries of the truths found in the revealed Word of God.

B. *The Names of God.*

The nature of God as taught in the Holy Scriptures, has been progressively revealed to man through the use of the divine names. These communicate in varying degrees a knowledge of the divine nature, and indicate something of the unsearchable mystery which surrounds His Being. The first name by which God has revealed Himself is the generic term *Elohim*, which may be traced to the simple root word meaning "power." It signifies, therefore, that God is the possessor of every form of power. For this reason the word is generally used in the plural form to express the fullness and glory of the divine powers, and the majesty of the Being in whom these powers inhere. The second name by which God has revealed Himself is *Jehovah* or *Jahweh*. Instead of being a generic term, this name is a proper noun, and was interpreted to Moses as I AM THAT I AM. Hence the term unites in a single concept what to man is past, present and future, and thus reveals the personal and spiritual relationship which exists between God and men.

Because Jehovah signifies the faithfulness of God to His people, it became a custom among the Jews to form compound names expressive of personal and national triumphs. Thus we have the names *Jehovah-jireh,* "the Lord will provide"; *Jehovah-nissi,* "The Lord my banner"; *Jehovah-shalom,* "the Lord send peace"; *Jehovah-shammah,* "the Lord is there"; *Jehovah-tsidkenu,* "the Lord our righteousness." *Elohim* and *Jehovah* are frequently combined as *Elohim-Jehovah,* and as such reveal God as both Creator and Redeemer. Another term applied to Deity is *El Shaddai,* from the root word "shad" or breast. As such it means the "Nourisher" or "Strength-giver"—One who pours Himself into believing lives. In the process of revelation the term came to signify the Spirit of Love, or the "Comforter." The word *Adonai* signifies Lord, and is used with the two original words *Elohim* and *Jehovah* since it expresses dominion in a way that the word *Jehovah* does not. Since *Jehovah* is the incommunicable name, the Jews held it in superstitious reverence and refused to pronounce it, always substituting the word *Adonai* or Lord. *Adonai* is used with *Elohim* in such expressions as "My Lord and my God" (John 20: 28).

C. *The Christian Conception of God.*

In addition to the divine names through which God revealed Himself in the Old Testament, there are certain predicates used by Christ and His apostles in the New Testament to express the nature of God according to the Christian conception. These predicates are as follows: (1) God is Spirit; (2) God is Life; (3) God is Light; and (4) God is Love.

1. *God Is Spirit.* St. John records the words of our Lord in which He declares that *God is a Spirit; and they that worship him must worship him in spirit and in truth* (John 4: 24). Perhaps the passage is more accurately translated, "God is Spirit." By the use of the term "Spirit" the statement is doubtless intended to affirm the personality of God, thus indicating a common relationship between God and man. This common relation-

ship in which "Spirit may with spirit meet" becomes the ground of spiritual communion, and the basis of all true worship. Christlieb points out that we have here "The most profound definition of Scripture as to the nature of God, a definition to the sublimity of which the presentiments and longings of no heathen people ever rose; . . . . man has spirit, God is Spirit. In Him the Spirit does not form merely a portion of His being; but the whole substance of His nature, His peculiar self is Spirit. Here we have the idea of God in His inner perfection, just as the names Elohim and Jehovah tell us mainly of His external position. As Spirit, God is the eternal, self-dependent brightness and truth, absolute knowledge, the intelligent principle of all forces whose glance penetrates everything, and produces light and truth in all directions." If we but consider the Divine Being as a Spirit, having the same dominion over the invisible universe that our own minds or spirits exert over every portion of our bodies, we shall perceive faintly at least the source of all power so visible in the universe.

2. *God as a Spirit Is Life.* Jesus declared that *The Father hath life in himself; so also hath he given to the Son to have life in himself* (John 5: 26). He said, *I am the way, the truth, and the life* (John 14: 6). By the term "life," as here used, we are not to understand mere being, but organized life, that is, an organism including the fullness of truth, order, proportion, harmony, and beauty. As Absolute Life, God is exalted above all passivity, diminution and transitoriness, as well as above all increase. Life is in some sense the substratum in which the attributes inhere. It may not in this sense be definable, but it is known in consciousness as thought, feeling and will; and, therefore, the source of all reason, emotion, and self-directed activity.

3. *God as Spirit Is Light.* St. John uses this term in its most general sense, not as "a light" but as "light." *God is light, and in him is no darkness at all* (I John 1: 5). As here used, the contrast between natural light and darkness is the symbol of a deeper contrast between holiness and sin. Light is the outshining of the Father's

intrinsically holy nature. While darkness is the consequence of moral depravity and sin. Two important doctrines grow out of this concept of life. (1) There is the idea of moral depravity as the absence of light. The Scriptures regard this as an ethical darkness, that is, it is the consequence of voluntarily shutting out the light. It is a contradiction against God and against one's own higher nature. Back of this voluntary opposition to God, St. Paul maintains, is Satan, who as the *god of this world* blinds *the eyes of them which believe not, lest the light of the glorious gospel of God should shine unto them* (II Cor. 4:4). (2) In the next place there is the idea of a positive content of light which issues from the holiness of God. *In him is no darkness at all.* This means that down to the infinite depths of His being there is no darkness, nothing undiscovered, nothing hidden, nothing that needs to be brought to perfection.

4. *God as a Spirit Is Love.* The third fundamental property of Spirit is love. St. John is explicit. He says, *God is love,* and again, *God is love; and he that dwelleth in love dwelleth in God, and God in him* (I John 4:8, 16). Love demands both a subject and an object, and also a free reciprocal relationship between them. Love, therefore, becomes the bond of perfection in the Godhead, and also the bond of union between God and man. Holiness belongs to the essence of God as the property that distinguishes him from all others; love belongs to the self-expression of His nature. To the Father primarily belongs life; to the Son, light; and to the Spirit, love.

CHAPTER VI

THE ATTRIBUTES OF GOD

"We are not to think of the divine attributes as merely passive perfections inhering in the divine nature; they are ever and eternally active,
especially those which relate to His moral government. Who can seriously
contemplate all these attributes inhering in one person, and inhering in
each other, and not be profoundly impressed with a sense of His great-
ness? *Great is the Lord, and highly to be praised: he is to be feared above
all gods* (Psalms 96:4). Great and incomprehensible as God is, the devout
Christian by simple faith, may look up and say, *Our Father, which art
in heaven, hallowed be thy name,* and in the depths of his soul feel that
This God is our God forever and ever. No sight on earth is more sublime than to see poor, frail, erring man on his knees worshiping this
great and only true God."—BISHOP WEAVER.

I. CLASSIFICATION OF DIVINE ATTRIBUTES

A. *Divine Attributes, Perfections, and Predicates.*

The attributes of God are those qualities and perfections which belong only to the divine nature. In strict
usage a distinction is made between attributes and perfections. By the attributes we mean the qualities which
human beings attribute to God as they think of Him.
The perfections are those qualities which belong to the
divine essence, and they are applied by God to Himself. However, in common speech the terms are used
interchangeably. It is helpful to make a careful distinction between the divine attributes and predicates. A
predicate is anything that may be affirmed of God, such
as sovereignty or creatorship, but which does not attribute to God any essential quality or characteristic.
Predicate is a wider term than attribute, and includes
the latter. However, the attributes do not include the
predicates.

B. *Errors to Be Avoided in Considering the Divine Attributes.*

There are two errors concerning which we need to
be on guard in our consideration of the divine attributes.
First, we need to guard against oversimplification of the
attributes in order to preserve the divine unity. It may

be admitted that the extended list of attributes found in many works on systematic theology is not quite germane to the simplicity of the Christian conception of God. But, to reduce the number of attributes unduly is to weaken our conception of the divine perfections. We should seek to know as much about God as possible, and to give attention to the full range of perfections as revealed in the Holy Scriptures. *Second,* we must not fall into the error of regarding God as the mere sum total of attributes arranged according to some principle of unity. In our separate discussion of the attributes we are not suggesting that the divine nature is divided into separate parts. Rather, all the attributes inhere in one essence. No attribute is from another, neither does one precede the other. All of the perfections of God are eternal.

C. *Classification of the Attributes of God.*

A proper classification is of great value in bringing out the distinctive features of the divine nature. One of the simplest forms of classification is the twofold division into the natural and the moral attributes. Under this classification the natural attributes are those which are essential to His nature, and which do not involve the exercise of His will. Examples of these are aseity, infinity, eternity, immensity, immutability, and like characteristics. The moral attributes are qualities of His character, and involve the exercise of His will. Justice, mercy, love, goodness, and truth are included in this category. The weakness of this classification is the fact that it gathers in one group the relative attributes of God in His relation to creation and those which apply to Him apart from His relation to the world.

A second classification arranges the attributes in a threefold division: (1) the absolute attributes, or those qualities which belong to God in His essence and apart from His creative work; (2) the relative attributes, or those arising out of the relation existing between the Creator and the created, and which of necessity require the creature for their manifestations; and (3) the moral attributes, of those which belong to the relation existing between God and the moral beings under His government—especially man. It is this latter classification which we adopt. It is the simplest method of arrangement, and at the same time it is the clearest form of presentation.

II. THE ABSOLUTE ATTRIBUTES OF GOD

By the absolute attributes we mean those qualities which relate to God's mode of *existence* in contradistinction to those which refer to His mode of *operation or activity*. They must be conceived, as far as is possible, without any relation to the creature. They are absolute in that they are unlimited by time or space, are independent of all other existence, and perfect in themselves. They have their basis in the fact that God is, in Himself, absolute Being. They are inherent in that they belong to spirit, and are essential to any right conception of the divine nature. They are attributes of a personal Being, and may be summed up as spirituality, infinity, eternity, immensity, immutability, and perfection.

A. *Spirituality as an Attribute of God.*

Our Lord Jesus Christ declared that *God is a Spirit* (John 4: 24). Being a Spirit, it follows of necessity that He is a real, living, incorporeal Person. He is distinct from that which He has created, and is a self-conscious, intelligent, and voluntary agent. Furthermore, it follows from the nature of Spirit that God is a moral as well as an intellectual being. Spirituality as an attribute is closely related to spirit as an essence; thus, first place is given to it in our consideration of divine perfections. The term spirituality is here used in the sense of aseity or self-substance, which sometimes includes both unity and simplicity. By aseity we mean self-substance, or the possession of life in Himself. It indicates the fact that God has the foundation of all being in Himself alone. *God that made the world and all things therein, seeing that he is Lord of heaven and earth, dwelleth not in temples made with hands; neither is worshipped with men's hands, as though he needed any thing, seeing he giveth to all life, and breath, and all things* (Acts 17: 24, 25).

The term simplicity is applied to pure, uncompounded spirit. "He is a Spirit, not body," says Watson, "mind, not matter. He is pure Spirit, unconnected even with bodily form or organs." This conception is embodied in the creed as revised by John Wesley, which declares that, "There is but one living and true God, everlasting, without body, parts, or passions." Concerning spirituality, Paley declares that it "Expresses an idea made up of negative and positive parts; the negative part consists in the exclusion of some of the known properties of matter, especially solidity, inertia, divisibility, and gravitation. The positive part comprises perceptive thought, will power and action, or the origination of motion; the quality, perhaps, in which resides the essential superiority of the spirit over matter—which cannot move unless it is moved, and cannot but move when impelled."

Spirit being simple and uncompounded gives us the idea of unity as applied to God. Unity is frequently regarded as a separate attribute. It is designed to teach that there is but one God, and that His unity is involved in His self-existence. One self-existent being forever supersedes the necessity of another for the reason that the possession of all perfections is implied. *There is no God but one* (I Cor. 8:4). It is the attribute of self-existence which establishes this position, and it is further sustained and fortified by the attribute of eternity.

The Scriptures of both the Old and New Testaments teach the unity and spirituality of God. *Hear, O Israel: the Lord our God is one Lord* (Deut. 6:4). *Thou art God alone* (Psalms 86:10). *Is there a God beside me? yea, there is no God; I know not any* (Isa. 44:8). *I am God, and there is none else* (Isa. 45:22). *The Lord our God is one Lord* (Mark 12:29). *And this is life eternal, that they might know thee the only true God, and Jesus Christ, whom thou hast sent* (John 17:3). *But to us there is but one God* (I Cor. 8:6). *One God and Father of all, who is above all, and through all, and in you all* (Eph. 4:6). *For there is one God and one mediator between God and man, the man Christ Jesus* (I Tim. 2:5). To reject the divine unity so clearly set forth in the foregoing passages is to fall into the error of paganism. While the spirituality of God may be largely incomprehensible to us, as viewed from the standpoint of aseity, simplicity, and unity, it is nevertheless an essential attribute. The idea of God as a personal Spirit is the only concept of religious belief which is consistent with man as a dependent and responsible being. "This," says one, "is one of the first, the greatest, the most sublime, and necessary truths in the compass of nature: There is one God, the cause of all things, the fountain of all perfection, without parts or dimensions, for He is eternal, filling the heavens and the earth, pervading, governing, and upholding all things, for He is an infinite Spirit."

B. *Infinity as an Attribute of God.*

By infinity we mean that there are no bounds or limits to the divine nature. It is a term which applies to God only, and as such is peculiarly applicable to the personal attributes of power, wisdom and goodness. Hence the statement of the creed that God is "of infinite power, wisdom, and goodness." Dr. Foster considers this attribute as the basis of the related attributes of eternity and immensity. In the words of St. Augustine, "He knows how to be everywhere in His whole being and to be limited by no place. He knows how to come without departing from the place where He was; He knows how to go away without leaving the place whither He has come. . . . . He is everywhere in His whole being, contained by no place, bound by no bound, divisible into no parts, mutable in no respect, filling heaven and earth with the presence of His power." The term "infinite" is applicable to Personal Spirit only, and the word should be used in its integrity as simply expressive of that which does not admit of limitation.

C. *Eternity as an Attribute of God.*

By eternity as an attribute of God we mean that He stands superior to time, free from temporal distinctions of past and future, and in whose life there can be no succession. This is expressed primarily in the name *I AM THAT I AM* (Exod. 3:14); or as expressed by St.

John, *Which is, and which was, and which is to come, the Almighty* (Rev. 1:8). Here not only the self-sufficiency of God is declared, but His eternity also. The doctrine is further asserted in the Scriptures as follows: *The eternal God is thy refuge, and underneath are the everlasting arms* (Deut. 33:27). *From everlasting to everlasting, thou art God* (Psalms 90:2). *Thou art the same, and thy years shall have no end* (Psalms 102:27). *For thus saith the high and lofty One that inhabiteth eternity, whose name is Holy* (Isa. 57:15). *Whose goings forth have been from of old, from everlasting* (Micah 5:2). *Now unto the King eternal, immortal, invisible, the only wise God, be honour and glory for ever and ever. Amen* (I Tim. 1:17). *And they rest not day and night, saying, Holy, holy, holy, Lord God Almighty, which was, and is, and is to come* (Rev. 4:8). The fact that God *always was,* and *ever shall be* is beyond the power of human comprehension. "These facts," says Bishop Weaver, "fix in the mind that there is with God a mode of being entirely different from our own; that all that is, or has been, or will be, is a part of His serene and ever present consciousness; that God is to what we call time that which He is to space; that He who inhabits immensity, also and equally inhabits eternity" (WEAVER, *Christian Theology,* p. 23).

D. *Immensity as an Attribute of God.*

As an attribute, immensity expresses the contrast between the space world and God's mode of existence, much in the same manner as eternity expresses the temporal contrast. As time is born out of eternity, so space is born out of immensity. This attribute is mentioned directly but once in the Bible, and this in two parallel passages found in II Chronicles 6:18 and I Kings 8:27, *Behold, the heaven and heaven of heavens cannot contain thee; how much less this house which I have built!* However, there are other passages which indirectly teach the same truth. *Thus saith the Lord, The heaven is my throne, and the earth is my footstool* (Isa. 66:1). *Can any hide himself in secret places that I shall not see him?*

saith the Lord. Do not I fill heaven and earth? saith the Lord (Jer. 23:24). The appeal of the Scriptures here is primarily devotional, and is intended to guard the worshiper against the danger of unduly localizing his thought of God.

E. *Immutability as an Attribute of God.*

This attribute expresses the changelessness of God, whether in essence or attribute, in purpose or consciousness. However, this does not mean a rigid sameness of being. It refers to the fact that His essence and attributes are always in harmony with His operations in creation and providence. He loves righteousness and hates iniquity, and hence His moral government is always in harmony with His nature as holy love. He regards a person now with displeasure and now with approval insofar as the person is disobedient or righteous. The divine immutability is vital to both morality and religion. Here again we have the right and satisfying teachings of the Holy Scriptures. *Thou art the same, and thy years shall have no end* (Psalms 102:27). *I am the Lord, I change not* (Mal. 3:6). *Every good gift and every perfect gift is from above, and cometh down from the Father of lights, with whom is no variableness, neither shadow of turning* (James 1:17). "This is the perfection," says Dr. Blair, "which perhaps more than any other distinguishes the divine nature from the human, gives complete energy to all its attributes, and entitles it to the highest adoration. From hence are derived the regular order of nature and the steadfastness of the universe. The Eternal God who revealed Himself as the I AM to Moses, is the I AM of today, infinite, eternal, unchangeable, in His being, wisdom, power, holiness, justice, goodness, and truth."

F. *Perfection as an Attribute of God.*

This is the attribute which brings to completion and harmonizes all the other perfections. Nothing is wanting in God's being which is needed for blessedness. This attribute is a unity. It is unique. It is absolute. Rather than the combination of individual perfections or the culmination of a process toward perfection, this attribute is the very source of all other perfection. It excludes all possibility of defect. When our Lord said, *Be ye therefore perfect, even as your Father which is in heaven is perfect* (Matt. 5: 48), He presented the Father as the *Summum Bonum* of all spiritual good and the chief end of man's enjoyment and devotion. As the Perfect One, the Father comprehends in His own being all that is needed for our eternal blessedness.

III. THE RELATIVE ATTRIBUTES OF GOD

The relative attributes are not to be regarded as essentially different from the absolute, but as the same perfections in another form. The point of view only is changed. Thus the divine self-sufficiency finds expression in omnipotence or the all-powerfulness of God, likewise the divine immensity considered in relation to space, and eternity in relation to time, with the closely related quality of immutability, finds expression in the omnipresence of God. However, omniscience does not appear to be so closely related to the absolute attributes as we have considered them. It belongs more especially to personality and becomes the logical transition point between the metaphysical and ethical or moral attributes.

A. *The Omnipresence of God.*

The divine immensity is the presupposition for the attribute of omnipresence. Dr. Dick distinguishes between them as follows: "When we call His essence immense, we mean that it has no limits; when we say that it is omnipresent, we signify that it is wherever His creatures are" (DICK, *Theology*, Lecture 19). But while God is omnipresent, He stands in different relations to His creatures. "God is present in one way in nature," says Bishop Martensen, "in another way in history; in one way in the Church, in another way in the world; He is not in the same sense present alike in the hearts of His saints, and in those of the ungodly; in heaven and in hell" (MARTENSEN, *Christian Dogmatics,* p. 94).

In the light of our previous discussion of God's unity, we also understand that God is always present at every point with His entire being. It is in this sense that the devout always worship Him as a very present help in time of need. *For thus saith the high and lofty One that inhabiteth eternity, whose name is Holy; I dwell in the high and holy place, with him also that is of a contrite and humble spirit, to revive the spirit of the humble, and to revive the heart of the contrite ones* (Isa. 57:15). *Am I a God at hand, saith the Lord, and not a God afar off? Can any hide himself in secret places that I shall not see him? saith the Lord. Do not I fill heaven and earth? saith the Lord* (Jer. 23:23-24). How transcendently great is God! *The Lord looketh from heaven; he beholdeth all the sons of men* (Psalms 33:13). He is not only a present help in time of need, but a restraining presence from sin. Sin cannot be committed where He is not. He knows not only every act performed or every word spoken, but also every thought or motive entertained and every feeling indulged.

> "O may these thoughts possess my breast
> Where'er I rove, where'er I rest!
> Nor let my weaker passions dare
> Consent to sin, for God is there."

B. *The Omnipotence of God.*

The omnipotence of God is related to the absolute attribute of aseity as personality expressed in will. Being an expression of the divine will, it is also directly and vitally connected with the moral attributes of God. Omnipotence is defined as that perfection of God by virtue of which He is able to do all that He pleases to do. This is the scriptural definition. *There is nothing too hard for thee* (Jer. 32:17). *But our God is in the heavens: he hath done whatsoever he hath pleased* (Psalms 115:3). Whatever is impossible to Him is not such because of a limitation of His power, but solely because His nature makes it so, in the same sense that His holiness is incompatible with sin.

The Scriptures are replete with expressions concerning the power of God. *God hath spoken once; twice have I heard this; that power belongeth unto God* (Psalms 62: 11). *Let all the earth fear the Lord: let all the inhabitants of the world stand in awe of him. For he spake and it was done; he commanded and it stood fast* (Psalms 33: 8-9). *All power is given unto me in heaven and in earth* (Matt. 28: 18). *The Lord God omnipotent reigneth* (Rev. 19: 6). No doctrine is more important in religious value than that of the divine omnipotence. It is the basis for a deep and abiding religious adoration of God, and is the ground and firm support for quiet trust and assurance. It led our Lord courageously to the cross in the confidence that through the omnipotence of God His cause would triumph even over death, the last enemy. It has given courage to the saints of all ages, and in spite of discouragement and apparent defeat has caused them to be more than conquerors. Indeed, He is *able to do exceeding abundantly above all that we ask or think, according to the power that worketh in us, unto him be glory in the church by Christ Jesus throughout all ages, world without end. Amen* (Eph. 3: 20, 21).

C. *The Omniscience of God.*

By omniscience is meant the perfect knowledge which God has of Himself and all things. It is the infinite perfection of that which in us is called knowledge. Consequently, we read that *his understanding is infinite* (Psalms 147: 5). *Yea, the darkness hideth not from thee, but the night shineth as the day: the darkness and the light are both alike to thee* (Psalms 139: 12). *I am God, and there is none like me, declaring the end from the beginning, and from ancient times the things that are not yet done* (Isa. 46: 9-10). *O the depth of the riches both of the wisdom and knowledge of God: how unsearchable are his judgments, and his ways past finding out!* (Rom. 11: 33). *All things are naked and opened unto the eye of him with whom we have to do* (Heb. 4: 13). *For if our heart condemn us, God is greater than our heart, and knoweth all things* (I John 3: 20). *And*

*all the churches shall know that I am he which searcheth
the reins and hearts* (Rev. 2: 23).

The attribute of omniscience occupies a critical and
important place in theology because of its close relation
to the moral government of God. There is something
about this attribute which is peculiarly perplexing. It
bears an intimate relation to the unique and divine Personality. The first problem which arises in connection
with this attribute is the question of divine knowledge
of contingent events, commonly known as foreknowledge. Contingent events are those which are liable but
not certain to occur, those which are subject to chance
or unforeseen conditions, and those which are dependent
on the free will of man.

Concerning the problem of divine foreknowledge,
both Arminian and Calvinistic theologians hold to the
scientia necessaria or the necessary and eternal knowledge which God has of Himself. Infinite Personality implies infinite consciousness or knowledge of self. Also,
both Arminian and Calvinistic theologians believe in the
scientia libera, or the free knowledge which God has of
persons and things outside of Himself. However, they
differ as to the foundation of this foreknowledge. In
general, Arminians maintain that God has a knowledge
of pure contingency. On the other hand Calvinistic
theologians connect this foreknowledge with the decrees
which God has purposed in Himself. There is a mediating position commonly known as the *scienta media* or
knowledge of the hypothetical. This is the conditional
knowledge by which God is exactly acquainted, not only
with all which will happen, but also with all which would
or would not happen under certain nonexistent conditions. Whether knowledge be free or conditional, we
may wisely conclude with Van Oosterzee that "absolutely nothing is excluded from the divine knowledge."
The second difficult problem associated with the omniscience of God is the relation between foreknowledge
and predestination. The Calvinistic position identifies
foreknowledge and predestination, maintaining that the

divine decrees are the basis for the occurrence of all events, including the voluntary actions of men. "He foresees future events," says Calvin, "only in consequence of His decree that they should happen." Arminians contend that this view is diametrically opposed to the freedom of man's will, and is therefore unacceptable.

The Arminian position holds that the power of contrary choice is a constituent element of human freedom, and that foreknowledge must refer to free acts, and therefore to pure contingency. Dr. Pope's statement on this point is worthy of careful consideration: "It is not the divine foreknowledge which conditions what takes place, but what takes place conditions the divine foreknowledge. . . . . Predestination must have its rights; all that God wills to do is foredetermined. But what human freedom accomplishes, God can only foreknow; otherwise freedom is no longer freedom" (POPE, Compend. of Chr. Theol., I, p. 318). Of the relation between divine omniscience and human freedom, Dr. Hills observes, "Some deny freedom as contradictory to omniscience. But the mere knowledge of God influences nothing, nor changes the nature of human choices in any way; for the simple reason that it is knowledge, and not influence or causation. It was known by God as certain a million years ago just how A.B. would make a free choice this afternoon. He knows that he was free in making it, and might have made it otherwise. But if he had, God would have foreknown it the other way. The foreknowledge of God takes its form from man's free choice and not the free choice from the foreknowledge. What a man freely did this afternoon, decided what his onlooking neighbors saw him do: it also decided what God foresaw him do. How God thus foreknows the future free decisions of man is a mystery, like all the other infinite facts of His nature" (HILLS, Fund. Chr. Theol., I, p. 209).

In concluding our discussion of the relation between divine foreknowledge and predestination, let us note a statement by William Newton Clarke: "In fact no one practically believes that God's knowledge of events is the real cause of the events, or destroys the reality of other causes. All men know, practically that it is not so. God must know whether the apple blossoms of a given year will fulfill their promise: but no one supposes that His knowledge takes the place of the natural forces that produce the fruit or prevent its production. So in the realm of free action. . . . . We should go against all experience and common-sense of mankind if we affirm that God's knowledge of our action renders that action unfree. To say that God's knowledge destroys the efficiency of the forces whose operation He foresees, especially when those forces are human wills, is to assert that there is only one will in the universe, the will of God, and thus to embrace humanity in a genuine fatalism. This has sometimes been maintained, and is sometimes implied in arguments for the sovereignty of God, when no such doctrine is intended. But no doctrine that abolishes the human will, can possibly be true" (CLARKE, *An Outline of Chr. Theol.,* p. 85).

D. *The Wisdom of God.*

As a divine attribute, wisdom is closely related to and dependent upon omniscience. However, it is frequently given separate treatment by Arminian theologians. As defined by Wakefield it is "That attribute of His nature by which He knows and orders all things for the promotion of His glory and the good of His creatures." While wisdom and knowledge are closely related, the distinction is clear. Knowledge is the apprehension of things as they are, and wisdom is the adaptation of this knowledge to certain ends. As knowledge is necessary to wisdom, so omniscience is necessary to His infinite wisdom. Both the Old and New Testaments contain many references to this attribute. *With him is wisdom and strength; he hath counsel and understanding* (Job 12: 13). *O Lord, how manifold are thy works! in wisdom has thou made them all* (Psalms 104: 24). *Christ the power of God, and the wisdom of God* (I Cor. 1: 24). *Now unto the King eternal, immortal, invisible, the only wise God, be honour and glory for ever and ever* (I Tim. 1: 17).

E. *The Goodness of God.*

The goodness of God is that attribute by reason of which God wills the happiness of His creatures. It is that excellence which moves God to impart being and life to finite things and to communicate to them such gifts as they have capacity to receive. The goodness of God is voluntary. It refers primarily to His benevolence or that disposition which seeks to promote the happiness of His creatures. It is related to love, but love is limited to responsive persons or to those capable of returning love, while goodness applies to the whole creation. Not a sparrow *is forgotten before God* (Luke 12:6). The psalmist seemed to take delight in meditating upon the goodness of God. *Surely goodness and mercy shall follow me all the days of my life: and I will dwell in the house of the Lord for ever* (Psalms 23:6). *The goodness of God endureth continually* (Psalms 52:1). *Oh how great is thy goodness, which thou hast laid up for them that fear thee* (Psalms 31:19). In the New Testament St. Paul speaks of the goodness of God as leading to repentance (Rom. 2:4), and in Gal. 5:22 and Eph. 5:9 mentions goodness as a fruit of the Spirit.

IV. THE MORAL ATTRIBUTES OF GOD

The moral attributes of God relate to His government over free and intelligent creatures. Since moral bonds are essential to the existence and continuation of society, the knowledge of God will ever be a determining factor in the community life of man. There is a marked difference between the metaphysical (absolute and relative) and the ethical or moral attributes. Both the metaphysical and ethical attributes may in a measure be comprehended by the finite understanding of man. However, the ethical depend more particularly upon a common experience for understanding. Man is made in the image of God and, as a rational being, is able within 'the limits of his finiteness to comprehend the natural attributes of God. However, man has fallen into sin, and thus lacks the inner personal basis for understanding God's moral and spiritual character. It is only the pure in heart who see God. God's holiness is a barrier to the approach of sinful man. There is no meeting place, no common basis for understanding. Only through the mediatorship of Jesus Christ can man become a partaker of the divine nature, and hence come to know God in the deepest and truest sense. Only thus can the holiness and love of God be truly understood.

The moral attributes of God may be analyzed in various ways. All of them may be resolved into two: His holiness and His love; or, they may be organized into three main groups: holiness, love, and grace. For our purposes, it is adequate to consider them singly in the following order: holiness, love, justice, righteousness, truth, and grace.

A. *The Holiness of God.*

Three general positions have been taken by theologians concerning the holiness of God: (1) it may be regarded as one attribute alongside of and co-ordinate with other attributes; (2) it may be regarded as the sum total of all other attributes; and (3) it may be considered as the nature of God of which the attributes are but an expression. "The holiness of God," says Wakefield, "is commonly regarded as an attribute distinct from His other perfections; but this we think, is a mistake. Holiness is a complex term, and denotes not so much a particular attribute, as that general character of God which results from all his moral perfections. . . . . The holiness of God is not, and cannot be, something different from under which all these perfections are comprehended." A similar position is taken by Dr. Dick who holds that "holiness is not a particular attribute, but the general character of God resulting from His moral attributes." Dr. Wardlaw defines holiness as "the union of all the attributes, as pure white light is the union of all the colored rays of the spectrum." Dr. Pope holds that the two divine perfections, holiness and love, may be called the moral nature of God, "Two ascendencies in their not yet fully the moral perfections of His nature, but is a general term explained union and harmony." He indicates that these are the only two terms which unite both the essence and attributes of God. As essence, they constitute the moral nature of God; as attributes, they are the revelation of this nature through the economy of divine grace.

One of the best definitions of holiness is that given us by Dr. William Newton Clarke: "Holiness is the glorious fullness of God's moral excellence, held as the principle of His own action and the standard for His creatures" (CLARKE, *An Outline of Christian Theology*, p. 89). Here are *character, consistency, and requirement. First,* holiness in God is the perfection of moral excellence, which in Him exists unoriginated and underived. *Who is like unto thee, O Lord, among the gods? who is like unto thee, glorious in holiness, fearful in praises, doing wonders?* (Exod. 15:11). *Holy, holy, holy is the Lord of hosts: the whole earth is full of his glory* (Isa. 6:3). *Unto thee will I sing with the harp, O thou Holy One of Israel* (Psalms 71:22). *And they rest not day and night, saying, Holy, holy, holy, Lord God Almighty, which was and is, and is to come* (Rev. 4:8). *Who shall not fear thee, O Lord, and glorify thy name? for thou only art holy* (Rev. 15:4).

Second, holiness is the principle of God's own activity: *Thou art of purer eyes than to behold evil, and canst not look on iniquity* (Hab. 1:13). *The Lord is righteous in all his ways, and holy in all his works* (Psalms 145:17). Of Christ it is said, *Thou hast loved righteousness, and hated iniquity; therefore God, even thy God, hath anointed thee with the oil of gladness above thy fellows* (Heb. 1:9). The holiness of God is both positive and negative, implying the possession of all positive goodness, and the absence of all evil.

Third, holiness is the standard for God's creatures. *I am the Lord your God: ye shall therefore sanctify yourselves, and ye shall be holy; for I am holy* (Lev. 11:44). *That he would grant unto us, that we being delivered out of the hands of our enemies might serve him without fear, in holiness and righteousness before him, all the days of our life* (Luke 1:74-75). *But as he which hath*

called you is holy, so be ye holy in all manner of con-
versation; because it is written, Be ye holy; for I am holy
(I Peter 1: 15-16). Man is therefore called upon to be
holy, not absolutely, for absolute holiness belongs to God
only, but relatively, with the holiness that God communicates to angels and men. But how can sinful man
be holy? This is possible only through the atonement of
Christ, which protects at once the holiness of God and
restores it to man by making him a partaker of the divine
nature.

In the Trinity, life is peculiarly the property of the
Father, light of the Son, and love of the Spirit. But basic
and fundamental to each is ascribed a nature characterized as holy, and the threefold ascription of adoration and
praise, *Holy, holy, holy, is the Lord of hosts,* is not on the
ground of life or light or love, but of holiness. We may
say, then, that holiness in the Father is the mystery of
life, separate, distinct, and unoriginated; holiness in the
Son is light, which down to the depths of His infinite being, reveals no darkness, nothing undiscovered, nothing
unfulfilled, nothing which needs to be brought to perfection; holiness in the Spirit is the disclosure of the love
which exists between the Father and the Son, and is by
St. Paul called the bond of perfectness. In the Father,
holiness is original and underived, the basis of reverence
and adoration, and the standard of all moral goodness.
In the Son, holiness is revealed, and through His propitiatory offering man may be made holy and enter into fellowship with the Father. In the Spirit, holiness is imparted or made accessible to men. It is through the Spirit
that we become partakers of the divine nature. Hence
the term "Holy Spirit" affirms not only the nature of the
Spirit as in Himself holy, but declares also that it is His
office and work to make men holy.

B. *The Love of God.*

St. John sets forth a profound truth in the statement
that *God is love; and he that dwelleth in love dwelleth*
in God, and God in him (I John 4: 16). The nature of
God is holy love. Both holiness and love are equally of

the essence of God. Holiness is descriptive of the purity, moral character, and excellence of the love of God. The holiness of God requires that He always act out of pure love, and love must always win its objects to holiness. The love of God is in fact the desire to impart holiness, and this desire is satisfied only when the beings whom it seeks are rendered holy. Consequently we read that *God commendeth his love toward us, in that, while we were yet sinners, Christ died for us* (Rom. 5:8); and again, *Herein is love, not that we loved God, but that he loved us, and sent his Son to be the propitiation for our sins* (I John 4:10).

The love of God is therefore the nature of God from the standpoint of His self-communcation to men. Schleiermacher defines love as "That attribute in virtue of which God communicates himself." Dr. Francis J. Hall defines it as "The attribute by reason of which God wills a personal fellowship with Himself of those who are holy or capable of being made so." William Newton Clarke combines both factors and defines the love of God as "God's desire to impart Himself and all good to other beings, and to possess them for His own spiritual fellowship." From these definitions it is evident that there are at least three essential principles in love: self-communication, fellowship, and a desire to possess the object loved. The love of God must come to expression in the twofold desire to possess other beings for Himself, and to impart to them Himself and all other good.

It is frequently pointed out that the self-sacrificing mother who gives herself for her child is the one whose longing for the answering love of the child is most deep and inextinguishable. However great the self-surrender and sacrifice of love, it is always accompanied by a desire for mutual response. But in the very devotion of a mother to her son, that mother affirms her distinct personality. The self-surrender and the self-assertion must be equal. Neither can increase without the other if love is to be maintained. If self-assertion is not accompanied by its equivalent in self-surrender, we have not love but selfishness under the guise of love; if self-surrender be not balanced by self-assertion, we have not love but weakness. So also we find in God the twofold impulse that makes up love—the desire to possess others, and the desire to impart Himself to them. As love develops it grows richer in self-sacrifice and increase its desire for the possession of the object loved. It is because love in God is perfect that we read in the familiar text, *God so loved the world, that he gave his only begotten Son* (John 3:16). When therefore St. John declares that *We love him, because he first loved us* (I John 4:19) he is giving voice to that reciprocal love which delights the heart of God.

Love is commonly viewed as having two main forms —the love of benevolence, and the love of complacency. "The love of benevolence," says Dr. Henry B. Smith, "is that disposition of God or that form or modification of the divine love which leads God to desire to communicate happiness to all His sentient creatures, which leads Him to delight in all their happiness. The love of complacency is that element in the divine love which leads God to communicate and delight in the holiness of His creatures. The love of benevolence may be considered as having respect to happiness, the love of complacency to holiness; but both make up the divine love, both together and not one alone. Complacency is taking pleasure in something. Benevolence is the disposition to do good to anyone" (H. B. SMITH, *System of Christian Theology*, p. 38).

There are two other subjects closely associated with the concept of divine love—the idea of blessedness, and the idea of wrath. Bishop Martensen defined blessedness as a term "expressive of a life which is complete in itself," or "the reflection of the rays of love back on God, after passing through His kingdom." The word is frequently translated happiness, but this is too weak to convey the full meaning of the original word. Two positions have been taken concerning the wrath of God; namely, that it is not incompatible with divine love, and that it is a mere mode of human speech without any reality in the nature of God. The first is the Christian position which holds that wrath is the obverse side of love, necessary to the Divine Personality, and even to love itself. Divine wrath must therefore be regarded as the hatred of iniquity, and is in a proper sense the same emotion which is exercised toward righteousness and known as divine love.

C. *The Justice and Righteousness of God.*

The attributes of justice and righteousness are closely related to holiness. Dr. Strong regards them as transitive holiness, by which he means that God's treatment of His creatures always conforms to the holiness of His nature. While closely related, justice and righteousness may be distinguished from one another and both from holiness. The term holiness refers to the nature or essence of God as such while righteousness is His standard of activity in conformity with that nature. Righteousness is the foundation of the divine law, justice is the administration of that law. When we regard God as the Author of our moral nature we conceive of Him as holy. When we think of His holy nature as the standard of His action we conceive of Him as righteous. When we think of Him as administering His law in the bestowment of rewards and punishments we think of Him as just.

The attribute of Justice is commonly divided into *legislative* justice which *determines* the moral duty of man and defines the consequences in rewards and penalties; and *judicial* justice, sometimes known as distributive justice, by which God *renders* to all men rewards and penalties according to their works. The justice by which He rewards the obedient is sometimes known as *remunerative* justice, while that by which He punishes the guilty is *retributive* or *vindicative* justice. But whether as legislator or judge, God is eternally and absolutely just. Of that there is no doubt.

Many of the Scripture references make no distinction between the terms justice and righteousness. However, the careful student will be impressed with the various ways in which these attributes are combined. *The judg-*

ments of the Lord are true and righteous altogether (Psalms 19:9). *Justice and judgment are the habitation of thy throne* (Psalms 89:14). *There is no God else beside me; a just God and a Saviour* (Isa. 45:21). *The just Lord is in the midst thereof; he will not do iniquity* (Zeph. 3:5). *Who will render to every man according to his deeds* (Rom. 2:6). *Great and marvelous are thy works, Lord God Almighty; just and true are thy ways* (Rev. 15:3).

D. *Truth as an Attribute of God.*

Like justice and righteousness, the attribute of truth is closely related to holiness. It is commonly treated as veracity and faithfulness. By veracity is meant that all of God's manifestations to His creatures are in strict conformity with His own divine nature. When the Scriptures speak of the God of truth they thereby convey the idea of His veracity. By faithfulness or fidelity we mean God's fulfillment of His promises whether these promises are directly given in His Word or whether they are indirectly implied in the nature and constitution of man. The Bible abounds with references to God's veracity. *Thou hast redeemed me, O Lord God of truth* (Psalms 31:5). *The sum of thy word is truth* (Psalms 119:160, R.V.). *I am the way, the truth, and the life* (John 14:6). The references to His faithfulness are also definite and numerous. *A God of truth and without iniquity, just and right is he* (Deut. 32:4). *The Word of our God shall stand forever* (Isa. 40:8). *Faithful is he that calleth you, who also will do it* (I Thess. 5:24). *If we confess our sins, he is faithful and just to forgive us our sins, and to cleanse us from all unrighteousness* (I John 1:9).

E. *Grace and Its Related Attributes.*

St. John speaks of Christ as "full of grace and truth" and thereby makes them co-ordinate perfections of the Divine Nature. *Grace* may be defined as "unmerited favor" and all the "graces" are but various forms of the goodness and love of God. *Mercy* is love exercised toward the miserable, and includes both pity and compassion (Matt. 9:36). *Forbearance* is love in the deferring or lessening of punishment. *Or despisest thou the riches of his goodness and forbearance and longsuffering; not knowing that the goodness of God leadeth thee to repentance* (Rom. 2:4). The love of God manifested toward men generally is known as *kindness* or *benevolence. But after that the kindness and love of God our Saviour toward man appeared* (Titus 3:4). The word translated righteousness is frequently used in the sense of benevolence also, and is by St. Paul included in the fruit of the Spirit (Gal. 5:22). The grace of God is universal and impartial. He gives to His creatures as much good as they have capacity to receive. *The Lord is good to all; and his tender mercies are over all his works* (Psalms 145:9). *For as the heaven is high above the earth, so great is his mercy toward them that fear him* (Psalms 103:11). *But thou, O Lord, art a God full of compassion, and gracious, longsuffering, and plenteous in mercy and truth* (Psalms 86:15).

We have given this extended treatment of the attributes for two reasons: *first,* because the delineation of these perfections in their harmony and proportion is the glory of theology; and *second,* because the heresies which have brought the greatest dissension in the Church have grown out of unworthy and perverted notions of the divine attributes. Therefore it is essential that every follower of Christ be thoroughly instructed concerning the existence and nature of God.

CHAPTER VII

THE TRINITY

"May God the Father adopt me fully for His child. May God the Son dwell in my heart by faith. May God the Holy Spirit purge my conscience from dead works, and purify my soul from all unrighteousness! May the holy, blessed, and glorious *Trinity* take me and mine, and seal us for His own in time and eternity!

"O thou incomprehensible Jehovah, thou eternal Word, thou ever-enduring and all-pervading Spirit; Father! Son! and Holy Ghost! in the plenitude of thy eternal Godhead, in thy light, I, in a measure, see Thee; and in thy condescending nearness to my nature, I can love Thee, for thou hast loved me. In thy strength may I begin, continue, and end every design and every work, so as to glorify Thee by showing how much thou lovest man, and how much man may be ennobled and beautified by loving Thee! Here am I fixed, here am I lost, and here I find my God, and here I find myself!"—DR. ADAM CLARKE.

The doctrine of the Trinity which holds that there are three Persons in the one Godhead is one of the most sacred truths of the Christian Church. It is not a mere speculative or theoretical doctrine but one which is bound up with our eternal salvation. God the Father sent His Son into the world to redeem us; and God the Holy Spirit applies the redemptive work to our souls. The Trinity is therefore vitally involved in the work of salvation, and it is from this practical and religious aspect of the doctrine that the truth must be sought.

The early Christians saw that if Christ was not divine they could not worship Him without becoming idolaters. On the other hand, He had saved them, and through Him had come the gift of the Holy Spirit. They recognized, therefore, that He must be divine. This brought the question of the deity of Christ and His relationships in the Trinity to the Church at a very early period. These and other vital questions concerning the Trinity did not arise from philosophical speculation, and they cannot be settled in this manner. They are truths of divine revelation, and we must turn to the Scriptures for our authoritative teaching on this important subject.

I. The Unity and Triunity of God

A. *The Unity of God.*

By the "unity of God" we understand that there is but one God in the universe, who exists as an infinite, eternal, and self-existent Being. This is a truth which is asserted or implied in the whole body of the Scripture. In the Old Testament, the Israelite confessed his faith in the words, *Hear O Israel: the Lord our God is one Lord* (Deut. 6: 4). In order to preserve His people from pagan polytheism, God gave them as the first and fundamental commandment, *Thou shalt have no other gods before me* (Exod. 20: 3); and to this was added the further admonition, *Know therefore this day, and consider it in thine heart, that the Lord he is God in heaven above, and upon the earth beneath; there is none else* (Deut. 4: 39).

In the New Testament we also find explicit statements concerning the unity of God: *And Jesus answered him, the first of all the commandments is, Hear, O Israel; the Lord our God is one Lord* (Mark 12: 29). *And this is life eternal, that they may know thee the only true God, and Jesus Christ, whom thou hast sent* (John 17: 3). *There is none other God but one. For though there be that are called gods, whether in heaven or in earth, (as there be gods many and lords many,) but to us there is but one God, the Father, of whom are all things, and we in him; and one Lord Jesus Christ, by whom are all things, and we by him* (I Cor. 8: 4-6). *Now a mediator is not a mediator of one, but God is one* (Gal. 3: 20).

B. *The Triunity of God.*

While the unity of God is held by both Unitarians and Trinitarians, there is a vast difference in the positions taken. Unitarians ascribe all the perfections of God to the Father as the sole Deity; while Trinitarians hold that "in the unity of the Godhead there are three persons of one substance, power, and eternity—the Father, the Son, and the Holy Spirit." However, this does not make three Gods. "There is," says Dr. Gill, "but one divine essence, though there are different modes of subsisting in it, which are called persons; and these possess the whole essence undivided. And this unity is not a unity of parts, which makes one compositum, as the soul and body of man do, for God is a simple and uncompounded Spirit."

1. *Anticipations of the Trinity in the Old Testament.* The doctrine of the Trinity is anticipated in the Old Testament, but, like other New Testament truths, was contained merely in germ or in embryonic form. Only with the full revelation of God in Christ could it come to its full development. Let us note some of these germinal truths. The use of plural names to designate Deity has ever been regarded as an anticipation of the Trinity. *In the beginning God (Elohim, or the Gods) created the heaven and the earth* (Gen. 1:1). *And God said, Let* us *make man in* our *image, and after* our *likeness* (Gen. 1:26). Again, *And the Lord said, Behold the man is become as one of us* (Gen. 3:22). Wakefield points out that the plural form is preferred even when the design is to assert, in the most solemn manner, the unity of God. This is illustrated in the call to ancient Israel, *"Hear, O Israel, the Lord* (Elohaynu, *our Gods) is one Lord* (Deut. 6:4). The thought of the Trinity is also contained implicitly in the Old Testament references to the "Angel of Jehovah." *Behold I send an Angel before thee, to keep thee in the way, and to bring thee into the place which I have prepared .... for my name is in him* (Exod. 23:20-21). Here Jehovah is mentioned; then the Angel or Messenger (the Word); and lastly, the Spirit (*my name is in him*). The Aaronic benediction uses the word Jehovah in a threefold sense. *Jehovah bless thee and keep thee. Jehovah make his face to shine upon thee. Jehovah lift up his countenance upon thee and give thee peace* (Num. 6:24-27). The three members of this form may correspond to the love of the Father, the grace of the Lord Jesus Christ, and the communion of the Holy Ghost (cf. II Cor. 13:14). Closely related to these is the *Trisagion,* or the threefold use of the word holy by Isaiah, *Holy, holy, holy, is the Lord of Hosts* (Isa. 6:3). This is an act of devotion in which the term holy is used equally and appropriately of each of the Persons of the adorable Trinity. Lastly, there are the numerous references to

the Messiah, only one of which will be cited. *And now the Lord God, and his Spirit, hath sent me* (Isa. 48:16). Here the Messiah manifestly declares Himself to have been sent by the Lord God and His Spirit.

2. *The Son and the Spirit in the New Testament.* There is no direct and immediate foreannouncement of the Son in the Old Testament because the Fatherhood of God was not fully revealed. Both the Fatherhood and the Sonship are New Testament revelations, and the one waited for the other. But the idea of sonship permeates the Old Testament, and is found especially in the use of the terms "Word" and "Wisdom" which express in a clearer manner the Divine Logos, or "Word" which was to become incarnate: *And the Word was made flesh, and dwelt among us, (and we beheld his glory, the glory as of the only begotten of the Father,) full of grace and truth* (John 1:14). We must therefore turn to the New Testament for the full revelation of the Son as the Second Person of the Trinity; and for the Personality and Deity of the Holy Ghost as the Third Adorable Person.

II. The Deity of Our Lord Jesus Christ

The Scriptures are rich with teaching concerning the deity of Christ. So extensive is the full range of such teaching that we must confine our discussion solely to a few outstanding proof texts. The deity of Christ is sustained by those scriptures which refer to: (1) His pre-existence; (2) His divine names and titles; (3) His divine attributes; (4) His divine works; and (5) those which present Him as the recipient of divine worship and homage.

A. *The Pre-existence of Christ.*

He that cometh after me is preferred before me: for he was before me (John 1:15). Such is the testimony of John the Baptist concerning Jesus Christ. Our Lord himself declared, *I am the living bread which came down from heaven* (John 6:51). *And now, O Father, glorify thou me with thine own self with the glory which I had with thee before the world was* (John 17:5). These texts make it sufficiently clear that Christ was not only pre-existent before His incarnation, but also before the foundation of the world.

B. *The Divine Names and Titles of our Lord.*

The deity of Christ is clearly taught in the names and titles given to Him in the Holy Scriptures. He is called Lord. *Prepare ye the way of the Lord* (Matt. 3:3). He is also called God. *In the beginning was the Word, and the Word was with God, and the Word was God* (John 1:1). *And of whom, as concerning the flesh, Christ came, who is over all, God blessed for ever. Amen* (Rom. 9:5). *Looking for that blessed hope, and the glorious appearing of the great God and our Saviour Jesus Christ* (Titus 2:13).

C. *The Divine Attributes of Jesus Christ.*

A whole galaxy of divine attributes are ascribed to our Lord. Among these are (1) Eternity: *But unto the Son he saith, Thy throne, O God, is for ever and ever: a sceptre of righteousness is the sceptre of thy kingdom* (Heb. 1:8). (2) Omnipresence: *For where two or three are gathered together in my name, there am I in the midst of them* (Matt. 18:20). (3) Omniscience: *In whom are hid all the treasures of wisdom and knowledge* (Col. 2:3). (4) Omnipotence: *All power is given unto me in heaven and in earth* (Matt. 28:18). (5) Immutability: *They shall perish; but thou remainest; and they all shall wax old as doth a garment; and as a vesture shalt thou fold them up, and they shall be changed: but thou art the same and thy years shall not fail* (Heb. 1:11-12). *Jesus Christ the same yesterday, and to day, and for ever* (Heb. 13:8).

D. *The Divine Works of Christ.*

The works of Christ as described in the New Testament are such as could be wrought only by God, "The evidence is overwhelmingly cumulative that the Christ of the Scriptures is God in essence, being, and attributes." The works of Christ as divine include (1) Creation: *All things were made by him; and without him was not anything made that was made* (John 1:3). *He was in the world, and the world was made by him, and the world knew him not* (John 1:10). St. Paul affirmed that *by him were all things created, that are in heaven, and that are in the earth, visible and invisible, whether they be thrones or dominions, or principalities, or powers: all things were created by him, and for him* (Col. 1:16). The evidence is clear and unequivocal that it was Christ who made the worlds. (2) Preservation and Conservation: *And he is before all things, and by him all things consist* (cohere or hold together) (Col. 1:17). In Hebrews 1:3 we read, *Who being the brightness of his glory, and the express image of his person, and upholding all things by the word of his power, when he had by himself purged our sins, sat down on the right hand of the Majesty on high.* (3) Forgiveness of sins: *When Jesus saw their faith, he said unto the sick of the palsy, Son, thy sins be forgiven thee. . . . . But that ye may know that the Son of man hath power on earth to forgive sins, (he saith to the sick of the palsy,) I say unto thee, Arise, and take up thy bed, and go thy way into thine house* (Mark 2:5, 10-11). Jesus thus vindicated His authority as God to forgive sins by healing the afflicted man. St. Peter affirms this truth in his statement concerning Christ: *Him hath God exalted with his right hand to be a Prince and a Saviour, for to give repentance to Israel, and forgiveness of sins* (Acts 5:31). (4) Finally, the deity of Christ is attested by His gift of the Holy Spirit to believers: *And, behold, I send the promise of my Father upon you: but tarry ye in the city of Jerusalem, until ye be endued with power from on high* (Luke 24:49). The coming of the Holy Spirit on the Day of Pentecost bears witness to the essential deity of our Lord Jesus Christ.

E. *Christ is the Recipient of Divine Worship and Homage.*

God alone is worthy of man's worship. When St. John, overcome by a glorious vision, fell down before the angel, the command was: *Worship God.* Yet Jesus Christ received such worship without hesitation or embarrassment. *They worshipped him, saying, of a truth thou art the Son of God* (Matt. 14: 33). The writer to the Hebrews informs us that even the angels worship Him: *And again, when he bringeth in the firstbegotten into the world, he saith, And let the angels of God worship him* (Heb. 1: 6). These facts testify that Jesus Christ, as God, is worthy of our homage and worship.

By express statement and implication the New Testament repeatedly teaches the essential oneness and equality of Jesus Christ and the Father. The skeptical Jews who heard Christ speak clearly understood that he claimed equality with the Father (John 5: 18). The baptismal formula (Matt. 28: 19) in which the name of the Son is linked with that of the Father and the Holy Ghost on a plane of equality is a further testimony to His deity. This equality was His by inherent right (Phil. 2: 6). The overwhelming impression that Jesus Christ made upon His contemporaries and upon multitudes since that day was that He was indeed and in truth the very Son of God.

F. *Significance of the Doctrine of the Deity of Christ.*

Is Jesus Christ truly and properly God? This is a far-reaching and profound question. The whole plan of salvation hinges upon it. It is a question which only the Word of God can settle, and, as we have seen, it is answered in the affirmative. The sacred writers make statements concerning our Lord Jesus Christ which cannot by any fair interpretation be made to mean anything less than that He is truly and properly God. Concerning the significance of this, we can do no better than to quote from Bishop Weaver: "The whole plan of human redemption through the merits of Jesus Christ rests upon the doctrine of Christ's supreme divinity, or that he was truly and properly God manifest in the flesh. Remove this cornerstone from our holy Christianity and immortality and eternal life disappear. Allow Jesus Christ to be God, and we have a solid rock upon which to build our hope of heaven. Deny this, and hope vanishes. The divinity of Christ, the divine Sonship, the deity of the

Holy Spirit, and the Trinity are all more or less wrapped up in mystery. Like the existence of God, the fact is revealed to us, but who can comprehend this eternity and spirituality? Concerning the mode of the divine existence we know nothing. That there are three distinct, but not separate persons in the one only true God the Scriptures abundantly teach. If it were a condition upon which our eternal salvation depended, that we must comprehend these great truths, we could never be saved. Happy for us that in coming to God we are not required to know what He is, but to believe that He is, and that He is a rewarder of them that diligently seek Him. Jesus Christ, the divine Son, the second person in the Holy Trinity, is God manifest in the flesh, and by this condescension is become the only medium through which eternal life can be secured." *To him be glory and dominion for ever and ever. Amen.*

III. THE PERSONALITY AND DEITY OF THE HOLY SPIRIT

This theme does not demand the extended treatment given to the foregoing topic, inasmuch as many of the same principles are involved. Yet, from the standpoint of worship, it makes much difference whether we believe that the Holy Spirit is an impersonal power or influence emanating from God or a divine Person with whom we may commune and who desires fellowship with us. It makes much practical difference whether the Holy Spirit is a mere power that we may or may not secure to use in our weakness, or whether He is a Personality—wise, holy, compassionate, all-powerful—who wishes to get hold of us and use us for His glory.

A. *The Personality of the Holy Spirit.*

That the Holy Spirit is a Person distinct from that of the Father and Son is clearly taught in the Scriptures. Let us note several lines of teaching on this subject as found in Holy Writ.

1. *Personal Names and Pronouns Referring to the Holy Spirit.* In addition to such terms as "the Spirit," "The Spirit of God," and "the Spirit of Glory," our Lord

refers to the Spirit as "the Comforter" or "another Comforter." This is not an impersonal term, but is also applied to Christ himself and translated "Advocate" in I John 2:1. It means comforter, guide, instructor, or "one who strengthens by being with." In His consolatory discourse to His disciples, Jesus spoke plainly and reassuringly to them concerning this Comforter who should take His place, continuing His work and abiding forever. Note some of these passages: *But the Comforter, which is the Holy Ghost, whom the Father will send in my name, he shall teach you all things, and bring all things to your remembrance, whatsoever I have said unto you* (John 14:26). *It is expedient for you that I go away: for if I go not away, the Comforter will not come unto you; but if I depart, I will send him unto you. And when he is come, he will reprove the world of sin, and of righteousness, and of judgment* (John 16:7, 8). *Howbeit when he, the Spirit of truth, is come, he will guide you into all truth: for he shall not speak of himself; but whatsoever he shall hear, that shall he speak; and he will show you things to come. He shall glorify me: for he shall receive of mine, and shall shew it unto you. All things that the Father hath are mine: therefore said I, that he shall take of mine, and shall shew it unto you* (John 16:13-15). Note that in these passages the masculine pronoun is used, and is directly applied to the Holy Spirit some fourteen times. This is even more significant in view of the fact that there is a disregard of ordinary Greek syntax in using a masculine pronoun (for example v. 14) when *pneuma*, the noun translated spirit, is in the *neuter* gender, and would ordinarily require a pronoun in the neuter gender in its place. This is a remarkable example of the way in which Bible teaching concerning the personality of the Holy Spirit dominates even grammatical construction.

2. *Personal Acts Ascribed to the Holy Spirit.* In the scriptural passages cited above there are at least ten personal acts ascribed to the Holy Spirit. The Holy Spirit is said (1) to be sent, (2) to teach, (3) to come, (4) to reprove, (5) to guide, (6) to speak, (7) to hear, (8) to

show, (9) to take, and (10) to receive. To this list of *personal* acts could be added many others of similar character, such as: inspiring men to utter the oracles of God (I Peter 1:11; II Peter 1:21); teaching and commanding (John 14:21; Acts 8:29); testifying of Christ (John 15:26); directing the affairs of the Church (Acts 13:2; 16:6-7); and acting as the agent in regeneration (John 3:6) and in entire sanctification (II Thess. 2:13). If the Holy Spirit were nothing more than an abstract influence, quality, attribute, or energy, how are we to account for these personal acts which are ascribed to Him?

3. *The Holy Spirit Receives Personal Treatment.* A final line of evidence regarding the personality of the Holy Spirit is to note that He is the recipient of treatment which only a Person could receive. Men may rebel against Him: *But they rebelled, and vexed his holy Spirit: therefore he was turned to be their enemy, and he fought against them* (Isa. 63:10). He may be lied to: *But Peter said, Ananias, why hath Satan filled thine heart to lie to the Holy Ghost, and to keep back part of the price?* (Acts 5:3). He may be blasphemed against: *Wherefore I say unto you, All manner of sin and blasphemy shall be forgiven unto men: but the blasphemy against the Holy Ghost shall not be forgiven unto men* (Matt. 12:31). It is unthinkable that men should rebel against, lie to, or blaspheme an impersonal force. Such activities relate to persons only.

Dr. John Owen has well illustrated our thought concerning the personality of the Holy Spirit in the following statement: "If a wise and honest man should come and tell you that in a certain country where he has been there is an excellent governor who wisely discharges the duties of his office, who hears causes, discerns rights, distributes justice, relieves the poor and comforts the distressed—would you not believe that he intended by this description a righteous, wise, diligent, intelligent person? Could you imagine him to mean that the sun or wind by their benign influences rendered the country fruitful and temperate, and disposed the inhabitants to mutual kindness and benignity; and that the governer is a mere figure of speech? It is exactly thus with the case before us. The Scriptures tell us that the Holy Spirit governs and disposes all things according to the counsel of His own will. Can any man credit this testimony and conceive otherwise of the Spirit than as a holy, wise, intelligent Person?"

B. *The Deity of the Holy Spirit.*

The deity of the Holy Spirit may be proved scripturally by a collation of texts as in the case of the divine Sonship. The name of God, His attributes, His works, and His worship are all applied to the Holy Spirit. A few representative texts will suffice to illustrate this line of truth. Among the attributes which belong to no being in the universe but God, and which are attributed to the Holy Spirit, are: (1) Eternity. *How much more shall the blood of Christ, who through the eternal Spirit offered himself without spot to God, purge your conscience from dead works to serve the living God?* (Heb. 9:14). (2) Omnipotence. *By word and deed, through mighty signs and wonders by the power of the Spirit of God* (Rom. 15:18, 19). (3) Omnipresence. *Whither shall I go from thy Spirit? or whither shall I flee from thy presence?* (Psalms 139:7). (4) Omniscience. *For the Spirit searcheth all things, yea, the deep things of God. For what man knoweth the things of a man, save the spirit of man which is in him? even so the things of God knoweth no man, but the Spirit of God* (I Cor. 2:10-11).

St. Peter charged Ananias with lying to the Holy Ghost, which he affirmed was lying to God, thus teaching that the Holy Ghost is God: *But Peter said, Ananias, why hath Satan filled thine heart to lie to the Holy Ghost? . . . . Thou hast not lied unto men, but unto God* (Acts 5:3, 4). A comparison of John 1:13 and John 3:5-7 reveals that the new birth—being born of God—is ascribed to God and to the Holy Spirit, thus teaching that the Holy Spirit is God. A number of New Testament references to Old Testament passages are of interest. The word "Lord" or "Jehovah" occurs in the Old

Testament, while in the New Testament citations the activity is specifically attributed to the Holy Spirit. In Isaiah 6: 8-10 the prophet declares that he heard the "voice of the Lord." Referring to this in Acts 28: 25-27, St. Paul declares, *Well spake the Holy Ghost by Esaias the prophet unto our fathers.*" In Exodus 16: 7 the children of Israel are pictured as murmuring against the Lord. In Hebrews 3: 7-9 the Israelites are described as having tempted and proved the Holy Ghost. It is evident that the Holy Spirit clearly occupies the position of Deity in New Testament thought.

Again, the name of the Holy Spirit is coupled with those of the Son and the Father in such a way as to imply a status of full and complete equality. This is true of the baptismal formula and the apostolic benediction, *Go ye, therefore, and teach all nations, baptizing them in the name of the Father, and of the Son, and of the Holy Ghost* (Matt. 28: 19). *The grace of the Lord Jesus Christ, and the love of God, and the communion of the Holy Ghost, be with you all. Amen* (II Cor. 13: 14).

Finally, the agency or work of the Holy Spirit attests His proper divinity. The creation and preservation of the inorganic universe is attributed to the Spirit of God (Gen. 1: 2, 3; Psalms 104: 29, 30; Job 33: 4). He bears witness to the truth concerning our Lord Jesus Christ (Acts 5: 30-32; John 15: 26). He convicts the world of sin, and of righteousness, and of judgment (John 16: 8-11). He regenerates believers (Titus 3: 5). He indwells and strengthens all who are true Christians (I Cor. 6: 19; Eph. 3: 16); bears witness that they are indeed children of God (Rom. 8: 16); enables them to possess and display Christlike graces of character (Gal. 5: 22-23); guides and teaches earnest believers (John 16: 13; I Cor. 2: 9-15); enables them to communicate effectively to others the truth that they themselves have received of God (Acts 1: 8); strengthens the devotional life (Jude 20; Eph. 6: 18; Rom. 8: 26); calls and guides believers in Christian service (Acts 13: 2; Acts 16: 6-7; Acts 8: 29); and purifies by faith (Acts 15: 9, 10). These and other activities of the Spirit of God bear witness to His complete deity and equality with the Son and the Father.

IV. Antitrinitarian Theories

There are two outstanding errors which have appeared in the Church from time to time. Both are the outgrowth of the earlier Monarchianism, which through a misapprehension of the nature of the divine unity, held that the doctrine of the Trinity was irreconcilable with it. These errors are Sabellianism and Arianism.

A. *Sabellianism.*

This form of Monarchianism takes its name from Sabellius (c. 250-260 A.D.), who held that there were not three Persons in the Godhead but that the one God manifested Himself in three modes or forms. God as Father is Creator; the same God as Son manifested Himself in the incarnation as the Redeemer; while the Spirit is the same God manifested in the spiritual life of the Church. It may be readily seen that this is not a Trinity of Persons, but only a trinity of manifestations. It is at base unitarian and not trinitarian. The principle is pantheistic in that it is God evolving Himself, first as Jehovah, then more clearly to His creatures as the Son, and still more fully and spiritually as the Holy Spirit. This doctrine is clearly opposed to the Scriptures, for there the Father is constantly addressing the Son, and the Son addresses the Father. Christianity therefore rightly rejected this teaching.

B. *Arianism.*

Arianism is also a form of Monarchianism, but at the opposite extreme to the former position. It takes its name from the presbyter Arius (256-336 A.D.) who held an important position in the Church at Alexandria. He was without doubt one of the most formidable enemies encountered in the development of Trinitarianism. Arius sought to find a place for Christ above that of creation, and yet outside the Godhead (See Chapter II, Sect. III). He held that when God would create the world, He found it necessary to first create the "Word" or Son as His Agent. The Son was therefore a creature and of a different essence from the Father. Instead of saying that the Son was God, he said only that he was "like God." According to Arius, Christ took only a human body in the incarnation, not a human soul, and the Holy Spirit bears the same relation to the Son that the Son does to the Father. Both were alike creatures. The Church therefore rightly rejected this teaching as being subversive of the true doctrine of redemption. It is clear also that an erroneous doctrine concerning the Person of Christ makes impossible a valid doctrine of the Trinity.

V. THE EVANGELICAL DOCTRINE OF THE TRINITY

The evangelical doctrine of the Trinity as generally held in the Church is best expressed in the words of the ancient creeds and confessions of faith. The Athanasian Creed has the most explicit statement: "We worship one God in Trinity, and Trinity in Unity; neither confounding the Persons, nor dividing the substance. For there is one Person of the Father, another of the Son, and another of the Holy Ghost; but the Godhead of the Father, of the Son, and of the Holy Ghost is all one, the glory equal, the majesty coeternal." The Thirty-nine Articles as revised by John Wesley declared that "in the unity of this Godhead, there are three Persons of one substance, power, and eternity—the Father, the Son, and the Holy Ghost." Therefore, we may say that the evangelical doctrine affirms that the Godhead is of one substance, and that in the unity of this substance there are three subsistences or Persons; and further, that this must be held in such a manner as not to divide the substance or confuse the Persons.

A. *The Unity of Substance or Essence.*

The term unity is applied to the substance or essence of God; trinity is applied to His personality. The distinction is in the persons and not in the substance. There are not three Gods in one Person, but three Persons in one God. The nature of which they partake is not divided. The Church has never taught that the one and the three are used in the same sense. It applies the term unity to the substance, and trinity to the Persons, or the distinctions within that one substance. The evangelical formula is: "One substance; three persons."

B. *The Trinity of Persons.*

The term "person" as used here is a translation of the Greek word *hypostasis*, and it must be carefully distinguished from the modern use of the word person as applicable to the whole of the being. When we speak of God as a Person, we are in reality using the modern term to express the nature of the one substance; when we speak of "persons" in the trinitarian sense, we are referring to the *Hypostases* or distinctions within that one substance. It is easy for confusion to arise from the use of a word in different senses or connotations, and we need to guard carefully a proper definition of these terms. The Church has always maintained that there is something more than an "economic" trinity of manifestations, such as Sabellianism teaches. It teaches that the Trinity not only expresses God's outward relation to man, but also His inner relation to Himself; and, therefore, that there is an "essential" as well as an "economic" Trinity.

Wakefield makes the following statement on the foregoing topic: "The term *person* signifies in ordinary language an intelligent being. Two or more persons, therefore, in the strict philosophical sense, would be two or more distinct intelligent beings. If the term *person* were so applied to the Trinity in the Godhead, a plurality of gods would follow; while if taken in what has been called a *political* sense, personality would be no more than a *relation* arising out of office. Personality in God is, therefore, not to be understood in either of the above senses if we pay respect to the testimony of Scripture. God is *one being.* But, He is more than one being in three *relations,* for *personal acts,* such as we ascribe to distinct persons, and which most unequivocally characterize personality, are ascribed to each person of the Trinity. The doctrine of the Scripture is, therefore, that the persons are not *separate,* but distinct, and that they are so united as to be but *one* God. In other words, that the divine nature exists under the personal distinction of Father, Son, and Holy Ghost, and that these three have equally, and in common with one another, the nature and perfections of supreme divinity" (WAKEFIELD, *Chr. Theol.*, pp. 178-179. See also W. N. CLARKE, *Outline of Chr. Theol.*, pp. 161-181).

C. *Conclusion Regarding Evangelical Doctrine of the Trinity.*

As previously indicated, the doctrine of the Trinity is not merely a speculative or philosophical theory, but a practical doctrine, revealed to us in the Holy Scriptures. It cannot be denied that therein is taught, (1) that there is but one true God; and, (2) that to both Jesus Christ and the Holy Spirit are ascribed attributes, titles, and predicates which belong only to this one true God. But we are ever brought back to the thought that the Being of God is by St. Paul termed a *mystery,* and we are commanded to *worship* the "Unity in Trinity and Trinity in Unity," not necessarily to understand it.

"The Bible doctrine of the Trinity," says Ralston, "is one of those sublime and glorious mysteries which the mind of man, at least while shrouded in clay, cannot penetrate. We may study and meditate until lost in thought, yet never can we comprehend the mode and nature of the divine being." Dr. Pope cautions, "It is well to be familiar with the terms that express the relation of the One to the Three-in-One. No thoughtful student will either discard or undervalue them. The Deity is the Divine Essence or Substance or Nature; the Three are Subsistences, *Hypostases,* and Persons. . . . . One of the results of careful and reverent study will be the discipline that shall make every word faithful to the equal honor of each of the Adorable Persons in the unity of the other two, and in the unity of the Godhead, adoring and praying to each with this sacred reservation."

Is it any wonder, then, that the Church has not only given us explicit doctrinal statements concerning this important truth, but for the purposes of worship, has set it to music in the matchless Gloria? Here is summarized all its teachings concerning the Trinity as they are to be used in the service of worship. May we not then reverently say, "Glory be to the Father, and to the Son, and to the Holy Ghost; as it was in the beginning, is now, and ever shall be, world without end, Amen."

UNIT III

THE DOCTRINE OF MAN AND THE PROBLEM OF SIN

Preview

In this unit we turn from our study of the nature of God and begin a consideration of His work or activity. The first aspect of this with which we deal is creation. The creative work of God, as recorded in the Book of Genesis, has been the subject of much controversy in recent years. However, it is heartening to observe that, as the Genesis account is studied carefully and without prejudice, it is found to be in remarkable harmony with the established *facts* of modern science. The superiority of the biblical account of beginnings to other such explanations is evident even to the casual observer.

A study of creation provides a natural transition from the doctrine of God to a study of man and his need of redemption. Man was the culmination of God's creative activity. We, therefore, give special attention to the origin of the human race, the nature of man, and original holiness, or the spiritual condition of man prior to the entrance of sin into the world.

Our study of primitive man leads in turn to a consideration of the doctrine of sin. It is difficult to overemphasize the necessity of correctly understanding and tenaciously holding scriptural views of this subject. Our conception of sin will largely determine our views of other Christian doctrines, particularly the doctrines concerning salvation.

Creation and man and sin: these are the themes for our study now. May diligence and honesty and the blessed Holy Spirit himself be our constant companions as we travel along in this unit.

UNIT III

THE DOCTRINE OF MAN AND THE PROBLEM OF SIN

Chapter VIII. *Cosmology*

I. THE SCRIPTURAL ACCOUNT OF CREATION

    A. The Nature of Cosmology.

    B. Theories of Creation.
        1. Physical or Materialistic Theory.
        2. Emanation or Pantheistic Theory.
        3. Theory of Natural Evolution.
        4. Theory of Continuous Creation.

    C. The Relation of God to Creation.
        1. Creation and the Trinity.
        2. Creation and the Attributes of God.
        3. Creation and the Logos.

    D. The Hymn of Creation.

    E. The Mosaic Cosmology.
        1. Varied Types of Interpretation.
        2. The Days of Creation.
        3. Primary and Secondary Creation.

    F. The Order of Creation.
        1. Primary Creation or Origination.
        2. Secondary Creation or Formation.
        3. The Creative Periods.

    G. The Purpose of Creation.

II. ANGELS AND SPIRITS

    A. Nature, Attributes, and Ministry of Angels.
    B. Satan.

III. THE RELATION OF GOD TO HIS CREATION

    A. Conservation.
    B. Preservation.
    C. Government.

Chapter IX. *Anthropology*

I. THE ORIGIN OF MAN

    A. The Nature of Anthropology.

    B. The Two Scriptural Accounts of Man's Creation.

       1. The First Account of Man's Creation.

       2. The Second Account of Man's Creation.

    C. The Origin of Woman.

    D. The Unity of the Race and its Community of Origin.

II. THE NATURE OF MAN

    A. The Constituent Elements of Human Nature.

       1. Theory of Dichotomy.

       2. Theory of Trichotomy.

    B. The Primitive State of Man.

    C. The Origin of the Soul.

       1. The Theory of the Pre-existence of Souls.

       2. The Theory of Creationism.

       3. The Theory of Traducianism.

    D. The Image of God in Man.

       1. The Natural Image of God in Man.

       2. The Moral Image of God in Man.

    E. The Nature of Primitive Holiness.

       1. Not a Mere Possibility of Holiness.

       2. Not Ethical Holiness.

       3. The Presence of the Holy Spirit.

Chapter X. *The Doctrine of Sin*

I. THE TEMPTATION AND FALL OF MAN

    A. The Genesis Account of the Fall of Man.

    B. The Necessity of Man's Probation.

    C. The Fall of Man.

II. SATAN AND THE ORIGIN OF SIN

    A. The Doctrine of Satan.

       1. The Origin of Satan.

       2. Satan as Antichrist.

       3. Satan and the Redemptive Work of Christ.

       4. The Kingdom of Satan.

    B. Summary of Scriptural Teaching Concerning the Origin of Sin.

III. THE NATURE AND PENALTY OF SIN

    A. Scriptural Terminology Regarding Sin.

    B. Definitions of Sin.

    C. The Consequences of Sin.

       1. The Nature of Guilt.

       2. The Nature of Penalty.

IV. ORIGINAL SIN OR INHERITED DEPRAVITY

    A. Terminology.

    B. The Fact of Original Sin.

    C. The Fact of Inherited Depravity.

    D. The Nature of Inherited Depravity.

    E. The Transmission of Original Sin.

    F. Depravity and Infirmity.

CHAPTER VIII

COSMOLOGY

"The glory of the Mosaic Cosmogony is its testimony to God, who reigns supreme in it from beginning to end, whether as the *Elohim* of the first chapter, or the *Jehovah-Elohim* of the second. He is the Absolute Creator of a universe which is not Himself, evolved according to laws which in this record are exhibited as successively communicated by a series of fiats or impulses. The beginning of each great development is marked, and nothing more. So long as we hold fast this principle we shall find the original document unassailable."—WILLIAM BURTON POPE.

I. THE SCRIPTURAL ACCOUNT OF CREATION

A. *The Nature of Cosmology.*

Cosmology is that study which deals with the origin and nature of the universe as an orderly system, or cosmos. However, in theology the term is usually limited to a consideration of nature apart from man. The study of the origin and nature of man is considered under separate categories as follows: Anthropology, which deals with man in his original state; and Hamartiology, which treats of man in his fallen or sinful state.

In very early times people seem to have had little conception of the world as such. But, as they began to give attention to the world in which they lived and to the heavens above them, the expression "the heavens and the earth" came to be used to describe the created universe. Nations living near the sea coast frequently spoke of "the heavens, earth, and sea."

Ancient people found considerable difficulty in explaining the origin of the basic or primary material out of which other things were formed. They commonly accepted the principle, "from nothing nothing comes," and could not therefore admit that the world was created out of nothing. As a result, they commonly believed in two eternal principles, God and self-existent matter, neither being dependent upon the other. Indeed, the principle "from nothing nothing comes" does appear to be entirely true as it applies to purely material causes, but it does not hold true when God is considered as the Efficient Cause. Generally the ancients believed that primordial matter was of the nature of thin air, or an ether, fluid and movable, out of which the earth was formed. In contrast to the foregoing concepts were the views of the Hebrews. They regarded the universe more after the pattern of a building of which God was the Creator of the materials as well as the Builder of the structure.

B. *Theories of Creation.*

The scriptural account of creation will be more meaningful if viewed against a background of various non-Christian views. In our discussion, brief mention will be made of the following theories: (1) The Physical or Materialistic; (2) The Emanation or Pantheistic; (3) The Theory of Natural Evolution; and, (4) The Theory of Continuous Creation.

1. *The Physical or Materialistic Theory.* This theory of creation presupposes the eternity of matter. The hypothesis of spontaneous generation is substituted for God as the Builder of the universe. It is an application of materialistic philosophy to the idea of creation, and arose out of nineteenth century rationalism. Any such theory as this, which omits God as the active personal Agent in creation, is obviously untenable in Christian theology.

2. *The Emanation or Pantheistic Theory.* This view holds that the world was neither created nor fashioned out of pre-existent material, but is to be regarded as an extension of the divine substance. It flows from God as a stream from a fountain, or as rays of light from the sun. The weakness of this theory is the weakness of Pantheism itself, with its denial of the personality of God, its failure to admit man's freedom and immortality, and its basis on assumptions which are not only unproved but unprovable.

3. *The Theory of Natural Evolution.* This theory is similar to, if not identical with, that of spontaneous generation. Naturalistic evolution, instead of solving the

problem of creation, merely pushes it back farther and farther in time. The question of origin remains unanswered. The theory breaks down at three vital points: (1) It has not been able to bridge the chasm between the inanimate and the animate. (2) It cannot pass from the diffused life of the vegetable realm to the conscious, somatic life of the animal kingdom. (3) It cannot span the gap from the somatic life of animals to the rational, self-conscious, spiritual life of man. Only the creative activity of God could have originated vegetable, animal, and personal life.

4. *The Theory of Continuous Creation.* This view challenges the idea of creation as a single completed act in favor of creation as a continuous process. This theory is often held by theistic evolutionists. It asserts that organic development is due, not to materialistic forces, but to divine power working within the organism. This divine activity is sometimes identified with the continuous creative process, and sometimes it is limited to certain crucial points in development.

C. *The Relation of God to Creation.*

The scriptural doctrine of creation maintains that the universe had a beginning; that it is not eternal in either matter or form; that it is not self-originated; and that it owes its origin to the omnipotent power and unconditional will of God. This is the Christian conception. It involves: (1) a belief in Almighty God whereby the world once began to be out of nothing, solely through the divine will; (2) the concept of God in the Trinity of His essence; (3) a display of the attributes of God—omnipotence, wisdom, and love; and (4) belief in creation through the divine Word.

1. *Creation and the Trinity.* The Scriptures plainly teach that in the work of creation the Son and the Spirit were associated with the Father. St. Paul speaks of the relation of the Father and the Son in creation as follows: *To us there is but one God, the Father, of whom are all things, and we in him; and one Lord Jesus Christ, by whom are all things, and we by him* (I Cor. 8:6). The

Spirit's role in creation is referred to by the psalmist in his declaration, *Thou sendest forth thy spirit, they are created* (Psalms 104:30). This confirms the Genesis record of the dawn of creation. Here the Spirit is portrayed as moving upon the face of the waters—brooding over the waters—bringing order and beauty out of chaos (Gen. 1:2). These and many other scriptural passages reveal that all of the Persons in the Trinity were active in creation.

2. *Creation and the Attributes of God.* Many of the attributes of God are revealed in creation. Thus we may say that the world is what it is because God is what He is. The very existence of a universe, so vast and complex as to stagger one's imagination, reveals His omnipotent power. Its order and perfection reflect His immeasurable omniscience. His wisdom and goodness are revealed in the preparation of all things for man's happiness and enrichment. The creation of man himself finds its origin in the overflowing love of God as He sought new objects upon whom that love could be bestowed. Everywhere nature reveals the perfections of our God. Well did the psalmist exclaim, *O Lord, how manifold are thy works! in wisdom hast thou made them all: the earth is full of thy riches* (Psalms 104:24).

3. *Creation and the Logos.* By what means did God create all things? To this the Scriptures give answer, *By the word of his power. By the word of the Lord were the heavens made; and all the host of them by the breath of his mouth* (Psalms 33:6). But this word must not be thought of as impersonal. It is Christ as the *Logos* or Word. He is the Mediator in creation as well as in redemption. *In the beginning was the Word, and the Word was with God, and the Word was God. . . . . All things were made by him; and without him was not anything made that was made* (John 1:1, 3). *For by him were all things created, that are in heaven, and that are in earth, visible and invisible, whether they be thrones, or dominions, or principalities, or powers: all things were created by him, and for him: and he is before all things, and by him all things consist* (Col. 1:16, 17). The Word

veiled in the Old Testament in such expressions as *God said,* and *Let there be* is seen in the New Testament to be not only the spoken Word but the speaking Word, even our Lord Jesus Christ. It is through Him that the Father's desires and plans in creation pass into reality. It is because the *Logos* or Word was the Mediator of both purpose and efficiency in the work of creation that the Word incarnate, Jesus Christ, became the Mediator of both the revealing and the enabling grace of redemption.

D. *The Hymn of Creation.*

The Book of Genesis opens with an inspired psalm, sometimes known as the "Hymn of Creation," or the "Poem of the Dawn." By this it is not meant that the account is an allegory or fiction, but a true historical description cast in poetical form. It is fitting that the harmony of creation, at which the morning stars sang together, and all the sons of God shouted for joy, should be revealed to us in the harmonies of poetical description. Here is the balanced rhythm, the stately movement, the recurrent refrains, and the blend of beauty and power which characterize great poetry. In commenting on this Dr. Thomas C. Porter says that "To him who could grasp the mighty idea and take in the whole at one view, the entire creation would appear like a solemn hymn, like some grand oratorio which starting on a few low, faint notes, gradually gains strength and fullness, and swelling louder and louder, rolls on from harmony to height of harmony until it reaches its loftiest outburst and expression, the diapason closing full in man."

E. *The Mosaic Cosmogony.*

The Christian account of the origin and ordering of the universe is set forth in the Hymn of Creation. In our study of this, attention will be directed to three themes: (1) Varied Types of Interpretation; (2) The Days of Creation; and (3) Primary and Secondary Creation.

1. *Varied Types of Interpretation.* The Mosaic account of the origin of the universe, including the earth and man, has been interpreted in various ways. Some

modern critics have regarded the account as mythological. But neither the tone nor the contents of the account
warrant this construction. Both Jesus and the apostles
treated it as sacred history (cf. Matt. 19:4). A second
type of interpretation, the allegorical method, was developed as a result of the influence of scholars located at
the great center of Greek learning in Alexandria. A
number of early Church fathers adopted this method.
It is scarcely less objectionable than the mythological
method. Still another method of interpretation is known
as the "vision hypothesis." This regards the Genesis
account as resulting from a series of visions given in
such a manner that the factual truth blended with the inner conceptions of the seer. This explanation has never
been accepted by the Church. The Christian view is that
the Mosaic account represents true history concerning
the origin of the world. Jesus Christ pronounced it holy,
and He appealed to it as divinely inspired. It is therefore
for us final and authoritative, however much interpretations may vary in detail or in emphasis.

2. *The Days of Creation*. The Genesis account of creation is primarily a religious document. It cannot be considered a scientific statement, and yet it must not be regarded as contradictory to science. The Hebrew word
yom which is translated "day" occurs no less than 1,480
times in the Old Testament, and is translated by over
fifty different words including such terms as "time,"
"life," "today," "age," "forever," "continually," and
"perpetually." With such a flexible use of the original
term, it is impossible to dogmatize or to demand un-
swerving restriction to one only of those meanings. The
best Hebrew exegesis has never regarded the days of
Genesis as solar days, but as day-periods of indefinite
duration. The doctrine of an immense time prior to the
six days of creation was a common view among the
earlier fathers and schoolmen. Augustine referred to
the periods as "God-divided" days in contrast to solar
or "sun-divided" days. He affirms that the word "day"
does not apply to the duration of time, but to the boun-
daries of great periods. Many other Church fathers,

learned Jewish doctors, and modern theologians hold to this same interpretation. Other writers, recognizing that the Hebrew word for "day" may mean either a definite or indefinite period of time, leave the question open.

3. *Primary and Secondary Creation.* The Mosaic account of creation makes a distinction between the first production of matter in the sense of origination, and secondary creation, or the formation of that matter by subsequent elaboration into an orderly universe. The primary creation is direct and immediate; the secondary creation is always indirect and mediate. In the former God brings into existence the raw building material; in the latter He forms and shapes it into specific objects. *Both* are *truly creative* acts of Deity: the one, direct; the other, indirect. These will be more fully explained in the following section.

F. *The Order of Creation.*

In considering the order of creation as given in the Book of Genesis several topics will be examined: (1) Primary Creation or Origination; (2) Secondary Creation or Formation: (3) The Creative Periods; and (4) The Restoration Theory.

1. *Primary Creation or Origination.* The word "created" is used three times in the Genesis account. It is a translation of the Hebrew word *bara* which signifies origination, or creation *de novo*. The word occurs in the following verse: *In the beginning God created the heaven and the earth* (Gen. 1:1). *And God created great whales* (leviathans or sea monsters) (Gen. 1:21). *So God created man in his own image, in the image of God created he him* (Gen. 1:27). It seems evident that the word "created" as here used clearly refers to the commencement of a thing's existence. That which was brought into being had not been in existence at any prior time or in any previous form.

Dr. Adam Clarke translates Genesis 1:1 as follows: "God in the beginning created the substance of the heavens and the substance of the earth," that is, the *prima materia,* or first element out of which the heavens and the earth were successively formed. The first step in creation was thus to bring into existence material substance or matter in its chaotic and unformed state.

The second origination was that of somatic or soul life, *And God created great leviathans* (or sea monsters) *and every living 'soul* (creature) *that moveth* (Gen. 1: 21). Here again is the appearance of an entirely new entity. It is called somatic life (from *soma,* a body). This new individualized life is given a body separate and distinct from the diffused life found in the vegetable realm. The word "soul" as used here refers to the immaterial entity, marked by sensation, feeling, and will, which characterized this new order of creation. The word is not synonymous with the word "spirit" which is used to indicate man's immaterial nature in its relations to deity and the moral order.

The third of God's creative acts, in the sense of origination, resulted in the appearance of a personal being. *And God created man in his own image, in the image of God created he him; male and female created he them* (Gen. 1: 27). Here is described the creation of a self-conscious man, one who knows and knows that he knows. He is a free moral agent who is responsible for his acts. He is one who bears the image of God.

2. *Secondary Creation or Formation.* In the foregoing section we discussed creation in the sense of origination. Three new entities—matter, soul, and spirit— were brought into being. But God is not only the Creator of the materials. He is also the Fashioner or Architect. He creates through formation out of previously existing materials. He creates through creation itself, though He does so by creative fiat as in the case of origination.

In the Genesis account we find a series of seven formative acts by which God transforms the chaotic and formless, but pre-existent and prepared materials, into an orderly, beautifully formed universe. These seven decrees of God constitute His secondary creation. They are as follows: (1) *Let there be light* (Gen. 1:3). This is the formation of cosmic light, sometimes regarded as radiant heat and light. (2) *Let there be an expanse* (or firmament) (Gen. 1:6). *Let the waters under the heaven be gathered into one place, and let the dry land appear* (Gen. 1:9). (3) *Let the land put forth vegetation* (Gen. 1:11). Here there is an introduction of a new force within matter, a vital element giving rise to vitalized germinal matter, and making possible the realm of living objects. Note that this new element is brought into being by Divine fiat, but not apart from the pre-existent earth. The statement is not "Let there be vegetation," but *Let the earth bring forth vegetation*. (4) *Let there be luminaries in the expanse of the heavens* (Gen. 1:14). At an appropriate time the light from these luminaries furnishes the necessary conditions for further development in the organic realm. (5) *Let the waters swarm forth swarming things, living souls, and let birds fly over the earth* (Gen. 1:20). (6) *Let the land bring forth living soul after its kind* (Gen. 1:24). In the fifth and sixth formative acts reference is made only to the creation of the material or physical organisms which embody the living souls created (in the sense of origination) at this point (Gen. 1:21) in the creative plan. (7) *Let us make man* (Gen. 1:26). Even the formative act in this instance is not exactly parallel to the preceding ones. Instead of "Let the earth bring forth man," it is *Let us make man*. The formative word *make* refers to man's material body, and it links him to the physical universe. In the word *create* (Gen. 1:27), as previously noted, we find the origination of man's spiritual being in the image and likeness of God. A logical and natural order is evident in the various stages of formative development. Each step prepares the way for those which follow. The whole is fittingly climaxed and gathered up in the final refrain, *And God saw everything that he had made, and, behold, it was very good* (Gen. 1:31).

3. *The Creative Periods.* Perhaps the outstanding feature of the Mosaic account of creation is the orderly arrangement in stages and periods known as creative

days. In the sense of origination, creation is instantaneous; but as formation, it is gradual and cumulative. There is a progressive revelation in an ascending scale of creative acts. Each stage is preparatory to that which succeeds it, as well as a prophecy of that which shall follow.

The study of the Genesis account reveals certain facts which take on added significance with each new scientific discovery. *First,* there are two great eras mentioned, each with three creative days—the Inorganic and the Organic. *Second,* each of these great eras begins with the appearance of light—the one with the creation of cosmic light, and the other with light emanating from created luminaries. *Third,* each of these eras ends with a day in which a twofold work is accomplished. The first is the completing or perfecting act or that which precedes it, and the second is a prophecy of that which is to be. This arrangement may be set forth in schematic form as follows:

The Inorganic Era

1st Day—Cosmical Light.
2nd Day—The Firmament—water and atmosphere.
3rd Day—Dry Land (or the outlining of land and seas).
        Creation of Vegetation (transitional and prophetic).

The Organic Era

4th Day—The Luminaries.
5th Day—The Lower Animals—fishes and birds.
6th Day—Land Animals.
        Creation of Man (transitional and prophetic).

The creation of vegetation which for physical reasons belongs to the third day, is the culmination of the Inorganic Era and the prophecy of the Organic Era which immediately follows. We may say also that Man, the culmination of the work of the sixth day, is likewise prophetic of another aeon, the new age in which the will of God shall be done on earth as it is in heaven.

With the rapidly increasing discoveries of science, the Genesis account was soon called in question by men who appeared to be authorities in their field of investigation. But Christian men, eminent in science also, after prolonged study and research, declared that not only was there no conflict between Genesis and modern science, but that there was a remarkable parallel between them. Hugh Miller, eminent in geology, found no misplacement of facts in the Genesis account. Professors Winchell, Dana, Guyot, and Dawson, among the earlier men of science, maintained that the order of events in the Scripture cosmogony corresponds essentially to the discoveries of modern science. Sir William Ramsay declared, "Between the essential truth of Christianity and the established facts of science there is no real antagonism." When one orients himself as to the first day of creation, then the other days follow in exact, scientific order. These periods of time have never been arranged by scientists in any other basic manner than that of the first chapter of Genesis. Palaeontological evidence substantiates the order and arrangement of life as laid down in Genesis. The creative fiat, in its triple expression in the first chapter of Genesis, is sufficient explanation for being, both living and nonliving, and with increasing discoveries of science it is being verified each day by earth's greatest minds.

4. *The Restoration Theory.* In order to account for the great geological periods, many Christian scholars interpret the first verse of the creative account as an introductory statement without reference to a time order. It is believed that an immense interval of time elapsed between this and the events recorded in the following verses. In this way the long creative periods which geology demands are accounted for without regarding the days of Genesis as other than solar days of twenty-four hours each.

Closely allied to the foregoing is the Restoration Theory which is held more or less extensively in the Church. According to this view the opening statement, *In the beginning God created the heaven and the earth,* represents an initial and perfect creation. The following statement, *Now the earth had become waste and wild* (or formless and empty) *and darkness was on the face of the abyss,* is said to refer to a great catastrophe in which everything upon the earth was destroyed. After a period of undetermined length God recreated the earth, revivifying it in a week of six solar days. In substantiation of this view the words of Isaiah are cited: *God himself that formed the earth and made it; he hath established it, he created it not in vain* (that is, He created it not a waste), *he formed it to be inhabited* (Isaiah 45: 18).

G. *The Purpose of Creation.*

The term *aeon* ("age" or "world") is used to describe the succession of epochs and periods running throughout the course of the ages and involving both the physical and ethical aspects of the world. The first *aeon* was that indefinite formative period which antedates the present heavens and earth. This period was characterized by the chaos of the geological ages, and by moral and spiritual confusion resulting from the apostasy of a portion of the angels.

The second age is the present economy. The Scriptures clearly teach that at its close mighty agencies now held in check will be released. The result will be drastic changes, and the appearance of a new heaven and a new earth. St. Peter describes these cataclysmic changes as follows: *But the day of the Lord will come as a thief in the night; in the which the heavens shall pass away with a great noise, and the elements shall melt with fervent heat, the earth also and the works that are therein shall be burned up. Seeing then that all these things shall be dissolved, what manner of persons ought ye to be in all holy conversation and godliness, looking for and hasting unto the coming of the day of God, wherein the heavens being on fire shall be dissolved, and the elements shall melt with fervent heat? Nevertheless we, according to his promise, look for new heavens and a new earth, wherein dwelleth righteousness* (II Peter 3: 10-13). From a spiritual and ethical viewpoint, the present age has been characterized by two momentous occurrences: the fall of man into sin, and the glorious incarnation of Jesus Christ in order that man might have a new spiritual beginning.

The third aeon will open with the second advent of Christ as He ushers in the age that is to be. From the physical aspect, the new age will find its expression in a new heaven and a new earth. On the ethical and moral plane, it will be an age free from sin and all moral disorder.

Thus theology finds the ultimate purpose of creation in the kingdom of God. This kingdom is at once a present possession of *righteousness, and peace, and joy in the Holy Ghost* (Rom. 14:17), and a future hope. Jesus Christ was Himself the perfect embodiment of the principles upon which the kingdom rests. Through His redemptive work men may now be delivered from sin; with the full fruition of this work, His people will be delivered from the consequences of sin. In the age to come, His kingdom shall be ushered in as the full realization of man's highest ethical and spiritual ideals. In the ultimate sense, therefore, the physical creation finds its meaning in the ethical and spiritual aspirations and possibilities of man as they find their full satisfaction in the completely realized kingdom of God.

II. Angels and Spirits

The Scriptures clearly teach that there is an order of intelligences higher than that of man; and further asserts that these beings are connected with man both in providence and in the redemptive economy. They are called *spirits* to denote their specific nature; and *angels* to denote their mission. Relatively little is known concerning these beings, and all of that is revealed in the Scriptures. They are created spirits, but the time of their creation is not clearly indicated.

A. *Nature, Attributes, and Ministry of Angels.*

Angels are frequently described as pure spirit, that is, incorporeal and immaterial beings. The general view of the Church is that angels do not possess bodies. Dr. Pope, however, insists that only God is pure, essential Spirit, and that angels are clothed with ethereal vestures such as St. Paul described in his statement, *There is a spiritual body* (I Cor. 15:44). If they do not possess bodies, the Scriptures teach that on occasion they assume human bodies, either in appearance or reality, in order to converse with men (Gen. 18:2; 19:1, 10). They are great in power and might (II Peter 2:11), and excel in strength (Psalms 103:20).

The Scriptures indicate that man enjoys a richness of experience that is denied to the angels. St. Peter speaks of those *that have preached the gospel unto you with the Holy Ghost sent down from heaven; which things the angels desired to look into* (I Peter 1:12). Both St. John and St. Paul refer to similar limitation of angelic experience. They are merely witnesses to the redemptive glory of man, but they themselves cannot partake of Christ in the same real manner. The hymn writer was no doubt correct when he observed "that angels never knew the joy that our salvation brings."

The attributes commonly ascribed to angels usually include indivisibility, immutability, illocality, and agility. Being indivisible and immutable, angels may be described as invisible, incorruptible, and immortal. They are not omnipresent, but are always present somewhere. They move quickly and with ease. They are to be regarded as individuals, but have no racial connection. They are not male and female, and they do not propagate their kind (Matt. 22:30). There are grades and ranks among angels, such as cherubim, seraphim, thrones, dominions, principalities, powers, and archangels.

The highest ministry of angels is to wait upon God. When it is said that *all the sons of God shouted for joy* (Job 38:7), the reference is to angels as sons. Their chief duty is to minister to the heirs of salvation. They were present at creation, at the giving of the law, at the birth of Christ, after the temptation in the wilderness, in

Gethsemane, at the resurrection, and at the ascension. Hence the author of Hebrews inquires, *Are they not all ministering spirits, sent forth to minister for them who shall be the heirs of salvation* (Heb. 1:14).

The angels in their original estate were holy beings, endowed with freedom of will and subjected to a period of probation. They were meant to choose voluntarily the service of God and be prepared for the free service of ministering to the heirs of salvation. They did not all keep their first estate, but some fell into sin and rebellion against God (Jude 6). Hence we read of the *condemnation of the devil* (I Tim. 3:6), who, as we gather from the Scriptures, was at the head of that portion of the angels that fell away. Satan for this reason is called the *prince of the power of the air* (Eph. 2:2), and his hosts are referred to as *spiritual wickedness in high places* (Eph. 6:12). We may believe that following their probationary period the good angels were confirmed in holiness and admitted to a state of glory wherein they always behold the face of God (Matt. 18:10). The fall of the wicked angels may be regarded as a voluntary apostasy, and it is surmised that their sin was pride (I Tim. 3:6). As a consequence of their sin, they are under the condemnation of God (II Peter 2:4), and shall be punished eternally (Matt. 25:41). Their disposition toward God is one of enmity, this evil purpose being centered in Satan who stands at their head.

B. *Satan.*

Satan is a personal being, the head of the kingdom of evil spirits. He is the essential antichrist. Two names are more frequently applied to him, both of which express his character. He is Satan, or adversary; and devil, or false accuser. Our Lord describes him as sowing the seeds of error and doubt in the Church (Matt. 13:39), and as being both a liar and a murderer (John 8:44). He is able to transform himself into an angel of light. This subject will be given further attention in connection with the origin of evil (see Chapter IX, Sec. II).

III. The Relation of God to His Creation

The God of creation is also the God of providence. He sustains and cares for the world which He has made, and His tender mercies are over all His works. His providence reflects His goodness, wisdom, power, and other attributes. Providence is ascribed to the Father (John 5:17), to the Son (Col. 1:17; Heb. 1:3), and to the Holy Spirit (Psalms 104:30). However, it is conventionally attributed to the Father.

Providence may be defined as that activity of the Triune God by which He conserves, cares for, and governs the world which He had made. The subject may be broadly divided into *General Providence,* by which is meant God's care for the world as a whole and everything in it; and *Special Providence,* which refers more especially to His care for the human race. At other times the subject is classified as *Ordinary Providence,* by which is meant the general exercise of God's care through established principles and laws; and *Extraordinary Providence* or God's miraculous intervention in the ordinary course of nature or history. We shall treat the subject of Providence under the following main divisions: *first,* Conservation, as referring to inanimate nature; *second,* Preservation, as referring to animate nature and the creaturely wants of the subhuman kingdoms; and *third,* Government, as it applies to man.

A. *Conservation.*

Conservation is God's preserving providence in the realm of the physical universe. It is concerned with the relation of God to the world. The Scriptures clearly teach that God is active in upholding all things with the word of His power. *He giveth to all life, and breath, and all things* (Acts 17:25). *For in him we live, and move, and have our being* (Acts 17:28). *And he is before all things, and by him all things consist* (Col. 1:17). Charles Wesley sums up evangelical belief in conservation in the following concise statement: "God is also the supporter of all things which He has made. He beareth, upholdeth, sustaineth all created things by the word of His power;

by the same powerful word which brought them out of nothing. As this was absolutely necessary for the beginning of their existence, it is equally so for the continuance of it; were His almighty influence withdrawn, they could not subsist a moment longer."

While the Church generally has maintained a belief in the immediate presence of God in the conservation of the material universe, it has likewise regarded the laws of nature as the observed principles of divine activity. The exact relation between God and His laws has not been easy to determine, and Christian thinkers have held a variety of views. While most of them recognize laws, principles, and secondary causes in the conservation of the world, they do not make these laws active agencies which would supersede God and banish Him from the universe.

B. *Preservation.*

The word preservation is used to designate the work of Providence in the animate realm, personal and impersonal. God's providential care extends into the lowest forms of life. He governs the lower orders of the animal kingdom largely by appetite and instinct. *The ants are a people not strong, yet they prepare their meat in the summer* (Prov. 30:25). *The eyes of all wait upon thee; and thou givest them their meat in due season. Thou openest thine hand, and satisfiest the desire of every living thing* (Psalms 145:15, 16). This providential care extends also to man in general as a creature of God. Our Lord Jesus Christ declared that the Father *maketh his sun to rise on the evil and on the good, and sendeth rain on the just and on the unjust* (Matt. 5:45).

C. *Government.*

Because man is a free moral agent, the relation of God to man in government differs from His relation to the material universe in conservation, and to the animate realm in preservation. God recognizes and honors man's freedom. He exerts influences upon man, but does not coerce the latter to the extent that freedom of action and responsibility are set aside. The resulting action is not properly the work of God but that of the creature to whom the act belongs. It has been customary to distinguish four modes of divine government. (1) *Permissive.* "When we say that God permits any event," says Wakefield, "we are not to understand the term to indicate that He allows it, or consents to it; but rather that He does not exert His power to prevent it. God permits sin, but He does not approve of it; for, as He is infinitely holy, sin must always be the object of His abhorrence. Accordingly, He testifies against the very sins into which He permits men to fall, denouncing His threatenings against them, and actually punishing them for their crimes" (WAKEFIELD, *Christian Theology*, p. 266), (cf. II Chron. 32:31; Psalms 81:12, 13; Hosea 4:17; Acts 14:16; Romans 1:24, 28). (2) *Preventative.* This is the restraining act of God by which He prevents men from committing sin (cf. Gen. 20:6; Gen. 31:24; Psalms 19:13). (3) *Directive.* God overrules the evil acts of man, and brings out of them consequences which are unintended by the evil agencies. This is sometimes referred to as an overruling providence. *As for you,* said Joseph to his brethren, *ye thought evil against me; but God meant it unto good, to bring to pass, as it is this day, to save much people alive* (Gen. 50:20; cf. also Psalms 76:10; Isaiah 10:5; John 13:27; Acts 4:27-28; Rom. 9:17, 18). (4) *Determinative.* By this is meant the control which God exercises over the bounds of sin and wickedness. *And the Lord said unto Satan, Behold, all that he hath is in thy power; only upon himself put not forth thine hand* (Job 1:12; cf. also Job 2:6; Psalms 124:2; II Thess. 2:7). One of the best known and most frequently quoted passages illustrates this truth: *God is faithful, who will not suffer you to be tempted above that ye are able; but will with the temptation also make a way to escape, that ye may be able to bear it* (I Cor. 10:13).

In conclusion, we may well remember that the root idea of the Christian doctrine of Divine Providence is that God rules over all in love. This reaches its triumphant expression in St. Paul who declares that *We know that all things work together for good to them that love God, to them who are the called according to his purpose* (Rom. 8: 28).

CHAPTER IX

ANTHROPOLOGY

And God said, Let us make man in our image, after our likeness. . . . .
So God created man in his own image, in the image of God created he
him. . . . . And the Lord God formed man out of the dust of the ground,
and breathed into his nostrils the breath of life; and man became a living
soul (Genesis 1:26, 27; 2:7).

When I consider thy heavens, the work of thy fingers; the moon
and the stars, which thou hast ordained; what is man, that thou art
mindful of him? and the son of man, that thou visitest him? For thou
hast made him a little lower than the angels, and hast crowned him with
glory and honour. Thou madest him to have dominion over the works
of thy hands: thou hast put all things under his feet (Psalms 8:3-6).

I. THE ORIGIN OF MAN

A. *The Nature of Anthropology.*

Anthropology is the science of man. As a science it
deals with questions relating to primitive man, the distinctions of races, and the factors which enter into man's
development and progress. In a theological sense, the
term is limited to the study of man in his moral and religious aspects, with particular emphasis on the state of
man before the fall. To understand these problems we
need to examine certain themes which relate more especially to anthropology in its broader definition as a
science. Among the subjects to which we shall devote
some attention are the following: (1) the origin of man;
(2) the constituent elements of human nature; (3) the
unity of the human race and its community of origin;
(4) the origin of the soul; (5) the image of God in man;
and, (6) the nature of primitive holiness.

B. *The Two Scriptural Accounts of Man's Creation.*

Apart from divine revelation, man has had only
vague mythological theories as to his origin. Men have
frequently regarded themselves as earth-born, spring-
ing from rocks, trees, wild animals, the gods, or evolving from some lower form of life. The revelation found
in the Holy Bible must ever be our authority concerning
the origin of mankind. The only authoritative account

of man's origin that we have are those which are found in the first and second chapters of Genesis.

1. *The First Account of Man's Creation.* In the first of these scriptural accounts of man's origin we find the creative fiat of Deity, *Let us make man in our image after our likeness.* The creation of man represents and is the culmination of all former creative acts. He is at once linked to these preceding acts as the crown of creation, and is distinct from them as a new order of being. The creation of man was the end toward which all previous creation pointed. God had providentially prepared all things for man's sustenance and enjoyment. All was arranged for the perfect development of man according to the divine ideal.

2. *The Second Account of Man's Creation.* The second and more elaborate account of the origin of man is found in Genesis 2: 4-35. It is intended to be the starting point for the specific consideration of man's personal history. Here is set forth a twofold creative act, *And the Lord God formed man out of the dust of the ground, and breathed into his nostrils the breath of life; and man became a living soul* (Gen. 2: 7). The first of these creative acts consists of the formation of man's body from the dust of the earth, and the chemicals which compose it. The word "formed" carries with it the idea of creation out of pre-existent materials. There is no inference here that would support the evolutionary view of man's slow development from the lower animal kingdom. At the moment the dust ceased to be dust it existed in the flesh and bone constituting the human body. Yet this account teaches us that in one aspect of his being man is linked to nature; and that on this lower side he is the culmination of the animal kingdom, and represents its perfection in both structure and form.

But the distinctive feature in the creation of man is found in the concluding statement, *breathed into his nostrils the breath of life; and man became a living soul.* Here is a new, unique creation, and not mere formation. God made man a spirit—a self-conscious and self-determining being, a person. By the divine inbreathing man became an immortal spirit.

C. *The Origin of Woman.*

In Genesis 2: 21-23 we have an account of the process by which generic man was elaborated into the two sexes. This statement has been a source of perplexity to many commentators, and many theories have been suggested in its interpretation. St. Paul tells us that *Adam was first formed, then Eve* (I Tim. 2: 13). By this he means that the male was first brought to perfection, and from him the Lord God took that out of which He made woman. This fact was recognized by Adam when he said, *This is now bone of my bones, and flesh of my flesh; she shall be called Woman, because she was taken out of man* (Gen. 2: 23).

The translation of the Hebrew word which is rendered "rib" in the Genesis account is unfortunate. The original word is found forty-two times in the Old Testament, and in no other instance is it rendered "rib." It is usually translated "side" or "sides." The Bible record clearly teaches that every individual of the race, including the first mother, has its antitypal representative in the first man. This generic aspect of the creation of man is presented not only from the physical viewpoint but as forming also the basis of the social structure in the marriage relationship. St. Paul builds upon this aspect of the Genesis account, and gives us one of the most beautiful and meaningful symbols of the relationship between Christ and His Church (Eph. 5: 23-32).

D. *The Unity of the Race and Its Community of Origin.*

The Scriptures affirm both the unity of the race and its community of origin. The word "Adam" was at once the name of an individual and of a family—the personal name of the first man and the generic name of mankind. St. Paul declares that *God hath made of one blood all nations of men for to dwell on all the face of the earth* (Acts 17: 26). With the establishment of the first pair the Bible teaches that all the races of mankind have descended from this common parentage (Gen. 3: 20).

Scientific evidence tends to support the scriptural
view of the unity of the race and its community of origin.
Among the supporting lines of evidence are the following: (1) similarity of physical characteristics found in
all peoples; (2) similar mental characteristics, tendencies, and capacities; (3) similar principles underlying
languages; and, (4) a common, basic religious life with
traditions which indicate a common dwelling place and
a unity of religious life. It is the considered judgment of
science, based on a wealth of cumulative evidence, that
the races of mankind had a common point of origin somewhere in the Near East, probably in Mesopotamia.

II. THE NATURE OF MAN

A. *The Constituent Elements of Human Nature.*

The twofold position of man, at once a part of nature
and a free spirit transcending nature, gives rise to perplexing questions concerning the elements which constitute his personality. Chief among these are the theories of *Dichotomy* and *Trichotomy* which regard man
under a twofold or threefold aspect.

1. *The Theory of Dichotomy.* This view holds that
man is composed of two kinds of essence—a material
portion (the body) and an immaterial portion (the
soul or spirit). The Dichotomist insists that man consists of two, and only two, distinct elements or substances—matter and mind, or the material and the spiritual. Usually a distinction is made between soul and
spirit. When viewed as the power animating the physical
organism or connecting the personality to the world of
sense, the immaterial portion of man is called the soul;
when viewed as a rational or moral agent connecting the
personality with the world of faith, it is called the spirit.
Dr. Strong compares the immaterial portion of the man
to the upper story of a house, but having windows
looking in two directions, toward earth and toward
heaven.

2. *The Theory of Trichotomy.* This theory holds that
man consists of three constituent elements: the rational
spirit, the animal soul, and the body. Many passages of

Scripture, especially in the New Testament, seem to indicate that the nature of man is threefold. Thus St. Paul prayed that the *whole spirit and soul and body be preserved blameless* (I Thess. 5: 23). It is generally held that such expressions were used to express the totality of the being of man's nature. Such usage was common in the early Church, being derived from Platonic philosophy.

While the Scriptures seem to bear out the theory of dichotomy, a practical trichotomy in both ordinary speech and scriptural usage seems clearly evident. Yet, it is always to be remembered that body, soul, and spirit are normally conjoined to form one integrated personality which functions as a unit.

B. *The Primitive State of Man.*

The Scriptures give no support to the evolutionary view that man's primitive state was one of barbarism from which he evolved by a slow process of development to a state of civilization. Rather, the Bible teaches that man was originally created in a state of maturity and perfection. This perfection was not of a kind which precluded further progress or development, but is to be understood in the sense of a proper adaptation to the end for which he was created. As for maturity, the Scriptures are unequivocally opposed to that teaching which regards early man as of crude physical condition and low mentality, slowly developing for himself a language and awakening only gradually to moral and religious concepts. For Christians the scriptural view here is decisive.

The Bible account also challenges the evolutionary hypothesis at the point of the antiquity of man. While the evolutionist posits the necessity of countless millions of years in order to give time for man's development, the Scriptures teach that a few thousand years at most is sufficient. Accepted chronologies, such as those of Ussher and Hales, differ somewhat because the genealogies upon which they are based are variable. However, it appears that the creation of man in the fifth or sixth millennium before Christ as set forth in these chronologies would allow sufficient time for all racial and linguistic developments, as well as for the population to increase to its present level.

C. *The Origin of the Soul.*

Men as "persons" are separate and distinct from one another, and must ever be. Yet, each is possessed of a common human nature, and together they form a living organism which constitutes the human race. Man is both an individual and a racial being. The relation of such individuals to the race is both a philosophical and a theological problem. The body is admittedly propagated by the race through parentage, but what shall be said as to the origin of souls? Not only does the question relate to the nature of man, but it also involves the extent to which God is immanent in the natural processes of the propagation of the race. We shall briefly examine three theories concerning the origin of souls which have dominated the thought of the Church: (1) The Theory of the Pre-existence of Souls; (2) The Theory of Creationism; and (3) The Theory of Traducianism.

1. *The Theory of the Pre-existence of Souls.* This view was inherited from Platonic philosophy, and was productive of a number of heretical opinions in the early Church. It was held by certain theologians who thus explained the possession of ideas by the soul which could not be derived from the sense world. Origen, who is the best representative of this theory, was apparently concerned with the disparity of conditions under which men enter the world, and he attempted to account for it by the character of their sin in a previous state. In modern times the theory has reappeared as an explanation of inborn depravity. It is contended by some that only a self-determined act in a previous state of being could result in this innate condition.

2. *The Theory of Creationism.* This maintains that God immediately creates each human soul, the body being propagated by the parents. This theory seems to be closely connected with attempts to emphasize the im-

portance of the individual as over against an emphasis upon racial continuity and solidarity. This is the characteristic emphasis of both the Roman Catholic and the Reformed Churches. Creationism is sometimes associated with trichotomy and sometimes with dichotomy. In the former instance, the spirit only is regarded as the direct creation of God, the soul being propagated with the body. When connected with dichotomy, the body alone is held to be propagated by the race, the spirit or soul being immediately created by God.

3. *The Theory of Traducianism.* This holds that the souls of men as well as their bodies are derived from their parents. It is asserted that new souls develop from Adam's soul like the shoots of a vine or tree. The theory has been widely held in the Protestant churches. It implies that the race was immediately created in Adam, both in respect to body and soul, and both are propagated by natural generation. Thus the expression, *Adam begat a son in his own likeness,* is interpreted to mean that it is the whole man who begets and is begotten. This theory seems to provide the best explanation for the transmission of original sin or depravity. Among Arminian theologians no great importance is attached to the question concerning the origin of souls.

D. *The Image of God in Man.*

The distinctive note in the scriptural account of man's origin is that he was created in the image of God. This distinguishes him from the lower orders of creation, and at the same time relates him immediately to the spiritual world. To more fully understand what is meant by the *image of God* we may conveniently divide our subject into (1) the Natural Image of God; and (2) the Moral Image of God.

1. *The Natural Image of God.* This refers to man's original constitution as regards that which makes him man, and thereby distinguishes him from the lower animal creation. This may be conveniently summed up under the term "personality." By virtue of his personality man possesses certain powers, faculties, and char-

acteristics. Among these are three of special significance: spirituality, knowledge, and immortality.

Spirituality is the deepest fact in the likeness of man to God. St. James speaks of *men which are made after the similitude of God* (James 3:9), thereby implying the indestructibility of the natural image of God in man. Spirit in man is like spirit in God, the one finite and the other infinite. The spiritual nature itself is the likeness of God.

Man's cognitive powers belong also to the original nature in which he was created. Knowledge, in both its intellectual and moral aspects, is included in this original image. However, knowledge in its intellectual sense belongs to the natural image, while knowledge as an ethical and spiritual quality belongs to the moral image of man.

The Scriptures teach and the Church has maintained that man was created immortal and that death entered solely as a consequence of sin. There have been many views and theories concerning the question as to whether or not the body of man was created immortal. Some have held that the body was naturally mortal. Others have taught that man as such was immortal, but that provision was made in his original constitution for the gradual or sudden spiritualization of his bodily frame. As regards the immortality of man's spirit, the Church has ever held that immortality belongs to the very essence of the soul. The spirit is itself the person, and human personality is undying. Protestantism has uniformly maintained that eternal life as a gift of Christ does not apply to existence as such but to the quality of that existence. The soul has existence regardless of the state or quality of that existence which we call life or death. It may exist in a state of sin and death, or in a state of life and righteousness, whether in this world or in the world to come.

2. *The Moral Image of God in Man.* While the natural image of God in man may be summed up in the word "personality," the moral image may be summed up in

the word "holiness." The first has to do with the powers given to man; the second has to do with the use made of those powers or the direction given to those powers. The natural image is never lost in any man, the moral image is amissible. The moral image, man's moral likeness to God, thus refers to the dispositions and tendencies within man. It has to do with the character or quality of personality—the rightness or wrongness of the use of the powers with which man is endowed. The moral image gives man his moral ability and makes possible a holy character. It is closely connected with the idea of primitive holiness which is considered below.

E. The Nature of Primitive Holiness.

Man was created holy. This holiness consisted of a spontaneous inclination or tendency toward the good— an inner disposition which always answered to the right. This included an enlightened understanding of God and spiritual things. Three observations may well be made concerning this state of primitive holiness: (1) it was not a mere possibility of holiness; (2) it was not ethical holiness; and (3) it was a state that was characterized by the continual presence of the Holy Spirit.

1. *Not a Mere Possibility of Holiness.* A mere possibility of holiness would have been a purely negative state—a nature free from either virtue or sin. Such a concept concerning Adam's original state would naturally lead to a denial of inherited depravity in his descendants. Rather, as already noted, this state of primitive holiness was a positive attitude of the soul. It was characterized by a spontaneous tendency to obey the right and reject the wrong.

2. *Not Ethical Holiness.* The newly created state of Adam was one of holiness, but this did not possess any true ethical quality. This primitive holiness did not result from Adam's moral choices. He was not responsible for the state, and there was therefore no reward or merit attached to it. It was a holiness of nature rather than a holiness of personal agency. As John Wesley declared, "A man may be righteous before he does what

is right, holy in heart before he is holy in life." Such was the case with Adam.

3. *The Presence of the Holy Spirit.* Not only did Adam possess an inner state which spontaneously responded to the right, but the Holy Spirit was ever present and operative in his life. He enjoyed blessed and intimate communion with his Maker. The divine spirit revealed to him a knowledge of God and urged him always to do that which was right. The presence of the Holy Spirit was thus an original and abiding element in the holiness of man. Only thus, as Dr. Miley points out, can the true nature of human depravity be realized. The fall of man was not only a loss of the subjective state of holiness, but it also involved the corruption of man's nature as a result of the operation of influences made possible by the withdrawal of the Holy Spirit.

The scriptural account of creation closes with a statement of divine approbation: *God saw everything that he had made, and, behold, it was very good* (Gen. 1: 31). This expresses divine approval of man's moral rectitude and uprightness by creation, and cannot refer to man's conduct subsequent to creation.

CHAPTER X

THE DOCTRINE OF SIN

"In every religion there is a principal truth or error which, like the first link of a chain, necessarily draws after it all the parts with which it is essentially connected. This leading principle in Christianity . . . . is the doctrine of our corrupt and lost estate; for if man is not at variance with his Creator, what need of a Mediator between God and him? If he is not a depraved, undone creature, what necessity of so wonderful a Restorer and Saviour as the Son of God? If he be not enslaved to sin, why is he redeemed by Jesus Christ? If he is not polluted, why must he be washed in the blood of the immaculate Lamb? If his soul is not disordered, what occasion is there for such a divine physician? If he is not helpless and miserable, why is he perpetually invited to secure the assistance and consolations of the Holy Spirit? And, in a word, if he is not born in sin, why is the new birth so absolutely necessary that Christ declares with the most solemn asseverations, without it no man can see the kingdom of God?"—FLETCHER OF MADELEY.

Hamartiology, or the Doctrine of Sin, is frequently treated as a branch of Anthropology, the science of man. As such it has to do with man in his fallen state. The word "Hamartiology" itself is derived from one of several Greek terms used to express the idea of sin—that of *hamartia* (ἁμαρτία). The term is applicable to sin, both as an act and as a state or condition. It signifies a deviation from the way or end appointed by God.

The fact of sin is fundamental in Christian theology. Since Christianity is a religion of redemption, it is greatly influenced by any variation from the biblical view concerning the nature of sin. For example, any tendency to minimize the seriousness of sin has its consequences in a less exalted view of the person and work of the Redeemer. The three great central truths of the Bible— God, sin, and redemption—are so interrelated that basic views held concerning any one of them profoundly influence the other two. The organic, vital relationship existing among Christian doctrines is thus revealed and illustrated.

I. THE TEMPTATION AND FALL OF MAN

A. *The Genesis Account of the Fall of Man.*

The account of the probation and fall of man found in Genesis 3: 1-24 is an inspired record of historical fact bound up with a deep and rich symbolism. All attempts to show that it consists of a series of myths, or that it is an allegorical account, fail before the evidence which insists that it is an integral portion of a continuous historical narrative. The account is assumed to be historical throughout both the Old and New Testaments. Our Lord referred to the fall only indirectly (Matt. 19:4, 5; John 8:44), but St. Paul clearly cites the Genesis record as historical (II Cor. 11:3; I Tim. 2:13-14). There are also undeniable allusions to the fall in the Old Testament (Job 31:33; Hosea 6:7).

Without doubt this historical account of the fall contains a large element of symbolism. Conditions in the paradisaical history of man were characterized by a degree of uniqueness which was probably more fully understood by our first parents than by us. Such facts as the inclosed garden, the sacramental tree of life, the mystical tree of knowledge, the one positive command representing the whole law, the serpent form of the tempter, and the flaming defenses of forfeited Eden—all were emblems possessing deep spiritual significance as well as facts. In defending the historical character of the Mosaic account of the fall, we must not fail to do justice to its rich symbolism.

Interpretation of the biblical account of man's temptation and fall has occasioned considerable controversy in the Church. Let us note briefly the following items in the record. (1) The Garden of Eden. We are told that *The Lord God planted a garden eastward in Eden, and there he put the man whom he had formed* (Gen. 2:8). Here was a special environment designed as a proper setting for the probationary period of the first pair. (2) The tree of life. This tree not only represents the communication of divine life to man, but also man's constant dependence on God. Possibly, as Dr. Adam Clarke suggests, the tree of life was intended as an emblem of that life which man should ever live, provided he continued in obedience to his Maker. (3) The tree of knowledge of good and evil. This represented a knowledge about evil, not a knowledge of evil in personal experience.

God's commandment with reference to its fruit was a constant reminder of man's position as a servant and steward. It called attention to the moral obligations which he owed to his Maker. (4) The serpent. This mystical figure has been the occasion of much speculation. The most widely accepted view is that the serpent was one of the higher created animals which Satan used as an instrument in securing the attention and making possible the conversation with Eve. Regardless of this, two things are evident: man was tempted by a spiritual being external to himself; and, the mystical figure of the serpent furnished the instrumentality through which the Tempter gained access to our foreparents.

B. *The Necessity of Man's Probation.*

If God was to be glorified by man's free service, the latter must be placed on probation, subjected to temptation, and this at the inevitable cost of the possibility of sin. Temptation was permitted because in no other way could human obedience be tested and perfected. The question immediately arises, How could a holy being sin? Adam was indeed created holy, but he was also endowed with the power to freely choose between moral alternatives. Through this freedom of the will his state of holiness could be lost. The biblical position in this respect is well stated in the *Westminster Confession* as follows: "God created man male and female, with righteousness and true holiness, having the law of God written in their hearts, and power to fulfill it: and yet under a possibility of transgressing, being left to the liberty of their own will, which was subject to change." The will of Adam was holy and was inclined in the right direction. Yet, it had the power of reversing its course and moving in the opposite direction, and this solely through its own self-determination.

Man by his very constitution is a self-conscious, self-determining being. He is a free moral agent, and hence has a capacity for performing moral action. Moral action in turn demands a law by which character is determined—a law which may be either obeyed or disobeyed by the subject. Otherwise there would be no moral quality, for neither praise nor blame could be attached to either obedience or disobedience. This would destroy the character of the moral agent. It is evident, therefore, that the power to obey or disobey is an essential element in a moral being, and hence God could have prevented the fall only by the destruction of man's free agency.

Despite man's holiness, there existed in him certain susceptibilities to sin. First, he possessed certain physical desires which, though lawful in themselves, may become the occasion of sin. Again, from the higher or spiritual side of his being, man became impatient with the slow process of divine Providence, and thus became susceptible to suggestions which would seem to hasten the accomplishment of God's purposes. The use of false means to attain good ends is a part of the deceptiveness of sin.

The occasion of the temptation was the tree of the knowledge of good and evil which the Lord God placed in the midst of the Garden. The fruit of this tree was prohibited. Possibly the tree served to remind man that some things were fit and others unfit to be done, and that man is under the necessity of constantly exercising wise choices.

The agent of the temptation was the serpent, who as the deceptive spirit, presented God's gifts in a false light. Satan had nothing to offer, and hence he must tempt man solely through a deceptive use of God's gifts. The deceitfulness of sin immediately appears. Presented in a false coloring, the temptation appeared good for food, pleasant to the eye, and a thing to be desired to make one wise. Led by the desire to think of its possible gratification, the good appeared to be that which God would wish to bestow; and, since wisdom was desirable in intelligent beings, its increase would make man more like God. Satan immediately injected the doubt, *Yea, hath God said?* In the false glamour of the glittering fruit the truth was obscured—did God really mean to forbid its use? would He fulfill His threats? or, could He even have intended His admonitions to be effective in prohibiting its use? The consequence is told in one brief sentence:

*She took of the fruit thereof, and did eat, and gave also
unto her husband with her; and he did eat* (Gen. 3:6).

C. *The Fall of Man.*

Sin began in the self-separation of the will of man
from the will of God. When the doubt, *Yea, hath God
said?* found a reception in man's thinking, sin had its
origin in the race. With the injection of this doubt, the
desire for legitimate knowledge passed into desire for
illegitimate knowledge—of being wise like the gods.
Such forbidden desire is sin (Rom. 7:7). With the
severance of the self from God, the outward act was the
look of lustful desire for the tree. This had in itself the
guilt of partaking, and was followed by the partaking as
an overt act.

The question, "Why did God permit man to sin?" is
frequently asked. In considering this, two factors need
to be kept in mind. *First,* the divine permission can in
no wise be considered as a consent to the fall, or a license
to sin. The only sense in which it can be allowed is that
God did not by His sovereign power effectually inter-
vene to prevent it. This brings us to the scriptural position that man fell solely because of his own free de-
termination to sin. Temptation was permitted because
in no other way could the moral life be developed and
perfected. Man sinned against the holiness of his own
nature, and despite the fact that he lived in a perfect environment, enjoyed perfect liberty, and communed
freely with his Maker. Sin belongs solely to man, and
thus the goodness of God is vindicated. *Second,* if God
had not placed the tree of knowledge in the garden, man
would still have been under the necessity of making
decisions. The placing of the tree was in reality an act
of kindness, intended to warn man against wrong
choices, and to serve as a constant reminder of his obligation to choose wisely.

The immediate consequences of man's sin were
estrangement from God, enslavement to Satan, and the
loss of divine grace. By this loss man became subject
to physical and moral corruption. Man no longer pos-

sessed the glory of his moral likeness to God. Having lost the abiding presence of the Holy Spirit, he began a life of external discord and internal misery. The earth itself was cursed, and man was compelled to earn his bread by the sweat of his face. Within man, sin resulted in the birth of an evil conscience and a sense of shame and degradation. Deprived of the Holy Spirit as the organizing principle of his being, there could be no harmonious ordering of his faculties, and hence his powers became disordered. From this disordered state there followed as a consequence: blindness of heart or a loss of spiritual discernment; evil concupiscence or unregulated carnal craving; and moral inability or weakness in the presence of sin.

II. SATAN AND THE ORIGIN OF SIN

A. *The Doctrine of Satan.*

1. *The Origin of Satan.* Man was tempted by a superhuman being, called in the Scriptures, the devil or Satan. Evil then must have had an existence previous to its origin in the human race, and external to it. The Scriptures plainly teach that in the purely spiritual realm there were angels which kept not their beginning or first estate. Thus there was a fall in the spiritual realm prior to that in the human race. There was among the angels a tempter who led them astray. It is with this tempter that the Christian view of evil terminates. This superhuman, yet created spirit, Satan, was originally good, but he fell from his high and holy estate and became the enemy of God. Evil is therefore personal in its origin. Beyond this reason cannot go, and revelation is silent.

2. *Satan as Antichrist.* St. John makes it clear that Satan is that spirit of antichrist which should come, and even now is in the world. The essential antagonism of this spirit to Christ finds its expression in the fact that he does not confess that Jesus Christ is come in the flesh (I John 4: 1-3). Furthermore, sin in the New Testament use of the term, is to be interpreted by the attitude which men take toward Christ (John 16: 8-11). Thus

the nature of Satan can only be properly understood when viewed in contrast to the nature of the Christ.

It was through Jesus Christ, the Word, that God created all things. In Him as the express image of the Father were comprehended all the principles of truth, order, beauty, goodness, and perfection. But in contrast to this peerless One is Satan, the antichrist. This "son of the morning" seems to have become envious of the Son, and sought to sit upon His throne. Lifted up with pride, he fell into condemnation. To this Jesus doubtless referred when he said, *I beheld Satan as lightning fall from heaven* (Luke 10: 18). St. Paul speaks of Satan as *the prince of the power of the air, the spirit that now worketh in the children of disobedience* (Eph. 2: 2). He also refers to Satan as *the god of this world* (II Cor. 4: 4). St. John writes that *the whole world lieth in wickedness*, or in the wicked one. Not that the world is inherently evil, but lying in the wicked one, it is perverted from the true purpose of its existence. This evil spirit as Satan is the "adversary," the "accuser," and "deceiver." As the devil, he is the "slanderer," the "calumniator," and the "destroyer of peace." As Belial, he is the "low," the "unworthy," and the "abject."

3. *Satan and the Redemptive Work of Christ.* Not having the power of creation himself, Satan is limited in his scope of activity to the perversion of those things which are the result of God's creative activity. It was concerning this perverter of the good that Jesus declared, *He was a murderer from the beginning and abode not in the truth, because there is no truth in him. When he speaketh a lie, he speaketh of his own: for he is a liar, and the father of it* (John 8: 44).

In creation man was so constituted that he was a creature dependent upon his Creator, and consequently a servant of God. Yet, in the physical realm man was the highest of all creatures, and therefore he was the lord of creation. When man in this intermediate position looked up to God, he saw himself as a servant; when he looked out upon creation, he saw himself as its lord. In the temptation, Satan made the lordship appear more attractive than the servantship. He said, *Ye shall be as gods* (Gen. 3:5). But that which Satan did not tell man was that the lordship was a delegated power, and that he held it by virtue of faithful stewardship. Thus when man fell, he ceased to be the servant of God, and became the servant of Satan. Hence our Lord said of the unbelieving Jews, *Ye are of your father the devil, and the lusts of your father ye will do* (John 8:44). God is the Father of all men, because he always acts as a Father; but men are not always the sons of God, because they do not act as sons. Losing his servantship, man lost his true lordship. Now he makes all things minister to himself. He views the world from a false slant. The things God committed to his care as a steward he holds as his own. Like his father, Satan, he has become a usurper of the throne. Man as a child of Satan and a servant of sin has been untrue to his divinely appointed trust.

But in spite of Satan's temporary success in thwarting the purpose of Deity for man, God will ultimately and forever triumph. He sent forth His own Son, who was made in the likeness of sinful flesh. He took upon Himself the form of a servant, and became obedient unto death, even the death of the cross (Phil. 2:6-8). By virtue of this true servantship, Christ brought man back into his original relationship with God. He re-established spiritual fellowship and communion. As the Captain of our salvation, He met the cross-currents of the world and suffered at every step. But He never faltered, and He overcame even the last enemy which is Death. As a servant, He came not to be ministered unto, but to minister and give His life as a ransom for many. Having met the demands of perfect servantship, He became the Lord of His people—not this time by creation, for that He never lost, but as their Redeemer, their Saviour, and Lord. Having triumphed, He received the promise of the Holy Spirit, which now as the Lord of the Church, he gives freely to all who believe. Thus we may say with all the redeemed, *Blessing, and honour, and glory, and power be unto him that sitteth upon the throne, and unto the Lamb forever and ever* (Rev. 5:13).

4. *The Kingdom of Satan.* We have seen that the work of Satan is to pervert the things of God. This perversion extends also to the concept of the kingdom. As surely as there is a kingdom of God and of heaven, so also there is a kingdom of Satan and evil. Hence the Bible refers to principalities, powers, and rulers of darkness, which can indicate nothing other than an organization of evil forces. These are under the leadership of *the prince of this world*, whom Jesus mentions as being *cast out* (John 12:31), as having nothing in Him (John 14:30), and as being judged (John 16:11). St. Paul speaks of Satan as *the prince of the power of the air* (Eph. 2:2). He also speaks of *the spiritual hosts of wickedness* (Eph. 6:12, R.V.). That there are a great number of evil spirits under the leadership of Satan is indicated in many scriptural passages, such as *my name is Legion* (Mark 5:9), and the lake of fire prepared *for the devil and his angels* (Matt. 25:41). This kingdom of evil shall not stand, for *the accuser of our brethren is cast down, which accused them before our God day and night. And they overcame him by the blood of the Lamb and the word of their testimony* (Rev. 12:10, 11).

B. *Summary of Scriptural Teaching Concerning the Origin of Sin.*

The Scriptures maintain that in neither a positive nor a negative sense is God the author of evil. The two basic factors which account for the origin of sin in the human family are the prior existence of evil in the person of Satan who tempted man to sin, and man's freedom of choice in the presence of moral alternatives. A great creed concisely states this Christian position concerning the origin of sin: "it comes from the devil and the evil will of man." This biblical view concerning *the mystery of iniquity* (II Thess. 2:7; Rev. 17:5) constitutes the most satisfactory answer that has ever been given to a question which has baffled and perplexed thinkers throughout the ages. In the final analysis, we see that sin has had its origin in the abuse of freedom in intelligent, responsible creatures. This was first true of Satan, and subsequently true of man. Sin in the human race was due to the voluntary self-separation of man from God. Man is therefore responsible for the dire and tragic consequences which result from sin. To these consequences we now direct our attention.

III. THE NATURE AND PENALTY OF SIN

A. *Scriptural Terminology Regarding Sin.*

One of the best approaches to the study of the nature of sin is by means of an analysis of the terms used in the Scriptures to express the idea. We have already mentioned the word *hamartia* (ἁμαρτία) from which the word "hamartiology" is derived. It carries with it the idea of missing the right way, or missing the mark. The word suggests the thought of sin as a disposition or state as well as an act. It conveys the idea that a man does not find in sin what he seeks therein, but, conversely, a state of delusion and deception. Carlyle was amazed, not at what men suffered, but at what they missed. Such is the tragedy of sin.

A second word is *parabasis* (παράβασις) which signifies sin as an act of transgression. This indicates that the idea of sin is limited by the idea of law, *for where no law is, there is no transgression* (Rom. 4:15). Reference is here made to the eternal moral order of God with its earliest manifestations in the claims made by conscience. Sin as the transgression of law is possible only to moral and rational beings. But when a man knowingly disowns the claims of the law under which he exists, in that instant sin is born. That law is not impersonal, and voluntary transgression subjects the offender to the wrath of the personal Law-giver *because the law worketh wrath* (Rom. 4:15). Virtue is therefore in the nature of obedience, and sin is disobedience to God. This is true even when the wrong committed is against one's neighbor. The sinner who thus violates the law of God becomes a rebel in the moral realm.

St. John contributes to our further understanding of the nature of sin by a penetrating definition: *all unrighteousness is sin* (I John 5:17). The key word in this passage, *adikia* (ἀδικία) signifies "crookedness," or the bending or perverting of that which is right. It not only refers to perverted acts but to a state of unrighteousness or disorder arising from such perversion. Sin, then, is self-separation from God in the sense of de-centralization, the place which should be occupied by God being assumed by self. The perfection of love as manifested in Christ was found in the fact that He did not seek to please Himself (Matt. 22:37-40); and that He did not seek His own (I Cor. 13:5). On the other hand, St. Paul declared that the acme of sin in the last days would be found in this that they were lovers of their own selves (II Tim. 3:1-2). The emphasis of St. John is that sin is a state or condition wherein the center around which a man's thoughts, affections, and volitions should revolve is displaced, and hence has become one of unrighteousness. For this reason he speaks of sins being forgiven, but unrighteousness as being cleansed.

An even stronger word for sin, *anomia* (ἀνομία) is used by St. John in the text, *Whosoever committeth sin transgresseth also the law; for sin is the transgression of the law* (I John 3:4). Again the state of sin, rather than the act, is emphasized. It is a condition characterized by "lack of conformity to law," or "lawlessness." Sin represents not simply a disordered state, but a confused state of rebellion against God.

The last word we shall mention in this analysis of the nature of sin is *asebeia* (ἀσέβεια) or ungodliness. It not only marks the separation of the soul from God, but carries with it the thought of a character unlike God, and a state or condition characterized by the absence of God. It is a strong term. St. Paul uses it in Romans 1:18, *For the wrath of God is revealed from heaven against all ungodliness and unrighteousness of men, who hold the truth in unrighteousness.* The term carries with it the thought of verging toward doom. Thus St. Jude declares, *Behold, the Lord cometh with ten thousand of his saints, to execute judgment upon all, and to convince all that are ungodly among them of all their ungodly deeds which they have ungodly committed, and of all their hard speeches which ungodly sinners have spoken against him* (Jude 14-15).

B. *Definitions of Sin.*

Some typical definitions of sin may appropriately be noted at this point. Theologians have defined sin in various ways, but rarely is the fact overlooked that sin exists both as an act and as a state or condition. This is important in any system of theology where the evangelical principle of salvation by faith is given prominence. It is even more important when the doctrine of entire sanctification as a second definite work of grace subsequent to regeneration is emphasized.

One of the most familiar definitions of sin is that of John Wesley, "Sin is a voluntary transgression of a known law." Dr. Raymond emphasizes the twofold nature of sin by observing, "The primary idea designated by the term sin in the Scriptures is want of conformity to law, a transgression of law, a doing of that which is forbidden, or a neglecting to do that which is required. In a secondary sense the term applies to character; not to that which one does, but to what he is." One of the clearest and most comprehensive definitions of sin is that of Dr. A. H. Strong, who says, "Sin is lack of conformity to the moral law of God, either in act, disposition, or state."

C. *The Consequences of Sin.*

The consequences of sin are guilt and penalty. Guilt is personal blameworthiness which follows the act of sin. It involves the twofold idea of responsibility for the act, and a liability to punishment because of it. Penalty carries with it the thought of punishment which follows sin. This punishment may come as the result of natural consequences, or it may arise out of a direct act of God.

1. *The Nature of Guilt.* Guilt is the state or condition of one who has transgressed the law. It takes the form of condemnation based upon God's disapproval. This is because opposition to the law of God means personal opposition to a personal God, in the degree and to the extent that He has been revealed to the offender.

Guilt as personal blameworthiness must be distinguished from the consciousness of that guilt. The fact that a person has committed sin carries with it a sense of guilt. But varying circumstances may increase or diminish the consciousness of that guilt. Sin not only deceives, but it hardens the heart. Usually a man has less compunction of conscience the farther he goes in sin. But, the guilt remains nevertheless, even though it is not fully realized in consciousness. Guilt also involves personal liability to punishment on account of sin. Thus it is related to penalty, but a distinction must be made between the liability for punishment and the punishment itself.

2. *The Nature of Penalty.* Penalty includes the consequences of all the various evils included in sin. Every form of sin has its own penalty. There are sins against law, against light, and against love—each having its own peculiar penalty. There are sins of ignorance and sins of presumption. Thus there may be degrees of both guilt and penalty, as in the case of sins of ignorance or infirmity as over against sins of knowledge (cf. Matt. 10:15; 12:31; Mark 3:29; Luke 12:47; John 19:11; Rom. 2:12). Penalty, therefore, is the punishment that follows sin, whether it be through the operation of natural, moral, or spiritual laws; or by direct decree of God. It should be emphasized that God is not limited to His ordinary laws in the punishment of sinners. He is a free Person, and He may by direct action employ various means to vindicate Himself and His government. However, penalty in all of its forms represents God's reaction against sin, and is based ultimately on His holiness.

The chief penalty of sin is death (Gen. 2:17), but the nature of this penalty has been interpreted in different ways. Arminian theologians have generally interpreted death to mean what is commonly known as the "fullness of death," that is, death physical, temporal, and eternal. While it is true that physical death is a consequence of sin, spiritual death is the tragic result which must ever be emphasized. Death in both respects is a result of the withdrawal of the Holy Spirit from man. As Henry Drummond pointed out, death is a lack of correspondence, a lack of mutual response between a person and his environment. The branch separated from the vine is dead, in that it is no longer connected with the source of life. The moment of man's separation from God brought in the reign of death. That man's earthly existence did not end immediately was due to God's purpose of redemption.

The Holy Spirit was the bond of union between the soul of man and his Maker. By the withdrawal of the Spirit, man immediately lost his fellowship with God. Negatively, this represented the loss of man's original righteousness or primitive holiness; positively, it meant a depravation of those powers which in their united action we call man's moral nature. This fallen human nature is called the "flesh," a term which is used to indicate that the whole being of man—body, soul, and spirit—has been separated from God and subjected to the creature. The result of this depravation of man's powers is seen in his idolatry, selfishness, inordinate desire, and inclination toward an ever-increasing degree of ungodliness.

Eternal death is the final judgment of God upon sin. It is the permanent and irrevocable separation of the soul from the only Source of spiritual life. It is the punishment of sin apart from the helpful influences of divine grace. It is the final consummation of that stark and tragic reality announced in Holy Writ, *The wages of sin is death* (Rom. 6: 23).

IV. ORIGINAL SIN OR INHERITED DEPRAVITY

We have seen that the penalty of sin is death. We have also noted that the effects of sin cannot be limited to the individual, but must include in their scope the social and racial consequences as well. It is to these consequences that the terms Original Sin and Inherited Depravity are applied.

A. *Terminology.*

Dr. Field indicates that the term "original sin" is not to be found in the Scriptures, but was first introduced by St. Augustine in his controversy with the Pelagians. In ordinary usage the terms "original sin" and "inherited depravity" are often used synonymously; that is, they are applied generally to the natural condition of man's spiritual nature apart from divine grace. This common usage is revealed in the following definition of original sin which is found in the Articles of the Church of England: "Original sin is the fault and corruption of every man whereby man is very far gone from original righteousness, and is of his own nature inclined to evil, so that the flesh lusteth always contrary to the Spirit; and, therefore, in every person born into this world, it deserveth God's wrath and damnation."

Despite the fact that the two terms, original sin and inherited depravity, are often used interchangeably as referring to the unregenerate condition of man, we may profitably make certain distinctions in the use of the terms. The term original sin carries with it the following points of emphasis: (1) the idea of the racial consequences of sin; (2) the question as to what extent original sin is a result of Adam's first transgression; and (3) the respects in which man's natural state is actually *sinful.* The term inherited depravity may be reserved to describe the moral conditions of natural man, without particular reference to the ultimate origin of this condition, or without special attention to the question as to the exact sense in which this condition is sinful. It is evident that the two terms are interwoven in meaning. The distinctions we make are primarily for clarity of analysis and description.

B. *The Fact of Original Sin.*

The Scriptures teach that the presence of death in the world, with all its attendant evils, is due to man's sin. Perhaps the most important scriptural passage on this subject is that of St. Paul, which reads as follows: *Wherefore, as by one man sin entered into the world and death by sin; and so death passed upon all men, for that all have sinned: (for until the law sin was in the world: but sin is not imputed when there is no law. Nevertheless death reigned from Adam to Moses, even over them that had not sinned after the similitude of Adam's trans-*

*gression, who is the figure of him that was to come. . . . .
For if by one man's offence death reigned by one; much
more they which receive abundance of grace and of the
gift of righteousness shall reign in life by one, Jesus
Christ.) Therefore as by the offence of one judgment
came upon all men to condemnation; even so by the
righteousness of one the free gift came upon all men
unto justification of life* (Rom. 5: 12-14, 17, 18). Here
it is clearly taught that before the fall of Adam, there
was neither sin nor death; after his fall there were both,
and these are regarded as the direct consequence of sin.
The apostle further declares that death as a consequence
of sin passed upon *all* men, that is, through racial propagation. Hence original sin and inherited depravity are
identical in fact. The propagation of the race was not
only in Adam's physical likeness but also in his fallen
moral image. St. Paul also asserts that death reigns over
even those who have not sinned as did Adam by an overt
act of disobedience. Hence death as a penalty for sin
must have been and is a consequence of sin as a depraved
nature, as well as sin as an act of disobedience.

C. *The Fact of Inherited Depravity.*

We have seen that all men are born under the penalty of death as a consequence of Adam's sin, and they
are also born with a depraved nature. The latter is generally termed inbred sin, or inherited depravity. The
following representative scriptural passages reveal this
condition: *Behold, I was shapen in iniquity; and in sin
did my mother conceive me* (Psalms 51: 5). *The wicked
are estranged from the womb; they go astray as soon as
they be born, speaking lies* (Psalms 58: 3). The first
of these verses employs the word "iniquity" which carries with it the thought of a perverted or twisted nature
from the very inception of life. The second verse carries the thought still farther—as an estrangement or
alienation from God which is clearly inherited because
it dates from birth.

New Testament references to the morally depraved
character of the human race are numerous. Our Lord

said, *That which cometh out of the man, that defileth the man. For from within, out of the heart of men, proceed evil thoughts, adulteries, fornications, murders, thefts, covetousness, wickedness, deceit, lasciviousness, an evil eye, blasphemy, pride, foolishness: all these evil things come from within, and defile the man* (Mark 7: 20-23). Thus Christ affirms that evil traits have their original source in the natural heart of man. St. Paul uses the term "flesh" repeatedly with reference to the depraved nature of man. *For they that are after the flesh do mind the things of the flesh* (Rom. 8: 5). *So then they that are in the flesh cannot please God* (Rom. 8: 8). *But ye are not in the flesh, but in the Spirit* (Rom. 8: 9). *If ye live after the flesh, ye shall die* (Rom. 8: 13). *They that are Christ's have crucified the flesh with the affections and lusts* (Gal. 5: 24). *Now then it is no more I that do it, but sin that dwelleth in me. For I know that in me (that is, in my flesh,) dwelleth no good thing* (Rom. 7: 17-18). All of these passages show that the bias to sin belongs to fallen human nature.

D. *The Nature of Inherited Depravity.*

The term inherited depravity is applied to the state or condition of man by birth. It expresses the moral depravity of man in his natural state. This condition belongs to the *whole* of man's person, not simply to one aspect of his being, such as his will. It is a disordered state of affairs at the very foundation of man's being from which arise evil tendencies, inordinate affections, and vicious impulses.

Human depravity is the result of a deprivation. When man sinned, he lost the moral image of God in which he had been created. This meant that the Holy Ghost withdrew from his being, and man lost his state of primitive holiness. The result of this deprivation or loss was that the tide of sin flowed in upon man, overflowing his whole nature. The controlling, enabling, sanctifying power of the Holy Spirit being lost, man became estranged from God, enslaved to irregular impulses and evil passions, and enthralled under the curse of the law.

By the total depravity of man we do not mean that he is so thoroughly depraved that there can be no further degrees of wickedness. Rather, the term is used in its *extensive* sense, and carries the thought that the contagion of sin is spread throughout man's entire being. It vitiates every power and faculty of spirit, soul, and body. The affections are alienated, the intellect darkened, and the will perverted: *The whole head is sick, and the whole heart faint* (Isa. 1:5). Natural man is destitute of all positive good. St. Paul affirms, *For I know that in me (that is, in my flesh,) dwelleth no good thing* (Rom. 7:18).

Apart from the gracious ability extended to all men by the Holy Spirit, depravity renders man totally unable in spiritual things. However, St. Paul declares that, *Therefore as by the offence of one judgment came upon all men to condemnation; even so by the righteousness of one the FREE GIFT came upon all men unto justification of life. For as by one man's disobedience many were made sinners, so by the obedience of one shall many be made righteous* (Rom. 5:18, 19). By this "free gift" which comes through Jesus Christ, mankind is preserved from sinking below the possibility of redemption despite the effects of sin. The Holy Spirit was restored to the race—not in the sense of the spirit of life in regeneration or the spirit of holiness in entire sanctification— but as the spirit of awakening and conviction. Thus the gracious aid of the Holy Spirit is placed over against man's total depravity and natural inability. All who will, therefore, may be restored to a state of holiness through our Lord Jesus Christ. All who will may turn from sin to righteousness, believe on Christ for pardon and cleansing from sin, and follow good works pleasing and acceptable in His sight. It is to be remembered, however, that this free agency that man enjoys is not mere natural ability, it is gracious, God-given ability.

E. *The Transmission of Original Sin.*

Granting that original sin or inherited depravity had its origin in the sin of Adam, we must consider briefly the manner in which this is transmitted to the individual members of the race. Various views have been held concerning this subject, the most acceptable one being the "Genetic Mode." This is simply an expression or application of the natural law of heredity. It is the law of organic life that everything reproduces its own kind, and that not only as to anatomical structure and physical characteristics, but also as to mental life and disposition. The law of genetic transmission determines the likeness of offspring to the parents. This is sufficient to account for the common native depravity of man.

The descendants of Adam were born under the curse of the law which has deprived human nature of the Spirit of God and which can be restored only in Christ. Hereditary depravity, then, is only the law of natural heredity, but it is that law operating under the penal consequences of Adam's sin.

Man is not responsible for the depraved nature with which he is born. Hence, no guilt or demerit attaches to it. Man is not guilty of inbred sin when he comes into the world. He becomes responsible for it only after having rejected the remedy provided by atoning blood. In this way he ratifies it as his own.

F. Depravity and Infirmity.

The term "flesh" as used by St. Paul included both the spiritual and physical natures of man as under the reign of sin. The corruption extends to the body as well as to the soul. The depravity of the spiritual nature may be removed by the baptism with the Holy Spirit, but the infirmities of the flesh will be removed only in the resurrection and glorification of the body. In a general way man has no great difficulty in distinguishing between the soul and the body, but the fine line of demarcation, the exact boundary between the spiritual and the physical cannot be determined. Could we know where this line of demarcation lies, we could with ease distinguish between carnal manifestations, which have their seat wholly in the soul, and physical infirmities, which are the expression of the physical constitution of man still under sin. Mental strain often weakens the body, and physical weakness in turn may becloud the mind and spirit of man. Certain diseases may lead to abnormal emotional predispositions or peculiar forms of expression. The lack of adequate rest, improper food, disturbances of the endocrine glands, and other factors may lead to periods of excessive irritability or of abnormal depression. Mental conflict often leads to a condition commonly known as nervous breakdown, during which wholly sanctified persons may act in abnormal ways. In view of this fact, that the line between the physical and the spiritual is not precise and clear in many instances, a spirit of charity toward all men is ever needful. At the same time every person should be realistic and honest concerning his own spiritual condition. He should resolutely face the facts in his own life and should thrust aside any temptations to rationalize away carnal manifestations as mere "physical weaknesses."

UNIT IV

THE DOCTRINE OF JESUS CHRIST

Preview

Ancient students of the pseudo-science of alchemy professed a threefold aim: the discovery of the philosopher's stone, the universal solvent, and the elixir of life. With the philosopher's stone they hoped to be able to transmute, easily and quickly, such base metals as iron or lead into noble and valuable metals such as gold or silver. With the universal solvent they expected to readily dissolve all insoluble substances. And, with the elixir of life they proposed to destroy the seeds of all disease so that a person would remain everlastingly youthful.

On the exalted level of man's spiritual life, our Lord Jesus Christ gloriously satisfies all three quests of the ancient alchemist. He is the Philosopher's Stone of Grace. Through His atoning work He is able to remove the dross, the earthy, the base, from our natures, and so transmute them that we become the treasured "sons of God." He is the Universal Solvent. His incomparable teachings furnish timeless principles which will solve every problem, personal or social, no matter how "insoluble" they may seem to be. He is the Elixir of Life. Through His resurrection from the dead, we who are His alone, may also look forward to the life that shall never know a lengthening shadow.

It is to the wonderful and unique person, the glorious offices, and the vicarious death of our Lord that we turn our attention in this unit. In His person we find the divine-human One, who was truly man, yet truly God. In His offices He is our Prophet, Priest, and King. In His atoning work for sin we find the central purpose of His coming and the foundation of our redemption. Let us adore and worship our blessed Christ— even as we study.

UNIT IV

THE DOCTRINE OF JESUS CHRIST
Chapter XI. *The Person of Christ*

I. SCRIPTURAL AND HISTORICAL BACKGROUND

  A. Events in the life of Christ and their Theological Significance.
    1. The Miraculous Conception and Birth.
    2. The Circumcision.
    3. The Normal Development of Jesus.
    4. Baptism.
    5. The Temptation.
    6. The Obedience of Christ.
    7. The Passion and Death of Christ.

  B. The Development of Christology in the Church.
    1. Ebionism.
    2. Docetism.
    3. Sabellianism.
    4. Arianism.
    5. Apollinarianism.
    6. Nestorianism.
    7. Eutychianism.
    8. Monophysitism and Monothelitism.
    9. Adoptionism.
    10. Socinianism.

  C. The Authoritative Statement Concerning the Nature of Christ.

II. THE MANHOOD OF CHRIST

  A. Characteristics of the Human Nature of Christ.
  B. The Sinlessness of Christ.
  C. The Sufferings of Christ.

III. THE DEITY OF CHRIST

  A. The Pre-existence of Christ.
  B. Christ Was the Jehovah of the Old Testament.
  C. The Unique Claims of Jesus for Himself.

IV. THE DIVINE-HUMAN PERSON

    A. The Nature of the Incarnation.

    B. The One Person.

    C. The Two Natures.

        1. The Chalcedonian Definition.

        2. The Orthodox Faith.

Chapter XII. *The Estates and Offices of Christ*

I. THE STATE OF HUMILIATION

    A. The Stages in Christ's Humiliation.

    B. The Communicatio Idiomatum.

    C. The Earlier Depotentiation Theories.

    D. The Later Kenotic Theories.

II. THE EXALTATION

    A. The Descent into Hades.

    B. The Resurrection.

    C. The Ascension.

    D. The Session.

III. THE OFFICES OF CHRIST

    A. The Prophetic Office.

    B. The Priestly Office.

    C. The Kingly Office.

Chapter XIII. *The Atonement*

I. THE NATURE AND NECESSITY OF THE ATONEMENT

    A. Definitions of the Atonement.

    B. The Necessity of the Atonement.

II. THE BIBLICAL BASIS OF THE ATONEMENT

    A. Foreshadowings of the Atonement in the Old Testament.

        1. The Primitive Sacrifices.

        2. The Sacrifices of the Law.

        3. The Predictions of the Prophets.

    B. The New Testament Conception of Sacrifice.

    C. The Motive or Originating Cause of the Atonement.

    D. The Vicarious Nature of the Atonement.

    E. Scripture Terminology.

III. Theories of the Atonement
    A. The Patristic Doctrine.
    B. The Anselmic Theory of the Atonement.
    C. The Theory of Abelard.
    D. The Scholastic Theories.
    E. The Tridentine or Roman Catholic Theory.
    F. The Penal Satisfaction Theory.
    G. The Governmental or Rectoral Theory.
    H. The Moral Influence Theories.
        1. Socinianism.
        2. The Mystical Theories.
        3. Bushnell's Theory of Moral Influence.
        4. The New Theology.
    I. The Ethical Theory.
    J. The Racial Theory.

IV. The Extent and Benefits of the Atonement
    A. The Universal Scope of the Atonement.
    B. The Unconditional Benefits of the Atonement.
        1. The Continued Existence of the Race.
        2. The Restoration of All Men to Salvability.
        3. The Salvation of Infants.
    C. The Conditional Benefits of the Atonement.
    D. The Intercession of Christ.

CHAPTER XI

THE PERSON OF CHRIST

"He is the very God; but in the revelation in Christ the very Godhead is never separated from the very manhood; the divine and human natures were never separated from each other, and never neutralize each other. We are to see in Christ . . . . *the fullness of deity framed in the ring of humanity;* not the attributes of the divine in their unbounded infinitude but the divine attributes embodied in the attributes of human nature. Instead of the omnipresence we have the blessed presence, concerning which the God-man testifies, *He that seeth me seeth the Father* (John 14:9); in the place of the omniscience comes the divinely human wisdom which reveals to babes the mysteries of the kingdom of heaven; in the place of the world-creating omnipotence enters the world-vanquishing and world-completing power, the infinite power and fullness of love and holiness in virtue of which the God-man was able to testify *All power is given unto me in heaven and in earth* (Matt. 28:18). For all heavenly and earthly powers, all the forces of nature and history find in Him their center of freedom, and serve the kingdom of which He is the head."—BISHOP MARTENSEN.

Christology is that department of theology which deals with the Person of Christ as the Redeemer of mankind. The subject is sometimes enlarged to include both the Person and Work of Christ, but in general the term Christology is applied to the former only, and the term Soteriology reserved for the latter.

It is in the study of the Person of Christ that we touch the very heart of Christianity. However we are not here so much concerned with doctrines about Christ, as we are with the presentation of Him to faith and worship as God manifest in the flesh. True Christology is rooted in the objective experience of Christ as He was known by the apostles, which experience is recorded in the Gospels, and interpreted in the other apostolic writings under the illumination and guidance of the promised Holy Spirit. The Gospels, therefore, afford the fundamental facts of Christology, in that they declare the incarnation of the divine Word, through whom alone we can have a knowledge of God. Furthermore, the facts thus presented are verifiable by historic methods, and furnish the basis for later dogmatic development. We shall best approach this central and important subject, therefore, through a consideration of the more outstanding events in the life of Christ, and the theological significance which is attached to them.

I. Scriptural and Historical Background

A. *Events in the Life of Christ and their Theological Significance.*

The events in the life of Christ which will be considered in their theological significance are the following: (1) The Miraculous Conception and Birth; (2) The Circumcision; (3) The Normal Development of Jesus; (4) The Baptism; (5) The Temptation; (6) The Obedience of Christ; and (7) His Passion and Death. The Descensus, the Resurrection, the Ascension and Session will be best considered in connection with the state of exaltation (Chapter XII, Section II).

1. *The Miraculous Conception and Birth.* St. Matthew mentions the virgin birth of Christ as the fulfillment of prophecy, while St. Luke regards it as a fundamental fact of historical revelation. This fact has at times been violently assailed, but those who deny it involve themselves in greater difficulties than those who freely admit its miraculous nature. Had Christ been born in the ordinary manner, He must necessarily have inherited the depravity and sin which is so characteristic of our fallen nature. For this reason, the Church has always maintained that Christ *was conceived of the Holy Ghost* and *born of the Virgin Mary*. But to establish the sinlessness of Christ is only one aspect of the mystery of His Person. His miraculous conception and birth was the assumption of human nature—sin excepted—by the divine and pre-existent Son. For this reason the Scripture speaks of *that holy thing* which was to be born, thus implying that a change was to be wrought in the very constitution of human nature. It was not merely the origin of another being within the race, but the pre-existent Son coming into the race from above; it was not merely another individualization of human nature, but a conjoining of the divine and human

natures in a new order of being—a theanthropic Person. In Jesus Christ there is the birth of a new order of humanity—a *new man, which after God is created in righteousness and true holiness* (Eph. 4: 24). Here is to be found the ground of His mediatorial work. The instant that human nature became conjoined with God in the Person of Jesus Christ, that nature was redeemed; and this redemption becomes the ground of our regeneration and sanctification.

2. *The Circumcision.* The rite of circumcision marked the official induction of a Jewish child into the blessings of the Abrahamic covenant. A sound Christology must hold that for Jesus, circumcision was something more than an empty religious rite. It signified a covenant of grace, in which the relation of God to man, and man to God, was lifted to a unique and exalted level. It was for Him the communion of two natures in one Person—the divine and the human. While the humanity of Jesus was spotless, and in some sense already redeemed in the Person of Christ, the application of this redemption to mankind apart from the incarnation, was not yet effected. This could come only through His passion and death, His resurrection and ascension. The significance of this rite for the work of salvation lies just here—that final perfection is not attainable through the kingdom of nature, but through the kingdom of grace.

3. *The Normal Development of Jesus.* Because of His exalted communion with the Father through the Holy Spirit, it was possible for the child Jesus to pass from the spotless purity of childhood, to an uncorrupted and undefiled manhood. In Him, unconscious innocence was transformed into conscious obedience; and the holiness of His nature never knew either the experience or contamination of sin. The uniqueness of Jesus as it concerns His growth and development, lies in this, that it was the unfolding of a pure and normal human nature apart from sin. In ordinary childhood, there is the disintegrating force of inherited depravity or a bias to sin, and consequently the development can never be wholly normal. But Jesus had none of the vitiating consequences of in-

bred sin. Under the tuition of the Holy Spirit, and in
spiritual communion with the Father, His development
was pre-eminently perfect. Nor did He evade any condition of humanity—infancy, childhood, youth or maturity, but sanctified every age, that in all things He
might have the pre-eminence.

4. *The Baptism.* The baptism of Jesus was His official
induction into the office of the Messiah or Christ. He was
not anointed with oil, but with the Holy Spirit which the
oil typified. In the circumcision, Jesus had unconsciously
submitted to the imputation of sin; now He becomes the
conscious representative of a sinful race. Let the reader
picture in his imagination, a long line of candidates
awaiting baptism by John—Jesus among them, and we
see the fulfillment of the ancient prophecy, *He was
numbered with the transgressors; and he bare the sin of
many, and made intercession for the transgressors* (Isa.
53:12). The baptism, therefore, marks the official beginning of Christ's redemptive ministry.

5. *The Temptation.* The temptation of Jesus was a
necessity of the mediatorial economy, and like His baptism is of universal import. Two factors are involved:
(1) Jesus must personally triumph over sin by voluntary opposition to it, before He could become the Author
of eternal life to others; and (2) He must not only conquer for Himself, but He must secure dignity and
strength for His kingdom. The temptation was both external and internal. It was external in that it originated
outside of, and apart from Himself. He was confronted
by Satan, representing the kingdom of evil. His temptation was not merely the confusion of cross purposes in
His own mind, as some have held. Internally, the temptation was a conscious pressure toward evil. We must
believe that Christ felt the full force of the suggestions
of Satan, and that He repelled them immediately.

6. *The Obedience of Christ.* During the time of our
Lord's ministry on earth, He was under the anointing
of the Holy Spirit, and went about doing good. He came
not to be ministered unto, but to minister, and to give
His life a ransom for many. When the first Adam was

tempted, it was through an appeal to self-interest. Created to have authority in the earth, when he looked up to God, he saw himself as a servant; when he looked down to the earth, he saw himself as its lord. Satan therefore said, *Ye shall be as gods*. What he did not tell them, was that this authority was a delegated power only. Losing the servantship, he therefore lost the lordship also. Christ came to perfect this servantship, and thereby regain for man, the lordship. Consequently we see a strange reversal in the ministry of Jesus. During His earthly ministry He was subordinate to the Spirit; but having perfected His servantship, He received of the Father the promise of the Holy Spirit as a gift to the Church. Now from His intercessory throne, He ministers the Spirit, and restores man again to the regnancy of his being which was lost through sin.

7. *The Passion and Death of Christ.* The perfected obedience is to be found in the humiliating circumstances of His death—particularly the death on the cross. While the sufferings of Christ may be distinguished from the precise manner of His death, the death itself cannot be separated from the crucifixion. For this reason, the cross was to our High Priest, simply the awful form which His altar assumed, when *His own self bare our sins in his own body on the tree* (I Peter 2: 24). *And for this cause he is the mediator of the new testament, that by means of death, for the redemption of the transgressions that were under the first testament, they which are called might receive the promise of eternal inheritance* (Heb. 9: 15).

B. *The Development of Christology in the Church.*

We have seen that the facts concerning Christ as given to us in the Gospels, are intensely significant. These facts, after much controversy, were finally developed by the Church into an accepted and authoritative statement. A brief historical survey of the various errors which appeared in Christology from time to time, and the manner in which the Church met them, is essential to a proper understanding of this important subject.

1. *Ebionism*. One of the first errors concerning the nature of Christ which appeared in the early Church, was that of the Ebionites. This Jewish sect within the Church, could not reconcile the deity of Christ with a strict monotheism, and hence rejected it. They maintained that at the baptism of Jesus, an unmeasured fullness of the Spirit was given to Him, and that this constituted Him the Messiah.

2. *Docetism*. The Docetae took their name from the Greek word meaning "to seem" or "to appear." They were closely related to the Gnostics, and hence held that Christ's body was a mere appearance or phantasm. Only by regarding the earthly life of Christ as an extended theophany, could they account for the unity of the divine and human in our Lord. Ebionism was the result of Jewish influence, Docetism the result of pagan philosophy.

3. *Sabellianism*. This error is a form of Monarchianism, and belongs more especially to the trinitarian controversies (cf. Chapter VII, Section IV). However, since it also affects Christology, it must be given brief mention here. Sabellius taught that there was but one God, who manifested Himself, first as Father, then as Son, and finally as the Holy Spirit. It is readily seen that here we have no real trinity—only a trinity of manifestations. It is at base panthetistic, for it teaches that the one God evolved Himself into different forms or manifestations. The Church condemns this position as heresy.

4. *Arianism*. Like the preceding, this heresy is also concerned primarily, with the doctrine of the Trinity. Arius was a presbyter of Alexandria in the fourth century, and taught that Christ was an incarnation of the pre-existing *Logos* or Word, but that this Word was an intermediate creature—the highest indeed of all created beings, yet outside the Godhead. This position was the forerunner of the earlier Socinianism and the more modern Unitarianism.

5. *Apollinarianism*. Apollinaris, bishop of Laodicea in the fourth century, is supposed to have taught the in-

completeness of Christ's human nature. Holding to a trichotomous division of human nature into body, soul and spirit, he ascribed to Christ a human body and a lower or animal soul, but not a human spirit or rational soul. This latter he held, was superseded by the *Logos* or divine Word, thus forming a divine-human being. On the dichotomous division of human nature into body and soul, this was equivalent to teaching that Christ had no human soul.

6. *Nestorianism.* Nestorius, bishop of Constantinople in the fourth century, went to the opposite extreme, and so separated between the two natures of Christ as to constitute them two persons, thus destroying the unity and uniqueness of Christ's person.

7. *Eutychianism.* Eutyches, the abbot of Constantinople in the fifth century, fell into an error similar to that of Apollinaris. He held that the human nature of Christ was converted into the divine nature by absorption, so that after the union, there was but one nature. For this reason the Eutychians were later known as Monophysites, in that they reduced the two natures to one.

8. *Monophysitism and Monotheletism.* While the Council of Chalcedon (451 A.D.) closed the Christological discussions in the West, the controversies still continued in the Eastern Church. Monophysitism, or the doctrine of one nature; and Monotheletism, or the doctrine of one will, were but later developments of Eutychianism. Both of these positions were in error, in that they did not do justice to the complete human nature of Christ.

9. *Adoptianism.* This error arose in Spain the latter part of the eighth century, and was similar to the earlier Nestorianism. Christ was regarded as an ordinary man, whose humanity was adopted into divinity by a gradual process. It therefore denied a real incarnation.

10. *Socinianism.* Laelius Socinus and Faustus Socinus, uncle and nephew, taught a form of unitarianism closely related to the earlier Arianism. Christ was regarded as an ordinary man, although of miraculous birth, to whom God gave extraordinary revelations, and

exalted Him to heaven after His death. He was, therefore, merely a divinized man. Here the error lies in a
denial of the deity of Christ, and therefore, effectually
destroys the ground of the atonement.

C. *The Authoritative Statement Concerning the Nature
of Christ.*

In the Councils of Nicea (325 A.D.), Constantinople
(381 A.D.), and Chalcedon (451 A.D.), the Church
sought to carefully guard the orthodox teaching concerning Christ from heretical opinions, and consequently
arrived at the following authoritative conclusion. The
right faith according to the Athanasian symbol is "That
our Lord Jesus Christ, the Son of God, is God and man;
God, of the substance of the Father; begotten before
the worlds: and man, of the substance of His mother,
born into the world; perfect God, and perfect man: of
a reasonable soul and human flesh subsisting; equal to
the Father, as touching His Godhead: and inferior to
the Father, as touching His manhood; Who although He
be God and man; yet He is not two but one Christ; One,
not by conversion of the Godhead into flesh: but by taking the manhood into God; One altogether, not by confusion of substance: but by unity of Person. For as the
reasonable soul and flesh is one man: so God and man is
one Christ."

The doctrine of Christ, therefore, involves the following truths which must be given proper consideration before giving attention to the Chalcedonian Christology:
(1) The Manhood of Christ; (2) The Deity of Christ;
and (3) The Divine-human Person.

II. The Manhood of Christ

Christ became incarnate in a manner that made Him
man. The Scriptures tell us that *the Word was made
flesh, and dwelt among us* (John 1: 14); and that *as the
children are partakers of flesh and blood, he also himself
likewise took part of the same* (Heb. 2: 14). We must
then, regard His human nature as true and entire, admitting no defect in any of its essential elements, nor
acquiring any additions by virtue of its conjunction with

Deity. Furthermore, our Lord's human nature was assumed under conditions which properly belong to man, and underwent a process of development in common with other men, sin only excepted. For this reason, He is called the *Son of man*, the perfect realization of the eternal idea of mankind.

A. *Characteristics of the Human Nature of Christ.*

The incarnation did not mean merely the assumption of a human body; for human nature does not consist in the possession of a body only, but of body and soul. In order, therefore, to conform to the teachings of the Scriptures concerning Christ's human nature, we must consistently maintain that His human nature was full and complete.

Christ had a human body. This was at first denied by the Docetae on the ground that matter is essentially evil, and therefore could not be conjoined with deity. They looked upon the body of Christ as an extended theophany, or appearance, similar to the appearance of the Angel of the Lord in the Old Testament. This heresy was condemned by the Church and soon disappeared. The Scriptures abound with proofs of the human nature of Christ. We have already discussed His supernatural birth, His circumcision, baptism and temptation. We are told that He was hungry (Matt. 4: 2), thirsty (John 19: 28), and weary (John 4: 6); that he suffered bodily pain in the garden and on the cross; and that He died and was buried (Matt. 27: 33-66; Mark 15: 22-47; Luke 22: 44; 23: 26; John 19: 16-42). St. John evidently intended to refute the opponents of Christ's humanity when he wrote, *That which was from the beginning, which we have heard, which we have seen with our eyes, which we have looked upon, and our hands have handled of the Word of life* (I John 1: 1). Here there seems to be a striking gradation in his proofs of the human body of Christ. First, we have hearing, and then seeing as more convincing than hearing; next he mentions looking upon, or contemplation, as more satisfactory than either hearing or seeing; and lastly, handling, as rendering the proof complete. Jesus spoke of Himself as a man when He said, *But now ye seek to kill me, a man that hath told you the truth which I have heard from God* (John 8: 40). Nothing can be clearer from the Scriptures than that Christ possessed a body of "flesh and blood" in common with all other men.

Our Lord had a human soul. This fact was called in question by Apollinaris, who substituted in his teaching, the *Logos* for the human soul of Christ—an error which has appeared from time to time in the Church, but has always been condemned as a heresy. In anticipation of His passion, our Lord said to His disciples, *Now is my soul troubled* (John 12: 27); and again, *My soul is exceeding sorrowful, even unto death* (Matt. 26: 38). Jesus said of Himself, *I am meek and lowly in heart* (Matt. 11: 29); and He *rejoiced in spirit* when the disciples returned from their successful mission. To deny that the acts, attributes and experiences natural to the human soul are not the evidences of a complete humanity, is to lay the foundation for a denial of His deity, as based on the acts, attributes, names and titles assigned to Him.

B. *The Sinlessness of Christ.*

There was no original sin in Christ's human nature. Inherited depravity is a consequence of the natural descent from Adam; but Christ's birth was miraculous, and hence without the natural or inherited corruption that belongs to the fallen nature of man. Sin does not belong to original human nature, and the nature which Christ took was untainted by sin. Having God alone as His Father, the birth of Christ was not a birth out of sinful nature, but a conjoining of human nature with deity, which in the very act sanctified it. Sin is a matter of the person, and since Christ was the pre-existent *Logos* or Word, the second Person of the adorable Trinity, He was as such, not only free from sin, but free from the possibility of sin. Christ was also free from actual sin. He *did no sin, neither was guile found in his mouth* (I Peter 2: 22). His earthly life was free from fault or blemish. As a child, He was filial and obedient (Luke 2: 51); as a youth, respectful and docile (Luke 2:52); and as a man, *holy, harmless, undefiled, separate from sinners, and made higher than the heavens* (Heb. 7:26). The great mystery is, that Christ should take our nature in such a manner, that while Himself without sin, He nevertheless bore the consequences of our sin.

C. *The Sufferings of Christ.*

The human nature of Christ was subject to the natural weaknesses incident to mankind, such as hunger, thirst, weariness, pain and suffering. These, however, were not by the necessity of His nature, but by the free choice of His theanthropic Person. The fact that Christ was God incarnate, lifted Him above the infirmities which attach to sinful human nature. But for the sake of "us men and our salvation," He voluntarily partook of the human weakness of mankind, and in all things was tempted or tried like as we are. Hence the author of the Epistle to the Hebrews declares that He *was made a little lower than the angels for the suffering of death, crowned with glory and honour; that he by the grace of God should taste death for every man* (Heb. 2:9). Again, he writes that *It became him, for whom are all things, and by whom are all things, in bringing many sons unto glory, to make the captain of their salvation perfect through sufferings* (Heb. 2:10). The Sufferer was at once God and man. As the same Person was united with both natures; and that Person the Son of God, we may say that the Son of God suffered. This suffering, however, is that of a divine Person and not the divine nature—the one Person that is God, being also man, suffered in His human nature.

III. THE DEITY OF CHRIST

There are two avenues of approach to the study of Christ's deity—the *textual* and the *historical*. The textual method approaches the subject through numerous proof texts referring to His divine names and titles, His divine acts, His divine attributes, and the fact that worship was ascribed to Him as a divine Person. With its many advantages, this method has one distinct disadvantage—the fact that proof texts may be interpreted in a wrong manner by prejudiced persons. It is, therefore, by the *historical* method that men have generally been convinced of the supernatural character of Christ, and have been led to the persuasion that He is very God. This is the method of the Gospels, and any attentive reader may share the wonderment of the disciples, their insights and their conclusions concerning the deity of their Lord. We shall not attempt then, to offer an elaborate system of proof texts in this connection, and will refer the reader to those already mentioned in our discussion of the Trinity (Chapter VII, Section II). It is sufficient here, to consider only those points which involve the incarnation and its relation to the redemptive work of Christ.

A. *The Pre-existence of Christ.*

The Church in all ages has affirmed the pre-existence of Christ. It has held, therefore, to His true deity as the *Messiah* of the Old Testament, and the *Christos* of the New Testament. Jesus himself said, *Before Abraham was, I am* (John 8: 58) ; and again, *No man hath ascended up to heaven, but he that came down from heaven, even the Son of man which is in heaven* (John 3: 13). The mere fact of pre-existence, however, is not in itself a sufficient proof of His deity, for the Arians held that He was of like essence with the Father, yet still a created being. Others have held that His pre-existence was only ideal, that is, an impersonal principle or potency which became personal only in Jesus. Again, we may ask, did He exist as the sole God—a simple and absolute personal unity, or did He exist as one of the essential and infinite Persons in a Triune Godhead? The Holy Scriptures and the conciliar actions of the church both affirm that Jesus of Nazareth was the Christ, the Son of the living God, and therefore the second Person in the adorable Trinity (cf. John 1: 1-5; Phil. 2: 5; Heb. 5: 6).

B. *Christ Was the Jehovah of the Old Testament.*

The deity of Christ finds abundant support in the Old Testament Scriptures, as was previously pointed out in our discussion of the Trinity. In order to show the continuity of the redemptive mission of the Son, however, it will be necessary to point out the fulfillment of two prophetic utterances concerning the Messiah. (1) The Angel of Jehovah, in whom was the divine name or nature, is a prophecy of Christ. Moses declared that *The Lord thy God will raise up unto thee a Prophet from the midst of thee, of thy brethren, like unto me; unto him shall ye hearken* (Deut. 18:15); and this prophecy was specifically declared by Stephen to have been fulfilled in Christ (Acts 7:37ff). (2) The Angel (or messenger) of the covenant is mentioned by Malachi as coming suddenly to His temple. As the Lord of a temple is the deity to whose worship it is consecrated, the act of our Lord in entering the temple, makes it evident that He was the Jehovah of the Old Testament to whom it was consecrated. The idea of a new covenant is mentioned by Jeremiah (Jer. 31:31-32), and also by Ezekiel (Ezek. 37:26)—a subject which is elaborated in the Epistle to the Hebrews as the specific work of Christ.

C. *The Unique Claims of Jesus for Himself.*
necessity, be His own claims. If it be argued that a man's claims for himself are worthless, it must be answered that this depends upon a prior question as to who the man is. To the objection of the Pharisees Jesus said, *Though I bear record of myself, yet my record is true; for I know whence I came, and whither I go. . . . . It is also written in your law, that the testimony of two men is true. I am one that bear witness of myself, and the Father that sent me beareth witness of me* (John 8:14-18). It is possible, however, to enumerate here only a few of the claims of Jesus—one of the most profound subjects that can engage the mind of man. Jesus claimed
The highest testimony to the deity of Christ must, of for Himself, (1) the possession of divine attributes, such as *eternity* (John 8:58; 17:5), *omnipotence* (Matt. 18:

20; 28:20; John 3:13), *omniscience* (Matt. 11:27; John 2:23-25; 21:17), and *omnipresence* (Matt. 18:20; John 3:13). (2) He claimed, and manifested the power to work miracles, or to empower others to perform wonderful works (Matt. 10:8; 11:5; 14:19-21; 15:30-31; Mark 6:41-44; Luke 8:41-56; 9:1-2). (3) He claimed divine prerogatives, such as being the Lord of the Sabbath (Mark 2:28); the power to forgive sins and to speak *as* God *for* God (Matt. 9:2-6; Mark 2:5-12; Luke 5:20-26). (4) He claimed to know the Father in a direct and perfect manner, as no other being can (Matt. 11:27; Luke 10:22), and to be the Son of God in a unique manner (Matt. 10:32-33; 16:17, 27). (5) He spoke words of infinite wisdom, for He spake as never man spake. (6) He accepted the homage of worship (Matt. 14:33); and (7) He claimed to be the final judge of all men (Matt. 7:21-23; 13:41-43; 19:28; 25:31, 33; Mark 14:62; Luke 9:26; 26:69-70).

IV. THE DIVINE-HUMAN PERSON

We have considered the scriptural proofs of the deity of Christ and also of His perfect manhood, and must now give attention to the union of these two natures in one Person. This union was effected by the incarnation, and the result was a theanthropic person or God-man, who unites in Himself all the conditions of divine and human existence. This one Person is the pre-existent *Logos,* or the divine Word, who assumed to Himself human nature, and in this assumption both personalized and redeemed it.

A. *The Nature of the Incarnation.*

The incarnation was not merely a stage in the mediatorial ministry of Christ, but the foundation of all. Without it there could have been no atonement and no intercessory ministry. Certain outstanding facts must be observed in any consideration of this important subject.

1. The incarnation was not a form of transmutation or transubstantiation. The Scriptures do not teach that the second Person of the Trinity ceased to be God when

He became man. When it is said that *the Word was made flesh*, it is equivalent to saying that Christ came in the flesh, thereby assuming a human nature that He might better enter redemptively into the human experiences of men.

2. It was the Word or *Logos*, the second Person of the Trinity alone, who became incarnate, and not the whole of the Godhead. To teach the latter leads to the error of patripassianism in which it is said that "the Father suffered," or "the Father died." One trinitarian Person may become incarnate, and yet that incarnation will not be of the whole Godhead, because the Godhead represents the divine essence or nature in three modes; and the essence in all three modes did not become incarnate. But since the whole essence or divine nature exists in each of the three modes, as Father, Son, and Holy Spirit, we may say that when the Son became incarnate, there dwelt in Him all the fullness of the Godhead bodily, but only in the mode of the second Person, or the divine Son.

3. The incarnation was a union of the divine Person with human nature, and not with a human person. The human nature which He assumed acquired personality by its union with Him. The Redeemer is therefore said to have laid hold on *the seed of Abraham* (Heb. 2: 16); and further, was called *the seed of the woman* (Gen. 3: 15), and *the seed of David* (Rom. 1: 3). These expressions can only mean that the human nature assumed by our Lord, was not as yet individualized. Christ's human nature was not impersonal except in this sense—it was not personalized out of the race by natural birth, but by becoming a constituent factor of the one theanthropic Person. The fact that He had no other personality than that which subsisted in the divine nature does not make Him an impersonal man. It only guards against the Nestorian error of an additional personality exclusively in the human nature. His was a full and complete humanity whose consciousness and will were developed only in union with the personality of the Logos.

4. The incarnation marked the beginning of the theanthropic Person. The God-man was a new Person as well as a unique one. There was no God-man until the union of the two natures in time. The precise beginning of this theanthropic Person must be placed at the instant of the miraculous conception. Previous to that instant, the only Person existing was the eternal Son; the human nature existing in the Virgin Mary being not yet personalized. Though beginning in time, the theanthropic Person of the Redeemer will continue forever. The term "Christ," therefore, is not the proper name for the unincarnate second Person of the Trinity, but only of the second Person incarnate.

5. The incarnation was necessary as the ground of our Lord's redemptive work. Previous to His assumption of human nature, the *Logos* could not experience human feelings because He had no human heart; but after the assumption he could enter more fully into all the experiences of mankind. Previous to the incarnation Christ could have no finite perception, because He had no finite intellect, but after it, He could think as men think. Previous to the incarnation, the self-consciousness of the Logos was eternal only, that is, without succession in time; but subsequently, it was both eternal and temporal, with and without succession in time. The union of the two natures, therefore, was necessary in order that Christ might become our merciful and faithful High Priest.

B. *The One Person.*

The union of the divine and human natures in Christ is a personal one, that is, the union consists in the abiding possession of a common Ego or Self—that of the eternal *Logos* or Word. In theology, this is termed the hypostatical union. The term *hypostasis* is from the Greek word ὑπόστασις, and is the term used to mark the distinction between the personal subsistences in the Godhead, as over against their common substance or essence. The two natures meet and have communion with each other, solely through the self which is common to both.

1. The possession of two natures does not involve a double personality, for the ground of the person is the eternal *Logos* and not the human nature. Christ, therefore, uniformly speaks of Himself in the singular person. Always and everywhere, the Agent is one. There is never any interchange of the "I" and "Thou" as in the Trinity. The varying modes of consciousness pass quickly from the divine to the human, but the Person is always the same. Hence He says, *I and my Father are one* (John 10:30), and again, *I thirst* (John 19:28).

2. A person may consist of one, two or three natures. A Trinitarian Person, as that of the Father, the Son, or the Holy Spirit, has but one nature, that of the divine substance or essence. A human person has two natures—a material body and an immaterial soul. Christ as the theanthropic Person, may be said to have three natures—the divine Logos or Word, a human soul, and a human body. The latter two are combined in thought when we speak of Christ as having two natures, the divine and the human. It is the person, therefore, which unites the natures, but these are not joined in a mere external or mechanical manner. It is a personal union, and therefore close and inseparable. In Christ we are to believe that the union between the divine and human natures, was even closer than that existing between the soul and body in man. In the latter, the soul and body may be separated by death; in the former, the divine nature was not for a moment separated from either soul or body.

3. That the personality of the God-man depended primarily upon the divine nature, is shown by the fact that it was not destroyed by death. At His death there was indeed, a temporary separation between soul and body, but there was not for an instant, a separation between the divine *Logos* and either the human soul or body. Between His death and resurrection, both the human soul and body were still united with the *Logos* or divine Word. It is for this reason that Christ's body never saw corruption.

C. *The Two Natures.*

The unity of Christ's Person finds its complementary truth in the diversity of the two natures. That the Godhead and manhood each retains its respective properties and functions, without either alteration of essence or mutual interference, is as necessary to a true conception of the incarnation as is their hypostatic union in Jesus Christ. While the acts and qualities of either the divine or the human nature of Christ may be attributed to the theanthropic Person, it may not be said that they can be attributed to each other. The properties which belong to a nature are necessarily confined to it. A material substance can have only material properties, and an immaterial substance can only have spiritual properties. So also, human nature can have only human properties, and the divine nature only divine properties. Natures, however, although heterogeneous, may belong to the same person.

1. *The Chalcedonian Definition.* The statement prepared by the Council of Chalcedon in 451 A.D. is as follows: "Following the holy fathers we teach with one voice that the Son (of God) and our Lord Jesus Christ is to be confessed as one and the same (Person), that He is perfect in Godhead and perfect in manhood, very God and very man, of a reasonable soul and (human) body consisting, consubstantial with the Father as touching His Godhead, and consubstantial with us as touching His manhood; made in all things like unto us, sin only excepted, begotten of His Father before the worlds according to His Godhead; but in these last days for us men and for our salvation born (into the world) of the Virgin Mary, the Mother of God according to His manhood. This one and the same Jesus Christ, the only begotten Son (of God) must be confessed in two natures, unconfusedly, immutably, indivisibly, inseparably (united) and that without distinction of natures being taken away by such union, but rather the peculiar property of each being preserved and being united in one Person and Hypostasis, not separated or divided into

persons, but one and the same Son and Only Begotten, God the Word, our Lord Jesus Christ, as the prophets of old time have spoken concerning Him, and as the Lord Jesus Christ hath taught us, and as the Creed of our fathers hath delivered to us."

2. *The Orthodox Faith.* The Chalcedonian Creed has furnished the Church with a true basis for its Christology, and has been accepted as orthodox by both Roman Catholics and Protestants with this exception—Protestants reject the word *Theotokos* (Θεοτόκος) or Mother of God. Here the two natures in Christ are not only affirmed, but their relations to each other are also adjusted in four main points—without *mixture* (or confusion); without *change* (or conversion); without *division;* and without *separation.* It may be admitted that these terms do not define, but they do furnish the guideposts for the preservation of the true doctrine. If then we would hold the true faith, we must believe (1) that the union of two natures in Christ does not confuse or mix them in a manner to destroy their distinctive properties. The deity of Christ is as pure deity after the incarnation as before it; and the human nature of Christ is as pure and simple a human nature as that of His mother or of any other human individual—sin excepted. (2) We must reject as unorthodox any theory that would convert one nature into the other, either the absorption of the human nature by the divine as in Eutychianism; or the reduction of the divine to the human, as in some of the modern kenotic theories. (3) We must hold the two natures in such a union that it does not divide the Person of Christ into two selves, as in Nestorianism, or such a blending of the two natures into a composite which is neither God nor man as in Apollinarianism. The resultant of the union is not two persons, but one Person who unites in Himself the conditions of both the divine and human existence. (4) We must hold to a union of the two natures that is inseparable. The union of humanity with deity in Christ is indissoluble and eternal. It is a permanent assumption of human nature by the second Person of the Trinity.

CHAPTER XII

THE ESTATES AND OFFICES OF CHRIST

"Christ alone was Prophet, Priest, and King; and possessed and exe-
cuted these offices in such a supereminent degree as no human being
ever did, or ever could do.

"Jesus is a Prophet, to reveal the will of God, and instruct men in it.
He is a Priest, to offer up sacrifice, and make atonement for the sin of
the world. He is Lord, to rule over and rule in the souls of the children of
men; in a word, He is Jesus the Saviour, to deliver from the power, guilt,
and pollution of sin; to enlarge and vivify, by the influence of His Spirit;
to preserve in the possession of the salvation which He has communicated;
to seal those who believe, heirs of glory; and at last to receive them into
the fullness of beatitude in His eternal glory."—Dr. ADAM CLARKE.

A consideration of the estates and offices of Christ,
forms a natural transition from the doctrine of His Person to that of His finished work, which is commonly
known as the Atonement. The estates and offices of
Christ are two—the State of Humiliation, and the State
of Exaltation. Theologically, these estates represent
varying emphases upon the two natures of the God-man.
As to the limits of the humiliation, different positions are
held. The Reformed Church holds that it extends from
the miraculous conception to the close of the descent into
Hades, while the Lutheran Church generally holds that
it closed with the words, *It is finished,* spoken by Christ
on the cross. The Arminians accept the latter position.
The offices of Christ are three—those of prophet, priest
and king. This threefold classification was worked out
carefully by Eusebius at an early date, and forms a principle of distribution in most modern theologies.

I. THE STATE OF HUMILIATION

The Scriptures present Christ in strikingly contrasted
conditions. The prophets saw Him subjected to the greatest indignities, and as seated on the most exalted of
thrones. Unable to reconcile these contrasts, the Jewish
exegetes sometimes affirmed the necessity of two Mes-
siahs. Much of the opposition to Jesus during His earthly
life, was based on His humble condition, and the reasons

given by His opposers are in exact correspondence with the nature of the humiliation which the prophets had foretold concerning Him. If in the light of modern exegetical studies, we inquire as to the nature of the humiliation, we shall find that it pertains generally, though not exclusively, to the limitations of His human nature, and its relation to the penalty of sin. The portion of Scripture which has furnished the basis for the numerous and widely divergent Christological theories is found in St. Paul's Epistle to the Philippians, *Let this mind be in you, which was also in Christ Jesus: who, being in the form of God, thought it not robbery to be equal with God: but made himself of no reputation, and took upon him the form of a servant, and was made in the likeness of men: and being found in fashion as a man, he humbled himself, and became obedient unto death, even the death of the cross* (Phil. 2: 5-8).

A. *The Stages in Christ's Humiliation.*

From the scripture just cited, it is evident that the two states of Christ's being—as pre-existent *Logos,* and as the Word made flesh—necessitated a twofold renunciation, that is, from the divine to the human, and from the human to the cross. Subsisting in the form of God, there was (1) a self-renunciation, *He thought it not robbery to be equal with God,* or as frequently translated, *not a thing to be grasped and held on to;* (2) a self-emptying or *kenosis, He made himself of no reputation,* that is, *He emptied himself;* and (3) *He took upon him the form of a servant, and was made in the likeness of men.* Subsisting in the form of man, there were likewise three well-defined steps in His earthly humiliation paralleling the former: (1) a self-renunciation, *He humbled himself;* (2) a subordination, *and became obedient unto death;* and (3) a perfecting of His humiliation as the Representative of sinners, *even the death of the cross.* Following the Reformation, the Lutheran and Reformed Churches took widely different positions concerning the humiliation, especially the *kenosis* or "self-emptying." The various theories may be classified as follows: (1) The *Communicatio Idiomatum;* (2) The Earlier Depotentiation Theories; (3) The Later Kenotic Theories; and (4) The Mystical Theories.

B. *The Communicatio Idiomatum.*

This was peculiarly a development within the Lutheran Church. It signifies the communication of the idiomata or attributes of the two natures of Christ to the one Person, and through that Person from one nature to another. It does not involve the merging of one nature into the other, but it does hold that all the attributes, whether of the divine or human natures, are to be regarded as attributes of the one Person and not of either nature independently of that Person. It holds also, a communion of natures in such a manner, that the attributes and powers of the divine nature are communicated to the human. This, however, is not reciprocal, for the human nature cannot communicate anything to the divine, which is unchangeable and perfect. Here again, no confusion of natures is allowed, but a permeation of the human by the divine, this permeation or *perichoresis* taking place through the Person which is the bond of union between the two natures. In the trinitarian controversies the question with which the Church was concerned was that of the relation of Christ to the Godhead; in the earlier Christological controversies, the problem was that of the relation of the two natures to the one Person; here the problem is the relation of the one nature to the other through the one Person. The Lutherans held that through the one Person, the resources of the divine nature were placed at the disposal of the human; and that an act of either nature is the act of the one Person, and hence participated in by the other nature.

C. *The Earlier Depotentiation Theories.*

The development of the *Communicatio Idiomatum* led finally to a controversy within the Lutheran Church itself. Starting from the *communicatio* as a common basis, both schools held that from the moment of His conception Christ possessed the attributes of omnipresence, omniscience and omnipotence. But they interpreted the humiliation in different ways. (1) the *kenotists* (from κενόω "to empty") were so-called because they held that there was a kenosis or emptying of the divine attributes during the earthly life of Christ. However, they made a distinction between the possession and the use of the attributes, and held that the kenosis applied to the latter. (2) The *kryptists* (from κρυπτὸς "hidden" or "secret") maintained that He possessed the divine attributes but that during His lifetime they were concealed. Hence the kryptists regarded the glorification as the first display of the divine attributes, while the kenotists viewed it as a resumption of them. The depotentiation theories took various forms, but there was a common element in them all—they believed that there was a literal merging of the deity of Christ into the spirit of the man Christ Jesus.

D. *The Later Kenotic Theories.*

During the earlier part of the nineteenth century, an attempt was made to unite the Lutheran and Reformed Churches on the basis of the kenotic Christology. The substance of this new position was to the effect that Christ in becoming incarnate, "emptied" Himself, and thereby brought the eternally pre-existent *Logos* within the limitations of human personality. But here again, the form and degree of the kenosis became a matter of dispute. Four distinct types of kenotic theory appear in the literature of the period.

1. Thomasius (1802-1876) held that the Lutheran conception of the two natures demanded, either that the infinite be brought down to the finite, or that the finite be lifted up to the infinite. The latter or *majestas* theory he declared, should be abandoned in favor of the former or *kenotic* theory. He taught that the Son of God during His earthly life, limited Himself to the form and content of consciousness which belonged to finite personality. We may say, then, that he believed that Christ emptied Himself of the relative attributes of omnipresence, om-

niscience and omnipotence, while still retaining the immanent or essential attributes of deity.

2. Gess (1819-1891) carried the kenotic theory still farther, teaching that the *Logos* not only emptied Himself of His relative attributes, but of His essential attributes as well. There was, therefore, an actual transmutation of the Logos into a human soul.

3. Ebrard (1818-1888) agreed with Gess in regarding the incarnate Logos as taking the place of the human soul in Christ, but differs from him in that he does not hold this to be a depotentiation. The attributes of omnipresence, omniscience and omnipotence are retained, and therefore the humiliation lay in the fact that He disguised His deity.

4. Martensen (1808-1884), a Danish bishop and theologian, advanced the theory of a "real but relative" kenosis, by which he means, that the depotentiation though real, applied only to the earthly life of Christ in the flesh, and not to the divine attributes. He also makes a distinction between the *Logos* revelation and the Christ revelation, and confines the kenosis to the latter. The *Logos* while continuing as God in His general revelation to the world, enters at the same time into the bosom of humanity as a holy seed, that He may rise within the race as a Mediator and Redeemer. As the *Logos,* He works in an all-pervading presence through the kingdom of nature; as Christ, He works in the kingdom of grace; and He indicates His consciousness of personal identity in the two spheres by referring to His preexistence.

It is evident from this discussion of the kenotic theories, that some of them must be classed as mere humanism, and others as pantheism. The earlier theories limited the depotentiation merely to the use or manifestation of the divine predicates; the later theories applied the kenosis directly to the *Logos*, some of them holding to such a depotentiation as reduced the divine *Logos* to a merely finite being. To the question, then, "Of what did the *Logos* empty Himself?" we must say that it was a divestment of the *glory* which He had with the Father before the foundation of the world, and which He again desired, as expressed in His high priestly prayer. Dean Alford says, "He emptied Himself of the μορφῇ Θεοῦ (or form of God), not the essential glory but the manifested possession . . . . the glory which He had with the Father before the world began and which was resumed at His glorification. He ceased while in the state of exinanition to reflect the glory which He had with the Father." We may then, with safety, interpret the divestment of the glory to mean the giving up of the independent exercise of His own divine attributes during the period of His earthly life. We may also confidently believe: (1) that the pre-existent *Logos* gave up the glory which He had before the foundation of the world, in order to take upon Himself the form of a servant; (2) That during His earthly life, He was subordinate to the mediatorial will of the Father in all things; yet knowing the will of the Father, He voluntarily offered Himself in obedience to His will. (3) That His ministry during this period was under the immediate control of the Holy Spirit, who prepared for Him a body, who instructed Him during the period of His development, who anointed Him for His mission, and who enabled Him at last to offer Himself without spot to God.

II. The Exaltation

The exaltation is that state of Christ in which He laid aside the infirmities of the flesh according to His human nature, and again assumed His majesty. As in the humiliation there were stages of descent, so also in the exaltation there are stages of ascent. These stages are (1) the Descensus or descent into Hades; (2) the Resurrection; (3) the Ascension; and (4) the Session.

A. *The Descent into Hades.*

The brief interval in redemptive history, between the death of Christ and the resurrection, is known as the *Descensus ad inferos*, or descent into Hades. The term is not found in the Scriptures, but in the Creeds,

and is there expressed as "He descended into hell."
The doctrine, however, is based upon such Scriptures as
*Thou wilt not leave my soul in hell, neither wilt thou
suffer thine Holy One to see corruption* (Psalms 16:10);
and *He seeing this before spake of the resurrection of
Christ, that his soul was not left in hell, neither did his
flesh see corruption* (Acts 2:27, 31). Closely connected
with these texts is another by the same apostle, which
states that *He went and preached unto the spirits in
prison; which sometimes were disobedient, when once
the long-suffering of God waited in the days of Noah,
while the ark was a preparing, wherein few, that is,
eight souls were saved by water* (I Peter 3:19-20). The
Greek word *Hades* (Αἴδης) and its Hebrew complement,
Sheol, signifies the hidden or unseen state, that is, the
realm of the dead. It has no reference to punishment
endured while in this hidden state. It was into this realm
of the dead that our Lord entered while His body was
concealed in the sepulcher.

We may safely believe, then, that when our Lord
uttered the cry *It is finished!* the humiliation ceased and
the exaltation began. His death was His triumph over
death, consequently death had no more power over Him
(Rom. 6:8-9). When, therefore, He entered into the
realm of the dead, it was as a Conqueror. Descending
into the lower parts of the earth, *He led captivity captive, and gave gifts unto men* (Eph. 4:8-9). As through
the incarnation, the Son of God took upon Him flesh and
blood, and thereby entered into the state of human life,
becoming obedient unto the humiliating death of the
cross, so He enters the realm of the dead—not to suffer
more, but as its triumphant Conqueror. This, then,
marks the first stage in His exaltation.

B. *The Resurrection.*

The second stage in the exaltation is the resurrection,
or that act by which our Lord came forth from the tomb.
Since the ascension marks the transition from His earthly
to His heavenly state, the resurrection is the last and
crowning event of our Lord's earthly mission. There are

two phases of the truth which must be given consideration. *First*, the historical fact of the resurrection is intensely significant. It is, therefore, attested by *many infallible proofs* (Acts 1: 3). The testimony of the apostles
and first disciples is of immense value. Christ appeared
alive to them in tangible "flesh and bones" by which
they recognized His body as that which had been crucified. Added to this, they also recognized that He had
acquired new and mysterious powers, which transcended
those manifested in the flesh during His earthly life.
Many appearances are recorded during the forty days
of His sojourn with His disciples. But one of the strongest evidences of the resurrection was the complete and
instantaneous change which took place in the minds of
the disciples. From discouragement and unbelief, they
were suddenly transformed into joyous believers. The
supreme evidence of the resurrection, however, must
ever be the gift of the Holy Spirit to the disciples, making them flaming evangels of the gospel of Christ. *Second,*
the resurrection must also be considered in its doctrinal
relations. Five things stand out clearly as basic in their
importance.

1. The resurrection of Christ was the self-verifica-
tion of the claims of Jesus. It was the divine attestation
of Christ's prophetic ministry, by which His claims were
not only vindicated, but His mission interpreted to the
apostles and evangelists.

2. The new humanity of Jesus being sinless, furnished the ground for the atoning sacrifice. In the incarnation, our Lord assumed flesh and blood that He
might taste death for every man; in the resurrection, He
achieved victory over death. It is for this reason that the
resurrection is called a birth (Col. 1: 18; Rev. 1: 5). It
was, in reality, a birth out of death, and therefore the
death of death. By taking our nature and dying in it,
then reviving or quickening it, this new and glorified
humanity becomes the ground of an eternal priesthood,
His death and resurrection being the consecrating basis.
It is, therefore, an event of progress, in which the Redeemer passes from a lower to a higher plane in the new

creation. It was not merely a return from the grave to the same natural status, it was a transcendent event.

3. The resurrection furnished the ground for our justification. Christ *was delivered for our offences, and was raised again for our justification* (Rom. 4: 25). It becomes, therefore, not only a vindication of His prophetic work, but also of His priesthood. He died for the transgressions that were under the first testament; He arose to become the Executor of the new covenant—by which will or covenant, we are *sanctified through the offering of the body of Jesus Christ once for all* (Heb. 10: 9-10).

4. The glorified humanity of Christ also forms the basis for a new fellowship. He was the *image of the invisible God, the firstborn of every creature* (Col. 1: 15ff); and this new humanity in Christ furnished the bond between Him and those who are adopted as children *by Jesus Christ to himself* (Eph. 1: 5). This new humanity is ethical and spiritual (Eph. 4: 22-24; Col. 3: 9-10), and as the basis of this new and holy fellowship, becomes the body of Christ or the Church.

5. The resurrection of Christ is the guaranty of our future resurrection. Christ is the *firstfruits of them that slept.* It is a vital part of the redemptive purpose of God in Christ, that man should not only be delivered from sin spiritually, but that he should also be made free from the consequences of sin physically.

C. *The Ascension.*

The ascension is the third stage in our Lord's exaltation, and marks the close of His life on earth. This transference from earth to heaven must not be understood to mean merely a removal from one part of the physical universe to another, but a local withdrawal into what is known as "the presence of God." The ascension was a passing into a new sphere of mediatorial action, the taking possession of the presence of God for us, and is, therefore, immediately associated with His High Priestly intercession. He appears *in the presence of God for us* (Heb. 9: 24). He has also consecrated for us, a new and living way through the veil *that is to say, his flesh;* His glorified body becoming the way of access through which His people have liberty or *boldness to enter into the holiest by the blood of Jesus* (Heb. 10: 19-20). Lastly, the ascension signifies the withdrawal of Christ in the flesh, in order to establish the conditions by which the Holy Spirit could be given to the Church. Having received of the Father the promise of the Spirit, the day of Pentecost witnessed the coming of the Comforter as an abiding Presence in the Church.

D. *The Session.*

The fourth and last stage of the exaltation is known as the session. It is closely related to the ascension and signifies primarily, the place of Christ at the right hand of the Father as an intercessory Presence. As the prophetical office of Christ was merged into His priestly work by His death and resurrection, so His priestly office is merged into His kingship by the ascension and session. As the resurrection was the divine attestation of His prophetical office, so the gift of the Holy Spirit is the divine attestation of both the ascension and session. Christ's presence on the throne is but the beginning of a supreme authority which shall end only when He *hath put all enemies under his feet* (I Cor. 15: 25). From His session our Lord will return to the earth the second time without sin unto salvation (Heb. 9: 28); and the ascension is the pattern of His return. His exaltation will be complete, only when all things shall be subdued under Him, and He himself is crowned Lord of all. *Then shall the Son also himself be subject unto him that put all things under him, that God may be all in all* (I Cor. 15: 28).

III. THE OFFICES OF CHRIST

The mediatorial process which began historically with the incarnation, and was continued through the humiliation and exaltation, reached its full perfection in the session at the right hand of God. The estates and offices, therefore, form the transition from a consideration of the complex Person of Christ, to that of His finished work in the atonement—the former linking the mediatorial work more directly to His Person, the latter more immediately to the finished work. As Mediator, the work of Christ is resolved into the threefold office of Prophet, Priest and King. Into these offices He was inducted at His baptism, and by a specific anointing with the Holy Spirit became officially the Mediator between God and man.

A. *The Prophetic Office.*

Christ as a prophet is the perfect revealer of divine truth. As the *Logos,* He *was the true Light, which lighteth every man that cometh into the world* (John 1: 9). In the Old Testament He spoke through angels, through theophanies, through types and by means of the prophets, to whom He communicated His Holy Spirit. As the incarnate Word, He faithfully and fully revealed to men the saving will of God. He spoke with inherent authority (Matt. 7: 28-29), and was recognized as a teacher come from God (John 3: 2). After His ascension He continues His work through the Holy Spirit, who now dwells in the Church as the Spirit of truth. In the world to come His prophetic work will be continued, for we are told that the city *had no need of the sun, neither the moon, to shine in it: for the glory of God did lighten it, and the Lamb is the light thereof* (Rev. 21: 23). It will be through His glorified manhood that we shall see and enjoy the vision of God to all eternity.

B. *The Priestly Office.*

The priestly office of Christ is concerned with objective mediation, and includes both sacrifice and intercession. *He offered up himself* (Heb. 7: 27). He was at once the offering and the Offerer, the one corresponding to His death, the other to His resurrection and ascension, and together issuing in the atonement. Based upon His sacrificial work is His office of intercession and benediction, which are together connected with the administration of redemption. It was on the eve of the crucifixion that our Lord formally assumed His sacrificial function—first by the institution of the Lord's Supper, and following this by His high priestly prayer of consecration (John 17:1-26). After Pentecost the priestly office became more prominent. Consequently the cross becomes the center of the apostolic gospel (I Cor. 1:23; 5:7); His death is the establishing of a new covenant (I Cor. 10:16; 11:24-26); and His sacrifice is regarded as a voluntary act of atonement and reconciliation (Eph. 5:2; I Peter 2:24; Rom. 5:10; Col. 1:20). After Pentecost the priestly work of Christ is continued through the Holy Spirit as a gift of the risen and exalted Saviour; and in the world to come our approach to God must ever be through Him as the abiding source of our life and glory.

C. *The Kingly Office.*

The kingly, or regal office of Christ is that activity of our ascended Lord at the right hand of God, ruling over all things in heaven and in earth for the extension of His kingdom. It is based upon the sacrificial death, and therefore finds its highest exercise in the bestowment of the blessings secured for mankind by His atoning work. As our Lord formally assumed His priestly work on the eve of the crucifixion, so He formally assumed His kingly office at the time of the ascension. We must not overlook the fact, however, that by anticipation Christ assumed to Himself the office of King during His earthly life, particularly at the time just preceding His death. But at the ascension, He said, *All power is given unto me in heaven and in earth. Go ye therefore, and teach all nations, baptizing them in the name of the Father, and of the Son, and of the Holy Ghost: teaching them to observe all things whatsoever I have commanded you: and, lo, I am with you alway, even unto the end of the world. Amen* (Matt. 28:18-20). Having already proclaimed His rule over the dead in the descensus; and having declared it to His brethren on earth, He ascended to the throne, there to exercise His mediatorial power until the time of the judgment, when the mediatorial economy shall end. God's efforts to save men will then have been exhausted, and the fate of all men, whether good or evil, will be fixed forever. This is the meaning of St. Paul, when He says, *Then cometh the end, when he shall have delivered up the kingdom to God, even the Father; when he shall have put down all rule and all authority and power. For he must reign, till he hath put all enemies under his feet* (I Cor. 15: 24-25). It is obvious that the kingly office as exercised for the redemption of mankind, applies only to the era of extending and perfecting the kingdom; and the regal office in this sense will end when that era is completed. Nor does this mean that the Son shall not continue to reign as the second Person in the Trinity; nor that His theanthropic Person shall cease. He shall forever reign as the God-man, and shall forever exercise His power for the benefit of the redeemed and the glory of His kingdom.

CHAPTER XIII

THE ATONEMENT

"As the first dawn of morning light is succeeded by an increasing brilliancy, till the earth is illumined by the full glories of midday, even so the great doctrine of redemption through the blood of the everlasting covenant, which at first faintly gleamed from the illustrious promise of *the seed of the woman,* continued to shine, with still increasing luster, through the consecrated medium of the types and shadows, the smoking altars, and bleeding victims, of the patriarchal and Mosaic dispensations; till, at length, under the superior light and more glorious developments of gospel day, we behold the clear fulfillment of ancient predictions, the infallible comment upon the divinely instituted types, and the most explicit revelation of the great mystery of salvation, through the merits of the vicarious and piacular oblation of God's Messiah."—DR. T. N. RALSTON.

The word atonement occurs but once in the New Testament (Rom. 5:11). However, the Greek word καταλλαγὴν from which it comes appears often, but is usually translated reconciliation. The Old Testament term for atonement is *kaphar,* which signifies primarily to cover or to hide. When used as a noun it signifies a covering. In theology, it is used to express the idea of satisfaction or expiation. In the English language, however, it is made to cover a wide range of thought. (1) It denotes that which brings together and reconciles estranged parties, making them at-one-ment, or of the same mind. (2) It denotes also, the state of reconciliation, or the one-mindedness which characterizes reconciled parties. (3) It is sometimes used in the sense of an apology or *amende honorable.* This is a penitential confession, as for instance, the suffering in connection with the beloved dead, because we cannot make "atonement" to them for the wrongs committed against them while they were with us. (4) The word is most frequently used in the sense of a substitute for penalty—a victim offered as a propitiation to God, and hence an expiation for sin. (5) The Old Testament idea as indicated, is that of a covering, and therefore applies to anything which veils man's sins from God. (6) It reaches its highest expression in the New Testament, where it is used to signify the propitiatory offering of Christ.

I. The Nature and Necessity of the Atonement

A. *Definitions of the Atonement.*

Mr. Watson defines the atonement as follows: "The satisfaction offered to divine justice by the death of Christ for the sins of mankind, by virtue of which all true penitents who believe in Christ are personally reconciled to God, are freed from the penalty of their sins, and entitled to eternal life" (Watson, *Dictionary*, p. 108). The definition of Dr. Summers is similar in its import but more specific. "The atonement is the satisfaction made to God for the sins of all mankind, original and actual, by the mediation of Christ, and especially by His passion and death, so that pardon might be granted to all, while the divine perfections are kept in harmony, the authority of the Sovereign is upheld, and the strongest motives are brought to bear upon sinners to lead them to repentance, to faith in Christ, the necessary conditions of pardon, and to a life of obedience, by the gracious aid of the Holy Spirit" (Summers, *Systematic Theology*, I, pp. 258-259). Dr. Miley gives us the following definition: "The vicarious sufferings of Christ are an atonement for sin as a conditional substitute for penalty, fulfilling, on the forgiveness of sin, the obligation of justice and the office of penalty in moral government" (Miley, *The Atonement in Christ*, p. 23).

B. *The Necessity of the Atonement.*

When speaking of the necessity of the atonement, we mean that it was indispensable to the exercise of mercy toward condemned sinners, and consequently without it, there could have been no salvation for them. We should, however, carefully guard against the thought that atonement was necessary in order to excite the love of God to man, for the atonement is the outgrowth or effect of the divine love. It was an antecedent love in God that was the originating cause of the atonement. It follows, then, that the necessity of the atonement originated in the obstacles which law and justice interposed, for law in and of itself contains no provision for pardon. The law having been transgressed demanded that the penalty attached thereto be exacted of the sinner, and justice concurred in the demand. Furthermore, the law being holy and just and good, holiness and justice and goodness all demanded that the penalty be inflicted. The law then rose up in terrible majesty, restrained the exercise of divine mercy and demanded the execution of the penalty. God could not in His wisdom and holiness and goodness affix a penalty to a law, and then permit disobedience to pass with impunity. Without some external intervention, the whole human race would have been hopelessly and eternally lost.

Again, the necessity of the atonement may be traced from the nature of sin to the nature of God. The nature of sin is such as to result in demerit. The sinner is personally blameworthy. The demand made by the law implies the intrinsic evil of sin and its ill-desert. If we ask why, we find the answer in the nature of God. Sin is antagonistic to the nature of God. Here in the nature—and we may say, the attributes of God—is the ground of the contest for or against the necessity of atonement. Those theories of the atonement which teach or present only the manward and not the Godward side, in some sense deny both the holiness and justice of God. Further still, the humiliation, suffering and death of the only-begotten Son of God prove that there was some necessity for it.

II. THE BIBLICAL BASIS OF THE ATONEMENT

It is to the Scriptures we must turn in order to establish the Christian idea of the atonement. Here will be found the preparatory stages of development as set forth in the Old Testament; and the New Testament conception of Sacrifice as revealed in the vicarious sufferings and death of our Lord Jesus Christ.

A. *Foreshadowing of the Atonement in the Old Testament.*

The doctrine of the atonement was gradually unfolded to the world, and is marked by three principal stages; (1) The Primitive Sacrifices; (2) The Sacrifices of the Law; and (3) The Predictions of the Prophets.

1. *The Primitive Sacrifices.* The Old Testament does not give us an account of the origin of the primitive sacrifices, but it does give us a history of sacrificial worship from the earliest dawn of history until the time when the sacrifices were done away by the atoning work of our Lord Jesus Christ. The work of the patriarchs was to keep alive the sense of dependence upon God, and the altar was regarded as an essential element in any approach to the Deity. The record of sacrificial worship as found in Cain and Abel, Noah, and Abraham; show conclusively that the blood sacrifices were regarded as expiatory in character.

2. *The Sacrifices of the Law.* The institution of stated sacrifices under the Mosaic economy, marked a further stage in the development of the idea of atonement. Dependence upon God was now interpreted to mean dependence upon His will, and hence took on a moral character. The fact that atonement attached to the religious community is deeply significant as indicating a common depravity out of which personal transgressions sprang, and for which atonement was needed. The offering of blood had a twofold significance also—it was a representation of the pure life which the sinner should have; and that atonement could be made expiatory through death only. Furthermore, the animal sacrifices pointed to Christ as the great Antitype—the Lamb of God, whose blood alone could take away the sin of the world.

3. *The Predictions of the Prophets.* These supplemented the sacrifices of the law, and more fully developed the Messianic idea, and with it the idea of His sacrificial sufferings and death. They saw in Him, a living totality of truth. Being the God-man, in whom deity and humanity are conjoined, He was conscious of the full range of truth, and was able to speak from this indivisible whole. For this reason He bore an essential relation to all men, and could therefore offer a vicarious and propitiatory sacrifice for them. Perhaps the highest reach of this spiritual truth in the Old Testament is to be found in Isaiah's remarkable prophecy concerning the suffering

Servant of Jehovah. *Surely he hath borne our griefs,
and carried our sorrows: yet we did esteem him stricken,
smitten of God and afflicted. But he was wounded for our
transgressions, he was bruised for our iniquities: the
chastisement of our peace was upon him; and with his
stripes we are healed* (Isa. 53: 4-5).

B. *The New Testament Conception of Sacrifice.*

The conception of Christ's atoning sacrifice as found
in the New Testament, is simply the completion of that
which was foreshadowed in the Old Testament. For this
reason Christ is said to have died according to the Scriptures. Our Lord represents His death as a ransom for
men. He laid down His life voluntarily, for no man had
power to take it from Him. Hence we must regard the
crucifixion as not merely an event brought about by
circumstances, but as the great end for which He came
into the world. He was not merely a martyr to truth;
His death was sacrificial and propitiatory. This brings us
at once to a consideration of the motive which underlies
the atonement, and also its vicarious nature.

C. *The Motive or Originating Cause of the Atonement.*

The motive for the atonement is found in the love of
God. This is sometimes known as the moving or originating cause of redemption. The most prominent text in this
connection is the epitome of the gospel found in John
3: 16, *For God so loved the world, that he gave his only
begotten Son;* and again in the following verse, *For God
sent not his Son into the world to condemn the world;
but that the world through him might be saved* (John
3: 17). Many other scriptures set forth this same truth.
The atonement, whether in its motive, its purpose, or its
extent, must be understood as the provision and expression of God's righteous and holy love. Christ's life and
death are the expression of God's love for us, not the
producing cause of that love.

D. *The Vicarious Nature of the Atonement.*

The term "vicarious" in a general sense, means "one
in the place of another." The vicarious atonement, there-

fore, means that the suffering and death of Christ were expiatory. In the words of Mr. Watson, "Christ suffered in our room and stead, or as a proper substitute for us." This is shown by those scriptures that declare that He died for men, or that connect His death with the punishment due our offenses. There are two Greek prepositions which are translated "for" in the Scriptures. The first is *hyper* (ὑπερ), and is found in the following verses: *It is expedient for us, that one man should die for the people* (John 11: 50); *Christ died for the ungodly. . . . . While we were yet sinners, Christ died for us* (Rom. 5: 6, 8); *If one died for all, then were all dead. . . . . And that he died for all, that they which live should not henceforth live unto themselves, but unto him that died for them, and rose again. . . . . For he hath made him to be sin for us, who knew no sin; that we might be made the righteousness of God in him* (II Cor. 5: 14, 15, 21) (cf. also Gal. 1: 4; 3: 13; Eph. 5: 2, 25; I Thess. 5: 9, 10). The second Greek preposition is *anti* (ἀντὶ) and is found in such verses as Matt. 20: 28 and Mark 10: 45, where Christ is said *to give his life a ransom for many.* It is sometimes objected that these Greek prepositions do not always signify substitution; that is, that they do not always mean *instead of*, but are sometimes used as *in behalf of*, or *on account of*. Thus we have the expression "Christ died for our sins," which cannot of course mean *instead of* in this instance. However, that these prepositions are generally used in the sense of substitution is generally admitted.

E. *Scripture Terminology.*

The Scriptures regard the sufferings of Christ as a propitiation, a redemption, and a reconciliation. As being under the curse of the law, the sinner is guilty and exposed to the wrath of God; but in Christ his guilt is expiated and the wrath of God propitiated. The sinner is under bondage to Satan and sin, but through the redemptive price of the blood of Christ, he is delivered from bondage and set at liberty. The sinner is estranged from God, but is reconciled by the death on the cross. These Scriptures are peculiarly rich and satisfying.

1. Propitiation is a term drawn from the *Kapporeth* or Mercy-seat as used in the Old Testament. To propitiate is to appease the wrath of an offended person, or to atone for offenses. The term *hilasmos* (ἱλασμός) is used in three different senses in the New Testament. (1) Christ is the *hilasmos*, at once the Propitiator and the virtue of that propitiation. *He is the propitiation for our sins; and not for ours only, but also for the sins of the whole world* (I John 2: 2); *He loved us, and sent his Son to be the propitiation for our sins* (I John 4: 10). (2) He is the *hilastarion* (ἱλαστήριον) or Mercy-seat as the word is used in the Septuagint. *Whom God hath set forth to be a propitiation through faith in his blood* (Rom. 3: 25). (3) Where the adjective is used, then the term *thuma* (θύμα) is understood as in Hebrews 2: 17, where the high priest is said *to make reconciliation for the sins of the people.* Here the term is ἱλάσκεσθαι, and the correct meaning is "to make propitiation or atonement for the sins of the people."

2. Redemption is from the word which means literally "to buy back." The terms *lutroo* (λύτρόω) and *apolutrosis* (ἀπολύτρωσις), meaning to redeem and redemption, respectively, were used by the ancient Greeks and also by the New Testament writers, to signify the act of setting a captive free through the payment of a *lutron* (λύτρον) or redemptive price. The term, therefore, came to be used in a broader sense of a deliverance from every kind of evil, through a price paid by another. This is the true spiritual meaning of the following texts: *Being justified freely by his grace through the redemption that is in Christ Jesus* (Rom. 3: 24); *For ye are bought with a price: therefore glorify God in your body, and in your spirit which are God's* (I Cor. 6: 20); *Christ hath redeemed us from the curse of the law, being made a curse for us; for it is written, Cursed is every one that hangeth on a tree* (Gal. 3: 13). (Cf. also Eph. 1: 7; I Peter 1: 18, 19; Rev. 5: 9). The death of Christ is the redemptive price—He gave *his life a ransom* (λύτρον) *for many*

(Matt. 20: 28); and *gave himself a ransom for all* (I Tim. 2: 6). Here the idea of substitution is clearly evident— one thing is paid for another, the "blood of Christ" for the redemption of captives and condemned men.

3. Reconciliation is a term derived from the verbs *katallasso* (καταλλάσσω) or *apokatallasso* (ἀποκαταλλάσσω), both of which are translated "to reconcile." The words denote primarily, a mere change from one state to another, but as used in the Scriptures, this is a change from state of enmity to one of reconciliation and friendship. The Apostle Paul used the term freely. *For if, whn we were enemies, we were reconciled to God by the death of his Son, much more, being reconciled, we shall be saved by his life. And not only so, but we also joy in God through our Lord Jesus Christ, by whom we have now received the atonement* (or reconciliation, καταλλαγὴν) (Rom. 5: 10-11). *And you, that were sometime alienated and enemies in your mind by wicked works, yet now hath he reconciled in the body of his flesh through death, to present you holy and unblameable and unreproveable in his sight* (Col. 1: 20-22). In this and similar scriptures, it is clearly evident that the reconciliation between God and man is effected by Christ. But reconciliation means more than merely laying aside our enmity to God. The relation is a judicial one, and it is this judicial variance between God and man that is referred to in the idea of reconciliation. Moreover, the reconciliation is effected, not by the laying aside of our enmity, but by the nonimputation of our trespasses to us. This previous reconciliation of the world to Himself by the death of His Son, is to be distinguished also from the "word of reconciliation" which is to be proclaimed to the guilty, and by which they are entreated to be reconciled to God.

III. THEORIES OF THE ATONEMENT

In any consideration of the theories which have been advanced to explain the atonement, two things must be constantly kept in mind: *First,* a sharp distinction must be made between the fact of the atonement, and the theory advanced to explain it. One may by faith be a partaker of the benefits of the atonement, and yet not hold a proper theory of its explanation; and on the other hand, it is possible to hold a correct theory of the atonement and still be a stranger to its saving grace. *Second,* the errors found in the theories of the atonement are due largely to an undue emphasis upon one of its essential elements to the minifying or exclusion of other equally essential factors. Three essential elements must enter into any adequate theory of the atonement: (1) the idea of propitiation or satisfaction; (2) the necessity of upholding the dignity of the divine government; and (3) the drawing power of divine love. It is the emphasis upon the first that gives us the Penal Satisfaction theory, or other theories of propitiation; upon the second that gives us the Governmental or Rectoral theory; and upon the third which gives us the various moral influence theories. We can give only a brief review of the more important theories of the atonement.

A. *The Patristic Doctrine.*

The apostolic fathers taught that Christ gave Himself for our sins, but they did not formulate their views into any definite theory of the atonement. The popular view, which seems to have been first advanced by Irenaeus (c. 200 A.D.), was that the atonement was a victory over Satan. Origen (185-254) was the first to convert this popular idea into a theory that the ransom price was paid to Satan. Athanasius was probably the first to propound the theory that the death of Christ was the payment of a debt due to God. Apart from Augustine and his followers, it was the common belief that Christ died for all, and that it was the unfeigned will of God that all men should partake of this salvation through faith in Christ. Augustine himself taught this, until after his controversy with Pelagius, when he adopted the extreme monergistic position of effectual calling (cf. Ch. XV, Sec. IB.).

B. The Anselmic Theory of the Atonement.

Anselm (1033-1109) in the latter part of the eleventh century, published his epoch-making book, "Cur Deus Homo," in which he gives the first scientific statement to those views of the atonement which from the beginning had been held implicitly by the fathers. Here the idea of satisfaction to divine justice became the leading formula, and the Satisfaction Theory is still called by his name. Anselm rejected the theory of a ransom paid to Satan. His own theory may be thus stated. "Sin violates the divine honor and deserves infinite punishment, since God is infinite. Sin is guilt or debt, and under the government of God, this debt must be paid. Man cannot pay it, for he is bankrupt through sin. Consequently the Son of God became man in order to pay this debt for us. Being divine, He could pay the infinite debt; and being both human and sinless, He could properly represent mankind. But as sinless He was not obliged to die, and owing no debt on His own account, He received as a reward of merit, the forgiveness of our sins." This makes the redeeming work of Christ to center in His voluntary death. The weakness of the theory lies in its narrow and external conception of satisfaction. For this reason it is sometimes spoken of as the "Commercial Theory." Anselm held that Christ paid the debt in the exact amount of suffering that would have been the lot of condemned sinners throughout all eternity; and thus stresses quantity rather than the quality or dignity of Christ's sacrifice.

C. The Theory of Abelard.

Abelard (1079-1142) differed widely from Anselm. He maintained that it was the rebellion of man that needed subduing, and not the wrath of God which needed propitiation. In place of a satisfaction to divine justice, he held that the atonement should be regarded as a winning exhibition of divine love. Abelard's position became the basis of the later Socinianism, and the more modern moral influence theories.

D. *The Scholastic Theories.*

The scholastic period is important in that it marks the beginning of those trends which later developed into the Tridentine soteriology of the Roman Catholic Church; or into the strict Penal Satisfaction Theory of the earlier Protestant Reformers. (1) Peter Lombard (1100-1164) in his *Liber Sententiarum* followed Abelard, and held that the work of Christ must be supplemented by baptism and penance. (2) Thomas Aquinas followed Anselm but was responsible for several new developments. He held that merit and demerit are strictly personal, and in order to substantiate the idea of vicarious satisfaction, proposed a *unio mystica,* or mystical union existing between Christ and the Church. Thus a sinner united by faith to the Saviour, may become the ground and cause of judicial infliction of penalty upon his atoning Substitute; and in turn, the incarnate Word may become the sinner's propitiation. His distinction between merit and satisfaction later developed into the doctrine of the imputation of Christ's active and passive righteousness; and his teaching concerning the superabundance of Christ's merit led directly to the Roman Catholic theory of supererogation, with a treasury of merit at the command of the Church. His doctrine of a relative, rather than an absolute satisfaction resulted later, in a theory of justification based partly upon the work of Christ, and partly upon the penitential works of the individual. (3) Duns Scotus followed Abelard rather than Anselm, and from this there arose in the Church, two opposing parties known as the Thomists and Scotists. He taught that the relation between the atonement and sin was merely an arbitrary one. God was pleased to accept this particular sacrifice as an offset or equivalent for human transgression, because He so pleased and not because of its intrinsic value. He might have accepted any other substitute, or He might have dispensed with a substitute, making forgiveness a matter solely of His divine authority.

E. *The Tridentine or Roman Catholic Theory.*

The Roman Catholic theory adopted by the Council of Trent, is the outgrowth of the principles of Bonaventura and Thomas Aquinas. The *unio mystica* of the latter identified in some sense, the incarnation and the atonement. This union is supposed to have sanctified the race by the transference of the merit of Christ to the sinner, and the guilt of the sinner to Christ. The sacraments were regarded as an extension of the incarnation, and therefore by partaking of the bread, the communicant is brought into immediate relation with the humanity of Christ and consequently becomes the recipient of divine grace. The *unio mystica*, however, gave rise to certain fundamental errors: (1) it contradicted the universality of the atonement in that redemption was limited to the believer configured to his Lord; and (2) it regarded personal penance as a form of expiation joined to that of Christ.

Growing out of the Reformation period, we have a number of theories, especially the Penal Satisfaction theory; the Governmental or Rectoral theory; and the various Moral Influence theories. Also in more modern times we have the Ethical theory of Dr. A. H. Strong, and the Racial theory of Dr. Olin A. Curtis. These now demand our attention.

F. *The Penal Satisfaction Theory.*

This is the theory generally held by the Reformed Churches, and is frequently known as the Calvinistic theory. Dr. A. A. Hodge sums up the theory in the following essential points: "(1) Sin for its own sake deserves the wrath and curse of God. (2) God is disposed, from the very excellence of His nature, to treat His creatures as they deserve. (3) To satisfy the righteous judgment of God, His Son assumed our nature, was made under the law, fulfilled all righteousness, and bore the punishment of our sins. (4) By His righteousness, those who believe are constituted righteous, His merit being so imputed to them that they are regarded as righteous in the sight of God" (A. A. HODGE, *Outline of Theology,*

p. 303). This theory emphasizes the substitutionary work of Christ, but in too narrow and mechanical a manner. It is frequently claimed by its advocates, as the only theory which admits of substitution, but the Governmental theory of Grotius, and the modified Propitiatory theory of Arminius and Wesley, holds this fact as fully, and more properly than does the Penal Satisfaction theory.

This form of satisfaction theory is open to several serious objections. (1) If Christ bore the sinner's punishment as a Substitute, then the sinner is unconditionally free from it, for both the sinner and the Substitute cannot be justly punished for the same offense. The theory, therefore, leads necessarily, either to universalism on the one hand, or unconditional election on the other. (2) Since the penal substitutionary theory denies that all men are unconditionally saved, as universalism maintains, it follows immediately that the atonement must be limited to the elect, whereas the Scriptures declare that Christ died provisionally for all men. (3) The Satisfaction theory leads logically also, to antinomianism, or a disregard of the law. It holds that Christ's active obedience is imputed to believers in such a manner, that it is esteemed by God as having been done by them. In a sense, this makes Christ's obedience superfluous, for if He has done all that the law requires, why should we be under the necessity of being delivered from death? Also, if Christ's active obedience is substituted for that of the believer, it shuts out the necessity of personal obedience to God. Lastly, this type of *satisfaction* cannot be called such in truth, for it is merely the performance of all that the law requires by one person in substitution for another.

G. *The Governmental or Rectoral Theory.*

The Governmental theory of the atonement arose in protest against the rigorous penal substitution theory mentioned above. The theory was first advanced by James Arminius (1560-1609) and his follower, Hugo Grotius (1583-1645), who together agreed to uphold, not the exactitude of divine justice wholly, or even mainly as in the Anselmic theory, but also the just and compassionate will of God as a true element in the atonement. Later Grotius departed from the earlier position in some points, especially in limiting the satisfaction made by Christ to the dignity of the law, the honor of the Law-giver, and the protection of the universe. In patterning his idea of the atonement after the method of civil law, he really transformed it into a new theory, now known as the Governmental or Rectoral theory of the atonement. The central idea of this theory is, that God is not to be regarded merely as an offended party, but as the Moral Governor of the universe. He must therefore uphold the authority of His government in the interests of the general good. Consequently the sufferings of Christ are to be regarded, not as the exact equivalent of our punishment, but only in the sense that the dignity of the government was thereby upheld and vindicated as effectively as it would have been, if we had received the punishment we deserved.

A modified form of the Governmental theory was held by Richard Watson, but with more emphasis upon propitiation. In modern times, Dr. John Miley is the outstanding proponent of the Governmental theory, but out of its fundamental principles, he constructs a theory which is distinctly his own. We may say that while moral responsibility is an essential element in the atonement, the evil goes deeper than merely that of a broken law. It strikes deep into the nature of God and therefore demands propitiation. It suffers, therefore, more as an inadequate than as an erroneous theory. Its greatest defect appears to be an emphasis upon expediency, rather than satisfaction.

H. *The Moral Influence Theories.*

The moral influence theories take their name from the basic assumption, that salvation comes through the appeal of divine love, rather than through a satisfaction of divine justice. These theories do not regard the sacrifice of Christ as influencing the divine mind, but as furnishing an appeal to the sinner. The atonement does not expiate sin, or placate the divine wrath by suffering, or in any wise satisfy divine justice. They maintain that the sole obstacle to the forgiveness of sins is to be found in the sinner's own unbelief and hardness of heart. Christ's death, therefore, was designed to be the appeal of love rather than a display of wrath against sin. These theories are numerous and can be given only brief mention here.

1. *Socinianism*. This theory was first advanced by Laelius and Faustus Socinus, and represents the seventeenth century attack of rationalism against the penal satisfaction theory. Dr. A. H. Strong calls it "The Example Theory of the Atonement," for it denies any idea of propitiation or satisfaction. It holds that Christ's death was merely that of a noble martyr, whose loyalty to truth and faithfulness to duty, furnish us with a noble incentive to moral improvement. We are saved, therefore, by following His example. God is free to forgive sin without any satisfaction to divine justice. Repentance is the sole ground of forgiveness, although the death of Christ as an exhibition of divine love is intended to remove the hardness of the sinner's heart as an obstacle to repentance. It is evident that this theory, instead of explaining, merely denies the necessity of an atonement.

2. *The Mystical Theories*. These represent the type of moral influence theory as held by Schleiermacher, Ritschl, Maurice, Irving and others of like faith. The mysticism lies in the identification of Christ with the race in the sense that He rendered the perfect devotion and obedience which we ought to have rendered, and which in some sense mankind did render in Him. Since atonement and incarnation are so closely identified, these theories are sometimes known as "Redemption by Incarnation." Dr. Bruce speaks of them as "Redemption by Sample." Like Socinianism, they deny the vicarious atonement, in that they represent Christ as suffering with humanity instead of for it. They also emphasize the love of God in such a manner as to exclude the demands

of His holiness. They must therefore, be regarded as erroneous theories.

3. *Bushnell's Theory of Moral Influence.* This theory is frequently referred to as the clearest and best statement of moral influence in relation to the atonement. Dr. Miley calls it the theory of "Self-propitiation by Self-sacrifice." It belongs to the class of mystical theories, in that it regards the race as identified with Christ, but is given separate mention because of its distinct character. Dr. Bushnell resolves Christ's priesthood into "sympathy"; that is, there are certain moral sentiments similar in God and similar in man, such as the repulsiveness of sin and resentment against wrong, which must not be extirpated, but mastered and allowed to remain. God, therefore, forgives just as man does. So God must propitiate the cost and suffering for our good. "This He did in sacrifice on the cross, that sublime act of cost, in which God has bent Himself downward in loss and sorrow, over the hard face of sin, to say, and in saying to make good 'Thy sins be forgiven thee' " (BUSHNELL, *Forgiveness and Law*, p. 35). There is here no propitiation by Christ's death, but only suffering in and with the sins of His creatures. The theory is strictly Socinian and Unitarian, although Bushnell himself was a trinitarian.

4. *The New Theology.* This is a term applied to the more systematized forms of the mystical theory of the atonement, as found in the writings of John McLeod Campbell (1800-1872) of Scotland, and the Andover School of New England. The former taught that Christ made a perfect confession and an adequate repentance of sin for us. For this reason Dr. Dickie calls this the theory of "Vicarious Repentance." Campbell held also that Christ was the Head of a new humanity, in which He lives as a quickening Spirit, imparting to it the same attitude toward God's holiness and love, as were realized in His own life. Christ, therefore, discovered in man an inestimable preciousness which He brought into manifestation. Whether rightly or wrongly, this was interpreted to mean that man has in him an element of the divine, and the difference is in degree not in kind. For

this reason the New Theology came into immediate conflict with the older orthodox beliefs. Two errors attached to this belief: (1) it lowered the conception of Christ's deity and led immediately to unitarianism; and (2) it precluded the idea of total depravity and therefore minified both sin and redemption. The Andover School held more nearly to the cosmological view of Christ's work, regarding Him as a representative of the race in the suffering for sin and repenting of it, but denies any propitiation or atonement for sin.

Aside from the three historical theories, the Satisfaction, Governmental, and Moral Influence theories, there are two other modern theories deserving of special mention. These are the Ethical Theory of Dr. A. H. Strong, and the Racial Theory of Dr. Olin A. Curtis.

I. *The Ethical Theory.*

The Ethical theory has sometimes inadvertently been confused with the Moral Influence theories, from which it widely differs. It is instead, a reinterpretation of the Penal Satisfaction theory. Dr. A. H. Strong arranges his material according to two main principles (1) *The Atonement as Related to the Holiness of God.* The Ethical theory holds that the necessity for atonement is grounded in the holiness of God, of which conscience in man is a finite reflection. The ethical principle demands that sin shall be punished. The atonement, then, must be regarded as the satisfaction of an ethical demand in the divine nature, through the substitution of Christ's penal sufferings for the punishment of the guilty. (2) *The Atonement as Related to the Humanity of Christ.* The Ethical theory maintains that Christ stands in such relation to humanity, that what God's holiness demands, Christ is under obligation to pay, longs to pay, and pays so fully that the claim of justice is satisfied. The atonement on the part of man, therefore, is accomplished through the solidarity of the race, of which Christ was its representative and surety; and yet who justly yet voluntarily bore its guilt, condemnation and shame as

His own (cf. STRONG, *Systematic Theology*, I, pp. 750-771).

J. *The Racial Theory.*

Here again we must guard against the error of supposing that Dr. Curtis is teaching the doctrine of universal salvation. In his excellent work entitled *The Christian Faith* (pp. 316-334), Dr. Olin A. Curtis introduces the subject by giving an account of his dissatisfaction with the three historical theories, and his attempt to combine the essential qualities of each by the method of eclectic synthesis. The main points of his theory may be summed up as follows: (1) The new race is by the death of Christ, so related to the Adamic race penally, that it must express in perfect continuity God's condemnation of sin. (2) The center of the new race is the Son of God himself, with a human racial experience completed by suffering. (3) The new race is so constituted that it can be entered only on the most rigid moral terms. (4) The race moves through history as the one thoroughly reliable servant of the moral concern of God. (5) This new race makes it possible for each human being to find a holy completion of himself in his brethren and in his Redeemer, in perfect service, rest and joy. (6) This new race will finally be the victorious realization of God's original design in creation.

IV. THE EXTENT AND BENEFITS OF THE ATONEMENT

A. *The Universal Scope of the Atonement.*

The atonement is universal. This does not mean that all mankind will be unconditionally saved, but that the sacrificial offering of Christ so far satisfied the claims of the divine law as to make salvation a possibility for all. Redemption is therefore universal or general in the provisional sense, but special or conditional in its application to the individual. It is for this reason that the universal aspect is sometimes known as the sufficiency of the atonement. Two Scripture texts taken in their relation to each other, stand out with peculiar distinctness. The first is the statement of our Lord, that

The Son of man came . . . . to give his life a ransom for many (Matt. 20: 28). The second is generally considered to be the last statement of St. Paul on this subject, and is evidently a quotation from the previous scripture. *Who gave himself a ransom for all* (I Tim. 2: 6). Note that each of the principal words is given a stronger connotation: the life becomes the self; the purchase price, the personal Redeemer; and the many, the all.

The scripture passages bearing upon this subject have already been presented in a general way, and we need here merely to give additional references. We group them according to the following simple outline. (1) Those scriptures which speak of the atonement in universal terms: (John 3: 16, 17; Rom. 5: 8, 18; II Cor. 5: 14, 15; I Tim. 2: 4; 4: 10; Heb. 2: 9; 10: 29; II Peter 2: 1; I John 2: 2; 4: 14). (2) Those which refer to the universal proclamation of the gospel and its accompaniments: (Matt. 24: 14; 28: 19; Mark 16: 15; Luke 24: 47; cf. also Mark 1: 15; 16: 16; John 3: 36; Acts 17: 30). (3) Those which distinctly declare that Christ died for those who may perish: Rom. 14: 15; I Cor. 8: 11; Heb. 10: 29).

Arminianism with its emphasis upon moral freedom and prevenient grace, has always held to the universality of the atonement; that is, as a provision for the salvation of all men, conditioned upon faith. Calvinism, on the other hand, by its doctrine of the decrees, its unconditional election, and its penal satisfaction theory, has always been under the necessity of accepting the idea of a limited atonement.

B. *The Unconditional Benefits of the Atonement.*

Closely related to the question concerning the extent of the atonement, is that of the benefits of the atonement. Within the range or scope of the redemptive work, all things are included, both spiritual and physical. Every blessing known to man is the result of the purchase price of our Lord Jesus Christ, and comes down from the Father of lights. These benefits may be summed up under two main heads, the Unconditional Benefits, and the Conditional Benefits.

The unconditional benefits of the atonement are those which belong to the race as a whole, and which are given to all men unconditionally. These include the continued existence of the race, the restoration of all men to a state of salvability, and the salvation of infants.

1. *The Continued Existence of the Race.* It is hardly conceivable that the race would have been allowed to multiply in its sin and depravity, had no provision been made for its salvation. Yet had it not been for the divine intervention, the immediate death of the first pair would doubtless have taken place, and with it the termination of their earthly career.

2. *The Restoration of All Men to Salvability.* The atonement provided for all men unconditionally, the free gift of grace. This included the restoration of the Holy Spirit to the race as the Spirit of enlightenment, striving and conviction. Thus man is not only given the capacity for proper probation, but is granted the gracious aid of the Holy Spirit.

3. *The Salvation of Infants.* We must regard the atonement as accomplishing the actual salvation of those who die in infancy. This we may admit is not stated explicitly in the Scriptures, and in the past has been the subject of much debate. The general tenor of the Scriptures, however, when viewed in the light of divine love and the universal grace of the Spirit, will allow no other conclusion. Dr. Miner Raymond sums up the generally accepted Arminian position as follows: "The doctrine of inherited depravity involves the idea of inherited disqualification for eternal life. The salvation of infants, then, has primary regard to a preparation for the blessedness of heaven—it may have regard to a title thereto; not all newly created beings, nor those sustaining similar relations, are by any natural right entitled to a place among holy angels and glorified saints. The salvation of infants cannot be regarded as a salvation from the peril of eternal death. They have not committed sin, the only thing that incurs such a peril. The idea that they are in danger of eternal death because of Adam's transgres-

sion, is at most nothing more than the idea of a theoretic peril. But if it be insisted that *by the offense of one, judgment came upon all men to* (a literal and actual) *condemnation,* we insist that from the condemnation, be it what it may, theoretic or literal, all men are saved; for *by the righteousness of one the free gift came upon all men unto justification of life,* so that the conditions and relations of the race in infancy differ from those of newly created beings solely in that, by the natural law of propagation, a corrupted nature is inherited. As no unclean thing or unholy person can be admitted into the presence of God and to the society of holy angels and glorified saints, it follows that if infants are taken to heaven, some power, purifying, sanctifying, their souls, must be vouchsafed unto them; the saving influence of the Holy Spirit must be, for Christ's sake, unconditionally bestowed. Not only their preparation for, but also their title to, and the enjoyment of the blessedness of heaven comes, as came their existence, through the shed blood of our Lord Jesus Christ" (RAYMOND, *Systematic Theology,* II, pp. 311-312).

C. *The Conditional Benefits of the Atonement.*

The conditional benefits of the atonement are: (1) Justification, (2) Regeneration, (3) Adoption, (4) The Witness of the Spirit, and (5) Entire Sanctification. These must furnish the subjects of our discussion of the states of salvation. Before taking up these subjects, however, we must first give attention to the offices and work of the Holy Spirit as the Administrator of the great salvation, purchased through the atonement of our Lord Jesus Christ.

D. *The Intercession of Christ.*

There is another transitional point which needs to be mentioned, in addition to the conditional benefits of the atonement mentioned above. This is the intercession of Christ. The New Testament does not teach that the work of Christ ceased with the coming of the Holy Spirit. It teaches that His finished work of atonement was only the ground for the work of administration, which He

himself was to continue through the Spirit. He died for
the sins of the past, that He might establish a new covenant; He arose that He might become the executive of
His own will. His continued activity consists in carrying
into effect through the Spirit, the merits of His atoning
death. As a consequence of Christ's intercession for us,
the Holy Spirit is given as an intercessory presence within the hearts of men. The intercession of Christ at the
right hand of God, and the intercession of the Spirit
within, are in perfect harmony, for the Spirit takes the
things of Christ and shows them unto us.

UNIT V

THE DOCTRINES OF SALVATION

Preview

Salvation! What a thrilling word that is! "Christ Jesus came into the world to save sinners." His coming was not primarily to teach men, or to show men how they should live by His matchless example, but to save those who were hopelessly lost in sin: *And thou shalt call his name Jesus, for he shall save his people from their sins.* To study the doctrines related to this joyous experience of freedom from sin is the purpose of this, our fifth unit.

We begin with an examination of the person and work of the Holy Spirit, the "Executive of the Godhead," by whose gracious ministrations all the benefits of Christ's atonement are made available to us. How utterly dependent we are on the blessed Spirit of God, in this, His dispensation! Our study then passes over into the preliminary states of grace with emphasis on the gospel call, repentance, and saving faith. That brings us to a consideration of the first great crisis of Christian experience, the new birth, or the "birth from above." This we examine in its various aspects: justification in the sight of God, regeneration or inner spiritual renewal, and adoption into the family of God.

We are then ready to consider the second crisis of Christian experience, heart holiness—the central idea and purpose of redemption. This gracious experience is analyzed in the concluding chapters of the unit under the dual terms "entire Sanctification" and "Christian Perfection." Much of the criticism of this state of grace is based upon sheer ignorance or willful misrepresentation. Here, then, we shall need to be humble, diligent, and teachable in our search to know the whole will of God—and do it. May the Spirit of Truth himself be our companion and teacher.

UNIT V

THE DOCTRINES OF SALVATION

Chapter XIV. *The Person and Work of the Holy Spirit*

I. THE PROGRESSIVE REVELATION OF THE HOLY SPIRIT
  A. The Holy Spirit in His Preparatory Economy.
  B. The Holy Spirit and the Incarnation.
  C. The Holy Spirit and the Earthly Ministry of Jesus.

II. THE DISPENSATION OF THE HOLY SPIRIT
  A. The Holy Spirit and Pentecost.
  B. The Offices of the Holy Spirit.
    1. The Fruit of the Spirit.
    2. The Gifts of the Spirit.
    3. The Holy Spirit and the Work of Salvation.
  C. The Holy Spirit and the Church.
  D. The Holy Spirit and the World.

Chapter XV. *The Preliminary States of Grace*

I. THE GOSPEL VOCATION OR CALL
  A. The General Nature of the Gospel Call.
  B. Election and Predestination.
    1. The Calvinistic View of Predestination and Election.
    2. The Arminian View of Predestination and Election.
  C. Elements in the Gospel Call.

II. PREVENIENT GRACE
  A. Grace and Prevenient Grace.
  B. The Nature of Prevenient Grace.

III. REPENTANCE
  A. The Importance of Redemption.
  B. The Nature of Repentance.
  C. Representative Definitions of Repentance.

Chapter XVII. *Entire Sanctification or Christian Perfection*

I. HISTORICAL APPROACH TO THE DOCTRINE OF ENTIRE SANCTIFICATION

    A. The Testimony of the Apostolic Fathers.

    B. The Teaching of the Later Church Fathers.

    C. The Teaching of the Mystics.

    D. Roman Catholic Doctrine.

    E. Calvinistic Views of Sanctification.

    F. The Teaching of Arminianism and Wesleyanism.

    G. Other Modern Views of Sanctification.

II. THE SCRIPTURAL BASIS OF ENTIRE SANCTIFICATION

    A. Holiness Is the New Testament Standard of Christian Experience.

        1. It Is the Will of God that His People Be Holy.

        2. God Has Promised to Sanctify His People.

        3. God Commands His People to Be Holy.

    B. Entire Sanctification as a Second Work of Grace.

    C. Tense Reading of the Greek New Testament.

III. THE MEANING AND SCOPE OF SANCTIFICATION

    A. Definitions of Entire Sanctification.

    B. Justification and Sanctification.

    C. The Existence of Sin in the Regenerate.

    D. Entire Sanctification Is Subsequent to Regeneration.

    E. The Divinely Appointed Means and Agencies in Sanctification.

    F. Progressive Sanctification.

Chapter XVIII. *Entire Sanctification or Christian Perfection* (Continued)

I. ENTIRE SANCTIFICATION

    A. Entire Sanctification as Purification from Sin.

    B. Entire Sanctification as a Positive Devotement to God.

    C. The Divine and Human Elements in Entire Sanctification.

II. Christian Perfection

CHAPTER XIV

THE PERSON AND WORK OF THE HOLY SPIRIT

"When our Lord cried *It is finished!* He declared that His work of atonement was accomplished. But it was accomplished only as a provision for the salvation of men. The application of the benefit remained for the administration of the Spirit from heaven; whose sole and supreme office it is to carry into effect every design of the redemptive economy or undertaking. As the spirit of the Christ had from the foundation of the world administered the evangelical preparations, so now He acts on behalf of the fully revealed Christ. Through Him our Lord continues His prophetic office: the Holy Ghost is the Inspirer of the New Scriptures and the Supreme Teacher in the new economy. Through Him the priestly office is in another sense perpetuated: the ministry of reconciliation is a ministration of the Spirit. And through Him the Lord administers His regal authority."—DR. WILLIAM B. POPE.

Our purpose in this chapter is to discuss the person and work of the Holy Spirit under two general themes. His progressive revelation; and His administrative work. We have already observed that there is in the Scriptures a step-by-step revelation of the Son. So also is there a corresponding and similar revelation of the Holy Spirit. Only at Pentecost was He fully revealed.

As the incarnate Son is the Redeemer of mankind by virtue of His atoning work, so the Holy Spirit, the Executive of the Godhead, is the administrator of that redemption. It is our high privilege to live in the Dispensation of the Holy Spirit. In this era the revelation of His Person and Work is full, clear, and personally significant. It is important, therefore, that we obtain an accurate understanding of these facts as they relate to the Plan of Redemption and our personal salvation.

I. THE PROGRESSIVE REVELATION OF THE HOLY SPIRIT

In our discussion of the Trinity (Ch. VII, Sec. III), we noted the abundance of scriptural teaching concerning the personality of the Holy Spirit. He is more than a sacred influence. Indeed, He is the third Person of the adorable Trinity. Personal pronouns are used with reference to Him in Holy Writ, personal activities are predicated of Him, and personal treatment is rendered to Him. In view of the fact that He is the Person who completes the Godhead, His revelation was of necessity the last to be made manifest. He could not come as the Administrator of Christ's atoning work until the earthly ministry of the Master was completed. He could not be fully revealed until after the death, resurrection, and glorification of Christ. Thus it was only at Pentecost that the Holy Spirit as a Person could be wholly revealed.

A. *The Holy Spirit in His Preparatory Economy.*

While the full dispensation of the Holy Spirit does not begin until Pentecost, the Spirit himself as the third Person of the Trinity was from the beginning operative in both creation and providence. It was the Spirit who brooded over the waters and brought order and beauty out of chaos (Gen. 1:2); and it was the Spirit who breathed into the face of man and made him a living soul (Gen. 2:7; Job 33:4). He has been the Agent in the production of all life, and is therefore, by prophetic anticipation, the Lord and Giver of life.

The relation of the Holy Spirit to mankind after the fall, and previous to the coming of Jesus Christ, assumes four principal forms of which Abel, Abraham, Moses, and the prophets are representative types. First, there is the direct striving of the Spirit with the consciences of men in a purely personal and private manner. Abel yielded to these strivings but Cain did not do so. The wickedness of men increased until at the time of the flood the condemnation of God was expressed in these fearful words, *My spirit shall not always strive with man for that he also is flesh* (Gen. 6:3). The second aspect of the Spirit's operation with man was through the family. The promise was made to Abraham and his seed (Gal. 3:16). The family forms a new order, a new locality for the Spirit's communications. The called-out family of Abraham was the church in germ, and therefore the first historical beginning of a religious community.

The third stage in the operation of the Spirit is found in the giving of the law through Moses. To the internal striving of the Spirit was added an external mode of appeal. This law was moral, ceremonial, and judicial. That portion known as the Ten Commandments is said to have been given by "the finger of God," an expression which is interchangeable with "the Spirit of God" (Matt. 12: 28; Luke 11: 20). The fourth and last method of the Spirit's operation in the preparatory economy is found in the voice of the prophets, *Holy men of God spake as they were moved by the Holy Ghost* (II Peter 1: 21). The law served to give permanence to the moral ideal and its violation involved guilt (Rom. 3: 20). But, the law being a fixed instrument, men soon began to give more attention to its outward forms than to its inward spirit. Hence the prophets arose. They appealed to the hopes and fears of men, and this gave inward content to the outward forms. Not only was appeal made to law, but the prophets furnished a devotional literature and directed men's attention to the promised Redeemer.

B. *The Holy Spirit and the Incarnation.*

The incarnation of Jesus Christ was accomplished by the Holy Spirit. As the bond of union between the Father and the Son, it was appropriate that He should effect the high and singular union between the uncreated and the created natures in the One Person of Christ. The angelic message to the Virgin Mary was to the effect that *The Holy Ghost shall come upon thee, and the power of the Highest shall overshadow thee: therefore also that holy thing which shall be born of thee shall be called the Son of God* (Luke 1: 35).

It is significant that the mystery of the incarnation made possible the unveiling of the Holy Spirit as the third Person of the Trinity. Until the Annunciation, the Holy Spirit had never been revealed as a distinct Personal Agent. Never before had He been called by His own name. Previous to that time He was always mentioned in connection with the other divine Persons. In the penitential Psalm it is *take not* THY *holy spirit from me*

(Psalms 51: 11); and in Isaiah, *they rebelled, and vexed his holy Spirit* (Isa. 63: 10). Consequently the term is used relatively and not in the absolute sense. The full disclosure of His personality and perfections was not made until the set time for His inauguration.

C. *The Holy Spirit and the Earthly Ministry of Jesus.*

During the earthly ministry of Jesus, He alone did not act through His humanity. This humanity was also the temple of the Holy Spirit, which God gave to Him without measure (John 3: 34). Whatever belonged to the Son as the Representative of man was under the immediate direction of the Holy Spirit. The Holy Spirit guided and sustained Him in every experience of His earthly life, presiding over His entire earthly ministry. This subordination of the Son to the Spirit ceased when the Redeemer laid down His life of Himself. After His ascension the Son received of the Father the promise of the Holy Spirit; and by a strange reversal, He who was presided over by the Spirit during His humiliation, now in His exaltation becomes the Giver of that same Spirit to the Church (Acts 2: 33).

The Holy Spirit as the future Agent of Christ's ministry was the object of prophecy during our Lord's earthly life. This appears first in the words, *How much more shall your heavenly Father give the Holy Spirit to them that ask him?* (Luke 11: 13). Here is the faint dawn of the pentecostal day. The second prediction took place at the close of the great day of the feast, when Jesus stood and cried, saying, *If any man thirst, let him come unto me, and drink* (John 7: 37). In a parenthetical expression, St. John explains that our Lord referred to the Spirit *which they that believe on him should receive: for the Holy Ghost was not yet given; because that Jesus was not yet glorified* (John 7: 39). The full and complete foreannouncement is found in the farewell discourses of Jesus (John 14: 16, 17, 26). Here it is declared that the Comforter, as the Spirit which dwelt in Christ, should dwell in His people also. This Comforter or Paraclete, is the Spirit of truth, and as such is the Revealer of the Person of Christ. He will not speak of Himself during the pentecostal age, but will glorify only the Son, taking the things of Christ and making them known to the Church. As the Son came to reveal the Father, so the Holy Spirit comes to reveal the Son. The farewell discourses of Jesus, therefore, in a peculiar sense, furnish us with a revelation of the Trinity—the unity of the one God in the distinction of the three persons.

II. THE DISPENSATION OF THE HOLY SPIRIT

A. *The Holy Spirit and Pentecost.*

Pentecost marks a new dispensation of grace—that of the Holy Spirit. This new economy is not to be understood as superseding the work of Christ but as ministering to, and completing it. Jesus indicated that *all things that the Father hath are mine: therefore said I, that he shall take of mine, and shall shew it unto you* (John 16: 15). As the Son revealed the Father, so the Spirit reveals the Son and glorifies Him. *No man can say that Jesus is the Lord but by the Holy Ghost* (I Cor. 12: 3). The work of the Holy Spirit as the Third Person of the Trinity is in connection with His offices as the Representative of the Saviour. He is the Agent of Christ, representing Him in the salvation of the individual soul, in the formation of the Church, and in the witnessing power of the Church in the world. But He is not the Representative of an absentee Saviour. He is our Lord's ever-present other Self. This is the meaning of the promise, *I will not leave you comfortless: I will come to you* (John 14: 18). It is through the Spirit that our Lord enters upon His higher ministry of the Spirit. For this reason, He declared, *It is expedient for you that I go away: for if I go not away, the Comforter will not come unto you* (John 16: 7).

Pentecost was the inauguration day of the Holy Spirit, and the pentecostal Gift was the gift of a Person— the Paraclete or Comforter. This Gift Jesus promised to His disciples as the Agent through whom He would continue His office and work in a new and more effective manner. As the advent of Christ was attended by miraculous signs, so also the inauguration of the Holy Spirit was attended by signs indicative of His Person and work. These signs were three: *first,* the sound as of a rushing mighty wind; *second,* the cloven tongues like as of fire resting upon the disciples; and *third,* the gift of other tongues. The *first* forecast His coming; the *second* indicated His arrival; and the *third* marked at once the assumption of His office as Administrator, and the beginning of His operations.

The first inaugural sign was that of the rushing mighty wind which filled all the house where they were sitting (Acts 2: 2). The sound came suddenly and seems to have reached its height immediately. The sound also came from heaven and was heard not only by the disciples but throughout the city: *When the sound was heard, the multitude came together* (Acts 2: 6, R.V.). This sign is indicative of the inner, mysterious, spiritual power of the Holy Spirit which was to characterize His administration in the Church and in the world. It is suggestive also of an intense eagerness on the part of the Spirit to carry into effect the great salvation purchased by the blood of Christ.

The second inaugural sign was the appearance of *cloven tongues like as of fire,* which sat upon each of them (Acts 2: 3). It is generally believed that a cloven or forked tongue *like as of fire* sat independently upon each of the disciples. These *cloven tongues* were glowing, quivering flames which gleamed like a corona above the heads of the spiritual Israel, recalling the signs of Mount Sinai, when the Lord descended in fire and the whole mount quaked greatly (Exod. 19: 18). The significance of this symbol is to be found in the purifying, penetrating, energizing, and transforming effect of the Spirit's administration. The cloven tongues signify the varied gifts communicated by the one Spirit to the different members of the mystical body of Christ.

The third inaugural sign occupies a unique position in the events of the day. It is described as follows: *And they were all filled with the Holy Ghost, and began to*

*speak with other tongues as the Spirit gave them ut-
terance* (Acts 2:4). This sign not only signifies the
Spirit's coming, but also the actual beginning of His
operations. By a miraculous operation He enabled the
disciples to declare the wondrous works of God in such
a manner that the representatives of the nations heard
them in their own languages. The words here translated
"other tongues" occur only in this instance in the entire
New Testament, and they connote the idea of rational
utterance or an intelligible language. They may signify
an ecstatic utterance but never a mere jargon of sounds
without coherence or intelligibility. This phenomenon
of Pentecost was clearly a miraculous gift of intelligible
languages.

B. *The Offices of the Holy Spirit.*

The Holy Spirit is both Gift and Giver. He is the Gift
of the glorified Christ to the Church, and abides within
it as a creating and energizing Presence. This center of
life and light and love is the Paraclete or the abiding
Comforter. Following His inauguration at Pentecost the
Holy Spirit became the Executive of the Godhead on
earth. He is now the Agent of both the Father and the
Son, in whom they hold residence (John 14:23), and
through whom men alone can have access to God. The
Holy Spirit as the Giver, or Administrator of redemption ministers in two distinct though related fields—
that of the fruit of the Spirit, and that of the gifts of the
Spirit.

1. *The Fruit of the Spirit.* The fruit of the Spirit is
the communication to the individual of the graces flowing from the divine nature, and has its issue in character rather than in special qualifications for service.
When St. Paul catalogs the nine graces (Gal. 5:22-23)
which constitute the fruit of the Spirit, he possibly had
in mind the parable of our Lord concerning the vine and
the branches (John 15:1-5). In the apostle's list of
graces there are three relating to God—love, joy, and
peace; three that relate to others—longsuffering, gentleness, and goodness; and three that relate to ourselves—

faithfulness, meekness, and temperance or self-control. These qualities of character result from continued and vital contact with the Vine. They are strongly contrasted with works of the flesh (Gal. 5: 19-23).

2. *The Gifts of the Spirit.* These are gifts of grace. They are the divinely ordained means and powers with which Christ endows His Church in order to enable it to properly perform its task on earth. Paul's summary concerning spiritual gifts is as follows: *Now there are diversities of gifts, but the same Spirit. And there are differences of administration, but the same Lord. And there are diversities of operations, but it is the same God which worketh all in all. But the manifestation of the Spirit is given to every man to profit withal. For to one is given by the Spirit the word of wisdom; to another the word of knowledge by the same Spirit; to another faith by the same Spirit; to another the gifts of healing by the same Spirit; to another the working of miracles; to another prophecy; to another discerning of spirits; to another divers kinds of tongues; to another the interpretation of tongues: but all these worketh that one and the selfsame Spirit, dividing to every man severally as he will* (I Cor. 12: 4-11); (cf. also Eph. 4: 11; Rom. 12: 6-8).

The gifts of the Spirit are supernatural endowments for service, and are determined by the character of the ministry to be accomplished. They are vital to the successful achievement of the mission of the Church. Such gifts are distributed as the Spirit wills. They are related to, but distinguished from, natural gifts and abilities. Not all members of the Church are similarly endowed. There is a diversity of gifts in the Church (I Cor. 12: 29-30). These divine bestowments upon individual members determine their functions in the body of Christ (I Cor. 12: 21-25), and constitute essential factors in the spiritual progress of the Church in every age.

3. *The Holy Spirit and the Work of Salvation.* The administrative acts or functions of the Spirit which pertain especially to the work of salvation may be classified under two general heads—the Holy Spirit as "the Giver

of life," and the Holy Spirit as "a sanctifying Presence." To the former belongs the birth of the Spirit or the initial experience of salvation; to the latter, the baptism with the Spirit—a subsequent work by which the soul is made holy. This is known as entire sanctification which is "wrought by the baptism with the Holy Spirit, and comprehends in one experience the cleansing of the heart from sin and the abiding presence of the Holy Spirit, empowering the believer for life and service" (*Manual*, Article X).

The birth of the Spirit is the impartation of divine life to the soul. It is not merely a reconstruction or working over of the old life; it is the impartation to the soul, or the implantation within the soul, of the new life of the Spirit. It is therefore a "birth from above." The Holy Spirit infuses life into souls dead in trespasses and sins, and thereby sets them up as distinct individuals in the spiritual realm. These individuals are the children of God. To them is given the spirit of adoption by which they are constituted heirs of God and joint heirs with Christ (Rom. 8: 15-17).

While the child of God as an individual possesses life in Christ, there is in him also the "carnal mind" or inbred sin, and this prevents him from entering fully into his New Testament privileges in Christ. Jesus as the Lamb of God came to take away *the* SIN *of the world.* There must therefore be a purification from sin. Analyzing this further experience of entire sanctification, from the viewpoint of the Agent rather than the work wrought, we notice a threefold operation of the Spirit in the one experience of the believer: the *baptism,* which in its restricted sense refers to the act of purifying, or making holy; the *anointing,* or the indwelling Spirit in His office work of empowering for life and service; and the *sealing,* or the same indwelling Presence in His witness-bearing capacity. When, therefore, we speak of the birth, the baptism, the anointing, and the sealing, as four administrative acts or functions of the Spirit, we are referring only to the two works of grace, but are considering the second, entire sanctification, under a threefold aspect. It should not be forgotten that these four administrative acts belong at once to Christ and the Holy Spirit. It is Christ who quickens dead souls into life by the Spirit; it is Christ who baptizes men and women with the Holy Spirit; and it is Christ, also, who both anoints and seals His people with the Spirit. We shall have occasion at subsequent points in our study to develop more definitely each one of these aspects of the work of the Holy Spirit.

C. *The Holy Spirit and the Church.*

Pentecost was the birthday of the Christian Church. As Israel redeemed from Egypt was formed into a church-state by the giving of the law at Sinai; so also from individuals redeemed by Christ our Passover, the Holy Spirit formed the Church at Pentecost. This was accomplished by the giving of a new law, written upon the hearts and within the minds of the redeemed. As the natural body is possessed of a common life which binds the members together in a common organism; so the Holy Spirit sets the members in the spiritual body as it pleases Him, uniting them into a single organism under Christ its living Head. The purpose of Christ is not alone the salvation of the individual, but the building up of a spiritual organism of interrelated and redeemed persons. This Church is *a chosen generation, a royal priesthood, an holy nation, a peculiar* (treasured) *people,* and the purpose of this organization is to *shew forth the praises of him who hath called you out of darkness into his marvelous light* (I Peter 2: 9, 10). In this Church the Holy Spirit is the common bond which unites the members of the body to each other, and all to their living Head.

D. *The Holy Spirit and the World.*

The Spirit represents Christ to the world. But since the world does not know the Holy Spirit and cannot receive Him in the fullness of His dispensational truth, Christ is therefore limited in His operations to the preliminary stages of grace. The nature of the Spirit's work is described by our Lord in the following words: *When he is come, he will reprove the world of sin, and of righteousness, and of judgment: of sin, because they believe not on me; of righteousness, because I go to my Father, and ye see me no more; of judgment, because the prince of this world is judged* (John 16: 8-11). The sin referred to here is the formal rejection of Jesus Christ as the Saviour; the righteousness is His finished work of atonement as the only ground of acceptance before a righteous God; while the judgment is the dethronement of Satan as the prince of this world, and hence the final separation of the righteous and wicked on the last day. If the prince be judged, then all his followers must suffer condemnation. In this relation between the Spirit and the world, He is to be regarded primarily as the Spirit of truth and His instrument as the Word of God. The relation of the Church to the Spirit's efficiency through the Word finds its highest expression in the Great Commission. Here the gospel is the proclamation of salvation, and this leads us directly to our next theme: the gracious call of the Spirit.

CHAPTER XV

THE PRELIMINARY STATES OF GRACE

"There are two central, universal facts of human nature, first, a universal corruption of human nature through the *Adamic* fall; second, the compensating, universal help of the Holy Spirit, that comes through Christ. *That was the true Light, which lighteth every man that cometh into the world* (John 1:9). What the moral state of humanity would be, if it had been left to the unrestrained and unalleviated consequences of the fall, can only be conjectured. We do not know what total depravity could bring us to, into what depths of sin and alienation from God we should fall, were there no counteracting grace; for the experiment has never been tried. The race has always had the remedial influence of the Holy Spirit, steadily pulling away at our hearts to draw us back to God."—Dr. A. M. Hills.

The finished atonement of our Lord Jesus Christ becomes effective in the salvation of men only when administered to believers by the Holy Spirit. The Spirit's work *in* us is as necessary to salvation as the provision of Christ *for* us. The redemption provided provisionally on Calvary becomes a living reality in personal experience only as it is worked out in us through the agency of the blessed Holy Spirit. The Spirit of God therefore continues the redemptive work of Christ on a newer and higher plane.

We now turn our attention to these gracious benefits of the atonement of Christ as they are made actual in human experience through the ministry of the Holy Spirit. The principal themes of this chapter are: The Gospel Vocation or Call, Prevenient Grace, Repentance, Saving Faith, and Conversion.

I. THE GOSPEL VOCATION OR CALL

A. *The General Nature of the Gospel Call.*

The Holy Spirit as the Agent of Christ makes known His divine purpose for the salvation of the world through what is commonly known in theology as the Gospel Vocation or Call. A distinction is also made between the universal call of the Spirit, and His immediate call. By the former we mean that secret influence which is exerted by the Holy Spirit on the consciences of men apart from the Holy Scriptures. St. Paul affirms that the law of God is written in the heart (Rom. 1:19; 2:15); and that God has never left Himself without a witness (Acts 14:17). The immediate call refers to that which is made through the Word of God. In the Old Testament this was largely limited to Israel, but in the New Testament, it is universal in its scope.

B. *Election and Predestination.*

The Gospel Call is closely related to the subject of predestination. The latter may be defined as the purpose of God to secure the salvation of some men but not all. In our historical sketch of theological development, mention was made of the fact that certain divergent schools of Protestant thought took form during the Reformation Period. One of the most influential of these was Calvinism. Among other doctrines, this system of thought emphasizes the sovereignty of God, and predestination. Against the Calvinism of the Reformation Era arose the Arminian or Remonstrant school of theological thought.

1. *The Calvinistic View of Predestination and Election.* In both Calvinism and Arminianism the elect are the called or chosen ones, but the two systems differ widely as to the manner of this election. Calvinists regard election as unconditional and dependent upon predestination, or the exercise of sovereign grace. "Predestination," says Calvin, "we call the eternal decree of God by which He has determined in Himself what He would have become of every individual of mankind, for they are not all created with a similar destiny; but eternal life is foreordained for some, and eternal damnation for others. Every man, therefore, being created for one or the other of these ends, we say he is predestinated either to life or to death. . . . . In conformity, therefore, to the clear doctrine of Scripture, we assert that, by an eternal and immutable counsel, God has once for all determined both whom He would admit to salvation and whom He would condemn to destruction" (CALVIN, *Institutes of the Christian Religion,* III, Ch. 21).

Thus election in the Calvinistic sense refers to the choice which God, in the exercise of sovereign grace, made of certain individuals of mankind to enjoy salvation by Jesus Christ. This necessarily involves the unconditional reprobation of all the rest of mankind. This is stated as follows in the Westminster Confession: "The rest of mankind God was pleased, according to the unsearchable counsel of His own will, whereby He extendeth or withholdeth mercy as He pleaseth, for the glory of His sovereign power over His creatures, to pass by, and to ordain them to dishonor and wrath for their sin, to the praise of His glorious justice."

2. *The Arminian View of Predestination and Election.* In contrast to the Calvinistic view just stated, Arminianism holds that predestination is the gracious purpose of God to save all mankind from utter ruin. It is not an arbitrary, indiscriminate act of God intended to secure the salvation of so many and no more. It includes provisionally all men in its scope, and is conditioned solely on faith in Jesus Christ. *For God so loved the world that he gave his only begotten Son, that whosoever believeth in him should not perish, but have everlasting life* (John 3: 16). Election differs from predestination in this, that election implies a choice, whereas predestination does not. In Ephesians 1: 4, 5, 11-13, it is said that God *hath chosen us in him before the foundation of the world, that we should be holy and without blame before him in love.* This is election. The gracious plan by which this is to be accomplished is predestination, *having predestinated us unto the adoption of children by Jesus Christ to himself, according to the good pleasure of his will.* Thus predestination is God's general and gracious plan of saving men, by adopting them as children through Christ; election pertains to the chosen ones who are holy and blameless before Him in love. The proofs of election are not in the secret counsels of God, but in the visible fruits of holiness. The Church is both predestinated and elected, the former referring to the plan of redemption as manifested in the universal call; the latter to the elect or chosen ones who have accepted the

offers of mercy. The elect are chosen, not by absolute decree, but by *acceptance of the conditions of the call.* And as the character of the elect consists of holiness and blamelessness before Him in love, so election is by those means which make men righteous and holy. Hence our Lord says, *I have chosen you out of the world* (John 15: 19). St. Paul explains it by saying, *God hath from the beginning chosen you to salvation, through sanctification of the Spirit and belief of the truth* (II Thess. 2: 13). St. Peter's teaching is to the same effect, *Elect according to the foreknowledge of God the Father, through sanctification of the Spirit unto obedience and sprinkling of the blood of Jesus Christ* (I Peter 1: 2).

Arminian theology has generally treated the subject of election under the threefold aspect. *First,* the election of individuals to perform some particular service. Thus Moses was chosen to lead Israel out of Egypt and Aaron to be the priest of the sanctuary. Cyrus was elected to aid in rebuilding the temple, Christ chose the twelve as apostles, and St. Paul was chosen as the apostle of the Gentiles. These offices were ordained to assist others, and not to exclude them from saving grace. *Second,* the election of nations or other bodies of men to special religious privileges. Thus Israel was chosen as God's first representative of the visible Church on earth. *Third,* the election of particular individuals to be the children of God and heirs of eternal life. This Arminianism always and rightly regards as conditional upon faith in Christ, and as including *all* who believe.

C. *Elements in the Gospel Call.*

The first step toward salvation in the experience of the soul begins with the gracious call of God which is both direct through the Spirit and immediate through the Word. The Agent of the call is the Holy Spirit and the Word is the instrument of His operations. The call is universal in scope and includes the proclamation, the conditions upon which the offer of salvation is made, and the command to submit to the authority of Christ (cf. Acts 5: 32; 13: 38-40).

Awakening is a term used in theology to denote that operation of the Holy Spirit by which men's minds are quickened to a consciousness of their lost estate. In this awakening process the Holy Spirit influences the hearts of men in two ways. First, the influence of the Spirit is indirect through the Word of God. But in addition to this, the Holy Spirit also exerts a direct influence on the hearts of men. Thus in Acts 16:14 we read, *Whose heart the Lord opened, that she attended unto the things which were spoken of Paul.* Here it is clearly declared that the understanding and the heart were opened by the Lord directly and not by means of the Scriptures.

Conviction is that operation of the Spirit which produces within men a sense of guilt and condemnation because of sin. To the idea of awakening there is added that of personal blame. Conviction is specifically stated to be one of the offices of the Spirit during the pentecostal dispensation. *And when he is come, he will reprove the world of sin, and of righteousness, and of judgment* (John 16:8). This conviction applies to the conscience as well as to the mind or reason, and is one of hope and not of despair. The Spirit not only reveals the sinfulness of human hearts, but the fullness and freeness of salvation in Christ. His purpose is not only to turn men from sin, but to lead them to a living faith in God. The conviction of the Spirit is thus one of hope for all who will truly repent of their sins and believe on the Lord Jesus Christ.

The gospel call reflects the divine intention that all men shall avail themselves of their blood-bought privilege in Christ Jesus. The call is not fictitious but genuine. It is not only an external offer of salvation, but is accompanied by the internal grace of the Spirit sufficient for its acceptance. Yet the call may be resisted; and even after having been accepted, obedience may be forfeited. Of such, the term reprobation is used, but never in the sense of a fiat or arbitrary decree. The reprobate are those who do not retain the knowledge of God, or who finally resist the truth. *Know ye not your own selves how that Jesus Christ is in you, except ye be reprobates?* (II Cor. 13:5). The word "reprobate" has reference primarily to failure under test.

II. Prevenient Grace

A. *Grace and Prevenient Grace.*

Grace has been defined as "love in God regarded as free and unpurchased, coming out of its own accord to bless the undeserving"; or simply, "the unmerited favor of God." The grace of God is infinite. It is not limited to His redemptive work, unspeakably great as this is. It existed in His sacrificial love from the foundation of the world; was revealed in the beauty, order, and utility of creation; and will be consummated in the final restoration of all things.

When we speak of "prevenient grace" we think of the grace which "goes before," preparing the soul for its entrance into the initial state of salvation. It is the preparatory grace of the Holy Spirit exercised toward man helpless in sin. As respects the guilty, it may be considered mercy; as it respects the impotent, it is enabling power. It is that manifestation of the divine influence which precedes the full regenerate life.

The idea of grace is fundamental in both the Old and New Testaments. Thus the Prophet Zechariah made clear our dependence on the favor of God when he wrote, *Not by might, nor by power, but by my spirit, saith the Lord of hosts* (Zech. 4:6). Our Lord himself declared, *No man can come to me, except the Father which hath sent me draw him* (John 6:44); and *Without me ye can do nothing* (John 15:5). With St. Paul the idea of grace was foundational. This is revealed in such scriptures as: *For when we were without strength, in due time Christ died for the ungodly* (Romans 5:6); *By grace are ye saved through faith; and that not of yourselves: it is the gift of God* (Eph. 2:8) and, *For the grace of God that bringeth salvation hath appeared to all men, teaching us that, denying ungodliness and worldly lusts, we should live soberly, righteously, and godly in this present world* (Titus 2:11-12). These are but a few of the many references which might be cited as presenting the fundamental truth of salvation through grace.

B. *The Nature of Prevenient Grace.*

Having mentioned the general nature of prevenient grace, it is now necessary to analyze it more carefully. This is another point in theology at which the differences between Calvinistic and Arminian thought are brought into sharp focus. In general Calvin's ideas concerning grace were derived from St. Augustine. The latter made original sin the very foundation of his whole system of theology. The fall having bereft mankind of all capacity for good, salvation must be solely of grace without any measure of human co-operation. Augustine maintained the freedom of the will, but only in the sense of freedom to evil. Grace therefore operates directly on the will. This necessitated a belief in the divine decrees which determined the exact number of those who were to be saved. To these as the elect, efficacious grace was applied. This included irresistible grace for the beginning of the Christian life, and persevering grace for its close. From these views of the necessity of divine grace, the theory of predestination was gradually evolved. With Augustine the system of divine decrees amounted to a form of fatalism. It remained for John Calvin, with his sternness of character and extraordinary ability, to systematize the doctrines of Augustine into a closely knit logical system.

Against some of the ideas of grace as held by Augustine and Calvin, the Arminians vigorously remonstrated. Both Arminians and Calvinists admit the depravity of human nature, and insist that man is powerless and unable to save himself. Thus both magnify the grace of God in salvation. However, Arminians hold that man's natural state is in some sense a state of grace. Regarding this, John Wesley declared, "Allowing that all the souls of men are dead in sin by nature, this excuses none, seeing there is no man that is in a mere state of nature; there is no man, unless he has quenched the Spirit, that is wholly devoid of the grace of God. No man living is destitute of what is vulgarly called natural conscience: it is more properly termed preventing grace" (WESLEY, *Sermon: Working Out Our Salvation*).

This prevenient grace is comprehensive, including all human desires after God, all drawings of the Father, all convictions of the Holy Spirit. If we yield to these impulses toward God they increase more and more. If men stifle such impulses, their reality tends to fade in consciousness.

Arminianism also holds to the truth of the co-operation between divine grace and the human will. The Spirit works through and with man's concurrence. In this co-operation, however, divine grace is always given the pre-eminence. Arminianism insists that salvation is all of grace. Every movement of the soul toward God is initiated by grace, yet at the same time there is a recognition that man is a free agent. The human will ultimately determines whether the divine grace proffered to man is accepted or rejected.

In setting forth the relationship between free grace and personal agency, Arminianism holds that grace is exercised upon man's entire being, and not upon any particular element or power of his being. Grace does not operate merely upon the intellect, the feelings, or the will, but upon the person or central being which is beneath or behind all affections and attributes. Thus a legitimate belief in the unity of personality is preserved. The Arminian position is therefore psychologically sound. Prevenient grace operates on the unified, integrated personality of man. That person is viewed as a free and responsible agent, yet enslaved by sin and possessed of a "bent to sinning." Grace is needed to awaken the soul to reality and enlist the heart upon the side of truth. In all of this there is continuous co-operation between grace and the human will until prevenient grace is merged into saving grace.

III. REPENTANCE

A. *The Importance of Repentance.*

The doctrine of repentance is fundamental in the Christian system and should be carefully studied in the light of God's Word. Christ said of Himself, *I am not come to call the righteous, but sinners to repentance* (Matt. 9: 13). Both John the Baptist and Jesus preached repentance as a basic condition of entrance into the kingdom of God (Matt. 3: 2, 8; 4: 17). God seeks to lead men to repentance both by His admonitions (Rom. 2: 4; II Tim. 2: 25; Rev. 2: 5, 16), and by His judgments (Rev. 9: 20, 21; 16: 9). Repentance constituted a major theme of preaching in the early Christian Church. St. Paul is reported as *Testifying both to the Jews, and also to the Greeks, repentance toward God, and faith toward our Lord Jesus Christ* (Acts 20: 21). St. Peter affirmed that *The Lord is not slack concerning his promise, as some count slackness; but is longsuffering to us-ward, not willing that any should perish, but that all should come to repentance* (II Peter 3: 9).

As the conditions of salvation, repentance toward God and faith in our Lord Jesus Christ are always conjoined. Both proceed from prevenient grace, but they differ in this, that the faith which saves is the instrument as well as the condition of salvation. Faith, therefore, flows from grace and follows repentance. It is for this reason that it is frequently stated that faith is the sole condition of salvation, and repentance the condition of faith. Both are properly introductory to the state of salvation, but saving faith is alone the point of transition where conviction passes into salvation.

B. *The Nature of Repentance.*

Two Greek words are rendered "repent" in our English New Testament. One of these denotes the soul recollecting its own actions, and that in such a manner as to produce sorrow in review, and a desire of amendment. It is strictly a change of mind, and includes the whole of that alteration with respect to views, disposition and conduct which is effected by the "power of the gos-

pel." The second word which is translated "repent" refers
more properly to contrition, and signifies a sorrowful
change of mind. Dr. Field suggests that the two words
may be said to signify "afterthought" and "afterconcern."
"Afterthought" signifying such a change or alteration
of mind as implies a return to right views, right feelings,
and right conduct; "Afterconcern" on account of something that has been amiss (FIELD: *Handbook of Chr.
Theology*, pp. 193-194). It will be seen that repentance
involves the whole of man's personality: a change of
mind, a godly sorrow, and a resolution of amendment.

C. *Representative Definitions of Repentance.*

Among the many definitions of repentance, we select
a few which are representative. John Wesley says, "By
repentance I mean conviction of sin, producing real desires and sincere resolutions of amendment." According
to Mr. Watson, "Evangelical repentance is a godly sorrow wrought in the heart of a sinful person by the Word
and Spirit of God, whereby from a sense of sin, as offen-
sive to God, and defiling and endangering his own soul,
and from an apprehension of the mercy of God in Christ,
he with grief and hatred of all his known sins, turns them
to God as his Saviour and Lord." Dr. Pope declares that
"Repentance is a divinely wrought conviction of sin, the
result of the Holy Spirit's application of the condemning
law to the conscience or heart. It approves itself in contrition, which distinguishes it from mere knowledge of
sin; in submission to the judicial sentence, which is the
essence of true confession; and in sincere effort to amend,
which desires to make reparation to the dishonored
law. Hence it must needs come from God and go back
to Him: the Holy Spirit, using the law, being the Agent
in producing this preliminary divine change." Finally.
Dr. Nevin says, "Real repentance consists in the heart's
being broken for sin and from sin."

D. *The Divine and Human Elements in Repentance.*

Two factors are involved in genuine repentance—the
divine and the human. To suppose that repentance is a

purely human act, accomplished by the unassisted exercise of the sinner's own powers, is to presume upon God; while to look upon it as the work of God alone, is to sink in carelessness and despair. A correct understanding of this subject is necessary in order to preserve one from either extreme. God is said to be the author of repentance, but He does not repent for us; He gives or grants repentance (Acts 4:31; 11:18) in the sense of making repentance possible. An extreme emphasis upon the divine element in repentance leads to a curious interpretation of scriptural passages dealing with the necessity of repentance. Thus Dr. William Evans, a prominent Bible teacher of Calvinistic views, declares that the reason men are universally called to repentance is to reveal to them their own inability to do just that.

Repentance is, indeed, the result of the gracious work of the Holy Spirit upon the souls of men. The goodness of God leads to repentance (Rom. 2:4). The means by which it is effected is the divinely wrought application of the holy law. The first effect of the Spirit's work is contrition, or godly sorrow for sin. Thus true repentance is not a sorrow for sin apart from forsaking it, which St. Paul terms *the sorrow of the world* (II Cor. 7:10); nor is it a reform apart from godly sorrow. It involves a new moral consciousness of sin in which the sinner identifies himself with God's thoughts about it. He hates sin and from the center of his being abhors it. While certain sins may be at the focus of consciousness, true repentance involves an abhorrence of *all* sin as against a holy God. Repentance is characterized by a feeling of utter helplessness before the law of God, and an acceptance of the just judgments imposed as a result of the violation of that law.

It should not be forgotten that repentance is an act of the sinner himself in response to the conviction and appeals of the Spirit. The power indeed is given to him of God, but the act is necessarily his own. God, by His Spirit, applies the truth to the sinner's heart, unveils to his mind the number and aggravations of the sins he has committed, and the exposure to everlasting wrath which he has incurred. In view of this revelation, and of the grace bestowed upon him, he is commanded to repent and turn to God. He may accept the truth or he may resist it; but if he does not repent it is because he will not. To summarize: genuine repentance involves a conviction that we have sinned and are guilty before God; it includes contrition or a *broken and contrite heart* on account of our sin; it produces confession of sin; and implies reformation, a turning from sin to God and a bringing forth of fruits meet for repentance.

E. *The State of Penitence.*

Repentance is an act, penitence is a state of the soul consequent upon that act. It is that attitude which belongs to every person recovered from sin, and as such will not only exist in every subsequent stage of life but will have place also in heaven. True repentance results in lasting change in the entire personality which has undergone an inner revolution. As a natural man, he was spiritually blind, but now he sees truths which had never before penetrated his mind. Things are seen in a new light, with a new perspective. He now hates what he once loved, and loves what he formerly hated. Once he was bound by the chains of darkness and sin, now he finds his will freed from its fetters and able to function in the spiritual realm. True repentance brings a change of mind, which followed by an act of saving faith, brings the soul into the state of initial salvation. The continuance of penitence as a state makes possible the reception of further benefits and an abiding communion with God.

F. *The Necessity of Repentance.*

Repentance is essential to salvation. From Christ, our highest possible authority, we have the weighty words, *Except ye repent, ye shall all likewise perish* (Luke 13:3). This is not an arbitrary requirement, but arises from the nature of sin itself. Sin is rebellion against God. There can be no salvation, therefore, without a renunciation of sin and Satan. Sin is as inconsistent with happiness as it is with holiness. Until there is a deep feeling

of the evil of sin, and an utter renunciation of it, the soul
is unprepared for spiritual exercises or holy joy. Repentance is indeed bitter; yet the remembrance of the
bitter cup will be an occasion of praise to the redeemed
forever.

IV. SAVING FAITH

Repentance leads immediately to saving faith, which
is at once the condition and the instrument of salvation.
Faith forms the connecting link between prevenient
grace and the initial state of salvation. The term "saving
faith," however, is used in a particular sense, and must
be distinguished from the principle of faith generally as
it belongs to human nature, and from the assurance of
faith which is the outflow of the Christian life.

A. *The Nature of Faith in General.*

Faith is that principle of human nature which accepts the unseen as existing and which admits as knowledge that which is received on evidence or authority.
This general principle of faith, when directed to the
gospel and exercised under the prevenient grace of the
Spirit becomes saving faith. The Christian idea of faith
roots back in the Old Testament and has been modified
by Greek and Roman usage. The Hebrew word translated "faith" in its simple form means "to support, to
sustain, to uphold." In the passive form it means "to be
firm, stable and faithful." At the heart of its meaning is
the idea of reliance upon Jehovah. Thus Dr. Oehler defines the Old Testament concept of faith as "the act of
making the heart firm, steadfast and sure in Jehovah."
The Greek word for faith means "to trust," or "to be
persuaded" that its object, whether a person or thing, is
trustworthy. Several Latin words are translated "faith."
They mean "to believe," "to trust," and, "to place confidence in another." From all the various words for faith,
it is evident that the primary element is trust. The
older theologians commonly defined faith as the assent of
the mind, the consent of the will, and recumbency or re-
clining, by which was meant the element of trust. But the

comprehensive meaning of faith must ever be trust—
that which sustains our expectations and never disap-
points us. It is therefore opposed to all that is false, un-
real, deceptive, empty, and worthless.

Faith implies a previous knowledge of its object. This
applies to the intellectual element, or the assent of the
mind. It is in this sense of "belief" that knowledge must
be regarded as antecedent to faith, but it is only so as to
specific acts. A proposition to be believed, must be either
expressed or implied; and it must carry with it sufficient
evidence, either real or supposed. Faith also operates in
the emotional and volitional life to the degree that the fact
or proposition believed is judged to be important. If
faulty judgments arise from a failure to discriminate
between real and supposed evidence, the emotional and
volitional elements of the mind may sometimes be moved
more by false judgments than by true. Herein is the deceptiveness of sin and the human heart. Only grace
can awaken the mind to the truth as it is in Jesus. Thus
St. Paul wrote, *We look not at the things which are seen,
but at the things which are not seen: for the things which
are seen are temporal; but the things which are not seen
are eternal* (II Cor. 4:18).

There are also degrees of faith. This is due not only
to a limited apprehension of truth but also to varying
degrees of strength in faith itself. Our Lord said to His
disciples, *O ye of little faith* (Matt. 6:30); while to the
woman of Canaan, He said, *O woman, great is thy faith*
(Matt. 15:28). St. Paul speaks of *Him that is weak in
the faith* (Rom. 14:1); and to the brethren at Thessa-
lonica, he said, *Your faith groweth exceedingly* (II Thess.
1:3). We may well pray with the disciples, *Lord, increase our faith* (Luke 17:5).

B. *The Nature of Saving Faith.*

By the term "saving faith" we do not mean a different
kind of faith, but faith considered as the condition and
instrument of salvation. We have seen that the primary
element of faith is trust; hence saving faith is a personal
trust in the Person of the Saviour. The efficient cause

of this faith is the operation of the Holy Spirit, and the instrumental cause is the revelation of the truth concerning the need and possibility of salvation. Concerning saving faith, John Wesley declared, "Faith is a divine evidence and conviction not only that *God was in Christ, reconciling the world unto himself,* but also that Christ loved me, and gave Himself for *me.*" Mr. Watson states that "the faith in Christ, which in the New Testament is connected with salvation is clearly of this nature; that is, it combines assent with reliance, belief with trust." Dr. Pope also bears witness to this twofold aspect of faith. "Faith as the instrument of appropriating salvation is a divinely wrought belief in the record concerning Christ and trust in His person as a personal Saviour, these two being one" (POPE, *Compend. Chr. Th.,* p. 376).

Saving faith consists of both a divine and a human element. It is a "divine evidence and conviction" or a "divinely wrought belief." Concerning the relation of the divine and human elements in faith we have a splendid statement by Dr. Adam Clarke, "Is not faith the gift of God? Yes, as to the grace by which it is produced; but the grace or power to believe, and the act of believing are two different things. Without the grace or power to believe no man ever did or can believe; but with that power the act of faith is a man's own. God never believes for any man, no more than He repents for him; the penitent, through this grace enabling him, believes for himself: nor does he believe necessarily or impulsively when he has that power; the power to believe may be present long before it is exercised, else, why the solemn warnings with which we meet everywhere in the Word of God, and threatening against those who do not believe? Is not this a proof that such persons have the power, but do not use it? They believe not, and therefore are not established. This, therefore, is the true state of the case: God gives the power, man uses the power thus given, and brings glory to God: Without the power no man can believe; with it, any man may" (CLARKE, *Christian Theology,* pp. 135, 136. Also, *Commentary,* Heb. 11:1).

Saving faith is the act of man's entire being under the influence of the Holy Spirit. It is not merely the assent of the mind to truth, nor a feeling arising out of the emotions; nor is it alone the consent of the will to moral obligation. True faith is the act of the whole man. It is the highest act of his personal life—an act in which he gathers up his whole being and in a peculiar sense goes out of himself and appropriates the merit of Christ. It is for this reason that the Scriptures declare, *with the heart man believeth unto righteousness* (Rom. 10:10). Here the heart is understood as the center of personality, and as involving all its powers. Thus saving faith is *far more* than a mere assent of the mind to truth; it is more than the consent of the will giving rise to mere outward reformation; and it is more than a comfortable state of the emotions. Saving faith must embrace all these. It is an unshaken trust in God. It is the acceptance of the propitiatory offering of Christ which is set forth for the salvation of both Jews and Gentiles. It is a firm reliance upon the merits of the blood of atonement. This firm and unshaken trust in the atoning work of Jesus Christ must ever be the crowning exercise of saving faith.

Saving faith is based upon the truth revealed in the Word of God. It is for this reason that St. Paul defines the gospel as *the power of God unto salvation to every one that believeth* (Rom. 1:16). Our Lord laid the foundation for faith in revealed truth when He said, *Neither pray I for these alone, but for them also which shall believe on me through their word* (John 17:20). St. John says of his own Gospel, that *These are written that ye might believe that Jesus is the Christ, the Son of God; and that believing ye might have life through his name* (John 20:31). St. Paul also declares that God hath chosen us to salvation *through sanctification of the Spirit and belief of the truth* (II Thess. 2:13); and again, *Faith cometh by hearing, and hearing by the word of God* (Rom. 10:17). Through His providence and His grace, God gives to mankind the ground of saving truth in His eternal and unchangeable Word. He gives also the gracious influences of the Holy Spirit to awaken, convict, and lead the soul to Christ. A firm belief in the Christian revelation leads the soul to trust in the Christ who is the object of that revelation. Thus the proper and ultimate ideal of faith is a divine Person, and personally trusting our Lord Jesus Christ, our belief in His Word is strengthened.

Saving faith is vitally related to good works. The relation is well expressed by John Wesley as follows: "Although good works, which are the fruits of faith, and follow after justification, cannot put away our sins, and endure the severity of God's judgment; yet they are pleasing and acceptable to God in Christ, and spring out of a true and lively faith, insomuch that by them a lively faith may be as evidently known as a tree is discerned by its fruit." Good works pleasing unto God are performed according to His will, wrought through the assistance of divine grace, and are done for His glory.

St. Paul teaches that faith on man's part is not to be regarded as a work of merit, but as a condition of salvation. Hence man could be saved only by faith: *For by grace are ye saved through faith; and that not of yourselves: it is the gift of God* (Eph. 2: 8). Salvation is now, and always has been by grace through faith. The act of faith by which man is saved becomes the law of his being as saved; and hence good works flow from the principle of living faith.

C. *Faith as a Grace of the Christian Life.*

Saving faith is that act by which the prevenient grace of the Spirit passes over into the regenerate life of the believer. Thus the faith which saves becomes the faith which is a law of our being. The initial act becomes the permanent attitude of the regenerate man. *As ye have therefore received Christ Jesus the Lord, so walk ye in him: rooted and built up in him and stablished in the faith"* (Col. 2: 6, 7). This faith becomes *the law of the Spirit of life in Christ Jesus* (Rom. 8: 2). St. Paul mentions faith as the seventh fruit of the Spirit (Gal. 5: 22), and catalogs it as one of the gifts of the Spirit (I Cor. 12: 9). As the former it is a quality of the regenerate life and therefore a gracious result and an abiding privilege of believers. As a gift of the Spirit, faith is a special gift bestowed by the Spirit for the profit of those to whom it is given (I Cor. 12: 7).

Faith as the law of the Christian life is always operative. It works by love (Gal. 5: 6) and purifies the heart. Otherwise there is danger of faith becoming merely a formal assent to the conditions of salvation. It is this against which James warns us. *Thou believest that there is one God; thou doest well. . . . . But wilt thou know, O vain man, that faith without works is dead? For as the body without the spirit is dead, so faith without works is dead also* (James 2: 19, 20, 26). True faith is, therefore, a working faith.

V. CONVERSION

Conversion is the term used to designate the process by which the soul turns from sin to salvation. In common usage the term is used in an undifferentiated sense to express the initial state of salvation including justification, regeneration, and adoption. In the Scriptures, however, conversion usually refers to the human act of turning away from sin. Thus our Lord quotes the prophecy of Isaiah, that *they should not see with their eyes, nor understand with their heart, and be converted, and I should heal them* (John 12: 40). He also said, *Except ye be converted, and become as little children, ye shall not enter into the kingdom of heaven* (Matt. 18: 3). To Peter, He said, *When thou art converted, strengthen thy brethren* (Luke 22: 32). St. James declared, *Brethren, if any of you do err from the truth, and one convert him; let him know, that he which converteth the sinner from the error of his way, shall save a soul from death, and shall hide a multitude of sins* (James 5: 19, 20).

In Calvinistic theology, "conversion is the human side or aspect of that fundamental spiritual change, which viewed from the divine side, we call regeneration." But holding as they do that regeneration is an effectual calling by the decree of God, men are first regenerated, and then are able to turn themselves to God.

Dr. Pope, eminent Arminian theologian, defines conversion in a similar manner: "The process by which the soul turns or is turned, from sin to God, in order to its acceptance through faith in Christ." While these definitions are similar, if not identical, there is a vast difference between the Calvinistic and Arminian positions as regards conversion. The former holds that man is regenerated by absolute decree and then turns to God. Arminianism holds that through grace, preveniently bestowed, man turns to God and is *then* regenerated. This is the scriptural position.

CHAPTER XVI

JUSTIFICATION, REGENERATION, AND ADOPTION

"Justification is a cardinal doctrine in Christian theology. All evangelical denominations agree on this. Martin Luther styled it the 'article of a standing or a falling church. It spreads its vital influence through the whole body of theology; runs through all Christian experience, and operates in every part of practical godliness.' This doctrine relates preeminently to the way, and the only way, of a penitent sinner's acceptance with God. It is one link in the chain which leads to a full and complete reconciliation to God. Drop it out, and the whole system of Christianity is marred and incomplete. Justification, regeneration, and adoption mutually imply each other; and one cannot occur without the others, and yet neither is the other. They are distinct, but not separate doctrines."—BISHOP JONATHAN WEAVER.

I. JUSTIFICATION

In the foregoing quotation Bishop Weaver has cogently stated the vital importance of the doctrine of justification in Christian theology. A further observation on this subject from Bishop Merrill may well be cited: "Here God's life and spirit and power come into efficient contact with awakened consciences and penitent hearts, bringing the throbs of a new life and the gleams of a new day to the soul lost in darkness and sin. Destroy this link in the chain and the whole is useless. The name of Christ, if retained, will have lost its charm. His blood will be robbed of its meritorious efficacy, and His Spirit will be reduced to a sentiment or a temper, with no power to quicken the soul into the life of righteousness. Along with this displacement of Christ will come an undue exaltation of human virtues and the diminution of the turpitude of sin, till the presence of guilt shall cease to alarm, and the need of humiliation become a dream. Then the pomp of worship will take the place of inward groaning for salvation, and the services of the sanctuary will be required to charm the senses, to minister to the esthetic tastes, and to nourish the vanity of the heart, without disturbing the emotions or stirring the depths of the soul with longings after God and purity."

A. *Definitions of Justification.*

Dr. Bunting has given a splendid definition of justification which reads as follows: "To justify a sinner is to account and consider him relatively righteous; and to deal with him as such, notwithstanding his past unrighteousness, by clearing, absolving, discharging and releasing him from various penal evils, and especially from the wrath of God, and the liability to eternal death, which by that past unrighteousness he had deserved; and by accepting him as if just, and admitting him to the state, the privileges, and the rewards of righteousness." The Manual gives the following definitive statement: "We believe that justification is that gracious and judicial act of God, by which He grants full pardon of all guilt and complete release from the penalty of sins committed, and acceptance as righteous, to all who believingly receive Jesus Christ as Lord and Saviour" (Article IX). We may sum up the various aspects of the truth concerning this great doctrine in the following statement: Justification is that judicial or declarative act of God, by which He pronounces those who believingly accept the propitiatory offering of Christ, as absolved from their sins, released from their penalty, and accepted as righteous before Him.

B. *The Nature of Justification.*

In the Scriptures the idea of justification is presented under such terms as justification, righteousness, non-imputation of sin, and the reckoning or imputation of righteousness—all of which have substantially the same meaning but with certain shades of difference. Among the more important passages dealing with this subject are the following: (1) *Be it known unto you therefore, men and brethren, that through this man is preached unto you the forgiveness of sins: and by him all that believe are justified from all things, from which ye could not be justified by the law of Moses* (Acts 13:38-39). (2) *Being justified freely by his grace through the redemption that is in Christ Jesus: whom God hath set forth to be a propitiation through faith in his blood, to declare his righteousness for the remission of sins that are past, through the forbearance of God; to declare, I say, at this time his righteousness: that he might be just, and the justifier of him which believeth in Jesus* (Rom. 3: 24-26). (3) *But to him that worketh not, but believeth on him that justifieth the ungodly, his faith is counted for righteousness. Even as David describeth the blessedness of the man, unto whom God imputeth righteousness without works, saying, Blessed are they whose iniquities are forgiven, and whose sins are covered. Blessed is the man to whom the Lord will not impute sin* (Rom. 4: 5-8). These passages illustrate the variety of terms by which the Scriptures set forth the concept of justification.

1. *Evangelical Justification.* The Scriptures employ the term justification in at least three different senses. *First,* it is applied to one who is personally right or just, and against whom no accusation is brought. This is *personal justification* (cf. Matt. 11:19; Luke 7:29; Rom. 2:13). *Second,* the term is applied to one against whom accusation has been made but not sustained. This is *legal* justification (cf. Deut. 25:1). *Third,* it is applied to one who is accused, is guilty, and condemned. How can such a one be justified? In one sense only—that of pardon. By the act of God, his sins are pardoned for Christ's sake, his guilt cancelled, his punishment remitted, and He is accepted before God as righteous. He is therefore declared righteous, not by legal fiction, but by judicial action, and stands in the same relation to God through Christ, as if he had never sinned. This is *evangelical* justification, and is possible only through the redemption that is in Jesus Christ.

It is to be emphasized that evangelical justification is the remission of sins as an act of mercy; it is not an exercise of the divine prerogative apart from law, but consistent with law. It is thus distinguished from mere forgiveness.

2. *Justification Is Both an Act and a State.* Justification is an act of God whereby men are declared to be just or righteous; and it is a state of man, into which he

is introduced as a consequence of this declaration. But whether as an act or a state the word is never validly used in the sense of making men holy or righteous, but only in the sense of *declaring* or *pronouncing them* free from the guilt and penalty of sin, and therefore righteous.

3. *Justification Is a Relative Change.* Justification is not the work of God by which we are *actually* made *just* and *righteous.* We can do no better than to quote John Wesley on this point: "But what is it to be justified? What is justification? It is evident from what has been already observed that it is not being made actually just and righteous. This is *sanctification;* which is indeed, in some degree, the immediate fruit of justification, but, nevertheless, is a distinct gift of God, and of a totally different nature. The one implies what God does *for us* through His Son; the other what He works *in us* by His Spirit. So that, although some rare instances may be found wherein the term justified or justification is used in so wide a sense as to include sanctification also; yet, in general use, they are sufficiently distinguished from each other, by both St. Paul and the other inspired writers" (WESLEY, *Sermon on Justification by Faith*).

4. *Justification and Sanctification.* By viewing justification as a relative change we mean that it is an *actual* change in *relationship* to God, whereas sanctification is a change in the moral nature of the individual. The relation of a sinner to God is that of condemnation; when justified, this relation is changed through pardon to acceptance or justification. Now it is evident that if sanctification or the inward change preceded the outward, then we should have holiness or inward righteousness in those who stood in a relation of condemnation before God. Hence Protestantism has always held that the first act of God in the salvation of man must be justification, or a change of relation from condemnation to righteousness. In experience the outward relative change, and the inward, moral change occur simultaneously, and are but two aspects of the same experience; but in thought at least, justification must precede.

The failure to discriminate between justification and sanctification is one of the errors of Roman Catholic theology. In their Tridentine Decrees (1547 A.D.) it is stated, "Justification is not the mere remission of sins, but also the sanctification and renovation of the inward man through the voluntary reception of grace and gifts of grace." The result of this position is reflected in two other statements of the Council of Trent—one denying the instantaneousness of justification; the other its assurance. Thus justification becomes a process in which one grows justified more and more, yet "No one affirms with confidence and certainty that his sins are remitted." Justification, thus erroneously viewed, becomes a gradual process of the infusion of righteousness. Little wonder, then, that this Council took the following unscriptural position in the form of an anathema: "If anyone shall say that justifying faith is nothing but confidence in the divine mercy remitting sin on account of Christ, or that this faith is the sole thing by which we are justified: let him be accursed."

5. *Justification Is Both a Judicial and a Sovereign Act.* We have seen that justification and forgiveness are closely related. Strictly speaking, justification is more than mere forgiveness. Essentially, justification is a *judicial* act. God does not justify sinners merely of His own good pleasure, but only on account of the righteousness of Christ: *being justified freely by his grace through the redemption that is in Christ Jesus* (Rom. 3:24). The sinner is thus justified by the judicial act of God.

But justification also involves the pardon of sins. While only God as *Judge* can pronounce the sinner righteous, only God as *Sovereign* can pardon or forgive. Thus, viewed negatively, justification is the forgiveness of sins; when viewed positively, it is the acceptance of the believer as righteous. God acts in the work of justification in His character as *both* Ruler and Judge. By His sovereign grace He forgives the sins of the penitent; and by a judicial act He remits the penalty and pronounces him righteous.

6. *Justification Is Personal, Comprehensive, and Instantaneous.* Justification is an actual work performed, in which God changes the relation of the sinner from that of condemnation under law, to that of righteousness in Christ. This work is instantaneous in that it is a definite and immediate decision consequent upon faith, and not a sentence extending through years or a gradual infusion of righteousness. The moment a true penitent believes on the Lord Jesus Christ he is justified. It is personal in that it is experienced only by those who seek it earnestly by prayer and faith, and who obtain this grace for themselves. It is comprehensive, in that it is the remission of all the sins of the past, through the forbearance of God.

C. *The Ground of Justification.*

The ground of justifying faith is the mediatorial work of Jesus Christ. More explicitly, the evangelical plan of justifying the ungodly rests upon three things: *first,* the full satisfaction of the divine justice through the propitiatory offering of Christ as man's Representative; *second,* the divine honor placed upon the merit of Christ by virtue of His redeeming work; and *third,* the union of these two in a righteous and gracious economy, wherein it is possible for God as Ruler and Judge to show mercy in the forgiveness of sins, on terms consistent with justice. The sole ground of justification then is the propitiatory work of Christ received in faith.

The method of orthodox Protestantism in its attempt to relate the work of Christ to the justification of the believer is known as imputation. Here again differences in Calvinistic and Arminian thought come into sharp contrast. In general, the Calvinistic position is that the righteousness of Christ, both His doing and suffering, is accounted or imputed to us "as if it were our own." Thus the elect are rendered legally as righteous as if they themselves had perfectly obeyed the law of God. The elect are therefore righteous by proxy. The Antinomian tendencies of this type of theology are peculiarly subtle and dangerous. It rightly makes a distinction between the "standing" of the believer legally, and his "state" or condition spiritually; but too frequently it has so widely separated between the two, and so strongly emphasized the "standing," as to overlook and undervalue the inner work of the Holy Spirit in the actual impartation of righteousness.

Arminianism holds that imputation is always accompanied by inward sanctification. It maintains that justification, regeneration, adoption, and initial sanctification are concomitant blessings, all of which are included in the broader term, conversion.

The Antinomianism that would lead a soul to a reliance upon the imputed righteousness of Christ, without the inward impartation of righteousness by the Spirit, is a dangerous perversion of the truth of God. Only as Christ is made unto us wisdom, and righteousness, and sanctification, and redemption do we rest securely in the grace of God.

What, then, is the true scriptural position regarding imputation? It is the imputation of faith for righteousness. This is the only view of the subject which fully accords with the Scriptures, and with the great tenet of the Reformation that we are justified by faith alone. *By him all that believe are justified from all things* (Acts 13:39). *Abraham believed God, and it was counted unto him for righteousness* (Rom. 4:3). *Therefore it was imputed to him for righteousness* (Rom. 4:22); and *for us also, to whom it shall be imputed, if we believe on him that raised up Jesus our Lord from the dead* (Rom. 4:24). *Christ is the end of the law for righteousness* (justification) *to every one that believeth* (Rom. 10:4).

From the foregoing scriptures it is clear that (1) it is faith itself, as the personal act of the believer, and not the object of that faith that is imputed for righteousness. (2) Faith is the condition of righteousness. It does not constitute personal righteousness, which would make faith a subtle form of works having merit, but is simply the condition of righteousness. (3) The faith that justifies is not faith in general but a particular faith in the propitiatory work of Christ. *Being justified freely by*

his grace through the redemption that is in Christ Jesus:
whom God hath set forth to be a propitiation through
faith in his blood (Rom. 3: 24-25).

II. REGENERATION

Christian sonship, which involves both regeneration
and adoption, is vitally related to justification by faith.
Yet there are significant points of difference between
them. The necessity for justification lies in the fact of
guilt and penalty, while that of regeneration is due to
the moral depravity of human nature after the fall. The
former cancels guilt and removes penalty; the latter re-
news the moral nature and re-establishes the privileges
of sonship. However, justification, regeneration, adoption, and initial sanctification are concomitant in personal experience, that is, they are inseparable, and occur
at the same time.

A. *The Nature of Regeneration.*

The term *regeneration* as used in the Scriptures
means literally "to be again." It is, therefore, to be understood as a reproduction or a restoration. The term is
generally applied to the moral change which is set forth
in such scriptural expressions as: *born again* (John 3: 3,
5, 7); *born of God* (John 1: 13; I John 3: 9; 4: 7; 5: 1, 4,
18); *born of the Spirit* (John 3: 5, 6); *quickened* (Eph.
2: 1, 5); and, *passed from death unto life* (John 5: 24;
I John 3: 14). In His conversation with Nicodemus, Jesus
used comparable words in His insistence on the necessity
of a birth "from above." St. Paul refers to the same
experience in such statements as the following: *If any*
man be in Christ, he is a new creature (II Cor. 5: 17).
And you, being dead in your sins and the uncircumcision
of your flesh, hath he quickened together with him, hav-
ing forgiven you all trespasses (Col. 2: 13). Both St.
John and St. Paul stress the fact that regeneration is dependent upon faith. Thus to *as many as received him,*
to them gave he power to become the sons of God, even
to them that believe on his name (John 1: 12).

St. Paul indicates that men are saved *by the washing*
of regeneration, and renewing of the Holy Ghost (Titus

3: 5). Here the *washing of regeneration* is an allusion to the rite of baptism; although in a narrower sense, the "washing" may refer to the rite, and the "regeneration" to the spiritual renovation which it symbolizes. The "renewing of the Holy Ghost" must be regarded as a comprehensive term, referring in one sense to the basic work of regeneration, and in another to the subsequent work of entire sanctification. As related to regeneration, this renewing is a restoration of the moral image of God in which man was originally created. But it is more than this. It is also the renewing of the original purpose of man's life in its full devotement to God. Hence St. Paul exhorts us to *put on the new man, which after God is created in righteousness and true holiness* (Eph. 4: 24); and again to *put on the new man, which is renewed in knowledge after the image of him that created him* (Col. 3: 10). Here it is evident that man is "renewed" or created anew in regeneration; and that the subsequent knowledge, righteousness, and holiness constitute the end for which he was renewed.

B. *Definitions of Regeneration.*

A few representative definitions of regeneration may be helpful in clarifying our thought on this vital subject: John Wesley defines regeneration as "that great change which God works in the soul when he brings it into life; when He raises it from the death of sin to the life of righteousness. It is the change wrought in the whole soul by the Almighty Spirit of God, when it is created anew in Christ Jesus; when it is renewed after the image of God in righteousness and true holiness" (WESLEY, *Sermon on the New Birth*). According to Mr. Watson, "Regeneration is that mighty change in man, wrought by the Holy Spirit, by which the dominion which sin had over him in his natural state, and which he deplores and struggles against in his penitent state is broken and abolished; so that with full choice of will and the energy of right affections, he serves God freely, and runs in the way of His commandments" (WATSON, *Theological Institutes*, II, 267). If a simpler definition is desired, the following seems definitive: Regeneration is the communication of life by the Spirit to a soul dead in trespasses and sins.

C. *The Operations of God in Regeneration.*

Our Lord indicated that there is an element of mystery connected with the exact nature of the new birth when He said, *The wind bloweth where it listeth, and thou hearest the sound thereof, but canst not tell whence it cometh, and whither it goeth: so is every one that is born of the Spirit* (John 3:8). However it is helpful to study this gracious experience from a survey of the scriptural terms which represent God's operation in the soul of man. The first and simplest term is that of a "begetting." John indicates that *everyone that loveth him that begat loveth him also that is begotten of him* (I John 5:1). St. Peter uses the expression *begotten us again* (I Peter 1:3); while James declares that *Of his own will begat he us with the word of truth* (James 1:18). Closely related to, if not identical with "begotten" are the terms "born again" and "born from above." The emphatic statement of Christ was *Except a man be born again, he cannot see the kingdom of God* (John 3:3, 6, 7). Regeneration is thus that impartation of spiritual life to the souls of men which sets them up as distinct individuals in the spiritual realm. The moral quality of this new birth is stressed by Jesus in the words *That which is born of the flesh is flesh; and that which is born of the Spirit is spirit* (John 3:6). The "new birth" carries with it, therefore, the idea of a bestowment of life, and is the result of that divine operation by which the souls of men are restored to fellowship with God.

A second term used in connection with regeneration is "quickening" or "making alive." Thus, *the Son quickeneth whom he will* (John 5:21); and *He hath quickened us together with Christ* (Eph. 2:5). This idea of a spiritual quickening or resurrection sets the new life in contrast with the previous state of sin and death. St. Paul emphasizes this when he says, *You hath he quickened, who were dead in trespasses and sins* (Eph. 2:1); and

You, being dead in your sins and the uncircumcision of your flesh, hath he quickened together with him, having forgiven you all trespasses (Col. 2: 13). Regeneration, then, is a spiritual quickening, by which the souls of men dead in trespasses and sins are raised to walk in newness of life. It is an introduction into a new life where there are new tastes, new desires, and new dispositions.

A third term presents the work of regeneration as "a creating" or "a creation." *Therefore if any man be in Christ, he is a new creature* (II Cor. 5: 17); and, *We are his workmanship, created in Christ Jesus unto good works* (Eph. 2: 10). As a "birth from above" regeneration must be understood to be a sharing of the life of Christ glorified. St. Paul affirms that *like as Christ was raised up from the dead by the glory of the Father, even so we also should walk in newness of life* (Rom. 6: 4). As a new creature, man is restored to the original image in which he was created. Christ is the great pattern and man is *renewed in knowledge after the image of him that created him* (Col. 3: 10-11).

D. *Errors Concerning Regeneration.*

Without extended discussion, it is profitable to point out certain errors which have been held regarding regeneration.

Regeneration is not water baptism. Baptism is the outward sign of an inward grace, and for this very reason cannot be regeneration. St. Peter tells us that baptism is *not the putting away of the filth of the flesh, but the answer of a good conscience toward God* (I Peter 3: 21); and this good conscience cannot be attained apart from an inward spiritual renewal. The identification of baptism and regeneration, commonly called "baptismal regeneration," has had a long history in the Church which cannot here be traced in detail. Suffice it to say that regeneration and adoption were confused in thought, and baptism was looked upon as the completing act in the appropriation of Christianity, and the seal of positive adoption into the family of God. Baptism being so closely

related to adoption and regeneration it came to be erroneously regarded as the instrument by which the inner
transformation was effected.

Regeneration is not a mere human achievement.
Through the centuries various views of regeneration
have been held which erroneously emphasize the human
element. Pelagianism, a heresy in the early Church, regarded regeneration as an act of the human will. Regeneration was said to be achieved through the illumination of the intellect by truth, and by mere imitation of
Christ and His life. A more modern form of this rationalistic tendency holds that regeneration is effected by the
power of truth alone. The error in these positions is
found in the denial of the immediate agency of the Holy
Spirit, who alone can effect the new birth.

Regeneration is not brought about unconditionally
by the Holy Spirit apart from any preparatory steps and
without man's co-operation. Calvinism falsely holds that
regeneration is the first step in salvation, and that it is
accomplished without the co-operation of man. The
latter is merely passive in the process. This amounts to
a denial of prevenient grace, the gracious influence of
the Holy Spirit exerted upon the heart previous to regeneration. But nothing is clearer in the Scriptures than
the fact that before one can be made a child of God by
regenerating grace, he must first make use of prevenient
grace by repenting, believing, and calling upon God
(cf. John 1: 12; Gal. 3: 26; Acts 3: 19). The Calvinistic
position is also objectionable in that regeneration is made
to precede faith, repentance, and conversion. Thus, according to this view, a regenerate person who has not yet
repented is not yet pardoned and hence is still a sinner.
A third objection to this Calvinistic view of regeneration is its emphasis on man's complete passivity. Yet in
the Scriptures we are commanded to seek, to ask, to repent, to open the heart, and to receive Christ. These
are requisites which cannot be met apart from human
agency and there can be no regeneration without them.
To deny these human conditions is to reassert the unscriptural position of unconditional election. A final

objection to the Calvinistic view of regeneration is one drawn from practical considerations. If men are made to feel that there are no conditions to regeneration on their part, they are led into carelessness or despair. Only as men have been made sensible of the presence of the Holy Spirit, and the necessity of obedience to His awakening and convicting influences, have revivals been promoted, and the work of salvation accomplished. We are, therefore, exhorted to seek the Lord while He may be found, and to call upon Him while He is near.

E. *Summary of Teaching Concerning Regeneration.*

In the following outline, we summarize certain fundamental truths concerning the vital doctrine of regeneration, setting forth the scriptural position on this subject.

1. Regeneration is a moral change wrought in the hearts of men by the Holy Spirit. It is a mighty change in the moral and spiritual nature of man. Both body and mind are influenced by this moral change but man still possesses his natural powers of body, intellect, feeling, and will. These powers, however, are given a new direction under the glorious spiritual transformation at the very core of his personality.

2. This radical change is wrought by the efficient agency of the Holy Spirit. It is an act of God. It is a new birth. While there are conditions which man must meet prior to the operation of the Spirit these only bring the soul to God. But it is the Holy Spirit by His omnipotent power who breathes new life into the soul dead in trespasses and sins. It is through this infusion of life that the moral and spiritual nature of the soul is changed.

3. Regeneration is a complete work and therefore perfect in its kind. While concomitant with justification and adoption, it is nevertheless distinct from them. Justification is a work which God does for us in the forgiveness of our sins and in changing the relation which we bear to Him; regeneration is the renewal of our fallen natures through the bestowment of life on the ground of this new relationship; while adoption is the restoration

of the privileges of sonship by virtue of the new birth. The necessity of justification is found in the fact of guilt; that of regeneration in the fact of depravity; that of adoption in the loss of privilege. All three, while distinct in nature and perfect in kind, are bestowed by the same act of faith and occur at the same time in personal experience.

4. Regeneration is accomplished through the instrumentality of the Word. It is not the power of the truth alone which regenerates; nor is it the action of the Holy Spirit apart from and independent of the truth. That the Spirit uses the truth as the instrument in both regeneration and sanctification is clearly set forth in the Scriptures (cf. Acts 16: 14; Eph. 6: 17; I Peter 1: 23). Concerning this relationship Dr. Daniel Fiske has written as follows: "In regenerating men, God in some respects acts directly and immediately on the soul, and in some respects He acts in connection with and by means of the truth. He does not regenerate them by the truth alone, and He does not regenerate them without the truth. His mediate and immediate influences cannot be distinguished by consciousness, nor can their respective spheres be accurately determined by reason."

5. Regeneration is related to sanctification. The life bestowed in regeneration is a holy life. It is for this reason that John Wesley spoke of it as the gateway to sanctification. In relation to regeneration, a distinction must be made between initial and entire sanctification. Initial sanctification accompanies justification, regeneration, and adoption, while entire sanctification is subsequent to it. The distinction arises from the fact that guilt, which as condemnation for sin is removed by justification, carries with it also an aspect of pollution which can be removed only by cleansing. For this reason Wesleyanism has always held that sanctification begins with regeneration, but it limits this "initial sanctification" to the work of cleansing from the pollution of guilt and acquired depravity, or the depravity which necessarily attaches to sinful acts. Entire sanctification, then, is subsequent to this, and from the aspect of purifi-

cation, is a cleansing of the heart from original sin or inherited depravity. The distinction, therefore, is grounded in the twofold character of sin—as an act, and as a state. Those who hold to the doctrine of entire sanctification sometimes take a position concerning regeneration which is logically opposed to it. They regard regeneration as such a "change of heart" as amounts to only a renovation of the old life. This renovation is regarded as complete, and hence no place is found for a further work of grace. But this is a misconception of the work of regeneration. It is not the remaking of the old life, but an impartation of new life. Regeneration, therefore, "breaks the power of cancelled sin and sets the prisoner free," but it does not destroy the inbeing of original sin. "What has occurred," says Dr. Raymond, "is not a complete removal of what is called the flesh, or its weakness, nor an entire removal of the carnal mind, but a bestowment of power to conquer it, to walk not after it, but to walk after the spirit, and so to conquer the flesh and live after the Spirit as to maintain a constant freedom from condemnation. The thing done is salvation from the reigning power of inbred or original sin; it is deliverance from captivity; he is free whom the Son maketh free; it is a bestowment, by the grace and power of God by which man is empowered to volitionate obedience" (RAYMOND, *Systematic Theology*, II, p. 358).

6. Regeneration makes possible to mankind the personal knowledge of God. The regenerated soul is changed fundamentally in moral and spiritual quality, and this change becomes the basis of a new personal relationship. The life communicated by the Spirit is a reproduction of the life of Christ. Its quality is of the nature of God. Hence only as man becomes the partaker of the divine nature, does he learn through experience the kind of being God is. Only through the character and quality of this life given in regeneration can man have a positive, vital acquaintance with God.

7. Regeneration is vitally related to the revelation of God in Christ. Jesus Christ is the supreme revelation of God. In Him the truth of God becomes visible, as if

projected for us upon the screen of humanity. He may be viewed as a Teacher, a Prophet or a Revealer, but He is more; He is our life (Col. 3:4). It is for this reason that men miss the true conception of the gospel when they view it merely as a system of ideas instead of a series of spiritual forces. It is indeed a system of truth, but it is truth vitalized into reality. The doctrinal system is but an attempt to give expression to this reality in a unified and systematic manner. Since Christ is the supreme Revelation of God, it is evident that the truth remains outside and apart from man experientially, until Christ is revealed in him as the hope of glory. This explains the fact that unregenerate man frequently fails to accept the revelation of Christ as set forth in the Holy Scriptures. With such it is purely a matter of intellectual investigation, but Christ can be understood only as we are made spiritually like Him. Hence these rationalists have closed the spiritual avenues of approach to the truth, and shut themselves off from that inner affirmation which comes solely through the new birth. It is for this reason that St. Paul declares that *If our gospel be hid, it is hid to them that are lost: in whom the god of this world hath blinded the eyes of them which believe not, lest the light of the glorious gospel of Christ, who is the image of God, should shine unto them* (II Cor. 4:3-4).

8. Regeneration is also related to the enabling power of the Holy Spirit. He not only reproduces the life of Christ in the regenerate as the Revealer, but also as the Agent of enabling grace. The life bestowed in regeneration is not only manifested in new light but in *new power*. It is a new spiritual beginning for man. It is an ethical change. It is a vitalizing of truth. It lifts the whole process out of the realm of theory into the realm of reality. Not only is a new goal set for man's attainment, but power is also given to free him from the bondage of sin, and to cause him to always triumph in Christ. This new life is devoted to God in sanctification, and he needs now to advance to the goal of entire sanctification, in which the heart is purified from all sin by the baptism with the Holy Spirit.

III. Adoption

A. *Meaning of Adoption.*

Adoption is the declaratory act of God, by which upon being justified by faith in Jesus Christ, we are received into the family of God and reinstated in the privileges of sonship. Adoption occurs at the same moment as justification and regeneration; but in the order of thought, logically follows them. Justification removes our guilt, regeneration changes our hearts, and adoption actually receives us into the family of God.

St. Paul occasionally uses the term adoption in a broader sense than indicated above. Thus he speaks of the special election of Israel *to whom pertaineth the adoption* (Rom. 9: 4). He also refers to the central purpose of the incarnation as culminating in our adoption as sons (Gal. 4: 5). Lastly, he uses the term for the full realization of man's restoration to his original estate: *Waiting for the adoption, to wit, the redemption of our body* (Rom. 8: 23). Despite these variations, St. Paul normally uses the term to express the privileges to which regeneration introduces believers under the terms of the new covenant.

B. *Benefits of Adoption.*

The blessings which flow from adoption into the family of God are many and desirable. These may be summarized as follows: (1) The privilege of sonship. We become *the children of God by faith in Christ Jesus* (Gal. 3: 26); *And if children, then heirs; heirs of God, and joint-heirs with Christ* (Rom. 8: 17). *Wherefore thou art no more a servant, but a son; and if a son; then an heir of God through Christ* (Gal. 4: 6-7). The kingdom of heaven has been described as "a parliament of emperors, a commonwealth of kings. Every humble saint in that kingdom is coheir with Christ, and hath a role of honor and a scepter of power and a throne of majesty and a crown of glory." (2) Filial confidence toward God. *For ye have not received the spirit of bondage again to fear; but ye have received the Spirit of adoption, whereby we cry, Abba Father* (Rom. 8: 15). The Spirit of

adoption brings deliverance from the bondage of sin.
Condemnation is removed, spiritual darkness is dis-
pelled, and God's approval placed upon the soul. (3) A
proprietary right in all that Christ has and is. *All things
are yours. . . . . And ye are Christ's, and Christ is God's*
(I Cor. 3: 21, 23). (4) The right and title to an eternal
inheritance. St. Peter speaks of this inheritance as *incorruptible, and undefiled, and that fadeth not away*
(I Peter 1: 4). It is called a *kingdom* (Luke 12: 32); a
better country (Heb. 11: 16); a *crown of life* (James
1: 12); a *crown of righteousness* (II Tim. 4: 8); and an
eternal weight of glory (II Cor. 4: 17). "Whatever God
now is to angels and glorified saints," says Dr. Dick,
"and whatever He will be to them through an endless
duration, for all this the adopted sons of God are authorized to hope. Even in this world how happy does the
earnest of the inheritance make them! How divine the
peace which sheds its influence upon their souls! How
pure and elevating the joy which in some select hour,
springs up in their bosoms! How are they raised above
the pains and pleasures of life, while, in the contempla-
tions of faith, they anticipate their future abode in the
higher regions of the universe! But these are only an
earnest!"

C. *The Evidence of Adoption.*

The doctrine of assurance or the witness of the Spirit
is one of the most precious doctrines of the gospel. As in
the case of the new birth, we may not understand the
Spirit's operations, but we may and can know the fact.
It is to the glorious fact of experiential religion that we
direct our attention in the following division.

IV. THE WITNESS OF THE SPIRIT

A. *The Scriptural Basis of the Doctrine.*

By the "witness of the Spirit" is meant that inward
evidence of acceptance with God which the Holy Spirit
reveals directly to the consciousness of the believer. The
Scriptures afford many illustrations of men who enjoyed the witness of the Spirit. In the Old Testament

we have the record of Abel (Heb. 11:4); Enoch (Heb. 11:5); Job (19:25); David (Psalms 32:5; 103:1, 3, 12); Isaiah (6:7); and Daniel (9:23). The New Testament likewise abounds with references to this doctrine (cf. Acts 2:46; 8:39; 16:34). As proof texts supporting this doctrine, the following may be mentioned, *The Spirit itself beareth witness with our spirit, that we are the children of God* (Rom. 8:16); *Ye have received the Spirit of adoption, whereby we cry, Abba, Father* (Rom. 8:15); *God hath sent forth the Spirit of his Son into your hearts, crying, Abba, Father* (Gal. 4:6); *He that believeth on the Son of God hath the witness in himself* (I John 5:10); *And it is the Spirit that beareth witness, because the Spirit is truth* (I John 5:6). These passages clearly teach that the Spirit testifies concerning the relation of believers to God.

B. *The Twofold Witness of the Spirit.*

The classical passage on this subject is found in Romans 8:16, *The Spirit itself beareth witness with our spirit, that we are the children of God.* It is evident that the apostle teaches here a twofold testimony: the witness of the divine Spirit and the witness of our own spirit. The first is commonly known as the direct witness, the second as the indirect witness. The passage is sometimes rendered "bear witness to" instead of "bear witness with" our spirit. This, however, does not change the meaning, but rather strengthens the former position. The very construction of the verse as given in the Greek implies a conjoint testimony of His Spirit and ours.

1. *The Witness of the Divine Spirit.* John Wesley, who was largely responsible for a modern revival of emphasis on the witness of the Spirit, held that "the testimony of the Spirit is an inward impression on the soul, whereby the Spirit of God directly witnesses to my spirit that I am a child of God: that Jesus Christ hath loved me, and given Himself for me; and that all my sins are blotted out, and I, even I, am reconciled to God." The value of absolute certainty in matters of such vital importance as the eternal salvation of the soul cannot

be overestimated. Here we must have the highest form of testimony. If there be no direct witness of the Holy Spirit then the whole matter becomes one of mere inference. But God has not left His people in darkness. He has given us of His Spirit that we may know the things that are freely given to us of God. For this reason Mr. Wesley exhorted his people not to "rest in any supposed fruit of the Spirit without the witness. There may be foretastes of joy, peace, and love, and those not delusive, but really from God, long before we have the witness in ourselves; before the Spirit of God witnesses with our spirits that we have redemption in the blood of Jesus, even the forgiveness of sins. If we are wise," he continues, "we shall be continually crying to God, until His Spirit cries in our heart, 'Abba, Father!' This is the privilege of all the children of God, and without this we can never be assured that we are His children. Without this we cannot secure a steady peace, nor avoid perplexing doubts and fears, but when we have once received the Spirit of adoption, this 'peace which passes all understanding,' will keep our hearts and minds in Christ Jesus" (WESLEY, *Sermons*, II, p. 100).

2. *The Witness of Our Own Spirit.* This is the indirect witness of the Spirit, and consists of the consciousness that individually we possess the character of the children of God. Mr. Wesley held that "It is nearly, if not exactly, the same with the testimony of a good conscience toward God; and is the result of reason and reflection on what we feel in our own souls. Strictly speaking, it is a conclusion drawn partly from the Word of God and partly from our own experience. The Word of God says everyone who has the fruit of the Spirit is a child of God; experience or inward consciousness tells me that I have the fruit of the Spirit; and hence I rationally conclude, therefore, I am a child of God. Now, as this witness proceeds from the Spirit of God, and is grounded on what He works in us, it is sometimes called the Spirit's indirect witness, to distinguish it from the other testimony, which is properly direct" (*Sermon* XI).

This indirect witness is confirmatory rather than fundamental. "Since, therefore, the testimony of His Spirit must precede the love of God and all holiness (in us), of consequence it must precede our inward consciousness thereof, or the testimony of our spirit concerning them." Filial love springs from the knowledge of filial relationships, and the direct witness of the Spirit must, therefore, precede the indirect. But the indirect is not thereby of less consequence. It is as indispensable as the first, for by it the direct testimony of the Spirit is fully confirmed. How am I assured," continues John Wesley, "that I do not mistake the voice of the Spirit? Even by the testimony of my own spirit; by the answer of a good conscience toward God: hereby I shall know that I am in no delusion, that I have not deceived my own soul. The immediate fruits of the Spirit, ruling in the heart, are love, joy, peace, bowels of mercies, humbleness of mind, meekness, gentleness, long-suffering. And the outward fruits are the doing of good to all men, and a uniform obedience to all the commandments of God" (WESLEY, Works, I, p. 92). We may say, then, that these two witnesses taken together establish the assurance of salvation. The one cannot exist without the other, and taken together, no higher evidence can exist.

C. The Common Privilege of Believers.

We have gone carefully over the scriptural grounds for belief in the witness of the Spirit; have shown that this testimony is inseparably connected with the spirit of adoption; that it is indeed essential to filial love; and, therefore, that it is as much a part of the common salvation as adoption itself. For this reason, we may safely affirm that the witness of the Spirit is the common privilege of all believers. Closely related to this is the question as to whether or not the witness of the Spirit can be held in uninterrupted enjoyment. As a matter of observation, it is well known that there are wide differences in the spiritual experiences of believers. Consequently we should expect the assurance of sonship to vary accordingly. Dr. J. Glenn Gould discriminates be-

tween the witness of the seeker's own heart, the witness
of God's Word, and the inner illumination of the Holy
Spirit. He points out that while the first two may remain
constant, the clarity of the latter may vary in consciousness at times (GOULD, *The Spirit's Ministry,* pp. 8-17).
John Wesley reviewed the whole subject with his usual
spiritual insight in his sermon on "The Wilderness
State." It should be remembered that the Scriptures set
forth the ideal of the *full assurance of understanding*
(Col. 2:2); the *full assurance of hope* (Heb. 6:11); and
the *full assurance of faith* (Heb. 10:22). These refer to
a perfect persuasion of the truth as it is in Christ, the
fulfillment of the promise of a heavenly inheritance and
entire trust in the blood of Christ. From these scriptures
we conclude that the full assurance of understanding,
faith, and hope is the privilege of every Christian, and
that none ought to rest short of his high calling in Christ
Jesus.

It is not only a wonderful but gracious provision in
the plan of human redemption that we may know beyond
a peradventure that we are the children of God by
adoption. To know that one's name is written in heaven
was declared to be of supreme value by the Master himself (Luke 10:17-20). Every Christian may know this
as certainly as he knows that he is living. Whenever
the Spirit himself beareth witness with his spirit that he
is a child of God, and adopted into His family, he knows
that his name is inscribed in the book of life.

CHAPTER XVII

ENTIRE SANCTIFICATION OR CHRISTIAN PERFECTION

"Holiness breathes in the prophecy, thunders in the law, murmurs in the narrative, whispers in the promises, supplicates in the prayers, sparkles in the poetry, resounds in the songs, speaks in the types, glows in the imagery, voices in the language, and burns in the spirit of the whole scheme, from alpha to omega, from its beginning to its end. Holiness! holiness needed! holiness required! holiness offered! holiness attainable! holiness a present duty, a present privilege, a present enjoyment, is the progress and completeness of its wondrous theme! It is the truth glowing all over, webbing all through revelation; the glorious truth which sparkles and whispers, and sings and shouts in all its history, and biography, and poetry, and prophecy, and precept, and promise, and prayer; the great central truth of the system. The wonder is that all do not see, that any rise up to question, a truth so conspicuous, so glorious, so full of comfort."—Bishop Foster.

Christian perfection and entire sanctification are terms used to express the fullness of salvation from sin, or the completeness of the Christian life. Other terms which are commonly used with similar intent are "full salvation," "holiness," "perfect love," the "baptism with the Holy Spirit," and the "second blessing." In addition to the common core of meaning, each of these terms has its own point of emphasis. *Christian perfection* stresses the completeness of Christian character and the possession of spiritual graces. *Entire sanctification* emphasizes cleansing from all sin, including the carnal mind, or indwelling sin. *Full salvation* suggests that the salvation of our Lord Jesus Christ is fully adequate for the entire sin problem. *Perfect love,* a term used much among the early Methodists, emphasizes the spirit and temper of the moral life of those who are wholly sanctified. It implies complete freedom from selfishness, utter devotion to God, and unselfish love toward all men. *The baptism with the Holy Spirit* stresses the gracious means by which the heart may be purged from all sin and filled with divine love. *The second blessing* ("properly so-called") is a term which was used with discrimination by John Wesley to point out the fact that entire sanctification is a second distinct work of divine grace subsequent to regeneration. The term *holiness* refers more particularly to the state or condition of the sanctified, rather than to the experience by which one is made holy. It describes a state of moral and spiritual purity, or complete soul health in which the image and spirit of God are possessed to the exclusion of all sin. Since spiritual truths can be discerned only by spiritual means the glorious work of divine grace to which the foregoing terms refer can be fully understood and appreciated only through personal experience.

Entire sanctification has been called the "central idea of the Christian system and the crowning achievement of human character." The entire Levitical system of the Old Testament is laid under tribute in an attempt to convey to the mind and heart the riches of this grace. The terms used embrace the altar and its sacrifices, the priesthood, the ritual with its sprinklings and washings, the ceremonies of presentation and dedication, the sealing and anointing, and the fasts and the feasts. All these point to the New Testament standard of piety—Christian perfection.

While entire sanctification is a fundamental doctrine of Christianity, and of vast importance to the Church, there are few subjects in theology concerning which there is greater variety of opinion. All evangelical Christians hold that it is a Bible doctrine, that it includes freedom from sin, that it is accomplished through the merits of Christ's death, and that it is the heritage of those who are already believers. There is much difference, however, as to its exact nature and the time of its attainment. For example, there are those who assert that this experience is concomitant with regeneration and is completed at that time. Others regard its attainment as a growth, extending throughout life; while still others hold that it is attained in the hour of death. The view which we believe to be the scriptural position is that sanctification begins in regeneration but is completed as an instantaneous work of the Holy Spirit subsequent to regeneration. This is commonly known as the Wesleyan view.

I. Historical Approach to the Doctrine of Entire Sanctification

Before beginning our analysis of the doctrine of entire sanctification, it is desirable to sketch the historical basis of the subject. This doctrine has come down to us from apostolic days as a sacred and uninterrupted tradition. Various periods of the Christian era have often been characterized by differences in terminology, but in no age has this glorious truth of Christian perfection been eclipsed.

A. *The Testimony of the Apostolic Fathers.*

The last words of Ignatius before his martyrdom were, "I thank thee, Lord, that Thou hast vouchsafed to honor me with a perfect love to Thee." Polycarp, speaking of faith, hope, and charity, says, "If any man be in these, he has fulfilled the law of righteousness, for he that has love is far from every sin." Clement of Rome states that "those who have been perfected in love, through the grace of God, attain to the place of the godly in the fellowship of those who in all ages have served the glory of God in perfectness.

B. *Teaching of the Later Church Fathers.*

St. Augustine at times rose to sublime heights in his conception of grace and at other times seemed to shrink from the full truth of his positions. He declares that "No one should dare to say that God cannot destroy the original sin in the members, and make Himself so present to the soul, that the old nature being entirely abolished, a life should be lived below as life will be lived in the eternal contemplation of Him above." Yet he believed that evil concupiscence remains throughout the natural life. Apart from this, he taught a full deliverance from all sin in this life. Macarius the Egyptian (c. 300-391 A.D.) wrote a series of homilies of Christian experience in which the idea of perfect love is given a prominent place. He says, "In like manner Christians, though outwardly they are tempted, yet inwardly they are filled with the divine nature, and so nothing injured. These degrees, if any man attain unto, he is come to the perfect love of Christ and to the fullness of the Godhead" (*Homily V*). "By reason of the superabundant love and sweetness of hidden mysteries, the person arrives to such degrees of perfection as to become pure and free from sin. And one that is rich in grace at all times, by night and by day, continues in a perfect state, free and pure" (*Homily* XIV).

C. *Teaching of the Mystics.*

The Mystics, notwithstanding their numerous errors and extravagances, served to preserve evangelical religion during the Middle Ages. Their contribution to this department of theology has been peculiarly rich in that the central idea of all mysticism is entire consecration to God. This demanded internal sanctity of heart, separation from the creature, and perfect union with God, the center and source of holiness and perfection. Their immemorial methods: the way of purification, the way of illumination, and the way of union correspond, respectively, to the evangelical doctrines of purification from sin, the consecration of the Spirit, and the estate of holiness in abstraction from self and earthly things in fellowship with God (cf. POPE, *Compend. Chr. Th.*, III, 75).

D. *Roman Catholic Doctrine.*

The Roman Catholic doctrine concerning sanctification is eclectic and took various forms from time to time. A good foundation for the doctrine is laid in the Tridentine Decrees which assert that negatively there is no bar to an entire conformity to law; and, positively, a complete satisfaction is necessary to salvation. Emphasis is also placed upon the power of the Redeemer "which effaces as well as forgives sin." However, purification of the individual is said to be accomplished in a twofold way. With some, purification is obtained in this life: with others, only in the life to come. Thus the idea of purgatory is introduced to provide for this cleansing after death. In practice, therefore, the Roman Catholic

Church fails to recognize the present power of the atoning blood of Christ for full and complete present cleansing.

E. *Calvinistic Views of Sanctification.*

As we have seen, the Reformers, especially those of
Calvinistic persuasion, tended to adopt certain theories
of imputation concerning justification. The same theories
were erroneously applied to sanctification. Since Christ
is our substitute, the Reformers held that not only a
complete justification, but also an entire sanctification
was thus provided for the believers, and applied to them
as a gift of covenant grace. But there is here an emphasis on what Christ has done *for* us to the minifying of
what He has wrought *in* us by the Spirit. Thus they held
to a belief in the imputation to Him of our sin, and to us
of His righteousness for our justification, and for our
sanctification also, insofar as it applied to the cleansing
from guilt. But sin itself cannot be done away by imputation; hence in the Calvinistic system it is necessary to
deny that it is actually done away. It is not imputed and
therefore, not reckoned to the believer. Thus he is sanctified by imputation, that is, by his "standing" in Christ,
although as to his actual "state," he still has the carnal
mind or inbred sin which imputation cannot take away.
Sin is not abolished as a principle or power, but instead,
Christ's righteousness is imputed as a substitute, and
inbred sin is hidden under the robe of an imputed righteousness. Here is the basis of the "standing and state"
theory which forms such a prominent part in some of
the modern theories of sanctification. The standing of
the believer is in Christ, that is by imputation; the actual
state is one in which sin is repressed, and, therefore, does
not reign; while sanctification is the process of bringing
the principle of sin into subjection to the life of righteousness. Sanctification, therefore, according to this theory,
is merely progressive while the soul dwells in the body,
and is completed only at death. The subtlety of a doctrine which holds that a man can be instantly sanctified
by an imputed standing, but not actually sanctified by

an impartation of righteousness and true holiness, makes
the error more dangerous. Anything that falls short of
an actual cleansing from all sin or the death of the "old
man" is anti-Wesleyan and anti-scriptural.

F. *The Teaching of Arminianism and Wesleyanism.*

The early Arminians wrote much on Christian perfection and their statements contain the germ of that
which was later developed in Wesleyanism. For example, Arminius defined holiness as follows: "Sanctification is a gracious act of God by which He purifies man,
who is a sinner, and yet a believer, from ignorance, from
indwelling sin, with its lusts and desires, and imbues
him with the spirit of knowledge, righteousness, and holiness. It consists of the death of the old man, and the
quickening of the new man."

The Wesleyan movement, which resulted in the organization of the Methodist Church, marks a revival of
the doctrine and experience of entire sanctification in
the eighteenth century. Wesley owed some of his inspiration to certain spiritual groups of the Reformation
Era, such as the Pietists and Moravians; although he dis-
agreed with Count Zinzendorf on his doctrine of imputation, and also rejected the idea that purification or
sanctification took place at conversion. However, the
chief impetus came from a study of the Scriptures themselves. Wesley tells us, "In 1729 my brother Charles
and I, reading the Bible, seeing we could not be saved
without holiness, followed after it, and incited others to
do so. In 1737 we saw that holiness comes by faith. In
1738 we saw that men are justified before they are sanctified, but still holiness was our pursuit—inward and
outward holiness. God then thrust us out to raise up a
holy people." Two years before his death, Wesley wrote,
"This doctrine is the grand depositum which God has
lodged with the people called Methodists; and for the
sake of propagating this chiefly He seems to have raised
us up." John Wesley was the founder of Methodism, and
his *Sermons* and *Notes*, together with the *Twenty-five
Articles*, form the standards of the doctrine. Charles

Wesley was the hymn writer of the movement, and John Fletcher, a member of the Anglican Church, its chief apologist. During the nineteenth century, a fresh impetus was given to the doctrine and experience of holiness by the great national camp meetings in the United States. The Wesleyan Methodist Connection was organized in 1843, the Free Methodist Church in 1860, and the National Association for the Promotion of Holiness in 1866. In order to both promote and conserve the truth of holiness, the latter part of the century witnessed the organization of the Church of the Nazarene by Dr. Phineas F. Bresee, the Pentecostal Association of Churches in the East, and a number of holiness movements in the South. These were later combined into one body, known as the Church of the Nazarene. This period witnessed also the combining of a number of other groups into the Pilgrim Holiness Church. These churches have sought to conserve the doctrine and experience of entire sanctification as a second definite work of grace subsequent to regeneration; and have persistently opposed the various fanatical groups that have obscured the pure truth and brought into ill-repute the doctrine and experience of full salvation.

G. *Other Modern Views of Sanctification.*

Among the more modern developments related to the doctrine of entire sanctification, aside from Wesleyanism, we mention the following: (1) The Oberlin Position; (2) The Theory of the Plymouth Brethren; and (3) the Keswick Theory.

(1) The Oberlin position is represented by President Asa Mahan, Charles G. Finney, and President Fairchild. According to this theory, there is a simplicity of moral action which makes sin to consist solely in an act of the will. Consequently, it is impossible for sin and virtue to exist in the same heart at the same time. Only one definition of sin is accepted, namely, "Sin is the transgression of the law." From these basic views, several erroneous positions logically follow. Inbred sin is denied as a state or condition. Instead an alternating theory of

moral character is asserted. There is also confusion between consecration and sanctification. Sanctification is made to consist in such an establishment in consecration as to prevent the further alternation of the will. Finally, sanctification is made a matter of growth and development. Thus President Fairchild asserts, "The growth and establishment of the believer, the development in him, of the graces of the gospel, is called sanctification."

2. The Plymouth Brethren originated about the same time in Dublin, Ireland, and Plymouth, England. In general, their theological positions are based upon the extreme imputation theories of hyper-Calvinism. They regard sin as having been condemned on the cross of Christ; and consequently hold that all sin—past, present, and future has by this act been done away—not provisionally, nor actually, but by imputation of men's sins to Christ. Having been done away by imputation to Christ, men are no longer responsible either for their sinful state or sinful acts. Holiness and righteousness are only imputed, never imparted. In this system faith becomes, not the condition of personal salvation, but simply a recognition of what was done by Christ on the cross. Justification likewise is not an act in the mind of God by which the sinner is forgiven, but a wholesale transaction on Calvary centuries ago, but just now recognized and accepted. Regeneration is regarded, not as an impartation of life to the soul, but as in some sense the creation of a new personality which exists alongside the old, both natures remaining unchanged until death. The person, or that which in man says "I," may put itself under the direction of either the "new man" or the "old man" without any detriment to his standing in Christ, except that in the latter case communion is interrupted. Whatever may be the deeds of the "old man," the believer is not held to be accountable for them—they were condemned on the cross.

The believer is not only made righteous in Christ, he is made holy also. The one act, viewed as righteousness, is justification; viewed as holiness, it is sanctification. One of their own writers states this position as follows: "He who is our Great High Priest before God is pure and without stain. God sees Him as such, and He stands for us who are His people, and we are accepted in Him. His holiness is ours by imputation. Standing in Him, we are in the sight of God, holy as Christ is holy, and pure as Christ is pure. God looks at our representative, and He sees us in Him. We are complete in Him who is our spotless and glorious Head." The individual's holiness and righteousness are only imputed, not inwrought by the Spirit. Sin continues until death, but this in nowise affects the "standing" of the believer. By contrast, the Wesleyan and scriptural position is that men may enjoy imparted holiness, that is, may be actually made holy in heart. No man is "in Christ" until he is cleansed from sin by the Holy Spirit. The mere intellectual assertion that a man is "in Christ" does not make it so. It is little wonder that those who hold such imputation theories regarding sanctification are particularly hostile to the scriptural and Wesleyan view.

3. The Keswick Movement originated in 1874 and was founded for the "promotion of scriptural or practical holiness." It has been popularized by a number of nationally known evangelists and has in it many sincere and earnest Christians. They believe in the lost condition of the race, and are zealous in their efforts for the salvation of men. They insist on the abandonment of all known sin, and a definite and complete consecration to Christ. They emphasize the necessity of an appropriation by faith of the power of God through Christ for both holy living and Christian service. This enduement for service is known among them as the baptism with the Holy Spirit, and is generally regarded as being subsequent to conversion. It is not, however, in the strict sense, a work of grace, for there is no cleansing from inbred sin. The latter is regarded as a part of the believer's humiliation, and in a sense as defiling his best deeds. It involves continuous suppression, and will continue to exist until death delivers from defilement. The enduement of the Spirit counteracts in some measure the carnal mind and assists the believer in repressing its

manifestations. The power of sin is merely broken. It is in no sense entire sanctification as Wesleyanism defines this term. Rather it is more closely related to the idea of positional holiness as taught by the Plymouth Brethren. The believer is holy in his "standing" but not in his "state." Holiness is thus a matter of imputation instead of impartation. Actual cleansing from all sin is rejected as being out of harmony with their general principles. The "standing" is eternal, and hence, like the theory of the Plymouth Brethren logically results in the so-called doctrine of "eternal security."

II. THE SCRIPTURAL BASIS FOR ENTIRE SANCTIFICATION

A careful study of the Holy Scriptures is the best apologetic for the doctrine and experience of entire sanctification. Limitations of space make it necessary for us to confine our citations to a limited number of the more prominent texts dealing with this vital theme.

A. *Holiness Is the New Testament Standard of Christian Experience.*

Here will be noticed those scriptures which refer to the will of God, His promises, and His commands.

1. *It is the Will of God that His People Be Holy. Wherefore be ye not unwise, but understanding what the will of the Lord is. And be not drunk with wine, wherein is excess; but be filled with the Spirit* (Eph. 5:17-18). This refers to the promised gift of the Holy Spirit, which the disciples received at Pentecost and of whom it is said, *they were all filled with the Spirit.* The implication is that the disciples had some measure of the Spirit prior to Pentecost, but that a cleansing was mandatory to the complete infilling of the Holy Spirit. *For this is the will of God, even your sanctification* (I Thess. 4:3). Here holiness or "the sanctification" is set in contrast to the misuse of the body. God's will is that His people shall be cleansed from all uncleanness, whether of the soul or of the body. *By the which will we are sanctified through the offering of the body of Jesus Christ once for all* (Heb. 10:10). The one great act of

atonement finds its supreme purpose in the sanctification of His people. The blood of Jesus Christ not only furnishes the ground of our justification, but is the medium of our sanctification also.

2. *God Has Promised to Sanctify His People.* *Come now, and let us reason together, saith the Lord: though your sins be as scarlet, they shall be as white as snow; though they be read like crimson, they shall be as wool* (Isa. 1:18). Scarlet is known as one of the most indelible of the dyes, and is here used to designate the stain of sin in the soul. The guilt of actual sin, and the pollution of inbred sin, can be cleansed only by the blood of Jesus Christ. *Then will I sprinkle clean water upon you, and ye shall be clean: from all your filthiness, and from all your idols, will I cleanse you* (Ezek. 36:25). The work of the Holy Spirit is here represented by the symbol of water as a cleansing agent. *For he is like a refiner's fire, and like fullers' soap: and he shall sit as a refiner and purifier of silver: and he shall purify the sons of Levi, and purge them as gold and silver, that they may offer unto the Lord an offering in righteousness* (Mal. 3:2-3). Christ is here portrayed by the prophets as the Great Refiner of His people. It is the sons of Levi who are to be purged, and the purpose of this cleansing is to enable them to make an offering in righteousness. *I indeed baptize you with water unto repentance: but he that cometh after me . . . . he shall baptize you with the Holy Ghost, and with fire. Whose fan is in his hand, and he will throughly purge his floor, and gather his wheat into the garner; but he will burn up the chaff with unquenchable fire* (Matt. 3:11-12). It is evident from this passage that the baptism with the Holy Spirit effects an internal and spiritual cleansing which goes far deeper than John's baptism. The latter is for the remission of sins, the former for the removal of the sin principle. The separation is not a separation between tares and wheat, but between wheat and the chaff, or that which by nature clings to the wheat. This chaff is not the wicked but the principle of sin which cleaves to the souls of the regen-

erate, and which is removed by Christ's purifying baptism.

3. *God Commands His People to Be Holy.* These commands embrace the three terms commonly applied to entire sanctification—holiness, perfection, and perfect love. *Be ye holy; for I am holy* (I Peter 1: 16). God requires that His people be holy and enjoins it by precept and example. Evangelical holiness is positive and real, not merely typical or ceremonial. There is a relative aspect of holiness, but it is never separated from that which is inwrought by the Spirit. Holiness in God is absolute, and in man derived, but the quality is the same in God and man. *The Lord appeared to Abraham, and said unto him, I am the Almighty God; walk before me and be thou perfect* (Gen. 17: 1). *Be ye therefore perfect, even as your Father which is in heaven is perfect* (Matt. 5: 48). This is the perfection of love, which comes from the purging of all the antagonisms of the soul, which war against it. *And thou shalt love the Lord thy God with all thy heart, and with all thy soul, and with all thy mind, and with all thy strength: this is the first commandment* (Mark 12: 30). The love mentioned here is not merely natural human love or friendship, but holy love, or the love created and shed abroad in the hearts of men by the Holy Spirit (Rom. 5: 5).

B. *Entire Sanctification as a Second Work of Grace.*

I beseech you therefore, brethren, by the mercies of God, that ye present your bodies a living sacrifice, holy, acceptable unto God, which is your reasonable service. And be not conformed to this world: but be ye transformed by the renewing of your mind, that ye may prove what is that good, and acceptable, and perfect, will of God (Rom. 12: 1-2). It is clear that this exhortation was addressed to those who were at the time Christians; that an appeal to the mercies of God would mean nothing to those who had not already experienced His pardoning grace; that the sacrifice was to be presented holy, as initially sanctified by the cleansing from guilt and acquired depravity; and that it was to be acceptable, that is, those who presented it must have been justified. Yet in the second verse it is admitted that there remained in the hearts of believers a bent toward worldliness, or a bias toward sin; that this tendency to conform to the world was to be removed by a further transformation or a renewal of their minds: and that they were thereby to prove, or experience, the good, and acceptable, and perfect will of God. *Having therefore these promises, dearly beloved, let us cleanse ourselves from all filthiness of the flesh and spirit, perfecting holiness in the fear of God* (II Cor. 7: 1). The holiness already begun in regeneration is to be perfected by the cleansing at a single stroke from inbred sin. This brings the soul into a state of perfected holiness. *Therefore leaving the principles of the doctrine of Christ, let us go on unto perfection* (Heb. 6: 1). The meaning here, according to Dr. Adam Clarke, is that of "being borne on immediately into the experience."

C. *Tense Readings of the Greek Testament.*

Dr. Daniel Steele in his *Milestone Papers* has an excellent chapter (V) on this interesting and important subject. He points out the contrast between the use of the present tense, as *I am writing,* or the imperfect as denoting the same continuity in the past, as *I was writing,* with the aorist tense, which in the indicative expresses simple momentary occurrence of an action in past time as *I wrote.* In all other moods, the aorist is timeless, or what is styled "singleness of act." When, therefore, the present tense is used, it denotes continuous action; but when the aorist is used, is without reference to time. There is in the English no tense like it. A proper understanding of this will greatly aid in the interpretation of important texts. Some examples are given below in outline form.

1. *Sanctify* (aorist imperative) *them* (once for all) *through thy truth: . . . . And for their sakes I sanctify* (present tense—am sanctifying or consecrating) *myself, that they also might be sanctified through the truth* (or truly sanctified) (John 17: 17, 19).

2. *Purifying* (aorist—instantaneously) *their hearts by faith* (Acts 15:9).

3. *I beseech you therefore, brethren, by the mercies of God, that ye present* (aorist—a single act not needing to be repeated) *your bodies a living sacrifice* (Rom. 12:1).

4. *Now he which stablisheth* (present—who is continually establishing) *us with you in Christ, and hath* (aorist, as a single definite act) *anointed us, is God; who hath also sealed us* (aorist) *and given* (aorist—gave as a single definite act) *the earnest of the Spirit in our hearts* (II Cor. 1:21-22). Here the establishing is constant, or continuous while the anointing, the sealing, and the earnest of the Spirit are momentary and completed acts of the one experience of entire sanctification.

5. *And they that are Christ's have crucified* (aorist—a single definite and completed act) *the flesh* (carnal mind or principle of sin), *with the affections and lusts* (Gal. 5:24).

6. *In whom also after that ye believed* (aorist), *ye were sealed* (aorist) *with the Holy Spirit of promise* (Eph. 1:13). Here both the believing and the sealing are definite, complete acts.

7. *And the very God of peace sanctify* (aorist) *you wholly; and . . . . your whole spirit and soul and body be preserved* (I Thess. 5:23).

8. *That he might sanctify* (aorist) *the people with his own blood, suffered* (aorist) *without the gate* (Heb. 13:12).

9. *If we confess* (present tense) *our sins, he is faithful and just to forgive* (aorist) *us our sins, and to cleanse* (aorist) *us from all unrighteousness* (I John 1:9). Here both forgiveness and the cleansing are spoken of as completed acts, and there is no more reason grammatically for believing in gradual sanctification than in gradual justification.

III. Meaning and Scope of Sanctification

An analytical study of the words in the Greek New Testament which refer to the truth of sanctification constitutes one of the most fruitful approaches to the subject. The scope of our study does not permit any detailed analysis of this aspect of the theme, other than to state that a careful study of the Greek word *hagios,* (ἅγιος) holy, and its derivatives reveals two fundamental facts. *First,* the idea of sanctification involves a setting apart, separation, or consecration; and, *second,* the concept includes a cleansing or purging from sin. The latter emphasis is particularly important in the New Testament. This dual meaning, consecration and cleansing, must ever be kept in mind if the New Testament standard of holiness is to be correctly understood. These two concepts have a clear scriptural basis, and from that authority there is no appeal (cf. WILEY, *Chr. Th.,* II, pp. 464-466).

A. Definitions of Entire Sanctification.

We believe that entire sanctification is that act of God, subsequent to regeneration, by which believers are made free from original sin, or depravity, and brought into a state of full devotement to God, and the holy obedience of love made perfect. It is wrought by the baptism with the Holy Spirit, and comprehends in one experience the cleansing of the heart from sin, and the abiding, indwelling presence of the Holy Spirit empowering the believer for life and service. Entire sanctification is provided by the blood of Jesus; is wrought instantaneously by faith; preceded by entire consecration; and to this work and state of grace the Holy Spirit bears witness. The following are some representative definitions of this experience:

Dr. E. F. Walker—"Sanctification, in the proper sense, is a work of grace, instantaneously wrought in the person of a believer, subsequent to regeneration, administered by Jesus Christ, through the baptism with the Holy Ghost purifying him from all sin, and perfecting him in divine love."

John Wesley—"Sanctification in the proper sense is an instantaneous deliverance from all sin, and includes an instantaneous power then given always to cleave to God."

Dr. John W. Goodwin—"Sanctification is a divine work of grace, purifying the believer's heart from indwelling sin. It is subsequent to regeneration, is secured in the atoning blood of Christ, is effected by the baptism with the Holy Ghost, is conditioned on full consecration to God, is received by faith, and includes instantaneous empowerment for service."

Dr. D. Shelby Corlett—"To be sanctified is nothing more or less than this one thing, the complete removal from the heart of that which is enmity to God, not subject to the law of God, neither indeed can be; and this enables the life to be fully devoted to God. Regardless of how perfect may be the consecration, no Christian is truly sanctified by Christ until the heart is made pure by His blood. This is a definite experience, a mighty work of grace, wrought by God in response to the faith of the consecrated Christian in Christ the Sanctifier. This experience marks a definite second crisis in spiritual life, it is the perfection of a spiritual relationship with God, the cleansing from all sin, when God works within us the devotedness He desires. Devotedness to God—sanctification—includes also a conscious fullness of the Holy Spirit dwelling within as the power of our love, enabling us to live in fellowship with Christ and in full obedience to Him, giving us glorious victory in the many conflicts of life. Holiness as devotedness to God involves the subordination of all other purposes to the one great purpose—the joyful acceptance and the happy doing of the will of God" (D. SHELBY CORLETT, "Holiness— the Central Purpose of Redemption," pp. 22-23).

B. *Justification and Sanctification.*

The nature of sanctification is revealed by a series of contrasts between justification and sanctification. Some of these distinctions are as follows:

1. Justification in a broad sense has reference to the whole work of Christ wrought *for* us; sanctification, the whole work wrought *in* us by the Holy Spirit.

2. Justification is a judicial act in the mind of God; sanctification, a spiritual change wrought in the hearts of men.

3. Justification is a relative change, that is, a change in relation from condemnation to favor; sanctification, an inward change from sin to holiness.

4. Justification secures for us the remission of actual sins; sanctification, in its complete sense, cleanses the heart from original sin or inherited depravity.

5. Justification removes the guilt of sin, sanctification destroys its power.

6. Justification makes possible adoption into the family of God; sanctification restores the image of God.

7. Justification gives a title to heaven, sanctification, a fitness for heaven.

8. Justification logically precedes sanctification, which in its initial stage, is concomitant with it.

9. Justification is an instantaneous and completed act, and therefore does not take place in stages, or by degrees; sanctification is marked by progressiveness in that partial or initial sanctification occurs at the time of justification, and entire sanctification occurs subsequent to justification. Both initial and entire sanctification, however, are instantaneous acts wrought in the hearts of men by the Holy Spirit.

C. *The Existence of Sin in the Regenerate.*

It has been the uniform belief of the Church that original sin continues to exist with the new life of the regenerate, at least until eradicated by the baptism with the Holy Spirit. As stated in the *Thirty-nine Articles,* "This infection of nature doth remain, yea, in them that are regenerated." John Wesley stated his view on the subject in a sermon entitled *Sin in Believers.* He says, in part, "By sin I here understand inward sin; any sinful temper, passion, or affection; such as pride, self-will, love of the world, in any kind or degree; such as lust, anger, peevishness; any disposition contrary to the mind of Christ. . . . . Is a justified or regenerated man freed from all sin as soon as he is justified? . . . . Was he not then freed from all sin, so that there is no sin in his heart? I cannot say this; I cannot believe it; because St. Paul says to the contrary. He is speaking to believers in general when he says, *The flesh lusteth against the Spirit, and the Spirit against the flesh: and these are contrary the one to the other* (Gal. 5:17). Nothing could be more expressive. The apostle here directly affirms that the flesh, evil nature, opposes the Spirit, even in believers; that even in the regenerate there are two principles, contrary the one to the other" (WESLEY, *Sin in Believers*). "The Scriptures affirm that there remains in man, after conversion, what is called 'the flesh,' 'carnality,' 'wrath,' —inherited predisposition—some call this predisposition, 'tendency to evil,' but it is evidently more; the apostle calls it 'the body of sin.' " (DR. P. F. BRESEE, *Sermons*, 46). The condition of the regenerate, previous to entire sanctification, is in a modified sense, a mixed state. There is within the heart of the believer both grace and inbred sin, but there is not, nor can there be commingling or blending of these antagonistic elements. They exist in the heart without admixture or composition. Otherwise we should have adulterated holiness.

D. *Entire Sanctification Is Subsequent to Regeneration.*

Regeneration considered in itself is a perfect work. It is the bestowal of divine life, and as an operation of the Spirit is complete in itself. But regeneration is only a part of the grace embraced in the New Covenant. Only in this sense may it be said to be incomplete. Regeneration is also the beginning of sanctification but only in the sense that the life bestowed in the new birth is a holy life. But we are not to infer from this that the mere expanding of this new life by growth will bring the soul to entire sanctification. Sanctification is an act of cleansing, and unless inbred sin be removed, there can be no fullness of life, no perfection of love. In a strict sense, regeneration is not purification. Initial sanctification accompanies regeneration but the latter is the impartation of life and the former is the cleansing from guilt and acquired depravity. It is true that a life of moral love is common to both regeneration and entire sanctification but the two works are separate and distinct, and consequently the latter is something more than the finishing touches of the former.

1. Why is redemption not comprehended in a single work of grace? Why two distinct works? It is impossible for us to say what God may or may not do. His Word, however, clearly reveals that He does not justify and entirely sanctify by a single work of grace. Doubtless the sinner does not realize his need of sanctification. His guilt and condemnation at first occupy his attention and only later does he come to see his need for further cleansing. Justification and sanctification deal with different phases of sin; the former with sins committed, or sin as an act; the latter with sin inherited, or sin as a principle or nature. It appears to be impossible to fully discover the latter condition without having experienced the former. Then, too, these works of the Spirit are in one sense directly opposite, the one being an impartation of life, the other a crucifixion or death. Finally, the experience of entire sanctification is obtained by faith which may be exercised only after meeting certain conditions, including entire consecration. Such conditions cannot be met by one who is in an unregenerate state.

2. What length of time must elapse between regeneration and entire sanctification? This depends wholly upon the experience of the individual. "This progressive work," says Luther Lee, "may be cut short and finished at any moment, when the intelligence clearly comprehends the defects of the present state, and faith, comprehending the power and willingness of God to sanctify us wholly, and do it now, is exercised" (LEE, *Elements of Theology*, p. 214).

E. *The Divinely Appointed Means and Agencies in Sanctification.*

We can properly appreciate the nature of entire sanctification only by taking into account the means and agencies which God employs to stamp His image anew upon the hearts of men.

1. The originating cause is the love of God. *Herein is love, not that we loved God, but that he loved us, and sent his Son to be the propitiation for our sins* (I John 4: 10).

2. The meritorious or procuring cause is the blood of Jesus Christ. *If we walk in the light, as he is in the light, we have fellowship one with another, and the blood of Jesus Christ his Son cleanseth us from all sin* (I John 1: 7).

3. The efficient cause or agency is the Holy Spirit. We are saved *by the washing of regeneration and the renewing of the Holy Ghost* (Titus 3: 5); we are said to be elected *through sanctification of the Spirit* (I Peter 1: 2); and, we are chosen to salvation *through sanctification of the Spirit and belief of the truth* (II Thess. 2: 13).

4. The instrumental cause is truth. *Sanctify them through thy truth: thy word is truth* (John 17: 17). The Holy Spirit is the spirit of truth and acts through its instrumentality. Hence St. Peter says, *Ye have purified your souls in obeying the truth* (I Peter 1: 22); and St. John declares that *Whoso keepeth his word, in him verily is the love of God perfected: hereby know we that we are in him* (I John 2: 5).

5. The conditional cause is faith. *And put no difference between us and them, purifying their hearts by faith* (Acts 15: 9); *That they may receive forgiveness of sins and inheritance among them which are sanctified by faith that is in me* (Acts 26: 18). When, therefore, we speak of sanctification as being wrought by the Father, or by the Son, or by the Holy Spirit; whether we speak of it as by the blood, or through the truth, or by faith,

we are referring merely to the different causes which enter into this glorious experience.

F. *Progressive Sanctification.*

The term progressive as used in connection with sanctification must be clearly defined. It means simply the temporal aspect of the work of grace in the heart, as it takes place in successive stages. Each of these stages is marked by a gradual approach and an instantaneous consummation. The stages together mark the full scope of sanctifying grace. Mention has already been made of "initial" sanctification, a concomitant of justification and regeneration. In this initial cleansing, the guilt and acquired depravity of the sinner are removed. Since that which removes pollution and makes holy is properly called "sanctification," this first or initial cleansing is "partial" sanctification. It does not refer to cleansing from original sin or inherited depravity. Not only so, but there is a preparatory, or gradual work effected by the Holy Spirit preceding the crisis of entire sanctification. This consists of a godly sorrow on account of indwelling sin, a renunciation of inbred sin, a loathing of the carnal mind. This is never found apart from the illuminating, convincing power of the Holy Spirit. When the child of God, through the Spirit, fully renounces inbred sin and trusts the blood of cleansing he may in that moment, by simple faith in Christ, be sanctified wholly. John Wesley describes this gradual preparation for the crisis of entire sanctification in the following words: "A man may be dying for some time; yet he does not, properly speaking, die until the instant that the soul is separated from the body. In like manner he may be dying to sin for some time, yet he is not dead to sin until sin is separated from his soul; and in that instant he lives the full life of love" (WESLEY, *Plain Account of Christian Perfection,* p. 51). The Scriptures clearly bear out the thought of the gradual preparation and instantaneous completion of entire sanctification. *Our old man, says St. Paul, is crucified with him, that the body of sin might be destroyed, that henceforth we should not serve sin*

(Rom. 6:6). Crucifixion as a means of death, tends to, and has its final issue in death. The "old man" must be kept on the cross until he dies; and when sin expires, in that moment the soul is entirely sanctified and lives the full life of perfect love.

There is still a third aspect in which sanctification is progressive. While entire sanctification is a definite, instantaneously complete act, it is also a completed and continuous act. We mean by this that we are cleansed from all sin, only as through faith, we are brought into a right relation to the atoning blood of Jesus Christ; and only as there is a continuous relation to atoning blood by faith, will there be a continuous cleansing, in the sense of a preservation in purity and holiness. It was with this thought in mind that Dr. Adam Clarke asserted that "It requires the same merit and energy to preserve holiness in the soul of man, as to produce it." Both the instantaneous and continuous aspects of sanctification are set forth by the Apostle John as follows: *But if we walk in the light, as he is in the light, we have fellowship one with another, and the blood of Jesus Christ his Son cleanseth us from all sin* (I John 1:7). Here there is a definite and instantaneous act by which the soul is cleansed from all sin, and a progressive sanctification whereby those who walk in the light are the recipients of the continuous merits of the atoning blood. The same truths are taught in I Peter 1:2, *Elect according to the foreknowledge of God the Father, through sanctification of the Spirit, unto obedience and sprinkling of the blood of Jesus Christ.* Here it is clear that salvation is through sanctification of the Spirit; that sanctification as an instantaneous act cleanses from all sin, and brings the believer to a place of obedience, internally and externally and that walking in this obedience, the elect dwell constantly under the sprinkling of the all-atoning and sanctifying blood. It is important to remember that we are cleansed by the atoning blood only as we are brought into right relation to Jesus Christ; and that we are continuously cleansed, or kept clean, only as these right relations are continued. We are sanctified by Christ, not separate from, but in and with Himself; not only by the blood of cleansing, but under the sprinkling of that blood. Faith is the vital bond of union with Christ, and the pure in heart abide in Him only by a continuous faith. If this connection be severed, spiritual life ceases immediately.

CHAPTER XVIII

ENTIRE SANCTIFICATION OR CHRISTIAN PERFECTION (CONTINUED)

"We count those things perfect which want nothing requisite for the end whereto they were instituted. Accordingly, man may be said to be perfect who answers the end for which God made him, and as God requires every man to love him with all his heart, soul, mind, and strength and his neighbor as himself, then he is a perfect man that does so—he answers the end for which God made him."—DR. ADAM CLARKE.

"What is Christian perfection? The loving God with all our heart, mind, soul, and strength. This implies that no wrong temper, none contrary to love, remains in the soul; and that all the thoughts, words, and actions are governed by pure love."—JOHN WESLEY.

In the chapter just concluded we examined the doctrine of entire sanctification from the standpoint of (1) its historical basis; (2) its scriptural foundation; (3) its meaning and scope; and (4) its nature as completed and progressive. In the present chapter we conclude our analysis of this great truth, and dwell at some length on the correlative term "Christian Perfection."

I. ENTIRE SANCTIFICATION

A. *Entire Sanctification as a Purification from Sin.*

As we have seen, entire sanctification is a term applied to the fullness of redemption, or the cleansing of the heart from all sin. The verb *to sanctify* is from the Latin *sanctus* (holy) and *facere* (to make). When used in the imperative mood it signifies literally *to make holy.* In the Greek we have the same meaning from the verb *hagiadzo,* which is derived from *hagios* (holy), and therefore also means *to make holy.* The first basic element, then, in entire sanctification is the purification of the believer's heart from inbred or inherited depravity.

Original sin must be viewed under a twofold aspect. It is the common sin that infects the race regarded in a general manner; and it is a portion of this general heritage individualized in the separate persons composing the race. As the former, or sin in the generic sense, original sin will not be abolished until the time of restoration of all things. Until that time, something of the penalty remains untaken away; and likewise something of the liability to temptation, or the susceptibility to sin, essential to the probationary state. But in the second sense, the carnal mind, or the sin that dwelleth in the me of the soul—the principle in man which has actual affinity with transgression, this is abolished by the purifying of the Spirit of holiness, and the soul kept pure by His indwelling Presence.

The extent of cleansing, according to the Scriptures, includes the complete removal of all sin. Sin is to be cleansed thoroughly, purged, extirpated, eradicated, and crucified; not repressed, suppressed, counteracted, or made void as these terms are commonly used. It is to be destroyed; and any theory which makes a place for the existence of inbred sin, whatever the provisions made for its regulation, is unscriptural. A study of the Greek terms used in this connection will make this clear.

1. One of the most common terms is *katharidzo*, which means to make clean, or to cleanse in general, both inwardly and outwardly; to consecrate by cleansing or purifying; or to free from the defilement of sin. "It is the very word from which we get our English derivative—cathartic. It literally means to purge, to purify, to remove dross and eliminate that which is foreign. It means nothing more or less than the actual cleansing of the nature of man from the virus of a sinful disposition" (Dr. H. V. Miller, *When He Is Come*). Some of the more prominent texts in which this word is used are the following: *And put no difference between us and them, purifying their hearts by faith* (Acts 15:9); *Having therefore these promises, dearly beloved, let us cleanse ourselves from all filthiness of the flesh and spirit, perfecting holiness in the fear of God* (II Cor. 7:1). *Who gave himself for us, that he might redeem us from all iniquity, and purify unto himself a peculiar (treasured) people, zealous of good works* (Titus 2:14); *But if we walk in the light, as he is in the light, we have*

fellowship one with another, and the blood of Jesus Christ his Son cleanseth us from all sin (I John 1: 7).

2. Another important word is *katargeo* which signifies to annul, to abolish, to put an end to, to cause to cease. *That the body of sin might be destroyed, that henceforth we should not serve sin* (Rom. 6: 6).

3. A strong term is *akrizoo* which means to root out, to pluck up by the roots, and, therefore, to eradicate. Thus the word *eradicate* appears in the original text but is veiled in the English translation. It is found in the word of our Lord to His disciples, *Every plant, which my heavenly Father hath not planted, shall be rooted up* (Matt. 15: 13). This is explained by St. John to mean that our Lord came *to destroy the works of the devil* (I John 3: 8); (cf. Matt. 13: 29; Luke 17: 6; Jude 12).

4. Perhaps the strongest term used in this connection is *stauroo* which according to Thayer means "to crucify the flesh, destroy its power utterly (the nature of the figure implying that the destruction is attended with intense pain)." It is used in Galatians 5: 24 *And they that are Christ's have crucified the flesh with the affections and lusts.*

5. Closely related to the previous term is the word *thanatoo* signifying to subdue, mortify, to kill, to destroy, to render extinct. *Wherefore my brethren, ye also are become dead to the law by the body of Christ* (Rom. 7: 4); *For if ye live after the flesh, ye shall die: but if ye through the spirit do mortify the deeds of the body, ye shall live* (Rom. 8: 13). A careful study of these terms should convince every earnest inquirer that the Scriptures teach the complete cleansing of the heart from inbred sin—the utter destruction of the carnal mind. "Sanctification goes even deeper than contradiction of wrong habits or evil conduct. It strikes not only at our customs and our ideals but it goes to the seat of wrong affections. It demands death to every wrong affection and to every wrong inner feeling and calls for the absorption of the will in the divine will. This is a glorious demand, but a costly one, and, therefore, it is unpopular. Sanctification calls for the death not only to sinful acts,

but sinful desires, sinful appetites and sinful affections. It goes to the center of human character to destroy the works of the devil" (Dr. R. T. Williams, *Sanctification*, pp. 30, 31).

B. *Entire Sanctification as a Positive Devotement to God.*

The work of sanctification involves not only a separation from sin, but a separation to God. This positive devotement, however, is something more than the human consecration of the soul to God. It represents, also, the Holy Spirit's acceptance of the offering, and, therefore, a divine empowering or enduement. It is a divine possession and the spring and energy of this spiritual devotement is holy love. The Spirit of God is able as the Sanctifier, not only to fill the soul with love, but to awaken love in return. Hence St. Paul declares that *the love of God is shed abroad in our hearts by the Holy Ghost which is given unto us* (Rom. 5:5); while St. Peter, approaching the subject from the opposite viewpoint says, *Seeing ye have purified your souls in obeying the truth through the Spirit unto unfeigned love of the brethren, see that ye love one another with a pure heart fervently* (I Peter 1:22). The former is a positive bestowal of divine love— bestowed by the Holy Spirit, and, therefore, holy love; the latter is such a purification as removes from the heart everything that is contrary to the outflow of perfect love. While entire sanctification considered from the negative point of view is the cleansing from all sin, from the positive standpoint it is the infilling of divine love.

Holiness consists in the deep, underlying unity of purity and perfect love. Holiness in man is the same as holiness in God as to quality, but with this difference, the former is derived while the latter is absolute. This unity of purity and love is best expressed in the words concerning Jesus, *Thou hast loved righteousness, and hated iniquity* (Heb. 1:9). Purity and love combine in a basic nature at the very heart of man's personality. It finds expression not so much in any particular virtue, or all the virtues combined, as it does in the recoil of the pure soul from sin and a love for righteousness.

"Holiness is the readjustment of our whole nature, whereby the inferior appetites and propensities are subordinated, and the superior intellectual and moral powers are restored to their supremacy; and Christ reigns in a completed renewed soul." Here is true integration of the personality!

C. *The Divine and Human Elements in Entire Sanctification.*

We have characterized entire sanctification as negatively, purification from sin, and positively, a full devotement to God. We have noted also that holiness embraces both of these at the very core of human personality and finds expression in an inherent spontaneous hatred of iniquity and love for righteousness. This is to view entire sanctification from the human side. How shall we characterize it from the standpoint of divine operations? It is the gift or baptism of the Holy Spirit. "This gift purifies the heart. That means the destruction of the body of sin, the removal of the carnal mind. It means also something further; it is more than housecleaning. The house is cleaned, purified, in order to receive the Guest. He makes it ready for His abode. . . . . Neither does heavenly enduement—aside from the indwelling personality—confer upon men power, either for Christian living or service. To make a man guiltless and pure—which God has provided for—is not sufficient. If left thus he would be an easy prey to the devil and the world, and utterly unable to do the work of bringing men and women to God. We stand by faith, which is heart loyalty to God, an intense longing, trustful gazing into His face; but this would not be sufficient, only that God provides that, into such a heart the divine presence comes, filling it with Himself. He keeps it. He acts in and through it. It becomes His temple and His basis of operations. The Bible insists upon, and we must have, holiness of heart, but we cannot trust in a holy heart; we can trust only in Him who dwells within it" (DR. P. F. BRESEE, *Sermons,* pp. 7, 8, 27). Entire sanctification embraces both the cleansing of the heart from sin and the abiding indwelling presence of the Holy Spirit empowering the believer for life and service. Here the experience of entire sanctification is set off distinctly from that of justification and regeneration which precede it; and it is equally guarded from the erroneous third blessing theory, which regards entire sanctification solely as a work of cleansing, to be followed by the baptism with the Holy Spirit as an added gift of power. The baptism with the Holy Spirit is, therefore, "the baptism with God. It is the burning up of the chaff, but it is also the revelation in us and the manifestation to us of divine personality, filling our being."

II. CHRISTIAN PERFECTION

Christian perfection in the critical sense, represents the more positive aspect of the one experience, known theologically either as entire sanctification or Christian perfection. Entire sanctification, as a term, applies more to the aspect of cleansing from sin or the making holy; while Christian perfection emphasizes the standard of privilege secured to the believer by the atoning work of Jesus Christ.

A. *Misconceptions of Christian Perfection.*

There are numerous misconceptions concerning Christian perfection which must be cleared away before there can be a right understanding or proper appreciation of this work of the Holy Spirit. The term seems to imply a standard of excellence which those who are rightly informed never claim for it. Rightly understood, there can be no objection either to the doctrine or the experience.

1. Christian perfection is not *absolute* perfection. This belongs to God only. In this sense, *there is none good but one, that is, God* (Matt. 19:17). All other goodness is derived. So, also, God alone is perfect; but His creatures may also be perfect in a relative sense, according to their nature and kind.

2. It is not *angelic* perfection. The holy angels are unfallen beings, and, therefore, retain their native fac-

ulties unimpaired. They are not liable to mistake, as is man in his present state of weakness and infirmity; and, therefore, have a perfection impossible to mankind.

3. It is not *Adamic* perfection. Man was made a little lower than the angels, and doubtless in his original state possessed a perfection unknown to man in his present state of existence.

4. It is not a perfection in *knowledge*. Not only was man's will perverted, and his affections alienated by the fall, but his intellect was darkened. Hence from this defective understanding may flow erroneous opinions concerning many matters, and these may in turn lead to false judgments and a wrong bias in the affections.

5. It is not immunity from temptation or the susceptibility to sin. These are essential to a probationary state. Our Lord was tempted in all points as we are, and yet He was without sin.

B. *Implications of the Doctrine of Christian Perfection.*

1. This perfection is *evangelical* as opposed to a legal perfection. *The law made nothing perfect, but the bringing in of a better hope did* (Heb. 7:19). Christian perfection is of grace in that Jesus Christ brings His people to perfection under the present economy. The term "sinless perfection" was one that Wesley never used because of its ambiguity. Those who are justified are saved from their sins; those who are sanctified wholly are cleansed from all sin; but those who are thus justified and sanctified still belong to a race under the doom of original sin, and will bear the consequences of this sin to the end of the age. The term perfection, however, is a proper one for by the grace of our Lord, sin is purged from the soul and the perfect love of God is shed abroad in the heart by the Holy Spirit.

2. Christian perfection is a *relative* term. It is a perfection, which when viewed in relation to the absolute perfection of God, may never be reached, either in this life, or that to come; but when viewed in relation to the present economy, marks a finality, in that it is the deliverance of the spiritual nature from the defilement of

sin. It is true that this redeemed and perfected spirit dwells in a body which is a member of a sinful race; but man's spirit may be lifted from darkness to light, while his body remains the same "muddy vesture of decay" that it was before his spirit was redeemed. Consequently it is still beclouded with weakness, in that the soul is under the influence of material things, and will be until the creature itself shall have put on incorruption and immortality.

3. Christian perfection is *probationary*. It is a state which is always under ethical law, and hence must be guarded by constant watchfulness, and maintained by divine grace. While we remain in this life, however deep our devotion, or fervent our religious life, there are sources of danger within us. In our nature, as essential elements of it, there are appetites, affections, and passions without which we should be unfitted for this present state of existence. These are innocent in themselves, but must be ever kept under control by reason, conscience, and divine grace. The danger and evil lies in the perversion of our God-given faculties to wrong ends. To argue that Christian perfection destroys or eradicates essential elements of human nature; or to believe that a man or woman may not enjoy perfection of spirit while these human elements remain, is to misapprehend entirely the nature of this experience. What Christian perfection does is to give grace to regulate these tendencies, affections, and passions, and bring them into subjection to the higher laws of human nature.

4. Christian perfection is *mediated*. It is not a triumph of human effort, but a work wrought in the heart by the Holy Spirit in answer to simple faith in the blood of Jesus. We are kept by His abiding intercession. *I pray not that thou shouldest take them out of the world, but that thou shouldest keep them from the evil* (John 17:15).

C. *The Fundamental Concept of Christian Perfection.*

The Christian's full privilege in Christ is reflected in the New Testament standard of love as fulfilling the law (Matt. 22: 40; Gal. 5: 14). *This is the covenant that I will make with the house of Israel after those days, saith the Lord; I will put my laws into their mind, and write them in their hearts: and I will be to them a God, and they shall be to me a people* (Heb. 8: 10). *This is the covenant that I will make with them after those days, saith the Lord, I will put my laws into their hearts, and in their minds will I write them; and their sins and iniquities will I remember no more. Now where remission of these is, there is no more offering for sin* (Heb. 10: 16-18). The point to be stressed in these passages is that the full life of love, made perfect in the heart by the agency of the Holy Spirit, constitutes the very essence of the New Covenant of God with His people. Pure love reigns supreme without the antagonisms of sin. Love is the spring of every activity. The believer, having entered into the fullness of the New Covenant, does by nature the things contained in the law, and hence the law is said to be written upon his heart. *Herein is our love made perfect, that we may have boldness in the day of judgment: because as he is, so are we in this world. There is no fear in love; but perfect love casteth out fear: because fear hath torment. He that feareth is not made perfect in love* (I John 4: 17-18).

St. Paul develops the idea of Christian perfection in connection with the attainment of spiritual adulthood (Heb. 5: 12-14; 6: 1). In contrast to the status of Christian childhood (Gal. 4: 1-2), the Christian adult, or "perfect one," has submitted to the baptism with the Holy Spirit (Matt. 3: 11-12; Acts 1: 5), which purifies his heart from all indwelling sin (Acts 15: 9), and fills it with divine love (Rom. 5: 5). In that instant he lives the full life of love. In him love is made perfect, and the conditions of the New Covenant are fulfilled in him. The law of God is written upon his heart.

We conclude that the Scriptures clearly teach that Christian perfection may be obtained in this life; that this perfection consists solely in a life of perfect love, or the loving God with all the heart, soul, mind, and strength; that this perfection of love has no reference to the degree or quantity of love, but to its purity or quality; that this state of perfect love is a consequence of the purification of the heart from all sin, so that love remains in soleness and supremacy; that this purification is accomplished instantaneously by the baptism with the Holy Spirit; and, that the resultant state of perfect love is regarded as adulthood in grace, in that the believer enters into the fullness of the privilege under the New Covenant.

D. *Important Distinctions Regarding Christian Perfection.*

It is necessary to note a few important distinctions concerning Christian perfection in order to preserve the doctrine from some of the erroneous objections which are sometimes urged against it.

1. Purity and maturity must be carefully distinguished from each other. Purity is the result of cleansing from the pollution of sin; maturity is due to growth in grace. Purity is accomplished by an instantaneous act. Maturity is gradual and progressive, and is always indefinite and relative. When, therefore, we speak of perfect love we have reference solely to its quality as being unmixed with sin, never to its degree or quantity. Dr. J. B. Chapman makes the following comment on this essential distinction: "Purity and maturity. The words are similar in sound, but they are very distinct in meaning. Purity may be found in the earliest moments after the soul finds pardon and peace with God. But maturity involves time and growth and trial and development. The pure Christian may even be a weak Christian, for it is not size or strength that is emphasized, but only the absence of evil and the presence of elementary good. Purity is obtained as a crisis, maturity comes as a process. One can be made pure in a twinkling of an eye; it is doubtful that anyone in this world should be listed as really mature. Growth continues while life lasts, and for aught we know, it may continue throughout eternity . . . . more faith, more love, more hope, and more patience incline

one to think that at some undefined time we will have
none of the opposites of these. But growth is not a process for purifying. Growth is addition, purifying is sub-
traction, and even though one may approach holiness by
ever so gradual a process, there must be a last moment
when sin exists and a first moment when it is all gone,
and that means that in reality sanctification must be instantaneous. At this or any given moment every Christian is either free from sin or he is not free from sin.
There can be no sense in which he is actually holy and
at the same time still somewhat defiled" (J. B. CHAP-
MAN, *Holiness the Heart of Christian Experience*, pp.
23, 24).

2. Infirmities must be distinguished from sins. Sin in
the sense used here is a voluntary transgression of a
known law. Infirmities are involuntary transgressions
of the divine law, known or unknown, which are the
result of ignorance or weakness on the part of fallen
man. They are inseparable from mortality. Perfect love
does not bring perfection in knowledge, and hence is
compatible with mistakes in both judgment and practice. Infirmities bring humiliation and regret, but not
guilt and condemnation. Both, however, need the blood
of sprinkling. Under the Levitical rites of purification
errors and infirmities were put away solely by the
sprinkling of blood (Heb. 9:7); while sin always demanded a special offering. It is for this reason that we
maintain that there is not only a definite act of cleansing from sin, but also a continuous blood of sprinkling
for our involuntary transgressions. The Scriptures take
into account this distinction between sins and infirmities. St. Jude says, *Now unto him that is able to keep
you from falling* (without sin) *and to present you fault-
less* (without blemish or unblamable) *before the presence of his glory with exceeding joy* (Jude 24). We may
be kept from sin in this life, we shall be presented fault-
less only in the glorified state.

3. Temptation is reconcilable with the highest degree of evangelical perfection. Jesus was holy, harmless,

undefiled, and separate from sinners, but was tempted in all points as we are, yet without sin. Temptation seems to be involved in the idea of probation. No temptation or evil suggestion becomes sin until it is tolerated or cherished by the mind. As long as the soul maintains its integrity it remains unharmed, however severe or protracted the temptation may be.

The question is sometimes raised as to the difference between the temptations of those who are entirely sanctified, and those who are not. The difference lies in this, that in the latter, temptation stirs up the natural corruption of the heart with its bias toward sin; while in the former, the temptation comes solely from without and the Tempter finds no responsive ally within the heart. This does not mean that the entirely sanctified Christian cannot yield to temptation and sin. He is still human and on probation. The royal road of Satan to the heart of man has always been the natural human desires and appetites of man. These he seeks to pervert to illegitimate ends. Freedom from indwelling sin serves to strengthen the bulwarks of the soul in the hour of temptation, and is an indispensable requisite to a life of constant victory over sin and Satan. *Blessed is the man that endureth temptation: for when he is tried, he shall receive the crown of life, which the Lord hath promised to them that love him* (James 1: 12; Heb. 12: 11).

E. *Christian Perfection a Present Experience.*

Christian perfection as we have shown is nothing more and nothing less, than a heart emptied of all sin and filled with pure love to God and man. As such, it is as a state, not only attainable in this life, but is the normal experience of all those who live in the fullness of the new covenant. It is the result of a divine operation of the Holy Spirit, promised in the Old Testament and fulfilled in the New Testament, by the gift of the Spirit as a Paraclete or Comforter. *The Lord thy God will circumcise thine heart, and the heart of thy seed, to love the Lord thy God with all thine heart, and with all thy soul, that thou mayest live* (Deut. 30: 6). *I*

indeed baptize you with water! declared the forerunner of Jesus, *but . . . . he shall baptize you with the
Holy Ghost, and with fire; whose fan is in his hand, and
he will throughly purge his floor, and gather his wheat
into the garner; but he will burn up the chaff with unquenchable fire* (Matt. 3:11-12). That these passages of
Scripture refer to a spiritual cleansing is confirmed by
St. Peter in these words, *And put no difference between
us and them, purifying their hearts by faith* (Acts 15:9).
As to the manner in which this work is wrought, the
Scriptures are clear, it is by simple faith in the atoning
blood of Jesus Christ; this blood of atonement being not
only the ground of what Christ has purchased for us, but
the occasion of that which His Spirit works within us.

What are the conditions for receiving the experience
of entire sanctification or Christian perfection?

1. A consciousness of inbred sin, and a hungering and
thirsting for full conformity to the image of Christ.
Catharine Booth declared, "God never gave this gift to
any human soul who had not come to the point that he
would sell all to get it," and R. A. Torrey asserted, "No
man ever got this blessing who felt he could get along
without it." This includes also a candid confession of
that need. This was reflected in Dr. Torrey's further
statement that "I cannot take another step in Christian
service until I know I am baptized with the Holy Ghost."

2. A firm conviction in the light of the scriptural provisions that it is not only a privilege but a duty to be
cleansed from all sin.

3. There must be perfect submission of the soul to
God, commonly known as consecration. "Search and
surrender, and research and surrender again, until you
get every vestige of self upon the altar." This is not the
consecration of something evil, but the offering to God,
unconditionally, of that which is good. It is comprehensive. As C. W. Ruth indicated, this consecration includes "all we have and all we expect to have; all we are
and all we hope to be; all we know and all we do not
know, with a promise of an eternal 'yes' to all the will
of God for all the future. It is not consecration to a work,

or consecration to a certain calling, but consecration to God. It is not simply a desire to consecrate or a willingness to consecrate, but the unconditional and irrevocable signing of the deed of all to God for time and eternity." It is not an act of feeling but of the will. It is a voluntary, unreserved, irrevocable, enlightened, and comprehensive dedication for the specific attainment of heart holiness.

4. An act of simple faith in Christ—a sure trust in Him for the promised blessing. "The voice of God to your soul is, Believe and be saved. Faith is the condition, and the only condition, of sanctification, exactly as it is in justification. No man is sanctified until he believes; and every man when he believes is sanctified" (WESLEY, *Works*, II, p. 224). "But what is that faith whereby we are sanctified, saved from sin and perfected in love? This faith is a divine evidence or conviction (1) that God hath promised this sanctification in the Holy Scriptures. (2) It is a divine evidence or conviction that what God hath promised He is able to perform. (3) It is a divine evidence or conviction that He is able and willing to do it now. (4) To this confidence, there needs to be added one thing more—a divine evidence or conviction that He doeth it" (WESLEY, *Sermons*, I, p. 390).

F. *Evidences of Christian Perfection.*

It is the uniform testimony of those who believe and teach the Wesleyan doctrine of Christian perfection, that the Spirit bears witness to this work of grace in the heart, exactly as He bears witness to Christian sonship. According to Wesley, "None ought to believe that the work is done till there is added the testimony of the Spirit witnessing his entire sanctification as clearly as his justification. . . . . We know it by the witness and by the fruit of the Spirit" (WESLEY, *Plain Account of Christian Perfection*, pp. 79, 118). Scriptural accounts of the sanctification of individuals or groups leave no doubt that the recipients knew with absolute certainty that the Spirit had come in His sanctifying power. The whole tenor of the Scripture is to the effect that men may know with certainty the realities of salvation. While the Scriptures stress the witness of the Spirit to Christian sonship (Ch. XVII, Sec. IV), yet it is evident that the sanctified soul may know by the testimony of his own spirit, and the witness of the Holy Spirit that the blood of Jesus Christ has cleansed him from all sin. Here we have the testimony of consciousness, which we can no more doubt than our own existence. And in addition to this, there is the direct and positive testimony of the witnessing Spirit. To all this is added the indirect testimony of a life of continuous victory through the power of the indwelling Spirit, and increased success in bringing forth the fruits of the Spirit (Gal. 5: 22-23).

UNIT VI

CHRISTIAN ETHICS AND INSTITUTIONS

Preview

Faith and works, the subjective and objective aspects of the Christian life, the experience of entire sanctification and the life of holiness: these pairs may be compared to the two oars of a rowboat. Both are essential to any worth-while progress. So also there must be the Christian experience within and the holy life without if advancement is to be made in spiritual things. It is both reasonable and scriptural to expect that the experience of Christian Perfection inwrought in the believer by the Holy Spirit should be consistently exemplified by a holy walk and godly conversation.

It is to this life of holiness that we give our first consideration in this sixth unit. What is the nature of Christian liberty? What part does conscience play in directing conduct? What duties do we owe to God? to ourselves? to others? These and other related questions will be answered as we examine the outworking of the experience of heart purity in the life of the believer.

As we study our Christian obligations, we soon discover that some are social in character. There are duties owed within the family, toward the state, and to the Church. This leads to our study of each of these institutions as God-given and God-ordained.

Of these institutions the Church is of special interest to us as Christians. Its nature is depicted under the two meaningful symbols: the Body of Christ, and the Temple of the Holy Spirit. Its organization, ministry, and worship constitute points of special emphasis. Lastly, our attention is directed toward the sacraments of the Church: Christian baptism and the Lord's Supper.

Are you a member of His Church? Are you of the Body of Christ? Then pray that you may envision the world's need as with His eyes; grasp true spiritual realities as with His mind; feel the world's heartbreak as with His heart; and minister to that need as His hands and His feet. *Now ye are the body of Christ and members in particular.*

UNIT VI

CHRISTIAN ETHICS AND INSTITUTIONS

Chapter XIX. *The Life of Holiness*

I. THE PRINCIPLES OF CHRISTIAN ETHICS
   A. Sources of Christian Ethics.
   B. The Scriptural Basis of Ethics.
   C. Christian Perfection and Ethics.
   D. The Law of Liberty.
   E. The Law of Love.
   F. Conscience as a Regulative Factor in Christian Experience and Conduct.

II. DUTIES TO GOD
   A. The Theistic Virtues.
   B. Reverence as the Fundamental Duty to God
   C. The Duty and Forms of Prayer.
   D. The Supreme Duty of Worship.

III. DUTIES TO ONESELF
   A. The Sanctity of the Body.
   B. The Culture of the Mind.
   C. The Development of the Spiritual Life.

IV. DUTIES WE OWE TO OTHERS
   A. Violations of Brotherly Love.
   B. The Christian View of the Rights of Man.
   C. Duties Owed Within the Family.
      1. Duties of Husbands and Wives.
      2. Duties of Parents and Children.
   D. Man's Duty to the State.

Chapter XX. *The Christian Church*

I. THE NATURE OF THE CHRISTIAN CHURCH
   A. The Church as the Body of Christ.
   B. The Church as the Temple of the Holy Spirit.
   C. The Founding of the Christian Church.
   D. Notes and Attributes of the Church.
   E. The Organization of the Christian Church.

CHAPTER XIX

THE LIFE OF HOLINESS

"What evidences indicate advancement in holiness? (1) An increasing comfort and delight in the Holy Scriptures. (2) An increasing interest in prayer, and an increasing spirit of prayer. (3) An increasing desire for the holiness of others. (4) A more heart-searching sense of the value of time. (5) Less desire to hear, see, and know for mere curiosity. (6) A growing inclination against magnifying the faults and weaknesses of others, when obliged to speak of their characters. (7) A greater readiness to speak freely to those who do not enjoy religion, and to backward professors of religion. (8) More disposition to glory in reproach for Christ's sake, and suffer, if need be, for him. (9) An increasing tenderness of conscience, and being more scrupulously conscientious. (10) Less affected by changes of place and circumstances. (11) A sweeter enjoyment of the holy Sabbath, and the services of the sanctuary. (12) An increasing love for the searching means of grace."—REV. J. A. WOOD.

After a consideration of the doctrine and experience of Christian perfection, it is proper that we devote some attention to its practical or ethical aspects. A holy heart is a necessary and fundamental condition for holy living. As the Scriptures declare, *We are his workmanship, created in Christ Jesus unto good works, which God hath before ordained that we should walk in them* (Eph. 2:10).

Most theologians devote some attention to the subject of ethics, even though it is to a considerable extent outside the normal field of theology. Theology seeks to answer the inquiry, what ought we to *believe?* Ethics seeks to answer the question, what ought we to *do?* Our purpose, therefore, is not to examine in detail the general field of ethics, but only to study more immediately the life of holiness as related to the doctrine and experience of entire sanctification.

I. THE PRINCIPLES OF CHRISTIAN ETHICS

A. *Sources of Christian Ethics.*

As in the case of theology, the sources of Christian ethics are dual in character. God has revealed Himself in two types of law—natural and positive. Natural law is that which God has written upon the heart of every man, or that which the light of reason teaches us is good or evil. Thus the Apostle Paul writes of the heathen, in contrast to the Jews, that *These, having not the law, are a law unto themselves: which shew the work of the law written in their hearts, their conscience also bearing witness, and their thoughts the mean while accusing or else excusing one another* (Rom. 2:14-15). They are a law unto themselves because they know in themselves what is good and what is evil through reason which is to them the herald of divine law. Both history and experience teach us that all nations acknowledge certain common principles of morality which cannot be entirely accounted for on the basis of education. These reflect a measure of divine revelation. Such universal maxims of conduct have their common source in natural reason, which is from the Light that lighteth all men coming into the world (John 1:9).

Far more important as a basis of Christian ethics is positive law which depends upon God's free will and can be known only through special revelation. Nature alone can no more furnish an adequate basis for ethics than it can for theology. The Christian revelation, culminating in the perfect life of our Lord Jesus Christ, becomes the foundation of Christian ethics. His words, deeds and spirit become the norm of all Christian conduct. His words furnish us with the knowledge of the divine will; His actions are the confirmations of the truth; and His Spirit is the power by which His words are embodied in deed.

B. *The Scriptural Basis of Ethics.*

Having indicated that the Christian revelation is the basis of ethics, a number of observations are in order. The question is often asked, Are the sources of Christian ethics to be derived solely from the New Testament, or are the Old Testament writings to be considered in this connection? This subject has been previously considered in another connection (Ch. IV, Sec. III B), and it is sufficient to say here that the Old Testament, insofar as it is applicable to the Christian life, is still binding upon men. Certain portions of it, however, especially the types or shadows of better things to come, had their perfect fulfillment in Jesus Christ; while others of a ceremonial or political nature were abrogated as belonging only to the Mosaic economy. But as to the moral law of Moses, the substance of which was embodied in the Decalogue, this was not superseded. Instead it was referred to by our Lord as of abiding authority without any special re-enactment. *Think not that I am come to destroy the law, or the prophets: I am not come to destroy, but to fulfil. For verily I say unto you, Till heaven and earth pass, one jot or one tittle shall in no wise pass from the law, till all be fulfilled. Whosoever therefore shall break one of these least commandments, and shall teach men so, he shall be called the least in the kingdom of heaven: but whosoever shall do and teach them, the same shall be called great in the kingdom of heaven* (Matt. 5: 17-19).

The ethical teaching of the Gospels center in the idea of the kingdom, entrance into which is based solely on the ground of repentance and faith. Acceptance of the call of God involves the subordination of all other loyalties: *Seek ye first the kingdom of God* (Matt. 6: 33). The Sermon on the Mount has been called the Magna Charta of the kingdom. Here the true inwardness of its nature is set forth in an attitude of spirit—of thought, feeling, and will which finds its highest expression in word and deed. The description which Jesus gives is not that of certain acts, but of a certain type of character. The true spring of obedience is found in divine love. When asked concerning the greatest commandment of the law, Jesus replied, *Thou shalt love the Lord thy God with all thy heart . . . . and with all thy mind. This is the first and great commandment. And the second is like unto it, Thou shalt love thy neighbour as thyself. On these two commandments hang all the law and prophets* (Matt. 22: 37-40). The children of the kingdom are to be as *wise as serpents and harmless as doves* (Matt. 10: 16). They are to *resist not evil* (Matt. 5: 39), and fear only him *which after he hath killed hath power to cast into hell* (Luke 12: 5). According to Jesus, the supreme test of love is this, *that a man lay down his life for his friends* (John 15: 13). In close connection with this is the practical application, *For whosoever will save his life shall lose it: but whosoever will lose his life for my sake, the same shall save it* (Luke 9: 24).

C. *Christian Perfection and Ethics.*

In our examination of entire sanctification or Christian perfection as the standard of New Testament experience, we found that it was a purification of the heart from sin in order to effect a full devotement of the whole being to Jesus Christ. Grace must first express itself in Christian experience; and from the communication of this new life and love, new standards of daily living will be formed. Doctrine may not always issue in experience; but experience, if it is to be maintained, must always issue in Christian living. Every doctrine has not only its experiential phase but also its ethical expression. God is a Person, and man is a person, hence all their relationships must be ethical. The dominant note of Christian perfection being that of a full devotement to God, this devotement becomes a fundamental principle in Christian ethics. The wholly sanctified person is *no longer his own,* and he lives by the principle expressed by St. Paul, *"Whether therefore ye eat, or drink, or whatsoever ye do, do all to the glory of God* (I Cor. 10: 31).

D. *The Law of Liberty.*

Through our Lord Jesus Christ, the life of the Christian is characterized by glorious freedom. St. James describes this new status as *the perfect law of liberty* (James 1: 25); and St. Paul speaks of it as *the law of the Spirit of life in Christ Jesus,* which makes us free from *the law of sin and death* (Rom. 8: 2). The external law ceases to be the law of sin and death, for the consciousness of sins is removed in justification; and the inner law of life by the Spirit furnishes the motive and the strength of obedience. This is the foundational fact of the New Covenant, *I will put my laws into their mind, and write them in their hearts* (Heb. 8:10). While this law within the Christian is supernatural, it is in some true sense the law of reason restored, and more than restored. The divine Spirit in the hearts of regenerate men seeks to work out obedience to the law of righteousness. Hence the believer unfolds in his spiritual life according to his own new nature, and not by means of outward compulsion. It is the rule of God's Spirit in a renewed self, according to the original idea of the Creator for man. Men are thus in their new natures under the authority of the Holy Spirit, and having their souls in subjection. They become a law unto themselves, *not without law to God, but under the law to Christ* (I Cor. 9:21). Thus the law is not made void, but established through faith (Rom. 3:31).

We are indeed delivered from the law of sin and death, but not from the law of holiness and life. While the law is written upon the heart, it is still a law, and therefore necessitates the dignity of an external standard also, in conformity with the inner law of life. The fundamental fact then, in Christian ethics is the law of life by which man is delivered from outward compulsion, and given the freedom to develop according to the new law of his nature. Thus he keeps the law, by the unfolding of his inner nature which is now in harmony with that law. In other words, he *does* right because he *wishes* to do so, not because he is compelled to do so. The keynote of his new inner nature is love, and thus love is the fulfilling of the law.

E. *The Law of Love.*

The basic motive to righteousness in Christian conduct is the law of love. Christian perfection is a purification of the heart from all that is contrary to pure love. Love is both the principle and the power of a perfect consecration to God. Charity or divine love, which has its source in the nature of God, and which is imparted to the individual soul by the Holy Spirit through Christ, becomes in its full ethical meaning the substance of all obligation—whether to God or man. Love is the crown of all the graces, the sum of all interior goodness, the bond of perfectness which unites and hallows all the energies of the soul, and the propulsive power of right-eousness. "It is a love," says Dr. Pope, "which neglects no injunction, forgets no prohibition, discharges every duty. It is perfect in passive as well as active obedience. It 'never faileth'; it insures every grace adapted to time or worthy of eternity. Therefore it is that the term per-fect is reserved for this grace. Patience must *have her perfect work;* but love alone is itself perfect, while it gives perfection to him who has it" (POPE, *Compendium of Christian Theology,* III, p. 177).

F. *Conscience as a Regulative Factor in Christian Ex-perience and Conduct.*

Conscience is a regulative factor in Christian ex-perience and conduct. St. Paul, speaking of conscience as an integral part of vital religious experience, declared, *Now the end of the commandment is charity out of a pure heart, and of a good conscience, and of faith un-feigned* (I Tim. 1:5). Here the apostle analyzes Chris-tian experience as follows: a stream of charity or divine love, flowing from a pure heart, regulated by a good con-science, and kept full and fresh and flowing by an un-feigned faith.

To understand more precisely the nature of con-science we need to remember that man is a moral being by virtue of being a person. Also, we should keep in mind the fact that the spirit as the controlling factor in man's complex being is a unit, and, consequently, is not divisible into parts. Thus, for example, both intellect and emotion are probably present to some extent in every activity. However, while the person acts as a unit, one form of activity, such as emotion, may so predominate at a given time, as to be discriminated and defined. For this reason we may define intellect as the soul thinking, and the will as the soul choosing. So, also, if we restrict our definition of conscience to certain modes of self-activity, we do not imply that the whole person is not active, but only that particular functions of the moral nature are predominant. We may, therefore, define conscience as "the self passing judgment upon its conformity or nonconformity, in character and conduct to the moral law, that is, as right or wrong, with the accompanying feeling or impulse to obey the judgment of the righteous" (ROBBINS, *The Ethics of the Christian Life,* p. 79). Conscience, thus defined, may be likened to a judge presiding over a court deciding that this desire, this affection, this purpose, this deed is in accordance with moral law, and therefore right. Upon this judgment a corresponding feeling follows, either impelling to action in accordance with the decision, or opposing any action not in harmony with it.

Conscience, as just defined, derives its authority from the law of God which is found primarily in the nature and constitution of man. Its authority is internal. Were men in their normal state, as was the case of man before the fall, the decisions of conscience would always be in conformity with the law of reason and, therefore, infallibly right. But man is not in his normal state. The law of his being is obscured and perverted as a consequence of original sin. Hence, although conscience always makes its decisions according to the law, the latter being obscured or perverted, the decisions will in these instances be erroneous. For this reason, God has given to man an external law as a transcript of his own true inner life and this law is found in the Word of God.

In our discussion of conscience to this point, two factors have been emphasized: the inner impulse to do right, and the moral judgment as to what constitutes the right. The former is conscience proper. It says, "Find the right and do it." The latter or moral judgment is, strictly speaking, not a part of conscience, but the standard by which conscience operates. Since this moral judgment is true only insofar as it is enlightened by the Word of God, we are led to the conviction that in the Christian life, the Scriptures are the only authoritative rule of faith and practice. Conscience in the broader sense, that is, as involving the whole moral process, is subject to education and development. Hence the Scriptures speak of a good or pure conscience; or of an evil or defiled conscience.

A good conscience is one which is enlightened by the Spirit of truth, and therefore always makes its decisions according to the standards of God's holy Word. The conscience also may be distinguished as pure (I Tim. 8:9; II Tim. 1:3); evil (Heb. 10:22); defiled (Titus 1:15); weak (I Cor. 8:7); and seared (I Tim. 4:2). To these are sometimes added such descriptive terms as steady or wavering, morbid or sound, and enlightened or dark when reference is being made to the state of the conscience.

II. Duties to God

Practical ethics involve the application of moral principles to the regulation of human conduct. In our discussion of this theme we shall observe the following outline: (1) Theistic Ethics or Duties to God; (2) Individual Ethics or Duties to Oneself; and (3) Social Ethics or Duties to Others.

Strictly speaking, all obligation must be to God as the Moral Governor, and all duties, therefore, are duties to God. The duties to self come second in order as essential to the formation of Christian character. Lastly, there is the regulation of external conduct toward others, as having its source in, and flowing from the character of the individual.

A. *The Theistic Virtues.*

The theistic virtues are faith, hope, and charity or love. These occupy first place in the Christian life and upon them all other virtues depend. By them we are actually united to God—to God as truth, by faith; to God as faithful, by hope; and to God as the supreme good, by love.

Viewed from the ethical standpoint, we may briefly analyze these three cardinal virtues as follows: (1) Faith is at once an act and a habit, in that it is a conscious repose in the merits of another. The sins against faith are infidelity, heresy, and apostasy. Infidelity is unfaithfulness to God; heresy is unfaithfulness to truth or persistence in error; while apostasy is a departure from religion. (2) Hope is that divine virtue which furnishes the motive whereby we trust with unwavering confidence in the word of God, and look forward to the obtainment of all He has promised to us. Hope may be viewed as either an act or a state. It relates to the future, and implies expectation of desirable objects. The sins against hope are despair on the one hand, and presumption or false confidence on the other. Despair is the abandonment of all hope of salvation. Presumption is taking advantage of God's goodness to commit sin. (3) Charity or divine love is the virtue whereby we give ourselves wholly to God as the sovereign good. It is a divinely infused virtue, the motive of which is God's goodness, and its object both God and our neighbor. It is that affection which wishes well to another, or desires what is good for him.

B. *Reverence as the Fundamental Duty to God.*

Reverence has been defined as a "profound respect mingled with fear and affection," or as "a synthesis of love and fear." As such, reverence is the supreme duty of man, the creature, to God, the Creator. It is the sentiment from which all worship springs. Reverence when expressed silently is known as adoration, and carries with it the added idea of homage or personal devotion. Praise is the audible expression which extols the Divine Perfections. Thanksgiving is expressed gratitude for the mercies of God. The duty of the devout spirit is to offer to God the adoration of the creature, the homage of the subject, and the praise of the worshiper.

In St. Paul's enumeration of the works of the flesh, two are mentioned that are violations of the duty of reverence. These are idolatry and witchcraft. Idolatry is commonly defined as the paying of divine honors to idols, images, or other created objects. It may also consist of excessive admiration, veneration, or love for any person or thing. Thus covetousness is regarded as

idolatry (Col. 3:5). Witchcraft is the practice of the
arts of a sorcerer or sorceress, which are commonly believed to be the consequence of intercourse with Satan.
The injunction forbids all enchantments, necromancy,
spiritism, or other so-called black arts.

C. *The Duty and Forms of Prayer.*

Prayer is a duty which is obligatory upon all men as
an expression of their dependence upon the Creator.
What the habitual sense of reverence is to adoration and
praise, the spirit of dependence is to prayer. Dr. Wakefield defines prayer as "The offering of our desires to
God through the mediation of Jesus Christ, under the
influence of the Holy Spirit, and with suitable dispositions, for all things agreeable to His will." Prayer must
be offered to God, through Christ, and in the Spirit to be
acceptable. It must also be offered for things agreeable
to the will of God, and the petitions must be presented
with faith in His promises.

There are a number of different forms or types of
prayer which are included under the general duty of
prayer.

1. Ejaculatory prayer is a term applied to "those
secret and frequent aspirations of the heart to God for
general or particular blessings, by which a just sense of
our habitual dependence upon God and of our wants and
dangers may be expressed while we are employed in the
common affairs of life." It denotes a devotional attitude
of mind and heart in which a constant spirit of prayer is
maintained. It includes all those impromptu expressions
of prayer and praise which flow from a heart which is
cultivated to *Rejoice evermore, pray without ceasing,*
and *in everything give thanks* (I Thess. 5:16-18). This
form of prayer was held by the fathers as a distinguishing mark of genuine piety, but the habit needs to be
guarded against any formality or excessive familiarity
which would leave the impression of irreverence.

2. Private prayer is expressly enjoined by our Lord
in the words, "But thou, when thou prayest, enter into

thy closet, and when thou hast shut thy door, pray to thy
Father which is in secret; and thy Father which seeth
in secret shall reward thee openly" (Matt. 6:6). The
duty of private prayer is further enforced by the example of our Lord and His apostles. The strict performance of private prayer has ever been regarded as one
of the surest marks of genuine piety and Christian sincerity.

3. Family or social prayer grows out of the nature of
the social structure itself. Family prayer is basic in the
whole system of Christian worship. The worship of
patriarchal times was largely domestic; and the sacred
office of father or master of the household passed from
Judaism to Christianity. Early Christian worship was
at first chiefly confined to the family, and only gradually took on a wider significance. Hence family worship
became an essential factor in the public services, by in-
culcating a spirit of devotion and by training in the
forms of worship. Parents may as well conclude, therefore that they are under no obligation to feed and clothe
their children, or to educate for lawful employment, as
to conclude that they are under no obligation to afford
them the proper religious instruction. "From all these
considerations, we conclude," says Dr. Ralston, "that
family prayer though not directly enjoined by express
precept, is yet a duty so manifest from the general principles of the gospel, the character of the Christian, the
constitution of the family, the benefits it imparts, and
the general promises of God, that it must be of binding
obligation on every Christian who is the head of a household" (RALSTON, *Elements of Divinity*, p. 780).

4. Public prayer includes every branch of public
worship, such as prayer, praise, the reading of the Scriptures, and the singing of psalms, hymns, and spiritual
songs. Public prayer was a part of the Jewish worship,
at least from the time of Ezra, and was performed in
the synagogues. Our Lord frequently attended and
participated in these services, and by this means placed
His approval upon the practice of public prayer. This

duty is also founded upon the express declaration of the Scriptures. St. Paul says, *I exhort therefore, that, first of all, supplications, prayers, intercessions, and giving of thanks be made for all men* (I Tim. 2:1); and again, *I will therefore that men pray everywhere, lifting up holy hands without wrath and doubting* (I Tim. 2:8). Public worship is designed to benefit each individual worshiper, to keep alive the sense of dependence upon God as the Giver of every good and perfect gift, and to publicly express the grateful remembrance of every material and spiritual blessing.

D. *The Supreme Duty of Worship.*

The union of all of the aspects of devotion constitutes divine worship. This is the highest duty of man. It includes the active offering to God of the tribute due Him, together with the supplication of His benefits. Worship blends meditation and contemplation with prayer, and these through the Spirit, strengthen the soul for its work of faith and labor of love. As worship marks the consummation of all ethical duty to God, so the end of all worship is spiritual union with God. This is the goal set for the Church by our Lord in His high-priestly prayer. He prayed *That they all may be one; as thou, Father, art in me, and I in thee, that they also may be one in us* (John 17:21). This is a personal spiritual union in which the identity of the individual is preserved. It is a union of affection, of like-mindedness, and identity of purpose. "Worship is the recognition of Christ," says Bishop McIlvaine, "and the ascription to Him of everything which is beautiful and glorious and desirable. It is the necessary tendency of all true worship to assimilate the worshiper into the likeness of the being worshiped." Thus the public and private worship of Christ becomes one of the chief agencies in our redemption. The thoughts and feelings of the heart demand for their completeness, a corresponding expression. Faith finds this expression in the worship services of the church and the duties of the Christian life.

III. Duties to Oneself

Individual ethics is that division of practical ethics which treats of the application of the moral law to the regulation of man's conduct insofar as it has reference to himself as an individual moral agent. These duties to self are essential in the formation of character, and thus are second in importance only to one's duties to God.

A. *The Sanctity of the Body.*

Since man's physical existence is essential to the fulfillment of his mission in this life, it is a first duty to conserve and develop all the powers of his being. Christianity regards the body, not as a prison house of the soul, but as a temple of the Holy Spirit. This gives sanctity to the body; and the preservation of this sanctity becomes a guiding principle in all matters of physical welfare. The specific duties pertaining to the body are as follows:

1. There must be the preservation and development of the bodily powers. This becomes a high and holy duty, for man's existence in the world depends upon this bodily organism. He who neglects his physical being, places his whole mission in jeopardy; he who destroys it, brings his mission to an end. Hence, self-murder is strictly prohibited. Wherever there is a morally enlightened conscience, men have agreed that suicide is contrary to the end for which life is given. So, also, self-mutilation is forbidden. This includes any bodily injury or dismemberment such as disfigures the body or prevents the complete functioning of the physical organism. Christianity is opposed to ascetic practices such as were found among the mystics of the Middle Ages, and as they are practiced in pagan countries at the present time. The fasts and self-denials which Christianity enjoins upon men are intended to invigorate rather than enfeeble the human body.

2. There must be the care and culture of the body through exercise, rest, sleep, and recreation. Both labor and rest are essential to man's well-being. The world owes no man a living who is able to earn it for himself.

Holiness dignifies labor and makes it delightful, whether with the hands, the head, or the heart. It also dignifies rest and makes the Sabbath a symbol of the spiritual "rest of faith." The tension of both mind and body resulting from the pace and complexity of modern industrial life emphasize the necessity of periods of rest and recreation as essential factors in the preservation of the body.

3. The appetites and passions of the body must be subjugated to man's higher intellectual and spiritual interests. Some have assumed that holiness implies the destruction or the near destruction of the physical appetites and pleasurable emotions. This is not according to the Scriptures. Holiness destroys nothing that is essential to man, either physically or spiritually. The appetites and passions remain but they are freed from the contamination of sin. The fact is that holiness fits one for the fullest enjoyment of all legitimate pleasures and satisfactions. The early disciples *did eat their meat with gladness and singleness of heart* (Acts 2: 46). One of the apostles warns against those *seducing spirits* who go about *forbidding to marry, and commanding to abstain from meats, which God hath created to be received with thanksgiving of them which believe and know the truth* (I Tim. 4: 1, 3).

Holiness does not necessarily provide immediately for a normal condition of the appetites and passions. Sometimes perverted appetites exist for considerable time in those who have clean hearts, but who have not had as yet, any light on these specific matters. However, both perverted and natural appetites are so subject to the power of God as to be corrected or regulated through faith. All appetite is instinctive and unreasoning. It knows nothing of right or wrong, but simply craves indulgence. It never controls itself, but is subject to control. Hence St. Paul says, *But I keep under my body, and bring it into subjection: lest that by any means when I have preached to others, I myself should be a castaway* (I Cor. 9: 27).

4. The care of the body demands proper clothing, not only for protection and comfort, but for propriety and decency. The question of dress not only concerns the welfare of the body, but becomes also an expression of the character and aesthetic nature of the individual. For this reason it is made a matter of apostolic injunction (cf. I Tim. 2: 9-10; I Peter 3: 3-4). Scriptural admonitions concerning adornment indicate that becoming taste should prevail in such matters; that dress should be appropriate to the wearer's age, the occasion, and the station in life; that modesty and sound-mindedness should govern the selection of appropriate adornment; and that all apparel should accentuate the modesty and beauty of the wearer. The apostle indicates that ornaments of gold, pearl, and other costly array are not in harmony with the spirit of meekness and modesty which is characteristic of the true Christian. In summary, Christians are admonished to dress in such a manner that the apparel will not attract undue attention either by reason of its eccentric plainness or gaudy expensiveness. Adornment should always contribute to the personal, social and spiritual effectiveness of the consecrated, sanctified Christian.

5. The body must be preserved holy. To render the body impure by devoting it to unholy service is sin. To give it over loosely to its own appetites, whether natural or abnormal, is also sin. Hence St. Paul says, *For this is the will of God, even your sanctification, that ye should abstain from fornication: that every one of you should know how to possess his vessel in sanctification and honour* (I Thess. 4: 3-4). During this life the body must be the object of sanctified care, and true holiness is always consistent with superior attention to it. The supreme reason for the sanctity of the body lies in the fact that it is the temple of the Holy Spirit. It is God's dwelling place. *What? know ye not that your body is the temple of the Holy Ghost which is in you, which ye have of God, and ye are not your own? For ye are bought with a price: therefore glorify God in your body, and in your spirit, which are God's* (I Cor. 6: 19-20). Whatever,

therefore, tends to injure the body or to destroy its
sanctity as the temple of the Holy Spirit is forbidden by
Christian teaching and practice.

B. *The Culture of the Mind.*

The word "mind" as used here refers generally to
the inner life, that is, the life of the soul in contrast to
the physical life of the body. Our Lord indicated the
necessity of developing all the powers of the mind in His
commandment, *Thou shalt love the Lord thy God with
all thy heart, and with all thy soul, and with all thy mind,
and with all thy strength: this is the first commandment*
(Mark 12:30). Here the "heart" refers to man's inmost
being, the seat of his affections; the love of the "soul"
refers to the glow of feeling which attaches to it; the
"mind" has reference to the intellectual powers through
which love is understood and interpreted; and "strength"
means the full devotion to God of all the powers of personality as thus developed. The love of the heart is
purifying, the love of the soul enriching, and the love
of the mind interpretative. The first has its object in
God as the supreme Good; the second, God as the
supreme Beauty manifested in order and harmony; and
the third, God as the supreme Truth or Reality.

1. The development of the intellect is essential to a
useful Christian life. The desire to know is human and
God-given, and in Christian experience, this desire is
greatly intensified. Ignorance is no part of holiness.
Christ is the truth, and hence the followers of Christ become "disciples" or learners. One who does not love
truth—scientific, philosophical or otherwise—has little
appreciation of the wonderful works of God. One who
has not a burning desire for spiritual truth may seriously
question any claim to the gift of the promised Comforter
who is expressly stated to be the Spirit of truth. The intellect and the understanding give vision to the soul.
Hence only with the broadening of the intellectual horizons, and a spiritual insight into truth can there be the
enrichment of the affectional nature and the deepening
of the spiritual life. Breadth of understanding also makes

for stability of character. Indecision and instability are frequently the consequences of short-sightedness. Wide intellectual horizons and far distances are essential to a continuity of purpose. St. Paul recognized this truth when he wrote that *Our light affliction, which is but for a moment, worketh for us a far more exceeding and eternal weight of glory; while we look not at the things which are seen, but at the things which are not seen: for the things which are seen are temporal; but the things which are not seen are eternal* (II Cor. 4:17-18).

2. The emotional or feeling aspect of man's inner life is intimately related to the intellect and the will. In religious experience, the perception of new truth, or of familiar truth in new aspects, results in emotional or feeling experiences. These emotional experiences are usually a composite of human and divine elements. Truths seen and realized through the aid of the Holy Spirit bring a glow of feeling. When that truth becomes familiar the glow of feeling is likely to subside or fade in consciousness. The result of the ebb and flow of emotional experience has often been an occasion of difficulty for young and inexperienced Christians. Many have unwisely sought for religious feeling as such. The essential factor, however, in the development of the emotional life of the Christian is to search the Word for new truth, or plead the Spirit's guidance into the deeper aspects of truth already known. Feeling apart from truth leads into dangerous fanaticism, but truth which gives rise to strong emotion becomes a supreme power in the life of holiness. The man who moves others is the man who is himself moved by truth. To act from principle is worthy, but to act from principle on fire is the high privilege of every New Testament Christian. While emotion has its legitimate and important place in Christian experience; it is to be remembered that faith in the eternal Word of God is central and basic. One can possess constant Christian certitude despite the ebb and flow of emotional experiences.

3. The moral nature requires development. Here we refer primarily to the development of the will with its

obligation and responsibility. It is only by proper choices that moral character is formed, and conduct is wholly dependent upon moral character. The impulses of the soul must be brought under the will and subordinated to the highest good. Correct moral standards are derived ultimately from the Word of God. They may be learned from teachers, from a study of the Scriptures or from works bearing on the subject, from the observance of correct social practices, or from the examples of good men. But they must be *learned*—they cannot be had otherwise. It is the duty of each individual, therefore, to cultivate the highest standards of ethical life, and to conscientiously observe every rule of moral obligation. This discipline of the will is effected only through controlled choices. Man learns to do by doing, and he gains facility only in constancy of action. Duty at first may cost much self-denial. There must be vigorous effort and eternal vigilance. However, with each duty done, new strength is acquired according to the law of habit and the pathway of duty becomes easier and lighter. Discipline, whether by the individual himself or by others, is exceedingly important. Without it there can never be developed that strength of purpose and ruggedness of character which becomes the true soldier of the cross.

4. Man has an aesthetic nature which also requires cultivation. The intellect, the emotions, and the will must not only be given attention, but Christian character demands that these be developed in such proportion as to result in a balanced, harmonious, and well-integrated personality. For this the psalmist prayed when he said, *Teach me thy way, O Lord; I will walk in thy truth: unite my heart to fear thy name* (Psalms 86:11). God reveals Himself through the beauty of the world: *Strength and beauty are in his sanctuary.* We are commanded to *worship the Lord in the beauty of holiness* (Psalms 96:6, 9). The beautiful and the sublime, whether in nature or the works of art are designed of God to elevate and ennoble the soul. Insensibility to the beautiful is indicative of incomplete development. The Christian is to cultivate a taste which is quick to discern

beauty, correct in the judgment of it, and catholic in the sense of recognizing and appreciating it wherever found.

C. *The Development of the Spiritual Life.*

The Scriptures abound with commands, instructions, injunctions, and exhortations concerning the development of the spiritual life. *But grow in grace, and in the knowledge of our Lord and Saviour Jesus Christ* (II Peter 3:18). *Giving all diligence, add to your faith virtue; and to virtue knowledge; and to knowledge temperance; and to temperance patience; and to patience godliness; and to godliness brotherly kindness; and to brotherly kindness charity. For if these things be in you, and abound, they make you that ye shall neither be barren nor unfruitful in the knowledge of our Lord Jesus Christ* (II Peter 1:5-8). St. Paul exhorts us to *Walk in the Spirit, and ye shall not fulfil the lust of the flesh* (Gal. 5:16). Through the indwelling presence of the Holy Spirit and due diligence given to the means of grace, the soul is not only preserved in holiness, but is led into the deeper unfolding of grace and truth.

The literature of devotion within and outside the Scriptures constitutes an invaluable aid in the development of the devotional life. In such inspired literature as the Psalms we have the record of God's dealing with the souls of men by means of which men have been able to voice the deepest emotions and highest aspirations of life. To the recognized devotional literature of the Bible may well be added the spiritual flights of the ancient prophets, the gracious words which fell from the lips of our Lord himself, and the inspired utterances of His holy apostles. All of these enable the souls of men to enter more deeply into communion with their Lord through the Spirit.

Space forbids any discussion of the wide field of devotional literature built up outside the Scripture. It was born from the broad and rich experiences of men who have entered deeply into the knowledge of God. To mention only a few classics among such works which have served to develop the spiritual lives of their readers would include: THOMAS A KEMPIS, *The Imitation of Christ;* FRANCES DE SALES, *An Introduction to the Devout Life;* MADAME GUYON, *Method of Prayer;* BUNYAN, *Grace Abounding,* and *Pilgrim's Progress;* BISHOP JEREMY TAYLOR, *Holy Living,* and *Holy Dying;* JOHN WESLEY, *Spiritual Reflections,* and *Plain Account of Christian Perfection;* and DR. THOMAS C. UPHAM, *Principles of the Interior Life.*

IV. DUTIES WE OWE TO OTHERS

As Christ summed up the first table of the law in one broad and comprehensive duty of love to God, so also He did likewise with the second table in an equally comprehensive duty of love to man (Matt. 22:37-40). This love which the Christian has for his fellow men is love that is shed abroad by the Holy Spirit, and is perfected only when the heart is purified from all sin. This Christian love does not mean that we are to love all men alike, irrespective of their characters or of the relation we sustain to them. We are required to love all men with the love of good will, and to love the unfortunate and distressed with the love of pity (Rom. 12:20). Those who are members of the family of God are to be loved with the love of complacency. Christians are under obligations to each other which do not bind them to other men (St. John 13:34-35). The New Commandment of Christ requires the love of character, or the love of a Christian as a Christian, and is based upon the example of Jesus Christ as the Redeemer.

A. *Violations of Brotherly Love.*

St. Paul declares that such passions and emotions as violate the law of love should be put aside, *Let all bitterness, and wrath, and anger, and clamour, and evil speaking, be put away from you with all malice* (Eph. 4:31). Whether expressed or not, such emotions are nevertheless contrary to the spirit of brotherly love. All censoriousness and evil speaking are likewise to be avoided (Eph. 4:29, 31; James 4:11). This includes unnecessary or unduly harsh criticism, lying, and deceptiveness (Col. 3:9; Rev. 21:8, 27). An unforgiving spirit itself is a serious violation of the law of love (Matt. 6:15). Revenge, also, is prohibited by express command. While it is lawful and right that offenders against society should be punished by properly constituted authority, private revenge is not permissible (Rom. 12:17, 19).

B. *The Christian View of the Rights of Man.*

Brotherly love has not only its prohibitions but has also due regard for the rights and privileges of others. These are generally summed up as the rights to life, liberty, and property. Man has the right to live, and this involves all that the Master included when He said, *I am come that they might have life, and that they might have it more abundantly* (John 10:10). Hence society is under obligation to provide the individual with the opportunity to secure proper food, clothing, and shelter; and also the opportunity for the cultural advantages of intellectual and spiritual development.

Man has a right to personal liberty. This liberty consists in freedom from compulsion or restraint, and applies to both mind and body. "Liberty of person," says Dr. Wakefield, "consists in exemption from the arbitrary will of our fellow men, or in the privilege of doing as we please, so as not to trespass on the rights of others." Such personal liberty, guaranteed under the laws of a social group, would include the freedom of speech, freedom of the press, and freedom to worship God according to the dictates of one's conscience.

Man has also a right to private property. This right is one of inestimable value, and any violation of it is justly condemned. It is secured by the divine commandment, *Thou shalt not steal* (Exodus 20:15). St. Paul expressly declares, *That no man go beyond and defraud his brother in any matter: because that the Lord is the avenger of all such, as we also have forewarned you and testified* (I Thess. 4:6). Such forms of dishonesty as theft, robbery, and fraud are all violations of the principle of justice, and are expressly forbidden by divine commandment. Christianity clearly recognizes and approves the institution of private property.

C. *Duties Owed Within the Family.*

The family is a social institution designed of God to perpetuate the race and enable each individual to enlarge his personality and usefulness. Marriage is the earliest form of human relationship, and the source and foundation of all others. It is primarily a divine institution (Gen. 2:18). Since the essence of the marriage contract is the mutual vows taken in the sight of God and in the presence of witnesses, it should not be entered into unadvisably, but "reverently, discreetly, and in the fear of God." The ceremony should be performed by a minister of Christ, for he alone is authorized to represent the law of God, and to receive and register the vows made in the divine presence. Marriage is also a civil contract and contributes to civil peace and strength in numerous ways. The state, therefore, rightly determines what marriages are lawful, and prescribes various regulations respecting it.

Marriage is the union of one man and one woman. It is thus opposed to polygamy and all other forms of promiscuity. The highest authority for this position is found in the words of our Lord himself when He said, *Have ye not read, that he which made them at the beginning made them male and female, and said, For this cause shall a man leave father and mother and shall cleave to his wife: and they twain shall be one flesh? Wherefore they are no more twain, but one flesh? What therefore God hath joined together let not man put asunder* (Matt. 19:4-6).

Marriage is a permanent institution and can be dissolved naturally only by the death of one of the parties. There are, however, unnatural methods by which this relation is severed. It is dissolved by adultery (Matt. 5:32). Protestantism has quite generally interpreted St. Paul to teach that willful desertion also dissolves the marriage bond (I Cor. 7:15), although such desertion probably implied adultery. It seems clear that the gospel does not allow divorce except for the single cause of adultery. Only through permanency can marriage contribute those moral and spiritual values for which it was designed of God.

1. *Duties of Husbands and Wives.* The marriage state demands first of all the duty of mutual affection. This requires that the husband and wife shall preserve the same tender regard for each other, as that which furnishes the basis of the marriage compact. Where this principle is duly regarded, mutual affection increases with the years, and becomes deeper and stronger as each seeks to become more unselfish, more self-sacrificing, and more lovely for the sake of each other. No higher standard of the marriage relation is conceivable than that found in the holy Scriptures. So sacred and exalted is this relation that St. Paul portrays it in his teaching concerning the relation between Christ and His Church (Eph. 5: 22-23). This mutual affection between husband and wife demands strict fidelity to the marriage contract, and forbids whatever would tend to lessen this mutual esteem. In addition to this basic duty of husband and wife, there are the further obligations of mutual co-operation, and division of responsibility. If the marriage relation and the family are to achieve their highest ends husband and wife must recognize their common purpose, and labor co-operatively together in a common cause. They should never cease to seek for common thoughts, common interests, and common joys. At the same time there must be a division of responsibility and labor if the family is to succeed in its God-given task (cf. Eph. 5: 22-23; Col. 3: 18-19; I Peter 1: 7; I Tim. 5: 8).

2. *Duties of parents and children.* The duties of parents to their children involves first of all parental affection in its purest and most unselfish form. Upon this depends the character and destiny of the children. In addition, there is the duty of parental care and training. This includes the proper nourishment of the body, the provision of a wholesome physical environment; the education of the mind in accordance with the gifts and abilities of each child; and the development of high

moral standards. Parents are commanded to bring up their children *in the nurture and admonition of the Lord* (Eph. 6:4). The importance of this early training is stated in the proverb, *Train up a child in the way he should go; and when he is old, he will not depart from it* (Prov. 22:6). Imperative in such training, if it is to be truly effective, is that the child be brought early to a knowledge of Jesus Christ as his personal Saviour. Finally, parents owe to their children the duty of family government. Such authority is to be adapted to the degree of development of the child, and while it must be firm, should always be administered in the spirit of Christ. This is implied in the words of St. Paul, *And, ye fathers, provoke not your children to wrath* (Eph. 6:4); and, *Fathers, provoke not your children to anger, lest they be discouraged* (Col. 3:21).

The duties of children to their parents may be summed up under two general heads: obedience and reverence. As to obedience, the scriptural injunction is, *Children, obey your parents in the Lord: for this is right* (Eph. 6:1); and, *Children, obey your parents in all things: for this is well pleasing unto the Lord* (Col. 3:20). It is the duty of the child to yield cheerfully to the instruction and direction which the superior wisdom of the parents may dictate. Parents are God's constituted officers to administer the government of their respective families; and to obey them in the exercise of their legitimate authority is to obey God. Like other rulers, parents may abuse their power, but in such a case the child is to obey only *in the Lord.* As to reverence as a duty to parents, this includes the respect due to all superiors, and especially parents: *Honour thy father and thy mother: that thy days may be long upon the land which the Lord thy God giveth thee* (Exod. 20:12). St. Paul calls this the *first commandment with promise* (Eph. 6:2). The word honor as here used includes affection, obedience, and gratitude. In it the Spirit of Christianity is particularly manifested.

D. *Man's Duty to the State.*

The state is the second of the social institutions ordained of God for the benefit of man. The chief design of the state is to furnish man a wider sphere of social activity. Since man's moral nature is in disorder, his unregulated development must of necessity lead to unjust interference with the rights of other men. Civil government, therefore, is intended to protect its citizens from all violence, and to secure to each individual the peaceable enjoyment of all his rights, to the best of its ability. The state must in the very nature of the case, exercise authority in regulating public conduct; and this it does by laws based upon the immutable law of right. Penalty must be used in the enforcement of the law if need be; guilt must be dangerous, and crime must become serious even to the criminal. It is important to note that the sovereignty of civil authority lies in the state itself, and not in any king or ruler whatever. This is established by the facts that the state existed before all rulers, and that rulers at the most are but its instruments.

Among the duties which man owes to the state are the following: (1) Prayer for rulers: *I exhort therefore, that, first of all, supplications, prayers, intercessions, and giving of thanks, be made for all men; for kings, and for all that are in authority; that we may lead a quiet and peaceable life in all godliness and honesty* (I Tim. 2:1). (2) Obedience to those in authority. *Put them in mind to be subject to principalities and powers, to obey magistrates, to be ready to every good work, to speak evil of no man, to be no brawlers, but gentle, shewing all meekness unto all men* (Titus 3:1-2). (3) Christians must be subject to government for conscience' sake. *Wherefore ye must needs be subject, not only for wrath, but also for conscience sake* (Rom. 13:5). (4) Government must be supported. *For this cause pay ye tribute also: for they are God's ministers, attending continually upon this very thing. Render therefore to all their dues: tribute to whom tribute is due; custom to whom custom; fear to whom fear; honour to whom honour* (Rom. 13:6-7). The obligations which man owes to government grow out of the fact that government is ordained of God. *Let every soul be subject unto the higher powers. For there is no power but of God: the powers that be are ordained of God. Whosoever therefore resisteth the power, resisteth the ordinance of God: and they that resist shall receive to themselves damnation* (Rom. 13:1-2). Thus rulers or other agents of the government must enforce the penalties of the law. *For rulers are not a terror to good works but to the evil. Wilt thou then not be afraid of the power? do that which is good, and thou shalt have praise of the same: for he is the minister of God to thee for good. But if thou do that which is evil, be afraid: for he beareth not the sword in vain: for he is the minister of God, a revenger to execute wrath upon him that doeth evil* (Rom. 13:3-4). St. Paul applies the principle of love to the affairs of state in the same manner that he does to those of domestic and social life. He sums up the whole matter in these words, *Owe no man any thing, but to love one another: for he that loveth another hath fulfilled the law* (Rom. 13:8).

In conclusion, it should be noted that the Scriptures clearly teach that no human authority is unlimited. The following observations concerning this aspect of state authority are cited from an excellent discussion of the subject by Dr. Charles Hodge. "The principles which limit the authority of civil government and of its agents are simple and obvious. The first is that governments and magistrates have authority only within their legitimate spheres. As civil government is instituted for the protection of life and property, for the preservation of order, for the punishment of evil doers for the praise of those who do well, it has only to do with the conduct, or external acts of men. It cannot concern itself with their opinions, whether scientific, philosophical, or religious. . . . . . The magistrate cannot enter our families and assume parental authority, or our churches and teach as a minister. Out of his legitimate sphere a magistrate ceases to be a magistrate. A second limitation is no less plain. No human authority can make it obligatory on a man to disobey God. If all power is from God, it cannot be legitimate when used against God. The apostles when forbidden to preach the gospel, refused to obey. . . . . When the civil government may be, and ought to be disobeyed is one which every man must decide for himself. It is a matter of private judgment. Every man must answer for himself to God, and therefore every man must judge for himself, whether a given act is sinful or not. . . . . When a government fails to answer the purpose for which God ordained it, the people have a right to change it. A father, if he shamefully abuses his power, may rightfully be deprived of authority over his children" (HODGE, *Systematic Theology*, III, pp. 357-360).

CHAPTER XX

THE CHRISTIAN CHURCH

"Conformable to the natural law of social integration, and resting on that intermediate Messianic community which Jesus organized, inspired and commissioned before His ascension into heaven, there arises by the advent of His Spirit another 'chosen communion,' a communion different in *kind* from every other organization, whether social, civil, or religious, a spiritual constitution, of which the incarnate Son, the glorified God-man, is the Head and of which men born of His Spirit become members."—DR. EMANUEL V. GERHART.

I. THE NATURE OF THE CHRISTIAN CHURCH

The word "church" as found in the New Testament is from the Greek word *ecclesia,* and in its simplest connotation means an assembly or body of "called out ones." The Christian Church is therefore the assembly of called out ones, made up of the divinely adopted sons of God. Christ is its glorious Head. From Him it receives its life through the indwelling Spirit, and as such, discharges a twofold function—as an institute of worship, and a depository of the faith. The Church is also the *Body of Christ,* thus constituting a mystical extension of the nature of Christ. Consequently it is composed only of those who have become partakers of that nature. The relation between Christ and the Church is vital, living, organic. The Church is not merely an organization. It is a living organism.

A. *The Church as the Body of Christ.*

The Church is the creation of the Holy Spirit. The Spirit, administering the life of Christ, makes us members of His spiritual body. Ministering in His own proper personality as the Third Person of the Trinity, the Holy Spirit dwells in the holy temple thus constructed. The Church, therefore, is not merely an independent creation of the Spirit, but an enlargement of the incarnate life of Christ.

As the body of Christ, the active or evangelistic aspect of the Church is emphasized. Under this symbol we give attention to the unity, the growth, and the varied types of ministry of the Church. The unity of the Church is the unity of the Spirit. It consists of more than mere natural ties, whether of family, nation, or race. No bond of outward relationship is capable of expressing the inward unity of the members of the Church, or their entire oneness of life, hence our Lord made His own oneness with the Father an illustration of it. He prayed, *That they all may be one; as thou, Father, art in me, and I in thee, that they also may be one in us* (John 17:21). Thus our Lord found no union short of that in the divine life by which to express His thought. They were to be one through the Spirit. The Holy Spirit being the bond of union in the Godhead, becomes likewise, the source of union in the Church, uniting the members to one another, to their exalted Head, and to Himself. St. Paul's most perfect illustration of the unity of the Church is, like that of his Master, patterned after the Trinity. He gives us a trinity of trinities—one body, one Spirit, one hope; *One Lord, one faith, one baptism; one God and Father of all, who is above all, and through all, and in you all* (Eph. 4:4-8).

Growth is the second aspect of this organism, the body of Christ. This growth is through the truth as ministered by the Spirit. Hence St. Paul says, *But speaking the truth in love, may grow up into him in all things, which is the head, even Christ: from whom the whole body fitly joined together and compacted by that which every joint supplieth, according to the effectual working in the measure of every part, maketh increase of the body unto the edifying of itself in love* (Eph. 4:15-16). Here it is indicated that the growth of the individual spiritually is to be interpreted, not by an increasing independency of action, but by a deeper and more joyful cooperation with other members of the body. Note also that the growth of the body is through the individual contributions of its members.

The third outstanding feature of the body of Christ is found in the varied types of its ministry. St. Paul tells us that the ascended Christ gave apostles and prophets as the foundational ministry, and evangelists, pastors, and teachers as the proclaiming or instructional ministry. The purpose of all this is *the perfecting of the saints, for the work of the ministry, for the edifying of the body of Christ"*: and the goal of attainment is, *"till we all come in the unity of the faith, and of the knowledge of the Son of God, unto a perfect man, unto the measure of the stature of the fullness of Christ* (Eph. 4: 12-13).

B. *The Church as the Temple of the Holy Spirit.*

The second symbol by which the spiritual Church of Jesus Christ is portrayed is that of a temple. St. Paul refers to this in Ephesians 2: 21-22: *In whom all the building fitly framed together groweth unto an holy temple in the Lord: in whom ye also are builded together for an habitation of God through the Spirit.* St. Peter uses the same figure of speech in a similar manner. He says, *Ye also, as lively stones, are built up a spiritual house, an holy priesthood, to offer up spiritual sacrifices acceptable to God by Jesus Christ* (I Peter 2:5). It is under the symbol of a temple that the Church is set forth as an institute of worship. In this connection we shall presently discuss the subject of worship, the means of grace, and the sacraments.

C. *The Founding of the Christian Church.*

The Christian Church is linked historically with the Jewish—sometimes called the *church in the wilderness* (Acts 7: 38). When our Lord, at the opening of His ministry, proclaimed that the kingdom of heaven was at hand, He by this means related His own work to the Jewish theocracy as to its inner spirit, though not to its outward form. The Church of the Old Testament was the first representative of the *ecclesia* or called out ones. It was a community of the Spirit. While manifesting itself through natural and social laws, it was nevertheless a supernatural organization. As such, it made a direct and positive contribution to the Christian Church in that it cultivated and matured the religion which should finally issue in the kingdom of God; and it was the community which gave Christ to the world.

The second step in preparation for the Church was the formation of the "little flock" by our Lord himself. This stood midway between the Mosaic economy and Pentecost. Two stages are evident in the formation of this intermediate community. The first comprised the group of disciples which clustered about John the Baptist as the forerunner of Jesus. The second included the group which was gathered about Jesus himself. This was made up of the Twelve, the Seventy, and an indefinite number of devout Jews—about five hundred. These believed that Jesus was the Christ, and were fused into an informal organization by their love for the Master and their faith in His words. Thus they were spiritually qualified to receive the gift of the Holy Spirit on the Day of Pentecost, and became the true nucleus of the Christian Church.

Pentecost was the birthday of the Church. The prepared disciples, in obedience to the command of their Lord, were assembled with one accord in Jerusalem when suddenly the Holy Spirit fell upon them, making the intermediate community in the truest sense of that term, "the new temple of the Triune God." Pentecost represents the ushering in of the fullness of the Spirit, and the fullness of the New Covenant in which the law of God is written upon the heart by the Spirit. Pentecost placed the Christian community under the jurisdiction of the Holy Spirit, who represents the invisible Head of the body now visible.

D. *Notes and Attributes of the Church.*

By the term "attributes" we refer to those characteristics of the Church which are set forth in the Holy Scriptures. By the "notes" we mean those attributes transformed into tests by which the true Church is supposed to be known. In the earlier creeds, such as the Apostles' and the Nicene, four notes are mentioned. These are suggested by the words, unity, holy, catholic, and apostolic. We examine each of these briefly.

The Church possesses both unity and diversity. There is one body, one Spirit, one hope, one Lord, one faith, one baptism. But this unity is one of manifoldness. The Scriptures nowhere speak of an outward or visible unity. There is no intimation of uniformity. The New Testament never speaks of the church of a province, but always of the churches. The unity is that of the Spirit. The diversity includes anything that is not out of harmony with that spiritual unity.

The term "holy" is applied both to the body of Christ, and to the members which compose that body. In either instance, it signifies being set apart from the world; and devoted to God. In the case of the individual person, there must of necessity be a preliminary work of spiritual cleansing in order to bring about this full devotement. The organization itself is regarded as holy on account of the purpose or end for which it exists. Yet this holy Church may yet include those who have not individually been made entirely holy. This is evident from the apostolic epistles which though addressed to "saints," contain much in rebuke of that which is unholy.

The idea of catholicity at first included merely the universality of the Church in design and destiny. The term was used in contrast to the Jewish conception of the Church as local and national. Later on the term "catholic" was taken over by the Roman Church which regarded all other groups, including the Eastern or Orthodox Church, as being outside the one only catholic Church. Related to the idea of catholicity is the distinction made between the Church visible and invisible. By the invisible Church is meant the mystical body of Christ as animated by His Spirit. The term catholic may be applied to either the invisible or the visible Church. As applied to the former, it is simply the universal body of believers. The invisible Church is frequently regarded as including, not only those now living, but also those of every age—past, present, and future. The term "catholic" as applied to the visible Church includes all those particular groups or organizations which make up the total body of professed believers in Jesus Christ. Roman Catholicism, while believing technically in an invisible Church, so exalts the visible aspect as to suppress almost entirely its invisible character. Hence it makes *exclusiveness* a characteristic of the visible instead of the invisible Church; and, therefore, holds that there can be no salvation outside the Roman Church. The opposite error is found among those smaller bodies which emphasize the invisible Church to the minimizing or exclusion of all external organization.

Another aspect of catholicity is that which regards the Church as militant and triumphant. The Church militant is the one body waging war with principalities and powers of evil; and the Church triumphant is the one body of believers who, having passed through death, are now in Paradise with Christ, awaiting the more perfect state which the Church shall enter at the end of the age.

The Church is also apostolic and confessional. It is apostolic in the sense that it is *built upon the foundation of the apostles and prophets, Jesus Christ himself the chief corner stone* (Eph. 2:20). It is confessional in that it requires for membership a confession of faith in Jesus Christ as Saviour and Lord. *For with the heart man believeth unto righteousness; and with the mouth confession is made unto salvation* (Rom. 10:10). The Roman Catholic view concerning the apostolic character of the Church involves two errors: the theory which merged the apostolic authority of the twelve into that of St. Peter; and the development of the so-called apostolic succession which resulted in the papacy. In contrast, Protestantism has substituted belief in the Scriptures for living apostolic authority. "The Church is apostolic, as being still ruled by the apostolical authority living in the writings of the apostles, that authority being the standard of appeal in all the confessions that hold the Head" (POPE, *Compendium of Christian Theology*, III, p. 285).

E. *The Organization of the Christian Church.*

Nothing is more clearly taught in the Scriptures than the fact of an external organization of the Church. This is shown from such facts as the stated times of meeting; a regularly constituted ministry known as bishops, elders or presbyters, and deacons; formal elections; a financial system for the local support of the ministry and for the more general interests of charity; disciplinary authority on the part of ministers and churches; and common customs and ordinances.

There are three general views concerning church organization. The first holds that the Church is exclusively a spiritual body and needs no external organization. The second theory is at the other extreme and maintains that the Scriptures give us a formal plan of organization for the Church. But even with those who hold this position, there is much controversy as to the form of government prescribed. There is a third and mediating theory which holds that the New Testament lays down general principles of organization, but prescribes no specific form of church government. This is the position generally taken by Protestant churches.

In general, there are five leading types of organization, or forms of church government, held by professed Christians. These are concerned primarily with the rightful authority of the visible Church. The Roman Catholic Church holds that supreme and final authority is with the pope and is, therefore, a papacy. At the other extreme, the Congregational churches hold that the authority is vested in separate congregations, and hence are known as independents. Between these extremes are the mediating positions: the Episcopalians, who hold that the authority is vested in a superior order of the ministry; the Presbyterians, who maintain that it rests with the ministry and laity jointly; and the Methodists, who assert that authority is vested mainly in the elders of the church. These five types may be reduced to three—the Episcopal, in which authority is vested in the ministry; the Congregational, in which it is vested in the congregation; and the Presbyterian, in which it is vested in both ministry and laity. "It is our opinion," says Bishop Weaver, "that the form of government in the New Testament was not exclusively Episcopal, Presbyterian, or Congregational, but a combination of certain elements of all—from a careful review of the whole question, we conclude that it is nearest in harmony with the practice and writings of the apostles to say that the authority in the visible Church is vested in the ministry and the laity taken together."

According to the Roman Catholic (Papal) theory, the Church is regarded as the one and entire visible organization throughout the world, and thus the local bodies are not churches in the truest sense of the word, but only parts of the one Church. At the other extreme is congregationalism or independency which holds strictly to the autonomy of the local church, and denies the title to any superimposed organizations. According to this view, the local body only is the Church; and the universal Church is merely a general term to express the totality of the churches, each perfect in itself and entirely independent.

The apostolic churches were voluntary associations. Those who joined themselves to them did so freely and of their own accord. No provision was made for any visible head of the one supposedly visible Church. Government was provided for the churches as they were founded by raising up within the churches themselves those whom the apostles ordained as ministers. The only unity of which the apostles speak is the unity of the whole Church in Christ its invisible Head. This unity is that of faith and fervent charity through the indwelling Spirit. Only toward the close of the second century were larger associations of churches founded. Yet the local churches in apostolic times were not completely independent. The apostles and evangelists exercised some control and general supervision over them. It appears, therefore, that the type of organization established by the apostles was a form of connectionalism in which the local churches retained a large degree of control over their own affairs, but were subject also in a general manner to a common government.

F. *Conditions of Membership in the Church.*

While regarding the Church as a voluntary and visible organization, we nevertheless insist upon the divine and invisible element also and, therefore, make regeneration the basic condition of membership. Since the Church is the fellowship and communion of believers, a confession of faith in the Lord Jesus Christ becomes the one essential requirement for admission to the visible organization. This confession Protestantism has interpreted to mean a "conscious Christian experience and life." The various denominations have generally adopted some form of covenant, including agreed statements of belief and practice, to which the applicant must be willing to conform. It is the duty of every Christian, not only openly to profess his faith in Christ, but to enter into fellowship with the body of believers in his community, and to take upon himself the responsibilities of church membership.

G. *The Function of the Church.*

As Christ assumed a body and came into the world to reveal God and redeem men, so the Church as His body exists in the world for the spread of the gospel. It is the sphere of the Spirit's operation, and finds its highest function in the great commission given to the Church by our Lord himself: *Go ye therefore, and teach all nations, baptizing them in the name of the Father, and of the Son, and of the Holy Ghost: teaching them to observe all things whatsoever I have commanded you: and, lo, I am with you alway, even unto the end of the world. Amen* (Matt. 28: 19-20).

H. *The Christian Ministry.*

Contrasting conceptions of the Christian ministry are held by Roman Catholics and Protestants. The former holds to a priestly or sacerdotal ministry; the latter to a prophetic or preaching ministry. In the early Church, the ministers were known indifferently as bishops, pres-byters, or elders. The Old Testament conception of the priesthood had little influence upon the churchly idea of the office. The sacrifices were abolished, and there could be no priest without a sacrifice. Consequently the whole congregation regarded itself as a body of priests to offer up spiritual sacrifices through Jesus Christ, its one great High Priest. Gradually, however, there grew up an un-scriptural distinction between the clergy and the laity, the former being known as *sacerdotes* to whom pertained a priestly function. This development in the Roman Catholic Church led to the priestly offering of the sacri-fice *for* the people, instead of *by* the people. With the coming of the Reformation the idea of the universal priesthood of believers was again brought to the front, and has been the dominant characteristic of Protestant-ism since that time. As such, it teaches the essential equality of all true believers, and their direct relation to Christ through the Spirit. Thus the true dignity of the individual Christian and the sanctity of corporate wor-ship are preserved.

Since the Church is a divinely appointed institution, that is, it is the will of God that men organize themselves into societies for mutual edification and divine worship, so it is the will of God that individual persons be ap-pointed to perform the duties and administer the sacra-ments of the church. This purpose of God in the selection of those who are to be leaders in His work was evident in the Mosaic dispensation, in the calling of the Twelve and the Seventy by our Lord, and in the experience of the early Church (cf. Luke 6: 13; Mark 3: 14; Luke 10: 1; Acts 9: 15; 27: 16-18; 14: 23). The ministry is a vocation or calling and not merely a profession. As it is the will of God that churches be formed, so it is His will also that particular persons be called to serve as ministers of these churches.

St. Paul enumerates the following classes in the New Testament ministry, as given to the Church by our ascended Lord: *And he gave some, apostles; and some, prophets; and some, evangelists; and some, pastors and teachers* (Eph. 4:11). From a further study of St. Paul's epistles we learn also of bishops, elders or presbyters, and deacons. Some of these terms pertain to the same person, that is, the person may be designated sometimes by one, and sometimes by another of these official terms. The five offices mentioned by St. Paul may be arranged in two main divisions: the extraordinary and transitional ministry, and the regular and permanent ministry.

The extraordinary and transitional ministry includes the apostles, the prophets, and the evangelists. The Church was founded by a specially chosen and qualified body of men. Their ministry was transitional, continuing the extraordinary ministrations of the Holy Spirit under the old economy, and bringing them to their full consummation in the service of the new order. The *apostles* were those who had been commissioned by our Lord in person, and were chosen to bear witness of His miracles and His resurrection. In order to lay the foundation of the Church in doctrine and practice, they were endowed with the gift of inspiration, and given the credentials or miracle working power. The prophets included those who in some instances foretold the future (Acts 11:28; 21:10-11). But the term generally refers to that body of extraordinary teachers who were raised up for the purpose of establishing the churches in the truth until such time as they should be under qualified and permanent instructors. They spoke under the immediate inspiration of the Spirit but in only a few instances were their revelations preserved. It was to this class that the pentecostal promise pertained (Acts 2:18), and the prophetic gift was exercised by both men and women (cf. Acts 21:9; I Cor. 14:24-25, 29-33, 37). It is in the sense of a foundational ministry only that the order was transitory. As a proclamation of the truth, it abides in the Church in the form of the regular ministry. The *evangelists* were the assistants of the apostles, and performed the apostolic offices of preaching and founding churches. Their power was delegated to them by the apostles, under whose supervision their duties were performed. Timothy and Titus are representatives of this class. They were given power to ordain elders in the church, but since they had no authority to ordain their successors, the office must be regarded as temporary. It passed away with the apostolate upon which it depended. As used generally in later church history, the term was applied at first to the writers of the Gospels, and then to the irregular ministry which is gifted in proclaiming the gospel to the unsaved.

The regular and permanent ministry was appointed to care for the church after the apostolic supervision should be withdrawn. Two classes of office are mentioned: the pastorate, pertaining especially to the spiritual oversight of the church; and the diaconate, devoted to the management of its temporal affairs. Those who served in the first office were known as elders or presbyters, and bishops; those in the second, as deacons.

The office of the pastorate has a twofold function—administrative and instructional; hence those chosen to fill this position were known as "pastors and teachers." Since the term pastor implies the duties of both instruction and government; and since elders or bishops were ordained in the various churches by the apostles or evangelists, it is evident that these are the pastors to which St. Paul refers in his Epistle to Ephesians. In apostolic times, it appears that the larger churches had several presbyters or elders as in the churches at Jerusalem (Acts 15: 4) and Ephesus (Acts 20: 17). There has been much controversy as to whether the terms bishop and presbyter refer to the same office, or whether the bishop represented a superior order of ministers with special authority and power to govern both presbyters and people. It is true that a distinction between the two terms arose very early, but biblical authority for the distinction in power seems lacking.

The deacons were concerned with administration of the temporal affairs of the church (Acts 6: 1-16). The qualifications of deacons and their wives are given by St. Paul in I Timothy 3: 8-13. Christian women were invested with this office (Rom. 16: 1), and the word *wives* is sometimes translated *deaconesses* (I Tim. 3: 11). In modern times the word "minister" which is equivalent to "deacon" has come into common use for the word elder or presbyter. For this reason, the deacon, in some churches is merely a presbyter on trial—a first step toward ordination as an elder.

The Scriptures clearly teach that the early Church ordained elders or presbyters by a formal setting apart to the office and work of the ministry. Numerous references indicate that elders were set apart by the imposition of hands. It is evident also that the power of ordination rested in the eldership itself; and that all candidates were to be adjudged as worthy or unworthy of the office only by those who had been themselves ordained. Ordination, however, does not make the elder an officer in a particular church. This can be done only as he is elected by the church and freely accepts this election. Thus the eldership is an order of the ministry from which pastors can be elected, but until so elected they are not pastors of particular churches. In fact, there are many and various offices in the church but only one order of the ministry—that of the elders.

The church through its ministers exercises three forms of administrative power. *First*, there is the administration of the laws of order and government. Such laws are necessarily scriptural and spiritual in character. *Second*, there are the didactic functions of the church. This involves the conservation and defense of the truth entrusted to the church, the preaching of the Word, and the instruction of the youth in spiritual matters. Finally, ministers are required to exercise proper discipline in the congregation. This does not include the use of civil authority or penalties, but is limited to censure, suspension, and expulsion from membership in the church.

II. Worship and the Means of Grace

We now turn our attention to the worship and ordinances of the Church. In doing so we consider the second meaningful symbol under which the Church is described by St. Paul, namely, the temple of the Holy

Spirit. With this new approach we also consider another aspect of the work of the ministry—its prophetic leadership.

A. *Worship in the Early Christian Church.*

In the Christian Church, previous to 100 A.D., the service of worship consisted of the *Eucharist* or Lord's Supper, preceded by the *agape* or love feast, and followed by "the liturgy of the Holy Spirit." It seems probable, that at first the *agape* was a real meal, which the people ate until they were satisfied; and that following this certain portions of the bread and wine having been set apart, were eaten solemnly as the Eucharist. Early abuses, however, were soon associated with this *agape* (I Cor. 11: 20-22), and it seems to have been finally merged into the Eucharist. It is for this reason that the early worship is commonly stated to be twofold—the eucharist service, and the free worship.

The first part of the service included the reading of the Scriptures and prayer, as well as the consecration and distribution of the elements. The sermon also formed a part of the service, as did the singing of psalms, hymns, and spiritual songs. The letters of the apostles were read, during the *agape*, or just before the communion service.

The second part, or so-called "free worship" held a very large place in the Christian service. After the Eucharist, inspired persons began to speak before the assembly and to manifest the presence of the Spirit who inspired them. The exercise of the prophetic gift seems to have been often in evidence.

B. *Individual and Social Aspects of Worship.*

Christian worship is both individual and social. Worship in its very nature is profoundly personal, but it is also the act of a person who is essentially social. The first words of the "Lord's Prayer" remind each individual worshiper of these social relationships. It is as "our" Father, not "my" Father, that he comes into the divine presence. However lonely the individual worshiper may appear to be, yet he stands as a member of the whole family of God. Corporate worship emphasizes the unity of the church. It exalts the body of Christ, rather than the free exercise of its many members. It checks religious egotism, breaks down devotional barriers, and confers the supporting and disciplinary benefits of life in a family. For this reason group worship is exceedingly important, whatever may be its outward form or manner of expression.

On the other hand, individual worship is basic. There is a true secret of worship which belongs to every child of God. The hidden and personal lives of prayer and devotion do not represent spiritual selfishness. It is the character of this personal devotion that gives strength to the corporate worship. A balance between the individual and social aspects of worship is essential. Separated from one another, the corporate or sacramental form of worship tends toward ritualism—with cathedral, altar, and priest; while the free individual worship, improperly governed, frequently results in the wildest forms of fanaticism. The simplicity of worship as found in the apostolic Church had in it both the sacramental phase with its emphasis upon unity, and the prophetic aspect with its freedom, enthusiasm, personal spontaneity, and intense ethical demands.

C. *The Order and Forms of Worship.*

The order of divine worship has reference to the principles according to which it must be conducted. These principles are fully set forth in the Holy Scriptures. Worship must be offered to the Triune God. This is a fundamental principle. Whatever of worship is paid to one member of the Trinity, must be offered to all—or must be offered to One in the unity of the other Two. Worship must also be mediatorial—"spiritual sacrifices, acceptable to God through Jesus Christ." Finally, worship must be spiritual, that is, it must be inspired by the Spirit to be acceptable unto God. *God is a Spirit: and they that worship him must worship him in spirit and in truth* (John 4:24). It is the touch of God upon the soul that is the source of all true worship.

The forms of worship are left to the discretionary powers of the church, insofar as they conform to the Scriptures. The time of worship is to be set by the church, but should not infringe upon the rights of the family or the individual. The church may appoint special seasons for prayer and fasting, for preaching, and for thanksgiving. The laws of decency and order require that public services be regulated. Spontaneity flowing from the presence of the Spirit in fresh anointing is to be commended, but all mere caprice is to be put away as out of harmony with the dignity of a divine service. Public services should also be characterized by simplicity. An elaborate ritual which distracts the soul from its one true function of spiritual worship is detrimental; but a careless and indifferent spirit is death to any form of spiritual worship.

D. *The Sabbath as a Means of Grace.*

The institution of the Sabbath is regarded as one of the permanent and divine ordinances of the church. Introduced as it was at the time of man's creation, the Sabbath belongs to the race generally and perpetually. Its original design was a rest from physical labor, and with it a spiritual design that man, ceasing from other occupations, might hold communion with his Creator. A right understanding of the Sabbath as an institution must regard it as a period of rest after six days of labor. It consists of two parts: the *holy rest,* and the *day* on which this rest is observed. The first part belongs to the moral law, and, as a perpetual institution, is ever binding upon all men. The second part, the day on which the Sabbath is to be observed, is purely positive, and may be altered by divine authority without altering the substance of the institution.

When our Lord said, "The sabbath was made for man," He referred to its original institution as a universal law, and not merely to the Jewish Sabbath as an enactment of the law of Moses. It belongs to all mankind, forms a part of the moral law as expressed in the Ten Commandments, and was never abrogated. It is as binding upon Christians as it was upon the Jews. Whoever denies the obligation of the Sabbath denies the whole Decalogue. Christians observe the Sabbath as truly as did the Jews but they celebrate it on another day.

When Jesus declared that *the Son of man is Lord also of the sabbath,* He doubtless intended them to understand that He had power to change the day on which the holy rest should be observed. The Scriptures clearly indicate that the Sabbath has been celebrated on different days. The first notice of the Sabbath is found in Genesis 2:2-3. Here, in the institution of the Sabbath, it is distinctly declared to be a day of holy rest after six days of labor; and further, in this instance, it is stated to be a memorial of creation. Now it is evident that God's seventh day would not be man's seventh day. "The seventh day which God blessed in Eden," says Dr. Whitelaw, "was the first day of human life, and not the seventh day; and it is certain that God did not rest from His labors on man's seventh day, but on man's first." Hence Adam's first day, and each succeeding eighth day would be his Sabbath—a reference strikingly similar to our Lord's appearance on the first and eighth days.

The next mention of the Sabbath is in connection with the giving of the manna (Exod. 16:14-31). Here it is stated that the twenty-second day of the second month was the first seventh day Sabbath celebrated in the Wilderness of Sin. That the Sabbath as a holy rest was reestablished at this time there can be no doubt; that it was celebrated on the same day as that of the patriarchal Sabbath has been a matter of controversy. Dr. W. H. Rogers holds that "The only change of the Sabbath by God's authority is for the Jews between the giving of the manna and the resurrection of Christ. The first day of the week, but always the seventh day after six working days, was the day of the holy rest from Adam to Moses. The Sabbatism was separated from idolatry by changing it from Sunday to Saturday among the chosen people *throughout their generations,* fifteen hundred years (cf. Exod. 31:13-14; Ezek. 20:12). At Christ's resurrection expired by statute limitation this peculiarity of exceptional change, leaving the divine rule for all mankind, requiring first-day Sabbath keeping, as had been the case for the first twenty-five hundred years of human history." With the coming of "the last Adam" (Christ) the Sabbath was restored to the original day on which it was celebrated by the first Adam.

That the Christian Sabbath or "Lord's Day" was restored, or at least changed to the first day, has been the teaching of the Church since apostolic times. Jesus placed approval upon the first day of the week by meeting with His disciples on that day. The resurrection took place on the first day of the week (John 20: 1). His first meeting with the disciples was on the evening of the resurrection day (John 20: 19); and the second on the evening of the eighth day. The apostles authorized the change, doubtless due to the unrecorded instructions of Jesus during the forty days (Cf. Acts 1: 2). Twenty-five years later St. Paul met with the disciples on the first day of the week (Acts 20: 7), and he gave instructions concerning the offering to be taken on this first day of the week (I Cor. 16: 1-2). St. John refers to the Sabbath as the "Lord's Day" (Rev. 1: 10) late in the first century of the Christian Era. Many of the early apostolic fathers, some of whom were associated with the apostles, indicate clearly that the first day of the week was the Lord's Day, and that it was set apart from other days in that it was the day of the resurrection. It was a holy day—a holy Sabbath.

From various scriptural references concerning the Sabbath as a holy rest day (Exod. 20: 9-11; Deut. 5: 12-15), we understand that the day is to be set apart for the worship of God, and devoted to the spiritual interests of mankind. For this reason all secular work is prohibited except that which is commonly known as a work of necessity or mercy (Isa. 58: 13). It is a cessation of labor whether of the body or the mind in order to permit time for spiritual things. Our Lord gives us two significant statements concerning the Sabbath. The first refers to the holiness of the day: *God is a Spirit: and they that worship him must worship him in spirit and in truth* (John 4:24). Here the true inwardness of the Sabbath is seen—a spiritual rest of the soul, from which flows that worship which is in Spirit and in truth. The second statement of Christ concerns man's interests: *And he said unto them, The sabbath was made for man, and not man for the sabbath: therefore the Son of man is Lord also of the sabbath* (Mark 2:27-28). Here it is clearly taught that those things which pertain to man's highest welfare, that is, his spiritual interests, are to be permitted on the Sabbath day; and this is a true and sure test as to the kind and extent of secular activity on this day of holy rest.

E. *Other Means of Grace.*

The means of grace are the divinely appointed channels through which the influences of the Holy Spirit are communicated to the souls of men. In this connection Protestantism stands midway between the Roman Catholic view which holds that the ordinances have power in themselves to confer grace, and the abstract position of the mystics who seek to do away with all external means.

The Word of God is one of the universal means of grace. The sufficiency of the Scriptures is everywhere affirmed, both in the Old and New Testaments. The Word of God is the *Sword of the Spirit*—the instrument by which He operates in converting and sanctifying the souls of men. Christians are begotten *through the gospel* (I Cor. 4:15), *Being born again, not of corruptible seed, but of incorruptible, by the word of God, which liveth and abideth for ever* (I Peter 1:23), and sanctified *through thy truth* (John 17:17). St. Paul makes the Word a means of grace by linking it directly to faith: *faith cometh by hearing, and hearing by the word of God* (Rom. 10:17). Resting securely on the basis of God's Word, faith opens the door to access to God, and lays hold of the purchased blessings. It is through the preached Word that grace is administered to the hearers. It is important that this preaching be *in the demonstration of the Spirit and of power* (I Cor. 2:4), for apart from the Spirit's operation upon the hearts of men, the Word has no power. It derives its efficacy as a means of grace only as it becomes the instrument of the Spirit. To be fully effective, the Word must be preached for *doctrine,* or instruction in the truths of the gospel; for *reproof* of neglect or failure; for *correction* of wrong tendencies; and for *instruction* in righteousness or the art of holy living (II Tim. 3:16).

Prayer, as combined with the Word, is also a universal means of grace. When the promises of the Word are pleaded in prayer they become effective in the spiritual life of the Christian. Prayer as defined by Mr. Watson is "The offering of our desires to God through the mediation of Jesus Christ, under the influence of the Holy Spirit, and with suitable dispositions for things agreeable to His will." Thus to be acceptable to God, prayer must be offered through the mediation of Christ; must be offered in faith and in a spirit of humility; and must be according to the will of God. The elements of a well-ordered prayer include *adoration,* which ascribes to God the perfections which belong to His nature, and which should be uttered in deep devotion, reverence, confidence, and affection; *thanksgiving,* or the pouring forth of the soul in gratitude; *confession,* or deep penitence, submission, and humility; *supplication,* or a prolonged and earnest looking to God in dependence for needed blessings; and *intercession,* or a pleading for our fellowmen, with sincere desires for their spiritual welfare (cf. I Tim. 2:1). Prayer is an obligation, a duty upon all men in private, in the family, and in public. If it be neglected or omitted, there can be no advance in spiritual things.

In both the Scriptures and the creeds Christian fellowship is represented as a means of grace. "The privileges and blessings which we have in association together in the Church of Jesus Christ are very sacred and precious. There is in it such hallowed fellowship as cannot otherwise be known. There is such helpfulness with brotherly watch care and counsel as can be found only in the Church. There is the godly care of pastors, with the teachings of the Word, and the helpful inspira-

tion of social worship. And there is co-operation in service, accomplishing that which cannot otherwise be done"
(*Manual,* pp. 214-215). (Cf. Heb. 3: 13; 13: 17; Gal. 6: 1.)

III. THE SACRAMENTS

A. *The Nature of a Sacrament.*

The term "sacrament" as used in theology signifies
an outward and visible sign of an inward and spiritual
grace given unto us, ordained by Christ himself as a
means whereby we receive the same, and a pledge to
assure us thereof. As understood by the early Christians,
the sacraments were religious rites which carried with
them the most sacred obligation of loyalty to the Church
and to Christ.

The Roman Catholic Church holds that there are
seven sacraments: baptism, the Lord's Supper, confirmation, ordination, extreme unction, penance, and
marriage. Protestant churches reduce the number to
two: baptism and the Lord's Supper. It is essential,
therefore, to understand the characteristics of a true sacrament. As given by Dr. A. A. Hodge, these marks include the following: (1) A sacrament is an ordinance
immediately instituted by Christ. (2) A sacrament always consists of two elements: an outward, visible sign,
and an inward spiritual grace thereby signified. (3) The
sign in every sacrament is sacramentally united to the
grace which it signifies, and out of this union the scriptural usage has arisen of ascribing to the sign whatever
is true of that which the sign signifies. (4) The sacraments are designated to represent, seal, and apply the
benefits of Christ and the new covenant to believers.
(5) They are designed to be pledges of our fidelity to
Christ, binding us to His service, and at the same time
they are badges of our Christian profession, visibly
marking the body of professors and distinguishing them
from the world.

There are three general opinions as to the manner in
which divine power is attached to the outward and
visible sign of the sacrament. (1) The Roman Catholic

or sacramentarian view holds that the sacraments contain the grace they signify; and, when administered, convey this grace of necessity, apart from and independent of the faith of the communicant. (2) The rationalistic view asserts that the sacraments are purely symbolical, and that any power derived from them is simply a result of their moral influence on the mind. (3) The mediating view, generally held by Protestant churches, regards the sacraments as both signs and seals: signs, as representing in action and by symbols the blessings of the covenant; and seals, as pledges of God's fidelity in bestowing them. Overemphasis on the sacraments as signs, that is, as visible and symbolical representations of the benefits of redemption, tends toward the rationalistic view: while undue emphasis on the sacraments as seals leads toward the sacramentarian position. The true Protestant, or mediating view, avoids the deficiencies of rationalism on the one hand, and the excesses of Roman Catholicism on the other.

B. *Baptism.*

"We believe that Christian baptism is a sacrament signifying acceptance of the benefits of the atonement of Jesus Christ, to be administered to believers, as declarative of their faith in Jesus Christ as their Saviour, and full purpose of obedience in holiness and righteousness.

"Baptism being the symbol of the New Testament, young children may be baptized, upon request of parents or guardians who shall give assurance for them of necessary Christian training.

"Baptism being the symbol of the New Testament, ing, or immersion, according to the choice of the applicant" (*Manual,* ¶ 18).

1. *The Institution of Christian Baptism.* Dr. Pope concisely defines baptism as "The right ordained by our Lord to be the sign of admission into the Church, and the seal of union with himself and participation in the blessings of the Christian covenants." The practice of water baptism as a sacred ordinance was not first introduced by Christ, but was long familiar to the Jews as a religious

rite. By means of it proselytes were inducted into the
Jewish religion, and thereby became partakers of the
benefits of the covenant. A second step in the development of the ordinance was the baptism of John. This was
a baptism "unto repentance" as a preparation for Christ
and the New Covenant. The third step in its development was Christian baptism which confesses that Jesus
as the Messiah has come, and also the Holy Spirit in
whose dispensation it is to be administered. Following
the Day of Pentecost, the rite of baptism was observed
in connection with conversion as an indispensable ordinance, there being no recorded instance of conversion
with which it is not connected. Thus St. Peter in his
pentecostal sermon exhorts the belivers to be *baptized
every one of you in the name of Jesus Christ* (Acts 2:
38), and *they that gladly received his word were baptized* (Acts 2:41). In later apostolic times baptism was
regarded as having superseded the Jewish rite of circumcision.

2. *Development of the Doctrine in the Church.* Great
importance was very early attached to the rite of baptism—not as a sign and seal of all Christian blessings,
but in that it was regarded as the means of conveyance,
by which those blessings were imparted. In the later
Ante-Nicene age baptism was universally regarded as
the rite of admission to the Church; and since it was held
that there could be no salvation apart from the Church,
baptism came to be associated with regeneration. At
first it was looked upon solely as the completing act in
the appropriation of Christianity—the seal of positive
adoption into the family of God. By the middle of the
second century, however, it was regarded as procuring
full remission of all past sins, and consequently we find
it spoken of as "the instrument of regeneration and illumination." Nevertheless the church fathers of this
era still held to the earlier belief that baptism was efficacious only in connection with a right inner disposition
and purpose on the part of the candidate.

In the Nicene and Post-Nicene periods certain views
held in the earlier period crystallized further. The idea

that divine life dwelt in the corporate body of the Church universally prevailed, and this life could be transmitted to its members only through the instrumentality of the sacraments. Baptism, therefore, came to be regarded as essential to salvation. Ambrose (c. 397) understood John 3: 5 to mean that "None can ascend into the kingdom of heaven except by the sacrament of baptism; indeed, it excepts none, neither infant nor him that is prevented by necessity." Augustine's more mature views regarding baptism included two propositions: first, that the rite carried with it not only the forgiveness of actual sins, but of original sin also; and, second, that in the baptism of infants the Church furnished a substitute faith, and the Holy Spirit implanted in the unconscious babe the germ of a new life, so that regeneration was wrought in the heart before the conscious conversion of the child.

3. *Summary of Basic Views Concerning the Nature of Baptism.* Roman Catholic views regarding baptism may be summarized by noting certain concepts asserted by St. Thomas. Baptism was held to impress an indelible character on the soul through regeneration. On the negative side, baptism was said to cleanse from all past sin, actual and original; and on the positive side, to incorporate the recipient with Christ, and bestow all the gifts and graces of the new life. On the question of infant baptism, it was held that babes do not believe through their own act, but through the faith of the Church in which they are baptized. The basic concept in the Roman Catholic view, to which Protestants later raised valid objection, was the doctrine that the mere administration of baptism saved the baptized person.

Protestant reformers, as suggested above, took radical exception to certain Roman Catholic views regarding baptism. This was particularly reflected in the Protestant insistence that faith was necessary on the part of the recipient in order to make the ceremony a means of grace. From this, as a starting point, certain differences developed among Protestants. The Lutheran position, as set forth in the Augsburg Confession, holds that bap-

tism is a perpetual witness that the forgiveness of sins
and the renewing of the Holy Ghost belong especially to
the baptized—the operating cause of this condition being
faith. Lutherans ordinarily regard baptism as essential
to salvation, since through it by divine appointment, the
blessings of remission and regeneration are conveyed
by means of faith and the Word.

The Reformed Churches started with the idea that
salvation is not dependent upon any external work or
ceremony. To them baptism was but the initiatory sign
which marks one as the follower of Christ. Zwingli attributed no sanctifying power to baptism *per se,* but only
to faith. Thus he did away entirely with mystery, and
viewed the sacraments partly as acts of confession, and
partly as commemorative signs. Calvin adopted the
principles of Zwingli, but in his development of them,
more nearly approached the Lutheran conception. To
him they were not merely memorials, but also pledges
of grace—that is, they were accompanied with an invisible gift of grace. This Reformed position, through the
medium of the Thirty-nine Articles of the Anglican
Church, became essentially the teaching of Methodism.
The latter holds that baptism is both a sign and a seal,
and therefore is not without its accompanying grace to
the recipient who complies with the conditions of the
covenant. The Baptist doctrine differs from Christianity
at large on two points—it maintains that baptism as a
rite belongs solely to adults as an expression of their
faith; and that the only valid mode of baptism is immersion in water.

4. *The Nature and Purpose of Christian Baptism.*
Christian baptism is a solemn sacrament signifying the
acceptance of the benefits of the atonement of Jesus
Christ, and it is a pledge with full purpose of obedience
in holiness and righteousness. By our Lord's express
command (Matt. 28: 19-20), and apostolic practice (Acts
2: 38, 41; 8: 12), we understand that baptism is a universal and perpetual obligation. It should be solemnly
and strictly observed. Being an initiatory rite it is to be

administered only once. It establishes a permanent covenant and is not therefore to be repeated.

Baptism is a sign and seal of the covenant of grace. As a sign it represents spiritual purification. Our Lord declared, *Except a man be born of water and of the Spirit, he cannot enter into the kingdom of God* (John 3:5). Here, evidently, the sign is the outward baptism with water, and the thing signified is the inner work of the Spirit. As a sign, baptism not only symbolizes regeneration, but also the baptism with the Holy Spirit which is the peculiar event of this dispensation. Baptism is also a seal. On God's part, the seal is the visible assurance of faithfulness to His covenant—a perpetual ceremony to which His people may ever appeal. On man's part, the seal is that act by which he binds himself as a party to the covenant, and pledges himself to faithfulness in all things; and it is also the sign of a completed transaction. "It is," says Dr. Shedd, "like the official seal on a legal document. The presence of the seal inspires confidence in the genuineness of the title-deed; the absence of the seal awakens doubts and fears. Nevertheless, it is the title-deed, not the seal, that conveys the title" (SHEDD, *Dogmatic Theology*, II, p. 574).

5. *The Mode of Baptism.* This subject has been one of long and serious controversy. Certain groups, such as the Baptists, contend that immersion is the only valid mode of baptism; while others, the great body of the Church in all ages, have ever maintained that it may be administered by sprinkling or pouring. The question is not whether immersion is a valid mode, but whether it is the only one authorized by the Scriptures. The Church generally has not found the evidence sufficient to establish immersion as the exclusive mode.

Immersionists contend that the Greek word $\beta\alpha\pi\tau\iota\zeta\epsilon\iota\nu$ always means *to dip* or *to plunge*. It is a fact, however, that the majority of lexicographers give it a broader meaning, including *to dip, to dye, to temper, to steep, to imbue*. Classical writers have on occasion, used the word to signify nothing more than moisten, tinge, and sprinkle. The word is clearly used in the Scriptures with meanings other than immersion. *Except they* (baptize) *wash, they eat not* (Mark 7:4). Here reference is made to the washing of the hands. St. Paul declares that the Israelites were baptized unto Moses in the cloud and the sea (I Cor. 10:1-2), using the word baptize as referring to the passing between the waters, overshadowed by the cloud. To contend that immersion is the only valid mode of baptism as a result of the use of the word βαπτίζειν in the Scriptures does not seem to be supported by the facts.

A study of the circumstances attending the recorded baptisms in the Scriptures, makes it clear, also, that baptism does not always signify immersion. For example, in the case of the baptism of Saul (Acts 9:18) it is stated that he arose and was baptized—literally, standing up he was baptized. In the case of the baptism of Cornelius and his friends, it is evident that they were baptized in the house and the implication is that water was brought for the baptism (Acts 10:47-48). Lastly, the baptism of the jailer and his household at night seems to have taken place in the jail, and cannot with certainty be said to have been administered by immersion (Acts 16:31-33). Space forbids an analysis of other biblical incidents (Matt. 3:5-6; 3:16; Acts 3:38-39) where the strength of the immersionist arguments rests on the prepositions used. Suffice it to say that the prepositions upon which the conclusions depend are actually used with a considerable variety of meaning in the Scriptures, and to base an argument on a single translation does not seem to be supported by sound exegesis.

Finally, the symbolism of burial has been a favorite argument with immersionists, and is based upon such scriptures as, *Therefore we are buried with him by baptism into death: that like as Christ was raised up from the dead by the glory of the Father, even so we also should walk in newness of life* (Rom. 6:4). The argument for immersion rests entirely upon the words *buried with him* BY or IN (Col. 2:12) *baptism. It is assumed* that the apostle *is* here speaking of water baptism, and, therefore defining the mode. A careful examination of the whole context, however, reveals that St. Paul was not referring to either water baptism or its mode. Throughout the whole passage he is speaking of spiritual death, burial, resurrection, and life. The whole argument shows that he is referring to the work of the Holy Spirit. It is manifestly impossible for water baptism to accomplish the extraordinary moral change of which the apostle speaks (cf. WAKEFIELD, *Christian Theology*, p. 582).

6. *The Subjects of Baptism.* All who believe in the Lord Jesus Christ, and have been regenerated, are proper subjects for Christian baptism. This is established by the direct statement of Jesus Christ, *He that believeth and is baptized shall be saved* (Mark 16: 16). But in addition to adult believers, the Church has always held that children are likewise the proper subjects of baptism. This position was called in question by the Anabaptists of the Reformation period, and their followers still object to it.

The history of infant baptism reveals that the practice has existed in the Church from the earliest times. This conclusion is supported by testimony of church fathers of the first and second centuries of the Christian era. Augustine in the fourth century says that "the whole Church practices infant baptism. It was not instituted by councils, but was always in use"; and, again, "I do not remember to have read of any person, whether Catholic or heretic, who maintained that baptism ought to be denied to infants." Evidently the practice has come down to us from the days of the apostles.

The principal scriptural warrant for the practice of infant baptism involves an analysis of St. Paul's teaching concerning the relation of the Christian Church to the Abrahamic covenant. Suffice it to say, that the Christian Church is the continuation of the Abrahamic covenant in its universal unfoldings, and in its highest degree. The initiatory rite of circumcision passed away with the rites and ceremonies peculiar to the Old Testament (cf. Col. 2: 10-12). Circumcision was mandatory under the Old Testament phase of the covenant, and stood as a constant reminder and confirmation of the same. In the New Testament baptism is an ordinance of comparable character. This phase of our subject is well summarized by Wakefield as follows: "We have shown that the Abrahamic covenant was the general covenant of grace; that children were embraced in that covenant, and were admitted into the visible church by circumcision; that Christianity is but a continuation, under a new form, of the covenant which God made with Abraham; and that baptism is now the sign and seal of the covenant of grace, as circumcision was under the former dispensation. From these premises it necessarily follows that as the infant children of believing parents, under the Old Testament, were proper subjects of circumcision, so the infant children of Christian believers are proper subjects of baptism" (WAKEFIELD, *Christian Theology*, pp. 569-570).

To the foregoing may be added the fact that in three different instances it is said that households were baptized (Acts 16: 15; 16: 33; I Cor. 1: 16). While there is no positive proof, we may regard the above incidents as at least presumptive evidence that there were children in the households of those who were baptized. Further still, we have from the lips of our Lord himself, the declaration that children belong to the kingdom of God (Mark 10: 4); and if so, they are entitled to this recognition as a witness to the faith of the parents in the words of their Lord. We maintain, therefore, that there is warrant for infant baptism, and that the arguments just given are a sufficient answer to the objections that are occasionally raised.

C. *The Lord's Supper.*

1. *The Institution of the Lord's Supper.* The circumstances under which this sacrament was instituted were solemn and impressive. It was the night of His betrayal, and Jesus and His disciples celebrated the Passover together. *And as they were eating, Jesus took bread, and blessed it, and brake it, and gave it to the disciples*

and said, Take, eat; this is my body. And he took the cup, and gave thanks, and gave it to them, saying, Drink ye all of it; for this is my blood of the new testament, which is shed for many for the remission of sins (Matt. 26: 26-28; cf. Mark 14: 22-24; Luke 22: 19-20). In addition to this historical account, St. Paul gives us a doctrinal interpretation in I Corinthians 10: 16-17: *The cup of blessing which we bless, is it not the communion of the blood of Christ? The bread which we break, is it not the communion of the body of Christ? For we being many are one bread, and one body: for we are all partakers of that one bread* (cf. also I Cor. 11: 23-28).

As baptism was substituted for circumcision, so also, the Lord's Supper superseded the Passover. Under the old covenant, the Passover was the eminent type of our Lord's redemptive sacrifice, which from age to age had represented the faith and hope of the ancient people. And since Christ himself as the true Passover was about to fulfill the Old Testament symbol, a new rite was necessary to commemorate this spiritual deliverance and confirm its benefits. That the Lord's Supper was intended to be permanent is evident from the fact that St. Paul received of the Lord the word which enjoined upon him the necessity of establishing it in all the churches which he founded (I Cor. 11: 23).

2. *Terminology.* During the apostolic age there were a number of terms used to express the meaning of the Lord's Supper, at least five of these words being found in the New Testament. (1) It was called the Eucharist ("to give thanks"), referring to Christ's taking the cup and giving thanks. On account of the appropriateness of this term it has always been popular among English speaking peoples. As such it is a solemn thanksgiving for the blessings of redemption. (2) It was known also as the Communion. St. Paul emphasizes this communion with one another as being inseparable from the communion with Christ (I Cor. 10: 16). (3) It was regarded as a memorial feast, a commemoration of the death of Jesus. This was closely associated with the redemptive death of Christ and the hope of His second coming. *For as often as*

ye eat this bread, and drink this cup, ye do shew the Lord's death till he come (I Cor. 11:26). (4) It was looked upon as a sacrifice—not in the sense of a repetition of Christ's sacrifice which was once for all (Heb. 9:25-26), but the community meal was itself called a sacrifice, in that it was a thank-offering or a *sacrifice of praise* (Heb. 13:15; cf. Phil. 2:17; 4:18); and also because it was attended by alms-giving for the poor. (5) It was called the presence, or the mystery. The first carried with it the idea of Christ as a host at His table, and is drawn from the Emmaus account, where Christ's presence was made known in the breaking of bread. The term *mystery* emphasizes the sacred food as a channel of grace and power. St. John is the primary witness here. Christ is the *bread of life* (John 6:53). However, it should be noted that the apostle is dealing with spiritual conceptions.

3. *The Nature of the Lord's Supper.* Various divergent views are held concerning the nature of the Lord's Supper. These are determined largely by the construction put upon the words, *this is my body,* and *this is my blood* (Matt. 26:26-28). These varying interpretations give us (1) The Roman Catholic doctrine of transubstantiation; (2) The Lutheran doctrine of consubstantiation; (3) The Zwinglian doctrine of commemoration; and (4) The Calvinistic doctrine of the Signs and Seals.

The doctrine of transubstantiation as held by Roman Catholics involves interpretation of the words *this is my body* and *this is my blood* in the most literal sense possible. It is believed that when our Lord pronounced these words, He changed the bread and wine into His own body and blood, and delivered it into the hands of the apostles. Since that time it is held that the priests through apostolic succession have the power of making a similar change by means of the prayer of consecration and pronouncement of the same words. The accidents of the bread and wine remain, that is, the bread tastes like bread, and the wine like wine; but the substance underlying these accidents is regarded as being changed, so that the bread is no longer bread, but the body of Christ;

and the wine is no longer wine, but the blood of Christ. Since the blood is included in the body, the laity receives only the bread, and the priest the wine. There are several important consequences which are related to this doctrine. (1) The bread and wine, having been changed into the body and blood of Christ, are by the priest presented unto God as a sacrifice. While this sacrifice differs from others as being without the shedding of blood, it is still regarded as a true propitiatory offering for the sins of both the living and the dead. (2) This body and blood contain within them the grace they signify, and therefore confer it *ex opere operato,* that is, they have intrinsic value in themselves and this grace is imparted to all through the mere partaking of the sacrament. No special disposition is necessary on the part of the recipient, not even faith, for the sacrament operates immediately upon all who do not obstruct it by mortal sin. (3) The bread having been changed into the body of Christ, any unused portion is sacredly kept as the "reserved host." (4) Since Christ's divinity was attached to His body, it is regarded as highly proper to worship the elements upon the altar; and further to carry them about that they might receive the homage of all who meet them. Against this unscriptural doctrine Protestants not only objected but revolted, and hence the Reformation doctrine is more simple and scriptural.

The doctrine of consubstantiation was adopted by Luther respecting the presence of Christ in the sacrament. While protesting against the Roman doctrine of transubstantiation, he yet felt the need of conserving in an objective manner the saving significance of the ordinance. He accepted, therefore, the words of institution in their literal significance, but denied that the elements were changed by consecration. He maintained that the bread and the wine remained the same, but that in, with, and under the bread and the wine, the body and blood of Christ were present in the sacrament for all partakers and not merely for believers. With the bread and wine, therefore, the body and blood of Christ are literally received by all communicants. Since Christ's presence is only in the use of the elements, the remnants are only so much bread and wine. It is in the use also, that the blessing is given to those who partake in faith.

The doctrine of the Lord's Supper as a commemorative rite was advanced by Zwingli, the Swiss reformer and contemporary of Luther. He objected to the literal interpretation of the words of institution as taught by Luther, and maintained instead, that when Jesus said, *This is my body, this is my blood,* He employed a common figure of speech, in which the sign is put for the thing signified. Instead of the elements representing the real presence, they are rather, the signs of the absent body and blood of Christ. The Lord's Supper, therefore, is to be regarded as merely a religious commemoration of the death of Christ, with this addition, that it is naturally adapted to produce helpful emotions and reflections, and to strengthen the purposes of the will. This view escapes the errors of the two former theories, but still falls short of the full truth.

The last theory to be mentioned is that of the Reformers as taught by Calvin. This is a mediating position between Luther and Zwingli, and is now the generally accepted creed of the Reformed churches. Calvin renounced both transubstantiation and consubstantiation. He taught that the body and blood were not locally, but only spiritually present in the elements. This doctrine is expressed in the first Helvetic Confession as follows: "The bread and the wine are holy, true symbols, through which the Lord offers and presents the true communion of the body, and blood of Christ for the feeding and nourishing of the spiritual and eternal life."

The doctrine which we hold is well summed up by Dr. Ralston in the following statement: "We conclude that, in this ordinance, (1) No change is effected in the elements; the bread and wine are not literally the body and blood of Christ. (2) The body and blood of Christ are not literally present with the elements, and received by the communicants. (3) But the elements are signs, or symbols, of the body and blood of Christ, serving as a memorial of His sufferings on the cross and a help to the faith of the communicant. (4) The elements also possess a sacramental character, being a divinely appointed seal of the covenant of redemption. As the blood of the paschal lamb served as a seal of this covenant under the old dispensation, pointing the faith of the Israelite to the coming Redeemer, it was fit that, as the old dispensation was now to be superseded by the new, the seal of the covenant should be correspondingly changed; hence at the conclusion of the last authorized Passover, the Holy Supper is instituted, as a perpetual memorial and abiding seal of the covenanted mercy and grace of God, till the Saviour shall appear the second time without sin unto salvation" (RALSTON, *Elements of Divinity*, p. 997). It will be observed that the above is in perfect agreement with Article XIV of the Manual, as well as the creedal statements of Protestantism in general.

4. *The Administration of the Lord's Supper.* A few observations may well be made in connection with the proper administration of the Lord's Supper. (1) The elements are bread and wine. While certain groups use leavened bread and fermented wine, our special rules state that "only unfermented wine and unleavened bread should be used in the sacrament of the Lord's Supper." (2) The sacramental actions are symbolical also. These are: (a) The prayer of consecration which includes the giving of thanks to God, the preparation of the hearts of the communicants, and the consecration of the elements; and (b) the breaking of bread. This is significant as representing the broken body of our Lord Jesus Christ. It is not essential, however, that it be broken as served. It is the common custom to pass it already broken to those who participate in the service. The cup is to be passed also, as an emblem of His shed blood. (3) The Lord's Supper is for all His people. Hence the invitation is, "Let all those who have with true repentance forsaken their sins, and have believed in Christ unto salvation, draw near and take these emblems, and, by faith, partake of the life of Jesus Christ, to your soul's comfort and joy. Let us remember that it is the memorial of the death and passion of our Lord; also a

token of His coming again. Let us not forget that we are one, at one table with the Lord." (4) The Lord's Supper should be observed with faithfulness and regularity until He comes again. It is both a privilege and duty for Christians to participate in this ordinance. "If a peculiar condemnation fall upon them who partake 'unworthily,' then a peculiar blessing must follow from partaking worthily; and it therefore becomes the duty of every minister to explain the obligation, and to show the advantages of this sacrament, and earnestly to enforce its regular observance upon all those who give satisfactory evidence of repentance toward God and faith in our Lord Jesus Christ" (WAKEFIELD, *Christian Theology,* p. 596).

UNIT VII

THE DOCTRINE OF LAST THINGS

Preview

In our concluding unit we study the subject of Eschatology, or the doctrine of last things. This truth is closely related to all of those doctrines which we have already considered. It is, as it were, the product or ripe fruit of Christian development and progress throughout the ages. In the Christian teaching concerning the last things we see God's ultimate and final purposes being achieved. God's designs, purposed in His mind before the foundation of the world, are here brought to fruition and completion.

Eschatology is also and particularly related to the office and work of our Lord Jesus Christ. It is in Him that the old creation and the new creation, redeemed from the dominion and stain of sin, are brought to completion. His Second Advent is therefore the central doctrine of this unit. After a brief consideration of the Christian meaning of death and biblical teaching concerning the intermediate state, we study in some detail the subject of the personal return of our Lord. In connection with this, we suggest, without dogmatism, what seems to be the scriptural teaching concerning the order of events of the "Lord's Day." Our attention is then directed toward the momentous developments which shall bring this age to a close—the judgment, the entrance of both wicked and righteous into their places of everlasting abode, and the final consummation of all things.

In keeping with the law of prophetic reserve, there are many aspects of future events which cannot now be fully known. As a result, intelligent and holy Bible scholars have often differed in the interpretation of certain points in Eschatology. A spirit of reverential humility may well characterize all of us in our study of these prophetic events.

At the same time many *facts* are before us with crystal clearness and awful certitude. Christ is coming again, and His coming may be at hand! Every man must stand before the judgment seat of Christ and give account. Men will either find their everlasting abode in the celestial bliss of heaven, or in the torments of a burning hell! These are stern realities which should grip every one of us, and incite us to holiness of heart and faithful service for Christ. *Therefore, be ye also ready: for in such an hour as ye think not the Son of man cometh* (Matt. 24:44).

UNIT VII

THE DOCTRINE OF LAST THINGS

Chapter XXI. *The Second Coming of Christ*

I. DEATH AND IMMORTALITY
  A. The Christian View of Death.
  B. The Immortality of Man.
  C. The Christian Victory through Christ.

II. THE INTERMEDIATE STATE
  A. Terminology.
  B. Varied Views Concerning the Intermediate State.

III. THE PERSONAL RETURN OF OUR LORD
  A. Christ Will Return in Person.
  B. The Sign of His Coming.
  C. The Manner of His Coming.
  D. The Purpose of His Coming.
  E. The Day of the Lord.
  F. The Second Advent and Millennial Theories.
  G. Christ's First and Second Advents.

IV. THE ORDER OF EVENTS OF THE LORD'S DAY
  A. The Rapture and the Revelation.
  B. The Investigative Judgment.
  C. The Destruction of the Wicked.
  D. The Fall of Antichrist and the Binding of Satan.
  E. The Establishment of the Kingdom.
  F. The Regeneration of the Earth.
  G. The Final Consummation.

Chapter XXII. *The Resurrection, Judgment, and Final Consummation*

I. THE RESURRECTION
  A. Scriptural Teaching Regarding the Resurrection.
  B. The Nature of the Resurrected Body.
  C. The General Resurrection.

II. The Final Judgment

    A. The Fact of the General Judgment.
    B. The Person of the Judge.
    C. The Principles of Judgment.
    D. The Purpose of the General Judgment.
    E. The Final Judgment Scene.

III. The Future State of the Impenitent

    A. The Scriptural Terms Denoting the Place of Punishment.
    B. The Doctrine of Eternal Punishment as Taught in the Scriptures.

IV. The Eternal Blessedness of the Saints

    A. Heaven Is Both a Place and a State.
    B. The Blessedness of the Saints.
    C. The Employments of Heaven.
    D. The Endless Duration of Heaven.

V. The Final Consummation

    A. Scope of the Final Consummation.
    B. The New Heavens and the New Earth.

CHAPTER XXI

THE SECOND COMING OF CHRIST

But of that day and that hour knoweth no man, no, not the angels which are in heaven, neither the Son, but the Father. Take ye heed, watch and pray: for ye know not when the time is. For the Son of man is as a man taking a far journey, who left his house, and gave authority to his servants, and to every man his work, and commanded the porter to watch. Watch ye therefore: for ye know not when the master of the house cometh, at even, or at midnight, or at the cockcrowing, or in the morning: lest coming suddenly he find you sleeping. And what I say unto you I say unto all, Watch.—Our Lord Jesus Christ (Mark 13:32-37).

We turn our attention in this last unit of our study to the subject of Eschatology or the Doctrine of Last Things. All of the doctrines of Christianity point to a final consummation, and all converge in one glorious hope—the Second Advent of our Lord. As preceding this event, we shall briefly consider the subjects of death and the intermediate state; and following it, the resurrection and the final judgment. Concerning these vital and important events of the future, the Word of God constitutes our only authoritative source of information.

I. Death and Immortality

A. *The Christian View of Death.*

In the Christian system, the concept of "death" is used in a number of connections with varied interpretations. Death in the physical sense, as the separation of the soul from the body, is viewed as the last event in the probationary history of man. As we noted in connection with our study of the fall, death is also to be interpreted as a penalty imposed on the human race because of sin; and the Scriptures also view death as spiritual and eternal. Death never means annihilation. In the physical sense, death refers simply to the separation of the soul from the body, not to the termination of existence. In the spiritual sense, death refers to the separation of both soul and body from God; and when the additional element of "eternal death" is considered, this separation is viewed as final and irrevocable.

The Scriptures teach that *As by one man sin entered into the world, and death by sin; and so death passed upon all men, for that all have sinned* (Rom. 5:12). Thus death is the penalty for sin, death physical, spiritual, and eternal. But the Scriptures teach with equal clearness that death as a penalty is abolished in Christ. *Therefore as by the offense of one judgment came upon all men to condemnation; even so by the righteousness of one the free gift came upon all men unto justification of life* (Rom. 5:18). Consequently, death as penalty, whether considered physically or spiritually, is abolished by Christ in two ways: provisionally for all men in that He tasted death for every man (Heb. 2:9); and actually for all who are in Christ. *He that believeth on the Son hath everlasting life: and he that believeth not the Son shall not see life; but the wrath of God abideth on him* (John 3:36). This abolition is both conditional, being dependent on faith in Christ, and gradual. We look forward in hope to the day when every trace of death shall be removed from God's created universe. Thus it is that physical death is still bound up with the divine purpose concerning the destiny of mankind, for *It is appointed unto men once to die* (Heb. 9:27). Also, for the Christian, death is a part of his probationary discipline, and is hallowed as a ground of fellowship with Christ. Physical death for the Christian is now transfigured to a simple departure from this life to another (cf. II Cor. 5:1, 4). It is the door through which he enters into the presence of Christ himself.

B. *The Immortality of Man.*

The life of man never ceases to be. The grave is only the tunnel through which men pass in order to reach the life beyond. The nature of this future existence is determined by the personal character; and this in turn by the attitude of the soul toward the atoning work of Jesus Christ. To the believer, it is eternal life; to the unbeliever, eternal death.

In addition to the fundamental conviction which is intuitively possessed by normal men concerning the fact of immortality, there are certain supporting arguments. The psychological argument is based on the nature of the soul as immaterial essence, indivisible and hence indestructible. The teleological argument holds that the human soul does not, and cannot fulfill all its promise in this world; and hence necessitates another world and continued existence in order to achieve its full complement of blessedness. Lastly, the moral argument, as presented in both its individual and social aspects holds that man in this world does not always receive justice. Thus mere annihilation would not permit degrees of punishment corresponding to the different degrees of guilt.

In the Old and New Testaments we have the only authoritative teaching concerning the immortality of man. No Hebrew writer, either inspired or uninspired, ever doubted the immortality of the soul. The spirit of man is distinguished from that of beasts, and the conviction of a life beyond for man is clearly set forth (cf. Eccles. 3: 21; Job 19: 25-26; Psalms 90: 10). The New Testament is rich with teaching concerning the fact of man's immortality. Our Lord himself declared, *And fear not them which kill the body, but are not able to kill the soul* (Matt. 10: 28). From this it is evident that the soul and the body are not identical, and that to kill the body does not kill the soul. This argument from the words of our Lord is conclusive (cf. also Luke 12: 4-5; Matt. 17: 3; 22: 31-32; Luke 16: 22-23; Luke 23: 43, 46; Acts 7: 59).

C. *The Christian Victory Through Christ.*

The resurrection of our Lord Jesus Christ was not only His own personal triumph over death but it was the triumph of His people also (Heb. 2: 14-15). Through His victory, He becomes the author of life to every believer. Death, therefore, which will eventually be swallowed up of life, is now a conquered enemy. This fact alone makes necessary a changed attitude toward death on the part of the believers. Death is to the Christian not now an abnormal event. In a sense it is a birth, not a spiritual birth into the kingdom of God, but a bursting forth of life into the post-earthly realm, a birth into the kingdom of glory. *But if the Spirit of him that raised up Jesus from the dead dwell in you, he that raised up Christ from the dead shall also quicken your mortal bodies by his Spirit that dwelleth in you* (Rom. 8:11).

II. THE INTERMEDIATE STATE

We turn now to the question of the conscious existence of the soul between death and the resurrection of the body. All who accept the teaching of the Scriptures as the Word of God accept also the fact of an intermediate state, but there is considerable difference of opinion regarding the nature of this state.

A. *Terminology.*

An understanding of three terms may be helpful in analyzing the teaching of the Scriptures concerning the intermediate state. *Sheol* is a Hebrew word which sometimes means indefinitely, the grave, or place or state of the dead; and at others, definitely, a place or state of the dead into which the element of misery and punishment enters, but never a place or state of happiness, or good after death. *Hades* is a Greek word which signifies the invisible world of departed spirits. It was used by the authors of the Septuagint to translate the Hebrew word *Sheol*, as in Psalms 16:10 and the Acts 2:27. The word *Hades* is used only eleven times in the New Testament and in every case but one is translated hell, and certainly always represents the invisible world as under the dominion of Satan, and as opposed to the kingdom of Christ. The third word, *paradise*, means a park or pleasure garden. It was used by the translators of the Septuagint to represent the garden of Eden (Gen. 2:8). It occurs only three times in the New Testament (Luke 23:43; II Cor. 12:4; Rev. 2:7), and the context shows that it is connected with the "third heaven" in one instance; and in the others with the "Garden of God" in

which grows the tree of life—all three passages necessarily referring to a life beyond physical death.

B. *Varied Views Concerning the Intermediate State.*

The common belief among the Hebrew people seems
to have been that all souls descended at death into Sheol,
which was a gloomy, subterranean abode; and in which
the inhabitants were shades, existing in a weak, powerless, and dreamy state. At other times Sheol is represented as divided into two departments—Paradise, a place of
positive bliss, and Gehenna, a place of positive torment.
In the former or Abraham's bosom, were the Jews, or
at least those who had been faithful to the law; in the
latter were the Gentiles.

Since the time of Gregory the Great, Roman Catholics have held to the doctrine of Purgatory as an intermediate place. This is regarded as the intermediate
abode of those who die in the peace of the church, but
who need further purification before entering the final
state of heaven. It is a state of suffering for the
purpose of both expiation and purification. The suffering in both length and intensity is said to be proportion-
ate to the guilt and impurity of the sufferer. Other than
the day of judgment, there is no known or defined limit
to the continuance of the soul in Purgatory. It is asserted
that souls in this place may be helped by the prayers of
the saints, and especially by the sacrifice of the Mass. It
is also claimed that the authorities of the Church, may
at their discretion, remit entirely or partially the penalty
of the sins under which souls there detained are suffering. This erroneous doctrine arises from the belief of
the Roman Catholic Church that the atonement of
Christ is available for us only in respect to original sin
and exposure to eternal death. That is, Christ delivers
us only from culpability, not from liability to punishment. For sins after baptism the offender must therefore make satisfaction by penance or good works. This
satisfaction must be completed in this life if the soul is
to enter heaven; if not, then this purification must be
completed in Purgatory.

Protestantism retains the idea of an intermediate state, but rejects generally the idea of an intermediate place. It is held that at death the souls of the righteous go immediately into the presence of Christ and of God. To be absent from the body is to be present with the Lord (II Cor. 5:6). These souls exist in a state of consciousness, and the moral and spiritual relationship to Christ is continuous and unbroken (Rom. 8:38). This is a state of blessedness and rest (Rev. 14:13). This state is not the final state of believers. Man is body as well as spirit, and hence in his disembodied state there is an element of imperfection which can be supplied only by the resurrection. The souls of the wicked are banished from the presence of the Lord where they, too, exist in a state of consciousness. This condition is one of suffering and unrest. It is not final but the wicked will also be raised, but to everlasting shame and contempt; and the judgment will fix their eternal doom.

The Scriptures leave undecided the question as to whether there is an intermediate place as well as a state. Some passages such as that dealing with the account of Dives and Lazarus (Luke 16:19-31); and the words of Christ to the dying thief, *Today shalt thou be with me in paradise,* seem to favor an intermediate place. Other texts such as the words of St. Stephen, *Lord Jesus, receive my spirit* (Acts 7:59), and the statement of St. Paul, *to be absent from the body, and to be present with the Lord* (II Cor. 5:8) clearly teach an intermediate state but not necessarily an intermediate place. It is the general belief of the Church that during the intermediate state the persons of men are incomplete while their souls and their bodies are separated, but this incompleteness is due to the state or condition, and not to the place. That is, the righteous and wicked each go to their place of final abode, but do not thereby enter upon their eternal state. This latter can take place only at the final judgment.

As to whether the intermediate state of the redeemed is characterized by progress, development, and activity the Word of God seems to suggest an affirmative answer. In the Apocalypse we are told that the spirits of the redeemed from among men, *follow the Lamb whithersoever he goeth* (Rev. 14: 4) ; and that having washed their robes and made them white in the blood of the Lamb, they *serve him day and night in his temple* (Rev. 7: 15). There is one instance in which the rapid development in the intermediate state is clearly set forth. St. John having heard the messenger of God says, *I fell at his feet to worship him. And he said unto me, See thou do it not: I am thy fellowservant, and of thy brethren that have the testimony of Jesus: worship God* (Rev. 19: 10). So transformed was the messenger, that St. John did not recognize him as a martyr, but supposed him to be a divine being to be worshiped. We may well believe then, on the authority of the Scriptures, that the intermediate state will be one of progress in righteousness for the righteous, and in wickedness for the wicked.

III. The Personal Return of Our Lord

In approaching the subject of our Lord's second advent we are about to enter one of the most delicate and controversial fields of theology. The subject is one which has periodically interested and agitated the Church especially during periods when man feels most his need of divine help. In times of disaster, war, pestilence or persecution the hope of His coming has always occupied the thoughts of men.

The glory of Christianity finds its highest expression in the return and reign of the God-man, who as the Christ or Anointed One, Creator and Redeemer, will establish Himself in a perfect world order—the kingdom of God in a new heaven and a new earth, wherein dwelleth righteousness.

A. *Christ Will Return in Person.*

Modern theology has frequently been too much inclined to deny the personal, visible return of our Lord, and to substitute instead, a belief in His spiritual presence only. However, the Scriptures clearly teach that as Christ once came into the world to effect man's redemption, so also, He will come again to receive His redeemed Church to Himself. This is expressly stated in the words, *Christ was once offered to bear the sins of many; and unto them that look for him shall he appear the second time without sin unto salvation* (Heb. 9:28). This second coming will be personal, visible, and glorious. *Behold, he cometh with clouds; and every eye shall see him, and they also which pierced him: and all kindreds of the earth shall wail because of him. Even so, Amen* (Rev. 1:7). His coming will not be merely to the eye of faith, but in the sight of heaven and earth—the terror of his foes, and the consolation of His people. This is confirmed by the incident on the Mount of Ascension. *And when he had spoken these things, while they beheld, he was taken up; and a cloud received him out of their sight. And while they looked steadfastly toward heaven as he went up, behold two men stood by them in white apparel, which also said, Ye men of Galilee, why stand ye gazing up into heaven? This same Jesus, which is taken up from you into heaven, shall so come in like manner as ye have seen him go into heaven* (Acts 1:9-11). According to Dr. Whedon, "This passage is an immovable proof text of the actual, personal, second advent of Jesus. It is the same personal, visible Jesus which ascended that shall come. The coming shall be in like manner with the going."

No testimony regarding His second advent is more important than that given by Jesus himself. In a solemn warning to the Jews, He said, *Behold your house is left unto you desolate. For I say unto you, ye shall not see me henceforth, till ye shall say, "Blessed is he that cometh in the name of the Lord* (Matt. 23:38-39). However, the climactic utterance is that which was made before the high priest when Jesus said, *Hereafter shall ye see the Son of man sitting on the right hand of power, and coming in the clouds of heaven* (Matt. 26:64).

With these clear statements of the Master himself as a foundation, it is not surprising that to the early Christians His second advent was the *blessed hope, and the glorious appearing of the great God and our Saviour Jesus Christ* (Titus 2: 13). St. Paul states that *Our conversation is in heaven; from whence also we look for the Saviour, the Lord Jesus Christ: who shall change our vile body, that it may be fashioned like unto his glorious body* (Phil. 3: 20-21). St. Peter gives us this exhortation, *Wherefore gird up the loins of your mind, be sober and hope to the end for the grace that is to be brought unto you at the revelation of Jesus Christ* (I Peter 1: 13); while St. James gives a like exhortation, *Be patient therefore, brethren, unto the coming of the Lord . . . . stablish your hearts: for the coming of the Lord draweth nigh* (James 5: 7-8). Perhaps the most loved text of all is that recorded by St. John, *Let not your heart be troubled: ye believe in God, believe also in me. In my Father's house are many mansions: if it were not so, I would have told you. I go to prepare a place for you. And if I go and prepare a place for you, I will come again, and receive you unto myself; that where I am, there ye may be also* (John 14: 1-3). In these clear statements of Christ and His apostles we have ample evidence of the fact of His personal second advent.

B. *The Sign of His Coming.*

In His reply to the question of His disciples, *What shall be the sign of thy coming, and of the end of the world?* our Lord predicted three classes of events which will mark the era of His second coming. *First,* there will be disturbances in the physical world, great political upheavals, and social disintegration. *For nation shall rise against nation, and kingdom against kingdom: and there shall be famines, and pestilences, and earthquakes, in divers places* (Matt. 24: 7). These our Lord declares *are the beginning of sorrows* (Matt. 24: 8). From the words, *but the end is not yet* (Matt. 24: 6), we may infer that this beginning of sorrows will precede the second advent by a considerable space of time. But our Lord predicts the deepening shadows of a greater tribulation as the end of the age approaches. This He introduces with warnings and exhortations of great moment (Matt.

24: 15-20) and concludes by saying, *For then shall be great tribulation, such as was not since the beginning of the world to this time, no, nor ever shall be. And except those days should be shortened, there should no flesh be saved: but for the elect's sake those days shall be shortened* (Matt. 24: 21-22). *Second,* the gospel will be preached in all the world prior to the second advent. To preach the gospel and bear witness of Christ is the supreme duty of the Church in this age (Acts 1: 7-8). Hence we are told that *This gospel of the kingdom shall be preached in all the world for a witness unto all nations; and then shall the end come* (Matt. 24: 14). *Lastly,* our Lord predicts that the era of His second return shall be characterized by an apostasy or falling away due to the deceptiveness of sin. *And then shall many be offended, and shall betray one another, and shall hate one another. And many false prophets shall rise, and shall deceive many. And because iniquity shall abound, the love of many shall wax cold* (Matt. 24: 10-12). Our Lord seems to indicate also, that as the tribulation deepens toward the end of the age, so also the deceptiveness of sin increases. *Then if any man shall say unto you, Lo, here is Christ, or there; believe it not. For there shall arise false Christs, and false prophets, and shall shew great signs and wonders; insomuch that, if it were possible, they shall deceive the very elect. Behold, I have told you before* (Matt. 24: 23-25). St. Paul also reveals that while there will be a great falling away in the last time, there will be also the revelation of a "man of sin" who, with wicked presumption, will assume the place of God and lay claim to the honor of divine worship. *Let no man deceive you by any means: for that day shall not come, except there come a falling away first, and that man of sin be revealed, the son of perdition; who opposeth and exalteth himself above all that is called God, or that is worshipped; so that he as God sitteth in the temple of God, shewing himself that he is God* (II Thess. 2: 3-4).

The increase in wickedness just described does not imply a gradual and necessary decline of Christ's kingdom. Christ does not teach, nor does the Church believe that His kingdom shall decline. Our Lord teaches that the same harvest season which ripens the wheat, ripens the tares also; that there is, therefore, a progress in wickedness as well as in righteousness; and that both the wheat and the tares are to *grow* together—not one grow and the other decline. But the true motive for evangelism as found in the Church, is not in the glory of outward success, but in a deep sense of obedience to a trust, and a fervent love for her Lord. As the end of the age approaches, we may expect an increase in righteousness and in wickedness, and the Church must gird herself for an aggressive and constant warfare against sin until Jesus comes.

C. *The Manner of His Coming.*

Here again our Lord's discourses must be the source of our authority concerning this eschatological event. Having warned against the deceptiveness of false Christs and false prophets, He instructs the disciples concerning the manner of His coming, in these words, *Wherefore if they shall say unto you, Behold, he is in the desert; go not forth: behold, he is in the secret chambers; believe it not. For as the lightning cometh out of the east, and shineth even unto the west; so shall also the coming of the Son of man be* (Matt. 24:26-27). He indicates also that there shall be disturbances of a cataclysmic nature in the physical universe immediately preceding or attending His second advent. *Immediately after the tribulation of those days shall the sun be darkened, and the moon shall not give her light, and the stars shall fall from heaven, and the powers of the heavens shall be shaken: and then shall appear the sign of the Son of man in heaven: and then shall all the tribes of the earth mourn, and they shall see the Son of man coming in the clouds of heaven with power and great glory. And he shall send his angels with a great sound of a trumpet, and they shall gather together his elect from the four winds, from one end of heaven to the other* (Matt. 24:29-31).

Our Lord teaches also, that a certain unexpected-ness will attend His coming. The time of the second advent is veiled in mystery. *But of that day and hour knoweth no man, no, not the angels in heaven, but my Father only* (Matt. 24:36). He instructs His disciples, therefore to give the utmost attention to watchfulness and faithfulness in the things of the kingdom. *Watch therefore: for ye know not what hour your Lord doth come* (Matt. 24:42); and again, *Therefore be ye also ready: for in such an hour as ye think not the Son of man cometh* (Matt. 24:44). He further declares that at the time of His second coming the world will be pursuing its ordinary course, unmindful of the great event which will take place suddenly and without special warning. *But as the days of Noe were, so shall the coming of the Son of man be. For as in the days that were before the flood they were eating and drinking, marrying and giving in marriage, until the day that Noe entered into the ark, and knew not until the flood came, and took them all away; so shall also the coming of the Son of man be* (Matt. 24:37-39). We may confidently believe, then, that the second advent will be a sudden and glorious appearance of our Lord, bursting in upon the ordinary course of the world as an unexpected cataclysmic event. To the righteous, who have through faith in His Word prepared themselves and are watching for His return, this appearance will be hailed with supreme joy; to the wicked who have rejected His words, saying, *Where is the promise of his coming?* it will be a time of conster-nation and condemnation.

D. *The Purpose of His Coming.*

Our Lord sets forth the purpose of His coming in two familiar parables, that of the ten virgins, and that of the talents. The outstanding truth emphasized in both of these parables is that of a coming judgment in which the righteous shall be rewarded and the wicked pun-ished. Following the second parable our Lord clearly states the purpose of His coming in the following words, *When the Son of man shall come in his glory, and all the holy angels with him, then shall he sit upon the throne of his glory: and before him shall be gathered all nations: and he shall separate them one from another, as a shepherd divideth his sheep from the goats: and he shall set the sheep on his right hand and the goats on the left. Then shall the King say unto them on his right hand, Come, ye blessed of my Father, inherit the kingdom prepared for you from the foundation of the world* (Matt. 25:31-34). Following this He depicts in vivid colors the scene of judgment, in which He pronounces sentence upon those on his left hand, saying, *Depart from me, ye cursed, into everlasting fire, prepared for the devil and his angels* (Matt. 25:41); and concludes the discourse with the solemn words, *And these shall go away into everlasting punishment: but the righteous into life eternal* (Matt. 25:46). From these words of our Lord concerning the second coming as directly related to judgment, there can be no appeal.

St. Paul places the second advent in close time relation to the resurrection, making the resurrection of the righteous dead to precede immediately the translation of the living saints. *For if we believe that Jesus died and rose again, even so them also which sleep in Jesus will God bring with him. For this we say unto you by the word of the Lord, that we which are alive and remain unto the coming of the Lord shall not prevent them which are asleep. For the Lord himself shall descend from heaven with a shout, with the voice of the archangel, and with the trump of God: and the dead in Christ shall rise first: then we which are alive and remain shall be caught up together with them in the clouds, to meet the Lord in the air: and so shall we ever be with the Lord* (I Thess. 4:14-17). Here it is evident that the coming of Jesus *with* His saints (the dead in Christ whose souls have already gone to be with Him), and the coming of Jesus *for* His saints (those which are alive and remain) must be associated not only with the same event, but must be regarded also, as indicating the order of the happenings in that event.

Not only does St. Paul present the second advent as closely related to the resurrection, but St. Peter places it in time relation to the final consummation of the present order. *But the day of the Lord will come as a thief in the night; in the which the heavens shall pass away with a great noise, and the elements shall melt with fervent heat, the earth also and the works that are therein shall be burned up. Seeing then that all these things shall be dissolved, what manner of persons ought ye to be in all holy conversation and godliness* (II Peter 3: 10-11).

As an event the second coming of Christ will therefore be associated in time with the resurrection, the judgment, and the final consummation. These and other related developments are sometimes referred to in the Scriptures as the "Day of the Lord."

E. *The Day of the Lord.*

As indicated in our discussion of the days of creation, the older Hebrew exegesis never regarded the days of Genesis as solar days, but as day periods of indefinite duration. The word "day" is frequently used in this same sense in the New Testament also. Thus our Lord says, *For as the lightning, that lighteneth out of the one part under heaven, shineth unto the other part under heaven; so shall also the Son of man be in his day* (Luke 17: 24). St. Peter speaks of *the day of the Lord* (II Peter 3: 10, 12, 13); and St. Paul mentions both the *day of the Lord* (I Thess. 5: 2, 4, 5), and the *day of Christ* (II Thess. 2: 1-2). This day of the Lord is generally, if not always, associated with the idea of judgment. We may confidently believe, then, that the day of the Lord is a period of time, marked by opening, intervening, and closing events. St. Paul views this day in relation to its opening event, the coming of Christ; while St. Peter regards it as the closing event in Christ's ultimate and triumphant accomplishment. It is a transitional period in which a time or season is preceded by other times or seasons. For this reason it is often difficult to distinguish the preparatory events from those of the final consummation to which they lead. Before turning our attention to the order of events in this day of the Lord it is advisable to examine the concept of the millennium.

F. *The Second Advent and Millennial Theories.*

The personal return of Christ was very early associated with the idea of a millennium, or a reign of Christ on earth for a period of a thousand years. Those who embraced this doctrine were known as Chiliasts. From the death of the apostles to the time of Origen, Chiliasm or premillennialism, was the dominant faith of the Church. This view asserted that the Scriptures taught us to look forward to a millennium or universal reign of righteousness on the earth; and that this millennial age will be introduced by the personal, visible return of the Lord Jesus. However, early in the fifth century, Augustine settled the fate of Chiliasm, for many centuries, by teaching that the church was the kingdom of God on earth. Such questions sank into insignificance when the Church won the protection of the state, and the doctrines of Chiliasm were not given prominence again until the time of the Reformation.

Only brief mention can be made of the various types of millennialism which have been taught since interest in the subject was revived in the sixteenth century. For convenience of analysis they may be divided into two groups: the literalistic theories, and the spiritualistic theories. The former include in general the premillennial theories of every type. These premillennial theories may be segregated also into two general types. *First,* there are those which regard the Church as complete, and therefore identify in point of time the second advent of Christ with the rapture and revelation, the first resurrection, and the conflagration, placing all these events before the millennium. This view is commonly known as the Adventist Theory. *Second,* there are those premillennial theories which regard the Church as incomplete at the time of the second advent. These theories separate the rapture and revelation on the one hand, and the conflagration on the other, making the millennium to lie between these two terminal points. This is often termed the Keswick Theory. The principal objection to this type of premillennialism centers largely in its emphasis upon a continuance of the work of salvation during the millennium. The ground of this objection is found in those scriptures which seem to indicate that when Christ comes the intercession will cease and the judgment begin (cf. Heb. 7: 25; 9: 12, 24-28). It is held by some that, "when the Advent arrives, the intercession is done; and when the intercession is done, salvation is done. When Christ appears the second time *to* us, He will cease to appear in the presence of God *for* us" (BROWN, *Christ's Second Coming*, p. 112).

The spiritualistic theories of the millennium are of two types. Roman Catholics hold to a view which is essentially that held by St. Augustine; namely, that the reign of Christ refers to the Church age, and the whole period of time between the first advent of Christ and the second. The millennium is thus identified with the whole gospel dispensation. The second type of spiritualistic theory is commonly known as postmillennialism. It is so called because it regards the second advent as following, rather than preceding the millennium. As to the personal visible return of our Lord, postmillennialists hold this as firmly, and cherish it as highly as do the premillennialists. The millennium is regarded as a reign of righteousness in the future. In this period the Church will flourish and holiness will triumph for a thousand years. The world will enjoy paradisaical blessedness while martyrs and saints in heaven will sympathize with its joy. The triumph on earth will be universal (cf. RAYMOND, *Systematic Theology*, II, pp. 493-494).

From what has been said, it is evident that premillennialism and postmillennialism represent opposite extremes of thought, and a totally different method of approach. The millennium as postmillennialists conceive it, is the flowering age of the Church—a time in which righteousness shall reign and peace spread throughout the world. This condition will be brought about by the present methods of evangelism, to which will be added, "the binding of Satan," or the restraining judgments of God. While the righteous are in the ascendancy, the millennium is, nevertheless, a mixed condition of saints and sinners — all in the flesh. One passage of scripture in particular, Revelation 20:1-11, has been interpreted in contrasting ways by premillennialists and postmillennialists. The latter interpret this apocalyptic statement as purely symbolical or figurative and thus the reign of Christ is looked upon as purely spiritual. In addition, the first resurrection is viewed as spiritual, and the second only, as bodily and literal. Premillenialists, on the other hand, interpret the passage in its literal sense on both points.

It is helpful to remember that the millennium is a transition period between the present temporal order, and the eternal order that shall be. It is due to this twofold aspect that much confusion arises. Being a transitional period the millennium looks both ways, and conjoins in itself, two widely different orders. It marks the transition from the natural to the spiritual, from the temporal to the eternal, from the immanent to the transcendent, and from grace to glory.

G. Christ's First and Second Advents.

There are certain interesting points of contrast between Christ's first and second advents which are worthy of our notice. In the first advent He came as a ministering servant; in the second, He will *sit upon the throne of his glory; and before him shall be gathered all nations* (Matt. 25:31-32). His first advent was in humiliation. He was despised and rejected of men (Isa. 53:3). *He came unto his own, and his own received him not* (John 1:11). But His second coming will be governed by the law of exaltation and not that of humiliation. His second advent thus will be marked by His people rising with joy to meet him in the air, and with an innumerable company of angels forming the convoy of their glorious Bridegroom on His return to earth. The purpose of His first advent was the deliverance of man from the guilt, power, and the being of sin, through His priestly sacrifice for sin. The second coming will be to remove the consequences of sin by means of the "all power" given to Him as our glorious King.

IV. The Order of Events of the Lord's Day

According to the law of prophetical reserve, there is enough given to us in the Scriptures to furnish the Church with a glorious hope; but the events of the future can never be entirely untangled until prophecy passes into history, and we view them as standing out clearly in their historical relation. Our purpose in dealing with the order of events of the Lord's day is not to speak with such a degree of positiveness as to exclude the sincere thought of Bible students who hold different positions. It is already evident to the reader that there is a wide variety of opinion concerning many of these matters. The material which we present is therefore suggestive rather than dogmatic, and we hope that it will serve to provoke further study and research on the part of the reader.

A. *The Rapture and the Revelation.*

The second coming of Christ is the opening event of the Lord's day. It will be attended by the resurrection of the righteous dead and the translation of the righteous living, both companies of the saints being caught up in the clouds to meet the Lord in the air. Here a distinction is made between the rapture and the revelation. The rapture is the catching away of the Lord's people to the meeting in the air. The revelation is Christ's return to the earth accompanied by the convoy of saints and angels. As to the relation of the rapture and the revelation there are widely different opinions. Some identify them, maintaining that when He comes every eye shall behold Him, the saints rising with joy to meet Him, and the nations of the earth wailing because of Him (Rev. 1: 7). Others separate between the rapture and the revelation, maintaining that the former is secret and known only to the saints; the latter alone being visible to the world. As to the time intervening between the two, most writers hold that it will be a period of three and one-half years. During this time the saints attend the marriage supper of the Lamb in the heavenlies, while the earth passes through a period of unparalleled tribulation at which time the Antichrist assumes full authority. The general fact of the rapture and revelation are clearly scriptural; the details just mentioned must be a matter of individual opinion and interpretation.

B. *The Investigative Judgment.*

Immediately following the return of Christ the investigative judgment will be set. For this we have the clear statement of our Lord himself (Matt. 25:31-34; 19:28). That this judgment related to the living nations at the time of the second advent is evidenced by His parable of the sower (Matt. 13:41-43). Postmillennialists identify the judgment described in Matthew 25:31-46 with the general judgment of the last day. Some premillenialists do likewise, while others apply it, as suggested above, to the nations living on the earth at the time of Christ's second coming.

C. *The Destruction of the Wicked.*

Closely associated with the investigative judgment is the destruction of the wicked. In addition to the scriptures previously cited, St. Paul gives us the following statement: *And to you who are troubled rest with us, when the Lord Jesus shall be revealed from heaven with his mighty angels, in flaming fire taking vengeance on them that know not God, and that obey not the gospel of our Lord Jesus Christ: who shall be punished with everlasting destruction from the presence of the Lord, and from the glory of his power; when he shall come to be glorified in his saints, and to be admired in all them that believe* (II Thess. 1:7-10).

D. *The Fall of Antichrist and the Binding of Satan.*

Included in the destruction of the wicked at the time of the second advent is the Antichrist, whom St. Paul calls that "Wicked" or the "Wicked One." *And then shall that Wicked be revealed, whom the Lord shall*

*consume with the spirit of his mouth, and shall destroy
with the brightness of his coming: even him, whose coming is after the working of Satan with all power and
signs and lying wonders* (II Thess. 2: 8-9). Satan also is
to be bound, *that he should deceive the nations no more,
till the thousand years should be fulfilled: and after that
he must be loosed for a little season.* (Rev. 20: 1, 3).

E. *The Establishment of the Kingdom.*

The Church Militant, in its full New Testament sense,
began with the Day of Pentecost, and will become triumphant with the rapture of the saints at the coming of
the Lord. The Church will then in some sense be merged
into the kingdom. In a mystical sense, *the kingdom of
God is within you* (Luke 17: 21). In that sense we are
now in the kingdom of God the Holy Spirit. The kingdom of God the Son will succeed this, when the inner
mystical kingdom shall find expression in outward glory.
Jesus, having overcome the world is now seated on His
Father's throne, awaiting the time when He shall return
to be seated upon the throne of His glory (Matt. 25: 31).

F. *The Regeneration of the Earth.*

It is a significant fact that our Lord connects the *regeneration* with His coming kingdom. *Verily I say unto
you, that ye which have followed me, in the regeneration when the son of man shall sit in the throne of his
glory, ye also shall sit upon twelve thrones, judging the
twelve tribes of Israel* (Matt. 19: 28). This statement
is very suggestive when we consider that regeneration
in the sense of "a new birth from above" stands for the
direct spiritual results which come from the grace of
God considered personally; and that here it refers to the
divine redemption of the earth, which when our Lord
appears, shall certainly be delivered from the bondage
of corruption (Acts 3: 19-21). Thus the curse of sin will
be removed from the present earth. Numerous changes
will result, the nature of which cannot be fully known,
but the Prophet Isaiah has suggested many interesting
aspects of the restoration. Among such innovations are:

an increased fertility of the earth (Isa. 55: 13), with large portions of the earth now uninhabitable becoming the abode of beauty and glory (Isa. 35: 1, 2, 6, 7); a miraculous restoration of wild animals to their normal instincts (Isa. 11: 6-9); an increased longevity of life (Isa. 65: 20-23); and certain possible changes in the astronomical heavens in their relation to the earth (Isa. 30: 26). The scriptures which we have just cited are fraught with intense spiritual significance, and have been the source of joy and strength to multitudes of God's holy people. While this is true, it does not necessarily forbid a conviction of their literal fulfillment also; nor does it detract from their spiritual meaning, but rather increases it.

G. *The Final Consummation.*

The final consummation or destruction of the world marks the close of the transitional period, and ushers in the new heavens and new earth of the eternal order. It is the closing event of the "day of the Lord." As in the beginning of this period, there is the rapture with its resurrection of the righteous dead, and the translation of the living saints, followed by the investigative judgment of the living nations; so also the day closes with an apostasy following the thousand years' reign, the resurrection of the wicked dead, the destruction of the heavens and earth by fire, and the final judgment with its rewards and punishments.

St. Peter describes the process by which the earth is to be renewed in the following words, *But the heavens and the earth which are now, by the same word are kept in store, reserved unto fire against the day of judgment and perdition of ungodly men* (II Peter 3: 7). He adds further that *The heavens shall pass away with a great noise, and the elements shall melt with fervent heat, the earth also and the works that are therein shall be burned up;* and again, *Looking for and hasting unto the coming of the day of God, wherein the heavens being on fire shall be dissolved and the elements shall melt with fervent heat* (II Peter 3: 10,12). St. Peter does not intend in these passages to teach the annihilation of the world by its fiery baptism. Rather, the word "dissolved" carries with it the idea of loosing the world from the bondage of corruption so that it may become what it was originally intended to be. As man's body is dissolved by death and becomes the subject of decay, out of which it shall be raised immortal, incorruptible, in power and glory; so this earth as man's habitation shall likewise be dissolved, but out of it shall appear in a comparable resurrection, the new heavens and the new earth wherein dwelleth righteousness (II Peter 3:13). *Then cometh the end, when he shall have delivered up the kingdom to God, even the Father; when he shall have put down all rule and all authority and power. For he must reign, till he hath put all enemies under his feet. The last enemy that shall be destroyed is death. For he hath put all things under his feet. But when he saith all things are put under him, it is manifest that he is excepted, which did put all things under him. And when all things shall be subdued unto him, then shall the Son also himself be subject unto him that put all things under him, that God may be all in all* (I Cor. 15:24-28).

CHAPTER XXII

THE RESURRECTION, JUDGMENT, AND FINAL CONSUMMATION

"Members of the consummated kingdom, sharing the glory which the Mediator has with the Father, they develop and fulfill with ever-increasing truth the threefold function of eternal life: declaring Him, serving Him, reigning with Him, in the transcendent communion of love with the Father in the Son through the Holy Spirit.

"The heaven of the saints will therefore not be a realm of shades, unsubstantial and indeterminate, but a kingdom substantial and real, where the faculties and functions of human personality will be active in the joy of righteous freedom. Like the capacities of the soul, the powers of the body will be commensurate with the law and vocation of the ever-lasting life. These are they which come out of great tribulation, and they washed their robes, and made them white in the blood of the Lamb. Therefore are they before the throne of God; and they serve Him day and night in His temple: and He that sitteth on the throne shall spread His tabernacle over them. They shall hunger no more, neither thirst any more; neither shall the sun strike upon them, nor any heat: for the Lamb which is in the midst of the throne shall be their shepherd, and shall guide them unto fountains of waters of life, and God shall wipe away every tear from their eyes."—DR. EMANUEL V. GERHART.

I. THE RESURRECTION

The resurrection which follows as an immediate effect of Christ's second coming is a distinctive and elementary truth of the Christian system. The term resurrection signifies a rising again, that is, a rising of that which was buried. It signifies also a restoration to life of that which was dead. Inasmuch as the soul does not die with the body, it cannot therefore be the subject of the resurrection. Thus it is the body of man which is resurrected.

A. *Scriptural Teaching Regarding the Resurrection.*

Teaching concerning the resurrection is found in the Old Testament, although it is not as explicit or full as in the New Testament. The fact of the resurrection was everywhere presupposed in the economy of the Old Testament, and a distinction is made between the immortality of the soul and the resurrection of the body. The psalmist, for example, speaks of the hope of redemption from Hades by indicating that *God will redeem my soul from the power of the grave: for he shall receive me* (Psalms 49:15). The Prophet Isaiah refers to the resurrection of the individual when he addresses a wonderful prophecy to the Church: *Thy dead men shall live, together with my dead body shall they arise. Awake and sing, ye that dwell in the dust: for thy dew is as the dew of herbs, and the earth shall cast out the dead* (Isa. 26:19). Here the dead are called "my" because they sleep in Him, their disembodied souls existing safely in His keeping. In the Book of Daniel we find that the doctrine of the resurrection is even more explicitly taught. *And many of them that sleep in the dust of the earth shall awake, some to everlasting life, and some to shame and everlasting contempt* (Daniel 12:2).

The New Testament is permeated with the truth of the resurrection, but here it is presented on a far higher level. St. Paul speaks of *the appearing of our Saviour Jesus Christ, who hath abolished death, and hath brought life and immortality to light through the gospel* (II Tim. 1:10). Only through the gospel does the Christian conception of the resurrection and the complete destruction of death find its highest expression. The basic testimony of the New Testament is found in the words of Jesus Christ himself. *Marvel not at this: for the hour is coming, in the which all that are in the graves shall hear his voice, and shall come forth; they that have done good, unto the resurrection of life; and they that have done evil, unto the resurrection of damnation* (John 5:28-29). The gospel announcement, therefore, includes the idea of the resurrection of the whole man, and of the whole race of men to an endless existence.

Christ also associates the resurrection with His own Person and work. He says, *I am the resurrection, and the life: he that believeth in me, though he were dead, yet shall he live: and whosoever liveth and believeth in me shall never die* (John 11:25-26). This is true because in Him there is life and power, *For as the Father hath life in himself; so hath he given to the Son to have life in himself* (John 5:26). St. Paul indicates that Christ's resurrection will be the pattern after which the bodies of the saints will be raised: *Who shall change our vile body, that it may be fashioned like unto his glorious body* (Phil. 3:21). It is union with the risen Christ as the source of life for both soul and body that is the secret ground and condition of the resurrection of believers.

While the resurrection of the just is unto everlasting life, that of the wicked is unto shame and everlasting contempt. St. Paul therefore, speaks of his *hope toward God, which they themselves also allow, that there shall be a resurrection of the dead, both of the just and the unjust* (Acts 24:15); and St. John testifies that he *saw the dead, small and great, stand before God. . . . . And the sea gave up the dead which were in it; and death and hell delivered up the dead which were in them: and they were judged every man according to their works* (Rev. 20:12-13).

B. *The Nature of the Resurrected Body.*

Speaking of the body, St. Paul writes, *It is sown in corruption; it is raised in incorruption; it is sown in dishonour; it is raised in glory: it is sown in weakness; it is raised in power: it is sown a natural body; it is raised a spiritual body. There is a natural body, and there is a spiritual body* (I Cor. 15:42-44). In this passage the subject "it" is used with reference to both the "natural" body and the "spiritual" body. For this reason the Church asserts that the body will rise, and that in some essential respects not entirely clear, it will be the same after the resurrection that it was before.

As to the nature of the perfected resurrected body, we know but little. Our Lord declared, however, that *The children of this world marry, and are given in marriage: but they which shall be accounted worthy to obtain that world, and the resurrection from the dead, neither marry, nor are given in marriage: neither can they die any more: for they are equal unto the angels; and are the children of God, being the children of the resurrection* (Luke 20:34-36); and St. Paul states that *Flesh and blood cannot inherit the kingdom of God; neither doth corruption inherit incorruption* (I Cor. 15:50).

From the scriptural passages cited above it appears that the resurrected body will be free from decay, dissolution, and death, as well as from anything which tends toward death, disease, pain, and suffering. The new body will be immortal in the fullest sense of that word. Beauty and glory beyond the power of human comprehension will doubtless characterize the glorious bodies of the redeemed for the promise is that *When he shall appear, we shall be like him; for we shall see him as he is* (I John 3: 2). It is likely also that new and exalted capacities and capabilities will be resident in the resurrected body, and most certainly those now in use will be immensely increased. In summary, we may say that the resurrected body will be of such a nature as to be perfectly adapted to the new environment in which the redeemed shall dwell. In that sense it will be a spiritual rather than a natural body and thus beautifully adapted to a spiritual mode of living.

C. *The General Resurrection.*

The term "general resurrection" refers to the belief commonly held in the Church, that at the second coming of Christ, all the dead, both the righteous and wicked, shall be raised simultaneously and immediately brought to judgment. Our own creed sets forth this belief as follows: "We believe in the resurrection of the dead, that the bodies of both the just and the unjust shall be raised to life and united with their spirits—'they that have done good, unto the resurrection of life; and they that have done evil, unto the resurrection of damnation' "(*Manual*, Art. XII, Sec. 1). The view that the resurrection of the righteous and wicked is simultaneous is based on our Lord's statement that *The hour is coming, and in the which all that are in their graves shall hear his voice, and shall come forth; they that have done good, unto the resurrection of life; and they that have done evil, unto the resurrection of damnation* (John 5: 28-29).

While the idea of a simultaneous resurrection of the wicked and righteous is the general opinion of both Reformed and Arminian theologians, some Bible students hold to a resurrection of both the righteous and the wicked, without regarding the two events as simultaneous. This is essential to the premillennial view of the second advent. We cannot here go into the detailed arguments set forth in support of this view. However, a study of the phrase "out of," or "from the dead" as used in such passages as Luke 20: 35-36; Mark 12: 25; Revelation 20: 5-6; Acts 4: 1-2; and Philippians 3: 11 strongly suggest that the resurrections mentioned are "out from among the dead." This is to say that a distinction is apparently taught between the resurrection of the righteous and that of the wicked. The former as followers of Christ are accounted worthy to attain the out-resurrection from the dead. It is clear that those who do not make this distinction between the two resurrections must hold to either a post- or a nilmillennial position.

II. THE FINAL JUDGMENT

A. *The Fact of the General Judgment.*

By the final judgment we understand a general judgment of all the righteous and all the wicked in one vast public assembly. This has been denied by some who think that the judgment of each man occurs at death; and by others who think that only the wicked will be judged at the last day. The Scriptures, however, clearly teach that there is a judgment day or period which is to be associated closely with the conflagration at the end of the world. *The heavens and the earth, which are now, by the same word are kept in store, reserved unto fire against the day of judgment and perdition of ungodly men* (II Peter 3: 7). It is expressly stated that *He hath appointed a day, in the which he will judge the world in righteousness* (Acts 17: 31). It is also referred to as *The day of wrath and revelation of the righteous judgment of God* (Rom. 2: 5); *The day when God shall judge the secrets of men by Jesus Christ* (Rom. 2: 16); *the day of judgment* (II Peter 2: 9); *the great day* (Jude 6); and *the great day of his wrath* (Rev. 6: 17). These scriptures clearly prove three things: there is to be a general judg-

ment; this is to take place at a fixed time; and this great
and terrible day is in the future.

As to the duration of the judgment, the indefinite
use of the term "day" forbids any statement of even its
probable length. The ancient fathers commonly believed
the period of judgment to be one thousand years in
length (cf. II Peter 3: 8). Others have suggested that,
considering the number of persons involved and the extent of the inquiries to be made, an even longer period
may be required. At the other extreme is the opinion of
those who believe that only a very short time will suffice
for God to accomplish the purposes for which the judgment is instituted.

Regardless of the length of time involved, the fact of
the judgment is clearly taught in the Word of God. In
Revelation 20: 11-13, 15, we find a plain and uncontest-
able prediction of a general judgment, at which all the
dead and all the living are to be assembled. That both
the righteous and the wicked will be present is evident
from the fact that those whose names are written in the
book of life will be saved, and those whose names are not
found there, will be cast into the lake of fire.

B. *The Person of the Judge.*

God alone is competent to perform the office of Judge
in the last great assize. He, only, is all-wise and to Him
alone are known the innermost secrets of men's lives. He
understands not only their actions, but their inward
thoughts and hidden motives—even their natures. But
this judgment is not by God as God, *For the Father
judgeth no man, but hath committed all judgment unto
the Son: that all men should honour the Son, even as
they honour the Father* (John 5: 22-23). The reason for
this is, that the Son is not only divine but human, and
His relation to humanity peculiarly qualifies Him for
this office. St. Paul preached to the Athenians that God
would *judge the world in righteousness by that man
whom he hath ordained* (Acts 17: 31). It appears from
this that judgment is to be exercised peculiarly by Christ
as man: *it is he which was ordained of God to be the*

Judge of quick and dead (Acts 10:42). The judgment of the world is represented as the last mediatorial act of Christ. After the execution of the final sentence, when the rewards of the righteous are bestowed, and the penalties of the wicked determined, He will deliver up the mediatorial kingdom to the Father, that God may be all in all (I Cor. 15:24-28).

C. *The Principles of Judgment.*

St. Paul enumerates the principles of judgment as follows: *To them who by patient continuance in well doing seek for glory and honour and immortality, eternal life: but unto them that are contentious, and do not obey the truth, but obey unrighteousness, indignation and wrath, tribulation and anguish, upon every soul of man that doeth evil, of the Jew first, and also of the Gentile: but glory, honour, and peace, to every man that worketh good, to the Jew first, and also to the Gentile: for there is no respect of persons with God* (Rom. 2:7-11). A careful study of this and other passages relating to this theme indicates that the measure of revealed truth granted to men will be the standard by which they are judged in the last day. Our Lord himself declared, *For unto whomsoever much is given, of him shall be much required* (Luke 12:48).

More specifically, the foregoing principle of judgment means that the heathen will be judged by the law of nature, or the law originally given to man as the rule of his conduct. Some portion of this law has been preserved among them, partly by tradition and partly by reason; and though the traces of it are in some instance obliterated, and in others greatly obscured, yet enough remains to render them accountable beings, and to be the foundation of a judicial trial (cf. Rom. 2:14-15). The Jews will be judged by the law of Moses and the teachings of the prophets. Our Lord's own words will be the standard for His own generation—*The word that I have spoken, the same shall judge him in the last day* (John 12:48). Christians in general will be judged by the Scriptures of the Old and New Testaments—especially the gospel as it confers on men superior privileges. If the Gentile who sins against the light of nature is justly punishable; if he who despised the law of Moses *died without mercy, ... of how much sorer punishment, suppose ye, shall he be thought worthy, who hath trodden under foot the Son of God, and hath counted the blood of the covenant, wherewith he was sanctified, an unholy thing, and hath done despite unto the Spirit of grace?* (Heb. 10:29).

D. *The Purpose of the Judgment.*

In order to understand the purpose of the general judgment it must be considered in its relation to God, Jesus Christ, and man. First, the judgment will furnish a worthy arena for the display of God's attributes. His justice, faithfulness, wisdom, omnipotence and other attributes will be witnessed and sanctioned by countless myriads of angels and men. Again, the glory of Christ's work will then appear—not only as Judge, but as Lord and King. As Lord, His dominion is now seen to be universal, and as King who has reigned in the hearts of His people, He now welcomes them into His joy, and invites them to participate in His glory. Lastly, as it concerns man the judgment is necessary for several reasons. (1) The condition of the righteous in this world is frequently such, that without the awards of the future, the justice and equity of God cannot be vindicated. (2) Only in the judgment can the total influence of man's life be summed up—either for good or evil. Men are social creatures, and are responsible for their influence on others. This influence goes on and on in an ever-widening circle even after an individual's death. Only in the final judgment can such influence be evaluated for good or evil. (3) The judgment is necessary in order that man's true character may be made manifest. *We must all appear* (or be made manifest) *before the judgment seat of Christ; that every one may receive the things done in his body, according to that he hath done, whether it be good or bad* (II Cor. 5:10). Thus in the judgment, God discriminates between the righteous and the unrighteous, and separates them from each other, that He may uncover or make manifest their true character.

E. *The Final Judgment Scene.*

The Scriptures describe the final judgment as a scene of awful solemnity and grandeur. St. John writes concerning it in the following words: *And I saw a great white throne, and him that sat on it, from whose face the earth and the heaven fled away; and there was found no place for them. And I saw the dead, small and great, stand before God; and the books were opened: and another book was opened, which is the book of life: and the dead were judged out of those things which were written in the books, according to their works. And the sea gave up the dead which were in it; and death and hell delivered up the dead which were in them: and they were judged every man according to their works. And death and hell were cast into the lake of fire. This is the second death. And whosoever was not found written in the book of life was cast into the lake of fire* (Rev. 20: 11-15).

III. THE FUTURE STATE OF THE IMPENITENT

The general judgment not only makes possible the bestowment of eternal blessedness upon the saints, but necessitates also the sentence of endless punishment upon the finally impenitent and wicked. The consideration of this subject brings before us one of the most solemn themes in the entire range of Christian theology. "This consideration should suppress trifling, inspire caution, and wake concern. Nothing could be more unnatural and shocking than to make this doctrine a subject of jesting or the theme of vehement and vindictive declamation. Let none touch the question unless, with becoming solemnity, they can treat it as a note of alarm, sounded in the ear of guilty men for the sole purpose of impelling them to take refuge in Christ" (LOWREY, *Positive Theology,* p. 269).

A. *The Scripture Terms Denoting the Place of Punishment.*

There are three words translated "hell" in the authorized version of the New Testament—Hades, Tartarus, and Gehenna. Hades refers to the realm of the dead, and the distinctions between place and state have already been discussed (Ch. XXI, Sec. II).

Tartarus is mentioned only in II Peter 2: 4, *For if God spared not the angels that sinned, but cast them down to hell* (Tartarus), *and delivered them into chains of darkness, to be reserved unto judgment.* We may, therefore, regard Hades as the intermediate state of wicked men, and Tartarus as the intermediate state of wicked angels. Gehenna is compounded from the two Hebrew words *Ge* and *Hinnom*, and means "the valley of Hinnom." In the New Testament it is called *Gehenna* and appears twelve times. Eleven of these references are in statements of Jesus Christ himself. In all twelve instances the word refers to torture and punishment in the future world. In Matthew 18: 9 the word Gehenna is associated with the punishment to be meted out at the judgment; and in the preceding verse, the words "everlasting fire" are used as its equivalent. In Mark 9: 43-44, Jesus says, *It is better for thee to enter into life maimed, than having two hands to go into hell, into the fire that never shall be quenched* (or inextinguishable): *where their worm dieth not and the fire is not quenched.* In Luke 12: 5, the words of Christ are, *Fear him, which after he hath killed hath power to cast into hell* (Gehenna). The word "hell," therefore, in the sense of Gehenna, refers to the place provided for the final punishment of evil angels and impenitent men, after the day of judgment.

B. *The Doctrine of Eternal Punishment as Taught in the Scriptures.*

The mere perusal of the words of Jesus Christ, without any note or comment, should convince the unprejudiced reader that He taught the doctrine of future punishment. Note carefully the following: *The Son of man shall send forth his angels, and they shall gather out of his kingdom all things that offend, and them which do iniquity; and shall cast them into a furnace of fire: there shall be wailing and gnashing of teeth* (Matt. 13: 41-42); *Then shall he say also unto them on the left hand, Depart from me, ye cursed, into everlasting fire, prepared for the devil and his angels: and these shall go away into everlasting punishment: but the righteous into life eternal* (Matt. 25: 41-46); *And if thy hand offend thee, cut it off: it is better for thee to enter into life maimed, than having two hands to go into hell, into the fire that never shall be quenched: where their worm dieth not, and the fire is not quenched* (Mark 9: 43-44); and *Marvel not at this: for the hour is coming, in the which all that are in their graves shall hear his voice, and shall come forth; they that have done good, unto the resurrection of life; and they that have done evil, unto the resurrection of damnation* (John 5: 28-29). The solemn truth taught in these scriptures is that those who reject Christ and the salvation offered through Him shall die in their sins and be separated from God forever. This present life is one of probation, and following it must be eternal consequences.

What will be the nature of future punishment? The terms which are used in the scriptures to express the idea of future punishment must of necessity be in part figurative. Only by comparing it with that which is within our mental grasp, are we able to understand even in a small measure this solemn truth. It is called the *second death* (cf. Rev. 21: 8; 20: 14-15). The fear of death brought the whole race of men into bondage (Heb. 2: 15). It is surrounded with gloom and terror, and is the source of tormenting fears. The second death is also that spiritual corruption of which physical death is a type. Apart from the mitigating and restraining influences of grace which were present in the life, the sinner becomes eternally exposed to the corruption of his own soul. Our Lord speaks of future punishment as *outer darkness,* and associates this with weeping and gnashing of teeth (cf. Matt. 8: 12;

22:13; 25:30). Dr. Wakefield speaks of this darkness as resembling "the deep midnight of the grave, lengthening onward from age to age, and terminated by no succeeding day." The everlasting state of the wicked is also described as a state of *positive punishment*. Our Lord informs us that the wicked shall be cast *into a furnace of fire: there shall be wailing and gnashing of teeth* (Matt. 13:42); while St. Paul speaks of the Lord as being *Revealed from heaven with his mighty angels, in flaming fire taking vengeance on them that know not God, and that obey not the gospel of our Lord Jesus Christ* (II Thess. 1:7-8). Attempts have been made to tone down the severity of these scriptures by regarding them as purely figurative. But the figure never fully portrays the reality; and the reasonable conclusion is, therefore, that the fire of future punishment, if not literal, will be infinitely more intolerable. Lastly, future punishment is described as *banishment from God*. This is the worst form of punishment conceivable—before which death, everlasting fire, and the blackness of darkness are as nothing. God is the author of every good and perfect gift, and the loss of God is the loss of all good. The words, *Depart from me, ye cursed* (Matt. 25:41) indicate a loss of light and love, of friendship, of beauty and song—the loss of even hope itself. To be banished from God is to be forever separated from heaven and all good. Such are the solemn representations which the Holy Spirit has seen proper to make concerning the state of the finally impenitent and the nature of their punishment.

Is future punishment eternal? Since this question has been answered in the negative by some, a careful consideration of the subject necessitates a study of the Greek word αἰώνιος which in the Scriptures is rendered *everlasting* or *eternal*. In one form or another, this word is used in each of the following scripture passages: *Wherefore if thy hand or thy foot offend thee, cut them off, and cast them from thee: it is better for thee to enter into life halt or maimed, rather than having two hands or two feet to be cast into everlasting fire* (Matt. 18:8). St. Mark uses this same scripture but adds the words

Into the fire that never shall be quenched: where their worm dieth not, and the fire is not quenched (Mark 9:43-44). He also says, *But he that shall blaspheme against the Holy Ghost hath never forgiveness, but is in danger of eternal damnation* (Mark 3:29). St. John says, *He that believeth on the Son hath everlasting life: and he that believeth not the Son shall not see life; but the wrath of God abideth on him* (John 3:36). In the description of the judgment scene found in Matthew 25:31-46, Jesus says to those on his left hand, *Depart from me, ye cursed, into everlasting fire, prepared for the devil and his angels;* and the scene closes with the words, *And these shall go away into everlasting punishment: but the righteous into life eternal.* If by these *statements our Lord does not mean eternal punishment,* what significance can possibly attach to them? "I have seen," says Dr. Adam Clarke, "the best things that have been written in favor of the final redemption of damned spirits, but I never saw an answer to the argument against this doctrine, drawn from this verse (Matt. 25:46), but that sound learning and criticism should be ashamed to acknowledge."

The objections which are urged against eternal punishment are usually that the punishment is disproportionate to the sin, and that God is too merciful to inflict everlasting punishment upon His creatures. Both of these objections represent a failure to recognize the fact that sin is infinite evil. An appreciation of the seriousness of sin can be attained only when we try to grasp the length to which God went in giving His Son to redeem man. Then it is that we become aware of the fact that punishment of endless duration is not disproportionate for those who willfully and finally reject the One who suffered—*The just for the unjust, that he might bring us to God* (I Peter 3:18).

IV. THE ETERNAL BLESSEDNESS OF THE SAINTS

The Scriptures have more to say of the eternal blessedness of the saints, than of the final state of the wicked; but the subject being less controversial, has generally occupied less space in theology. God's grace which warns the wicked against the day of wrath, assures the righteous also of their eternal blessedness.

A. *Heaven Is Both a Place and a State.*

That heaven is a state of eternal blessedness is admitted by all. But heaven is a place also. It is the abode of the righteous in their final state of glorification. Our Lord declared, *In my Father's house are many mansions; if it were not so, I would have told you. I go to prepare a place for you. And if I go and prepare a place for you, I will come again, and receive you unto myself; that where I am, there ye may be also* (John 14:2-3). The Scriptures speak of the *third* heaven where God dwells, and St. Paul writes of being caught up into this highest heaven. However, we need not think of the soul as having to travel long distances spatially in order to enter heaven. The distance is not to be conceived in terms of physical space, but of changed conditions. Heaven is just behind the veil, which so often but "thinly intervenes," as marking that which to us is invisible, and that which is beyond the range of mortal sight. The word *apocalypse* means an unveiling, and at death, the righteous pass through this veil into the beatific vision of Christ. This to the redeemed soul is heaven, the eternal abode of the redeemed of all ages.

B. *The Blessedness of the Saints.*

While the nature of future happiness cannot be known in this life, the Scriptures give us many intimations of what God has prepared for them that love Him. Heaven will be a place from which all sin and unrighteousness shall be banished forever. *There shall in no wise enter into it any thing that defileth, neither whatsoever worketh abomination, or maketh a lie* (Rev. 21: 27). No unholy thing shall ever enter the abode of the blessed, nor shall the saints ever feel the sinister influence of Satan or wicked men. It will be a place where the penal consequences of sin are all removed. *And God shall wipe away all tears from their eyes; and there shall be no more death, neither sorrow, nor crying, neither shall there be any more pain: for the former things are passed away* (Rev. 21: 4). Heaven will be a place where the saints enjoy the possession of all positive good. *The throne of God and of the Lamb shall be in it; and his servants shall serve him: and they shall see his face; and his name shall be in their foreheads. And there shall be no night there; and they need no candle, neither light of the sun; for the Lord God giveth them light: and they shall reign forever and ever* (Rev. 22: 3-5). Heaven will thus be the perfect answer to every holy desire. For those who are weary, it is everlasting rest; for the sorrowing, it is a place where God shall wipe away all tears; for the suffering, there shall be no more pain; for the mistakes and blunders of a sincere but imperfect service, the throne of God shall be there, and His servants shall serve Him—every deed being performed in His presence and under His approving smile; for those who are perplexed and bewildered by the uncertainties and disappointments of life, it is promised that there shall be no night there; for the Lord God giveth them light, and they shall reign with Him forever and ever.

Another source of blessedness to the saints will be their communion with each other and with their common Lord. We may be sure that the distinct personality of each redeemed saint will be preserved inviolate; and the social instincts which characterized them here will not be obliterated but rather intensified (cf. Heb. 12: 22-23; Matt. 8: 11). Also, the plain inference of Scripture is, that the saints shall recognize and mingle with their loved ones of earth, who like themselves have been saved through the blood of the Lamb. *Then shall I know,* writes St. Paul, *even as also I am known* (I Cor. 13: 12). Since memory remains, and the theme of our song is redemption, we may be assured that we shall also retain the knowledge of persons, places, and circumstances connected with our salvation (cf. I Thess. 2: 19). But highest and best, it is promised that without dimming veil. *They shall see his face; and his name shall be in their foreheads* (Rev. 22: 4); and St. John in an equally exultant strain exclaims, *Beloved, now are we the sons of God, and it doth not yet appear what we shall be: but we know that, when he shall appear, we shall be like him; for we shall see him as he is. And every man that hath this hope in him purifieth himself, even as he is pure* (I John 3: 2-3).

C. *The Employments of Heaven.*

While heaven will be a place of rest, we are not to suppose that it will be a place of inactivity. We may well suppose that such activities will be first of all spiritual. God, *who hath blessed us with all spiritual blessing in heavenly places in Christ Jesus* (Eph. 1: 3), will enable the souls of the redeemed to constantly expand in the ocean fullness of divine love. New views of divine grace, and fresh visions of His adorable person, will constantly burst in upon their enraptured minds and hearts. Their intellectual faculties will be enlarged and purified. "Before them shall lie the whole circle of creation," says Dr. Graham; "the system of providence and the character and attributes of God. His wisdom, love and power they shall be able to trace in the mysteries of nature and providence, which are now hidden from human eyes . . . . the enjoyments of the mind must make up a great part of the blessedness of heaven. The freed and expanded reason will no doubt delight in tracing the laws of the material universe and the supreme wisdom which ordained them, the rise and progress of the various kingdoms and empires, nations and races, which constitute the dominion of God; in tracing the wisdom, love and goodness of the Creator in every department of being, from the insect on earth to the seraph before the throne. Oh, what a field for that intellect!" (Graham, *On the Ephesians,* p. 72).

The crowning excellency of heaven is that its joys shall never end. Heaven is called *the city of God . . . . a city which hath foundations, whose builder and maker is God* (Heb. 11: 10); it is called a *better country, that is, an heavenly* (Heb. 11: 16); and it is spoken of as *a kingdom which cannot be moved* (Heb. 12: 28). The word eternity or some of its forms, is frequently associated with heaven. It is a *house . . . . eternal in the heavens* (II Cor. 5:1); *eternal glory* (I Peter 5:10); *everlasting habitations* (Luke 16:9); and *the everlasting kingdom of our Lord and Saviour Jesus Christ* (II Peter 1:11). When the saints enter into that eternal glory, they enter upon a life that shall never be finished, and of which it may be said of them, as it is of God himself, that their *years shall have no end.*

V. THE FINAL CONSUMMATION

A. *Scope of the Final Consummation.*

The final consummation marks the close of the history of this present world. In its place there will be a new heaven and a new earth, wherein dwelleth righteousness—destined through eternity to be the seat of the kingdom of God in its perfection of beauty. In this triumphant kingdom Christ will lay down the mediatorial work of salvation from sin, for the last enemy shall have been overcome. He will not, however, cease to be the Exalted One, for He shall still be the Firstborn among many brethren, our fountain of living waters, and our everlasting light. He shall forever be the mediate cause of our eternal life and light, our holiness and our happiness, even when He gives up the kingdom to the Father.

The final consummation brings to a close the probationary history of the individual—the final consequences being the future punishment of the wicked and the eternal blessedness of the saints. It also marks the perfection of the Church. Heaven will not be inhabited by an innumerable company of redeemed individuals only, but by the Church as an organic unity. The Church will be the most precious jewel in heaven. For this reason St. John speaks of the Church as the Bride of the Lamb, which he describes in the symbolism of a holy city—the new Jerusalem, coming down from God out of heaven (Rev. 21:2, 9, 10). No symbol is better adapted to express the complexity of social organization. In the present world, through the ill-adjustments of an imperfect social structure, the city becomes the seat of sin and wickedness, of want and penury, of pain and suffering. But in the city of God, the organization will be so perfect, as it affects the relation of the individual to the social order, that *There shall be no more death, neither sorrow, nor crying, neither shall there be any more pain: for the former things are passed away* (Rev. 21:4). The Church militant on earth becomes triumphant in heaven but she will never lose her identity. And when the Church shall have reached this perfection, and every enemy has been subdued and death itself shall be no more, then it is that the mediatorial kingdom as an agency of salvation must of necessity cease, and be absorbed in the endlessly blessed kingdom of God the Father, God the Son, and God the Holy Ghost.

The final consummation also includes the physical universe in its scope. There shall be a new heaven and a new earth. To this we give attention in our concluding section.

B. *The New Heaven and the New Earth.*

The Scriptures of both the Old and New Testaments look forward to a new creation, when the present heavens and earth shall have grown old, and are folded up as a vesture. Thus, *Of old hast thou laid the foundation of the earth: the heavens are the work of thy hands. They shall perish, but thou shalt endure: yea, all of them shall wax old like a garment; as a vesture thou shalt change them, and they shall be changed* (Psalms 102:25-26; cf. Heb. 1:10-12). The Prophet Isaiah waxes eloquent in contemplation of the new creation: *For behold, I create new heavens and a new earth: and the former shall not be remembered, nor come into mind. But be ye glad and rejoice forever in that which I create: for, behold, I create Jerusalem a rejoicing, and her people a joy* (Isa. 65:17-18; cf. Isa. 34:4; 51:6). In the New Testament, St. Peter draws a graphic picture of the changes which will take place and the new order which will emerge. He writes, *But the day of the Lord will come as a thief in the night: in the which the heavens shall pass away with a great noise, and the elements shall melt with fervent heat, the earth also and the works that are therein shall be burned up. . . . . Nevertheless we according to his promise, look for new heavens and a new earth, wherein dwelleth righteousness* (II Peter 3: 10, 13). Thus the Scriptures teach that God will at some future time set free certain forces which are now held in reserve, and use them to the purifying of that which has been defiled by sin. God destroys only that He may create something more beautiful; and upon the ruins of earth laboring under the curse He will raise up another, which shall bloom in unfading splendor.

The great consummation marks the restoration of harmony and order in the universe. It was to this, doubtless, that St. Peter referred when he said that the heaven must receive or retain Christ, *Until the times of restitution of all things, which God hath spoken by the mouth of all his holy prophets since the world began* (Acts 3: 21). This, of course, does not imply that all men might eventually turn to God and be saved. Our study of the duration of future punishment clearly reveals the opposite to be the case. The finally impenitent are hopelessly, and eternally lost. As the curtain is drawn on this present age the Word of God is that *He that is unjust, let him be unjust still: and he which is filthy, let him be filthy still: and he that is righteous, let him be righteous still: and he that is holy, let him be holy still* (Rev. 22: 11).

The consummation of the ages marks the glorious completion of the kingdom of God. Then the kingdom will have a new beginning, in a new heavens and a new earth made one. That kingdom shall be an everlasting kingdom, *For the Lord God giveth them light: and they shall reign for ever and ever* (Rev. 22: 5). But until that glorious and dread day shall come, when the destinies of men shall be fixed for weal or woe, for eternal life or endless death, the invitation of divine love rings clear and strong, *The Spirit and the bride say, Come. And let him that heareth say, Come. And let him that is athirst come. And whosoever will, let him take of the water of life freely* (Rev. 22: 17).

INTRODUCTION TO CHRISTIAN THEOLOGY
SELECTED ANNOTATED BIBLIOGRAPHY

The following list of selected books is designed for those who may desire a more complete study of theological subjects. The books mentioned do not necessarily express the views which have been presented herein. An attempt has been made to include in the list a few of the studies which are typical of the varying points of emphasis among Protestant theologians. The worth of each book and the validity of the ideas contained therein must be determined by the reader himself. In some cases the denominational affiliation of the author has been indicated.

BANKS, J. S., *A Manual of Christian Doctrine*, Eaton and Mains, New York, 1897 (Methodist).
A clear, brief statement of Arminian theology. Considerable attention given to doctrinal controversies in the early Church. Emphasizes distinction between doctrine and dogma.

BINNEY, AMOS, *Theological Compend Improved*, Methodist Book Concern, New York, 1902 (Methodist).
Essentially an outline of doctrine from the Wesleyan point of view. Widely used among holiness people a generation ago.

BOWIE, MARY ELLA, *Introduction to Systematic Theology*, Chicago Evangelistic Institute, Chicago, 1942.
A splendid syllabus. Well outlined and clearly expressed. Arminian in emphasis. In mimeographed form only at the present time.

CALVIN, JOHN, *The Institutes of the Christian Religion*, (2 Vols.), New York, 1819.
A classic in the history of Christian thought. Represents the Reformed type of theology as over against the Lutheran and Arminian types.

CHADWICK, SAMUEL, *The Way to Pentecost*, Light and Hope Publications, Berne, Indiana, 1937.
A dynamic presentation of the doctrine and experience of holiness. Short and readable.

CLARKE, ADAM, *Christian Theology*, Thomas Tegg and Son, London, 1835. (Methodist).
A clear statement of doctrine by a great scholar of early Methodism. Evangelistic and devotional emphasis often evident.

CLARKE, WILLIAM NEWTON, *An Outline of Christian Theology*, Scribners, New York, 1905 (Baptist).
A Baptist publication. Quite liberal in tone. Excellent as regards definitions. Always stimulating.

CURTIS, OLIN A., *The Christian Faith*, Eaton and Mains, New York, 1905, (Methodist).
A psychological and individualistic approach to the study of Christian doctrine.

EDERSHEIM, ALFRED, *Life and Times of Jesus the Messiah*, (2 Vols.), Longmans, Green and Company, New York, 1898.
A standard treatment of the life of Christ by one who was thoroughly familiar with Jewish life and customs.

ELLYSON, E. P., *Bible Holiness*, Nazarene Publishing House, Kansas City, 1938 (Nazarene).
A clear, brief treatment of a vital theme. Well organized. The author presents some rather original ideas on holiness.

FIELD, BENJAMIN, *The Student's Handbook of Christian Theology*, Eaton and Mains, New York, 1886 (Methodist).
Catechetical in form, clear in presentation, and post-millennial in emphasis as regards the second advent of our Lord.

FISHER, GEORGE P., *History of Christian Doctrine*, Scribner's, New York, 1911.
Excellent study of theological thought arranged according to historical periods.

FLETCHER, JOHN WILLIAM, *Five Checks to Antinomianism*, Hunt and Eaton, New York, 1891.
A thorough and devotional study of the Arminian and Wesleyan position in theology as over against the Calvinistic antinomian type. Worthy of careful study.

GERHART, EMANUEL V., *Institutes of the Christian Religion*, (2 Vols.), Funk and Wagnalls, New York, 1894 (Reformed).
Reformed type of theology. Rather tedious and laborious in style. Well organized. Suggestive as to content.

HARRIS, SAMUEL, *The Self-Revelation of God*, Scribner's, New York, 1887.
An older work, but thorough and helpful in the study of fundamental principles.

HARRISON, W. P., (Editor), *The Wesleyan Standards*, (Sermons by John Wesley), Publishing House of the Methodist Church, South, Nashville, 1894 (Methodist).
Selected sermons by John Wesley. The outlines and notes are especially helpful, as well as references to occasions and conditions under which certain sermons were delivered.

HILLS, A. M., *Fundamental Christian Theology*, (2 Vols.), C. J. Kinne, Pasadena College, Pasadena, California, 1931 (Nazarene).
Represents a type of Arminian thought similar to that of Dr. John Miley. Extremely anti-Calvinistic in spots. Rather discursive at times.

HODGE, CHARLES, *Systematic Theology*, (4 Vols.), Scribner's, New York, 1871 (Reformed).
The standard work of the Reformed type of theology. Thorough and comprehensive. Represents the older school of Calvinistic thought.

HOVEY, A., *Manual of Systematic Theology and Christian Ethics*, American Baptist Publication Society, Philadelphia, 1877 (Baptist).
A standard single-volume treatment of theology widely used as a text in Baptist training schools.

LOWREY, ASBURY, *Positive Theology*, Eaton and Mains, New York, 1853.
A dynamic, positive, forthright presentation of Christian doctrine from the Arminian point of view. Evangelistic and practical in tone and emphasis.

MACPHERSON, JOHN, *Christian Dogmatics*, T. and T. Clark, Edinburgh, 1898 (Presbyterian).
A scholarly, concise treatment of Christian doctrine with a Calvinistic emphasis.

MARTENSEN, H., *Christian Dogmatics*, T. and T. Clark, Edinburgh, 1898 (Lutheran).
Known as one of the mediating theologians. Lutheran, but in the latter part of his work he leans more toward the Reformed theology. Beautiful in style, suggestive in thought, and generally helpful.

MILEY, JOHN, *Systematic Theology*, (2 Vols.), Eaton and Mains, New York, 1892 (Methodist).
A thorough and strong work. Known especially for the type of governmental theory of the atonement which is developed.

MUELLER, JULIUS, *The Christian Doctrine of Sin,* (2 Vols.), Edinburgh, 1877.
One of the most thorough and comprehensive works on the doctrine
of sin.

ORR, JAMES, *Revelation and Inspiration,* New York, 1910.
The writer is a strong apologist for the fundamentals in the Christian
system of doctrine as over against modernistic trends.

PECK, JESSE T., *The Central Idea of Christianity,* Henry V. Degen, Boston,
1857 (Methodist).
A classic on the doctrine of holiness. Represented the early Methodist
position. Worthy of careful study.

POPE, WILLIAM BURTON, *A Higher Catechism of Theology,* Phillips and
Hunt, New York, 1884 (Methodist).
Catechetical in form. Highly condensed and well organized state-
ment of theology. Arminian and Wesleyan in emphasis.

POPE, WILLIAM BURTON, *Compendium of Christian Theology,* (3 Vols.),
Phillips and Hunt, New York, 1881 (Methodist).
The strongest and clearest exposition of Wesleyan doctrine since
Richard Watson. Devotional in tone. Scriptural in presentation.

RALSTON, THOMAS N., *Elements of Divinity,* (Edited by T. O. Summers),
Cokesbury, Nashville, Tenn., 1924 (Methodist).
An exposition of Methodist theology, widely known and extensively
used.

RUTH, C. W., *The Second Crisis in Christian Experience,* Christian Witness Co., Chicago, 1912 (Nazarene).
A clear statement of the "Second Blessing" position. Devotional and
evangelistic in tone.

SEISS, JOSEPH A., *Lectures on the Apocalypse,* Charles C. Cook, New York,
1901 (8th Ed.).
Written in excellent and attractive style. Widely known as representing one type of premillennialism.

SHELDON, HENRY C., *System of Christian Doctrine,* Methodist Book Concern, New York, 1903 (Methodist).
A Methodist theology of more modern type. Less emphasis upon the
distinctive Wesleyan doctrines of salvation.

SHELDON, HENRY C., *History of Christian Doctrine,* (2 Vols.), Harpers, New
York, 1886 (Methodist).
A careful and comprehensive study of Christian doctrine by periods.
Excellent for reference.

SMITH, HENRY B., *Introduction to Theology,* 1883, and *Systematic Theology,*
1884, Armstrong and Sons, New York.
Reformed type of theology arranged according to the Christocentric
plan. Known as the best representative of this Christocentric type of
theology.

STEELE, DANIEL, *The Gospel of the Comforter,* Christian Witness Co.,
Chicago, 1910.
A helpful study of the Person and work of the Holy Spirit. Clear,
original, and practical. Not too well organized as a whole.

STRONG, A. H., *Systematic Theology,* (3 Vols.), Griffith and Rowland,
Philadelphia, 1907 (Baptist).
The standard Baptist theology. Unique "Ethical Theory" of the
atonement. Excellent footnotes.

TAYLOR, RICHARD S., *A Right Conception of Sin,* Nazarene Publishing
House, Kansas City, 1939 (Nazarene).
A little book on an important subject. Clear, concise, readable. Anti-
Calvinistic in emphasis.

TIGERT, JOHN J., *Summer's Systematic Theology*, (2 Vols.), Publishing House of the Methodist Episcopal Church, South, Nashville, 1888 (Methodist).
A Methodist work on theology arranged on the basis of the Articles of Faith. Strong emphasis on the early Wesleyan position. Rather combative in tone.

TORREY, R. A., *What the Bible Teaches*, Revell, New York, 1898 (Congregational).
A usable collection of scriptural passages (R.V.) organized under doctrinal heads, and a large number of "propositions."

URQUHART, J., *The Inspiration and Accuracy of the Holy Scriptures*, Gospel Publishing House, New York, 1904.
An older work, but readable and fundamental

WAKEFIELD, SAMUEL, *Christian Theology*, Hunt and Eaton, New York, 1869 (Methodist).
A revision of Watson's *Institutes*, but with some excellent material added. A splendid study of the Wesleyan position in theology.

WATSON, RICHARD, *Theological Institutes*, (2 Vols.), Lane and Scott, New York, 1851 (Methodist).
The earliest and most authoritative work on Wesleyan theology.

WEAVER, JONATHAN, *Christian Theology*, United Brethren Publishing House, Dayton, Ohio, 1900 (United Brethren).
A brief, readable treatment of Christian doctrine. A fine devotional tone and practical emphasis. Many scriptural quotations (R.V.). Not well organized.

WESLEY, JOHN, *Plain Account of Christian Perfection*, Eaton and Mains, New York.
A classic statement of the doctrine of Christian Perfection by the founder of Methodism.

WILMERS, W., *Handbook of the Christian Religion*, Benziger, New York, 1891 (Roman Catholic).
A concise statement of Roman Catholic doctrine.

WINCHESTER, OLIVE M., *Christ's Life and Ministry*, Nazarene Publishing House, Kansas City, 1932 (Nazarene).
A brief survey of the life of our Lord Jesus Christ and His ministry written for popular study.

WOOD, J. A., *Perfect Love*, Christian Witness Co., Chicago and Boston, 1907.
An excellent treatment of the subject of Christian Perfection. Splendid devotional tone, and emphasis upon the practical and ethical aspects of entire sanctification.

GENERAL INDEX

SCRIPTURE INDEX

Compiled by David L. Mesarosh

OLD TESTAMENT

NEW TESTAMENT